Admiral Saumarez Versus Napoleon

THE BALTIC, 1807–12

The maritime war against Napoleon did not end with the Battle of Trafalgar, but continued right up to 1815, with even more British ships and sailors deployed after 1805 than before. One key theatre was the Baltic, where the British commander was Admiral Sir James Saumarez. He had had a highly successful career as a post-Captain, notably in a single-ship frigate duel for which he was knighted and at the two battles of Algeciras in 1801 as a newly-promoted rear-admiral. For five years from 1808 as Commander-in-Chief of a large Baltic fleet, with HMS *Victory* as his flagship, he played a very skilful diplomatic role, combining firmness and restraint, and working with Sweden contrary to the instincts of his superiors in London even when she declared war. Despite the determined efforts of Denmark's gunboats and privateers, he successfully kept British trade flowing in and out of the Baltic, undermining Napoleon's 'Continental System' – the economic blockade of Britain – and leading to Napoleon's fateful decision to invade Russia in 1812.

This book, based on extensive original research in both British and Scandinavian archives and making considerable use of Sir James' unpublished correspondence with his wife Martha, charts the maritime and political history of the war in the Baltic. It illustrates the highly successful, highly esteemed role the Admiral played and looks at the nature and motivation of the man himself revealed in his letters and in the private letters of Count von Rosen, Governor of Gothenburg and chief link between Saumarez and former French marshal Bernadotte, Crown Prince of Sweden, later to be crowned King Karl XIV Johan.

TIM VOELCKER gained his PhD in maritime history at the University of Exeter.

*Sir James Saumarez.   Mezzotint by H.T. Ryall of portrait by Samuel Lane
(in possession of the author).*
'There was always that pleasing smile on his countenance which was admirably
calculated to remove that diffidence which is natural to inferiors in their
approaches to men in exalted situation, and none who once approached him
had cause to feel the least apprehension of an unpleasant kind from a second
interview.' (*The Comet*, Guernsey, 13 October 1836)

Admiral Saumarez Versus Napoleon

THE BALTIC, 1807–12

Tim Voelcker

THE BOYDELL PRESS

First published 2008
The Boydell Press, Woodbridge

ISBN 978-1-84383-431-1

Transferred to digital printing

The Boydell Press is an imprint of Boydell & Brewer Ltd
PO Box 9, Woodbridge, Suffolk IP12 3DF, UK
and of Boydell & Brewer Inc.
668 Mt. Hope Avenue, Rochester NY 14620, USA
website: www.boydellandbrewer.com

A CIP catalogue record for this title is available
from the British Library

The publisher has no responsibility for the continued existence or accuracy of
URLs for external or third-party internet websites referred to in this book, and
does not guarantee that any content on such websites is, or will remain,
accurate or appropriate.

This book is printed on acid-free paper

In memory of Dr. Augustus Voelcker FRS
(1822–84)

Contents

Illustrations

Every effort has been made to contact all copyright holders. The publishers will be glad to make good in future editions any errors or omissions brought to their attention

Preface and Acknowledgements

In 1982 a friend staying with us visited nearby Shrubland Hall Health Clinic, then run by Lady Saumarez, the late mother of the present Baron, Eric de Saumarez. Our friend returned, bubbling with both health and news of boxes of unpublished private correspondence between the 1st Baron, James de Saumarez, and his wife Martha. Like most people I knew very little of Sir James' place in naval history so I read the Navy Records Society edition of his official Baltic correspondence by A.N. Ryan. It made me aware that he was a much more interesting and significant Napoleonic Wars admiral than his present lack of fame implied. As Ryan stated at the end of his general introduction, the archive 'shed new light on the war at sea, as well as upon European history, in the post-Trafalgar period of the Napoleonic war and upon the career of a distinguished officer whose unique contribution to the war was to keep open the gates of northern Europe after Napoleon had decreed that they be closed'.[1] The need to earn a living in the commercial world prevented me from pursuing the find until I was able to sell my wine business and turn to research the admiral in 2000.

I am most grateful to Baron de Saumarez for his permission to have access to the archive, to Bill Serjeant, former Suffolk County Archivist and archivist of the Saumarez family records, for his extensive and enthusiastic help, and to the friendly staff of the Suffolk Record Office where much of my time was spent transcribing the mass of documents. The other major source of unpublished documents has been the private letters of Count Axel Pontus von Rosen, Governor of Gothenburg, to Baron von Engeström, the Swedish Foreign Minister. I must thank Claes Tellvid, archivist at the National Archive in Stockholm for telling me of their presence in the Royal Library, for the help of Eva Dillman in the Manuscript section there, of Ingrid Karlsson in the War Archive and of Ingemar Carlsson on behalf of King Gustav at the Bernadotteska Archive in the Royal Castle.

Without Michael Ellis, former British Naval Attaché in Stockholm, I would not have met Commodore Jan Bring whose transcription and translation of 111 von Rosen letters has formed the core of my Swedish research, and Harriet Rydberg who both allowed me full access to her mother's earlier work on Saumarez, sadly never completed, and took me round Hanö and Karlshamn. To all three of them, I am eternally grateful. Nicolas Ellis of the Royal Swedish Society of Naval Sciences in Karlskrona provided some information in connection with the severe impact of scurvy on the Swedish fleet, as did Michael Helgesson of the County Museum in Karlskrona, who provided a transcript of a diary written in 1781 by a naval physician, Dr. Gersdorff, while acting as doctor to a naval exploration expedition. I am grateful also to Professor Emeritus Magnus Mörner for his information on the Spanish Division in Denmark commanded by the Marques de la Romana, prior to the publication in Spain of his book on the subject.

In Denmark, Ole Lisberg Jensen took me round the Royal Danish Naval Museum (Orlogsmuseet) and the Naval Dockyard with its great Mast Tower. I was also privileged to spend a couple of hours with Professor Ole Feldbaek in his home in Charlottenlund during which he asked me, not unkindly, how I hoped to add to the excellent works by Ryan which he had recently re-read. At that early stage of my researches, I had no clear answer. I hope I would be more convincing now. On a later visit to Copenhagen, I was glad to meet Jakob Seerup, Curator at Tøjhusmuseet, but neither there nor in the National Archive was there very much primary material that bore directly on this study. More relevant was a visit under sail to Christiansø off Bornholm as part of an Ocean Cruising Club rally to the Baltic. Brian Stigfeldt showed me over the Lilletårn Museum, a small but extremely well laid-out museum, and gave me a very different picture of the British attack in October 1810 to the one that the few English reports had depicted. Rasmus Voss resolved the mystery of why I thought there were two bombships and the Danes were sure there were three.

I have received a great deal of help from archivists and academics throughout England, especially the staff of the British Library, the Cambridge University Library, the Devon Record Office at Exeter, the Guildhall Library of the City of London, the Hampshire Record Office, Harewood House Trust and West Yorkshire Archive Service at Leeds, the Institute of Historical Research, the National Archives at Kew, the National Maritime Museum, Officers of the Society for Nautical Research and fellow post-graduate students at the University of Exeter. My thanks are especially due to Angela Harvey who told me of the Saumarez letters, to Andrew Baisley for his help with the illustrations, and to Michael Bosson, Brian Carpenter, Marianne Cisnik, Gareth Cole, Andrew Cook, Helen Dafter, Helen Doe, Andy Jackson, Richard Kennell, Seija Riitta Laakso, Alex Liddell, Professor Roger Knight, Peter Le Fevre, Janet Macdonald, The Marquis of Normanby, Dr. Roger Morriss, Dr. Thomas Munch-Petersen, Sir Richard Hyde Parker, Alan Readman, Sir John Meurig Thomas, Gina Turner, Dr. D.M. Williams, Joy Woodhead, and Sir Tony Wrigley, whom I was fortunate to have as my supervisor as an undergraduate at Peterhouse many years ago.

I am particularly grateful for the opportunity to see before publication the works on Saumarez of both David Greenwood and David Shayer, and for a copy of the massive Saumarez family tree going back to the thirteenth century put together by James Saumarez, descendant of another branch of the family.

I have also been helped by having a Guernsey brother-in-law, Peter Warry, whose hospitality has made visits to the island both easy and enjoyable, and who assisted me to obtain the help there of Nicholas Gold, David Mosely, Dr. Darryl Ogier, and Peter de Sausmarez. This branch of the family retains the 'de' and a second s. It is most encouraging that the present Lieutenant Governor of Guernsey, Vice Admiral Sir Fabian Malbon, has become an enthusiastic champion of Admiral Saumarez.

Professor Nicholas Rodger's wealth and breadth of knowledge have been of enormous benefit, as has his encouragement to someone who was very conscious of having to begin again in the academic world. Aided by the excellent catering of the British Library, supervisions have been almost too enjoyable. I must also gratefully acknowledge the constant enthusiastic support of Dr. Michael Duffy as Director of the Maritime Historical Department at the University of Exeter.

The list of names could continue, but I would like to end by mentioning the invaluable support of my wife Sally who has unselfishly put up with my living for the past seven years with another man, albeit long dead.

Abbreviations

Bernadotte	*La Correspondance de Bernadotte avec Napoléon, 1810–14*, ed. M. Bail (Paris, 1819)
BL	British Library, London
Byam Martin Letters	*Letters and Papers of Admiral of the Fleet Sir Thos. Byam Martin*, ed, Sir Richard Vesey Hamilton, 3 vols, Navy Records Society 12, 19 and 24 (1898–1903)
Mulgrave	Normanby Castle, Yorkshire, Private Correspondence of Lord Mulgrave
NA, Kew	National Archives, Public Record Office, Kew
Napoléon	*La Correspondance de Napoléon Ier 1769–1821*, ed. Jean-Baptiste Vaillant, 32 vols (Paris, 1858–69)
NMM	National Maritime Museum, Greenwich
Ross	Sir John Ross, *Memoirs and Correspondence of Admiral Lord Saumarez*, 2 vols (London, 1838)
Shrubland	Private Correspondence of Admiral Sir James Saumarez, formerly at Shrubland Hall, Coddenham, Suffolk, now at Suffolk Record Office, Ipswich; ref. SA/3/1/2/1 unless otherwise stated
SRO	Suffolk Record Office, Ipswich
Von Rosen	Von Engeström private correspondence with Axel Pontus von Rosen at Kungelige Biblioteket, Stockholm. (These letters were transcribed and translated by Commodore Jan Bring, Royal Swedish Navy, with minor emendation by the author)
WYAS	Harewood House Trust and West Yorkshire Archive Services, Leeds

Translations from French and Danish are by the author.

Introduction

'You are now the theme of every conversation, the toast of every table, the hero of every woman, and the boast of every Englishman.'[1] A favourite sister-in-law may perhaps be permitted to indulge in a little hyperbole, but there is no doubt that Admiral Sir James Saumarez was held in great esteem both by the general public and by his fellow-officers when he carved victory out of disaster in the two battles of Algeciras in July 1801. A letter of the same date from Earl St Vincent said:

> I hear nothing but praise and admiration from every quarter ... I have only to add my anxious wish that another opportunity will present itself, ere long, for a further display of that talent and intrepidity from which the country has, upon so many occasions, received important benefits.[2]

He was not to be disappointed. But it was to be in a very different way and under circumstances that St Vincent would hardly have imagined.

Saumarez lacked the charisma of Nelson: he also lacked the latter's flair for self-publicity. But in his ability and determination as a fighting captain, he showed himself throughout his early career to be the equal of any, combining these qualities with a skill in ship-handling and seamanship – born beside the tricky waters of the Channel Islands and hardened in years of blockade off Brest – that put him with Richard Goodwin Keats in a class of their own. He was the first to use Douarnenez Bay to shelter during westerly gales rather than running to Torbay, and claimed that not a single French ship escaped from Brest during his time. His predecessor, Knight, had recommended this tactic, and both Warren and Pellew had done so previously but were ordered not to use it by Lord Bridport.[3] But Saumarez backed his own judgement and went ahead on his own initiative, being congratulated afterwards by St Vincent: 'Your taking the anchorage in Douarnenez Bay during the late equinoctial gales has been of the utmost importance, and prevented the crippling of one or more of your squadron'.[4] Three years later, Admiral Cornwallis refused to use this anchorage, despite pressure from Lord Melville, the First Lord, since he considered it was not possible 'on nautical grounds'.[5]

However, what distinguishes him from the many other able captains and admirals of the French Revolutionary and Napoleonic Wars, was his diplomatic skill. This flowered during the five years that he was Commander-in-Chief of the Baltic Fleet from 1808 to 1812 when he played an exceptional part in that complex region, geographically on the fringe of the main battleground and yet at the very heart of the economic warfare to which Napoleon turned to challenge Britain when he had been forced to give up hopes of a successful invasion.

Saumarez' unpublished private correspondence has helped to reveal the nature of a man who had been transformed from a successful post-captain, participant in more fleet actions than Nelson and most of his other contemporaries,* as well as the victor of a single-ship frigate duel, into the diplomat and politician that he became during his Baltic command. It has also provided insight into the relationship between a commander-in-chief and his political masters at the Admiralty. Anchored in his flagship, HMS *Victory*, at Wingo Sand in the Kattegat, 14 miles offshore from the nearest Swedish town of Gothenburg, Saumarez could expect to receive a despatch from London under normal weather conditions in a week to ten days. When he was blockading the Russian Fleet in Rogervik at the entrance to the Gulf of Finland, fickle winds and adverse currents in the Belt could delay the packet ship for a month or six weeks. There was thus little chance of referring to the Admiralty on questions of policy if anything should arise which was not covered in the instructions he had been given on taking up command, as amended by any later despatches, which were few and far between.

Other than Ryan's edition of Saumarez' official Baltic correspondence (*The Saumarez Papers*) very little has been written about Saumarez. The one classic naval historian who did bring his weight to bear on Saumarez was Mahan and, in damning him with faint praise, he conditioned succeeding generations in their views. Mahan's article in *Atlantic Monthly* in 1893 looks at Saumarez' career in depth and praises him fully up to the end of the two battles of Algeciras of 1801: here, in his view, 'the story of Saumarez fitly terminates'. He largely dismisses Saumarez' time in the Baltic because he failed to do at Rogervik in 1808 what Mahan believed Nelson would have done – attack the enemy fleet instantly as at the Nile. As a result, Mahan felt 'it is impossible not to suspect in Saumarez the want of that indefinable, incommunicable something that we call genius', although 'for cool, steady courage, for high professional skill, for patient sustained endurance, Saumarez was unsurpassed'.[6] His assessment of him was as 'the accomplished and resolute division or corps commander'.[7] This was echoed by Ryan who picked on a remark made by Saumarez to his wife, Martha, when he was under Nelson scouring the Mediterranean for the missing Toulon fleet: 'fortunately I only act here *en second*; but did the chief responsibility rest with me, I fear it would be more than my too irritable nerves would bear'.[8] Ryan sees this as an assessment by Saumarez of himself, rather than as a

---

* Dogger Bank, Kempenfelt/De Guichen, Saintes, Belle Isle, St Vincent, Nile, Algeciras.

self-mocking aside in a private letter to his wife. However, Mahan's writings are curiously ambivalent. In the same year that the article in *Atlantic Monthly* came out, the second volume of his major study, *The Influence of Sea Power upon the French Revolution and Empire*, describes Saumarez as

> that most distinguished and admirable officer … it was chiefly owing to his representations to his own government, and to his steady conciliatory action, that the formal war [with Sweden] never became actual … Good feeling between the two nations centred around his attractive personality.[9]

Are greatness and genius necessarily the same? More often than not, genius may be accompanied by certain flaws whereas greatness may have more consistent all-round qualities. As Sir Walter Scott wrote of Canning: 'I think he alone [of contemporary politicians] has that higher order of parts which we call genius. I wish he had had more prudence to guide it.'[10]

Few would contest the attribution of genius to Nelson, but they might find it hard to deny his possession of flaws which could have been his downfall if he had survived Trafalgar. To the Swedes certainly, if not to the English, Saumarez possessed lasting greatness. Gunnar Fagrell subtitles his article 'Amiralen Sir James Saumarez' in *Unda Maris 1973–4*, 'Sveriges vänskapligaste fiende' [Sweden's friendliest enemy]. On Gothenburg's Town Hall there is a plaque in Saumarez' honour as saviour of the country, unveiled by the King of Sweden as recently as 1975. Bernadotte sent him a diamond hilted sword valued at £2,000 when he hauled down his flag in 1812 and, showing his portrait to his grandson (later to become King Oscar II), said: 'Look at the man who saved Sweden.'[11] A letter to Saumarez written from Sweden in August 1813, expressed it succinctly: 'you were the first cause that Russia had dared to make war against France: had you fired one shot when we declared war against England, all had been ended, and Europe would have been enslaved.'[12]

Strong words that need some explanation. There is some doubt over who wrote the letter. Sir John Ross attributed it to Baron von Platen, aide de camp to the Crown Prince and considered by Ross to be 'one of the most talented men in Sweden'.[13] The archivist who catalogued Saumarez' Baltic correspondence believes that the letter came from Count von Rosen. There are four copies in the archive, none of them have a signature and only one is dated. However, from internal evidence which links the letter to von Rosen, I believe the archivist is right.

Certainly, the policies that Saumarez followed during his five years in command in the Baltic proved successful, in both the short and the long term, just as those of Napoleon proved unsuccessful. What is not clear from earlier commentaries is how far this was attributable to him personally, whether there were other admirals who might have been equally successful and what difference another commander might have made would have been likely to produce the same results. How far did he create the policy of restraint as opposed to offensive use of his fleet of 20 ships of the line, or was he simply implementing orders from London, and did he have political weight that made it easier for him to take an independent line? Was his decision not to attack the Russian fleet at Rogervik a sign of weakness and indecision, or of mature judgement and political understanding, which was followed by his offer of terms to the Russian admiral and his letter to the czar suggesting that, in the light of the news from Spain, he might like to open negotiations for peace? Why were his initial suspicions of Swedish loyalty replaced by confidence that their actions would remain friendly, even when they had been forced to declare war and had as their new crown prince and effective ruler one of Napoleon's former marshals, Jean-Baptiste Bernadotte? How and why was it that Saumarez, the conventional fighting post-captain, developed into the diplomat and politician that he evidently became in his five years of command in the Baltic and how important in this were both his personal motivation and his feelings towards his wife and family? These are the questions that I will consider in the chapters that follow.

But since this is an area of naval and political history that is not widely known, having been so poorly covered in published works, it seems necessary not only to provide a detailed narrative of the events of the five years from April 1808, during which Saumarez flew his flag as Commander-in-Chief of the British Baltic Fleet, but also to set the scene in 1807, immediately prior to his arrival, which so largely determined many of the problems he had to face.

1

The Baltic in Autumn 1807*

To understand the situation in the Baltic in April 1808 when Saumarez took up his command, it is necessary to be aware of the dramatic political, diplomatic and military events that took place during 1807. In March 1807, the Ministry of All the Talents fell, having achieved the passage of the Act for the Abolition of Slavery, but little else in its brief life. When Pitt had died in January 1806 there had been four obvious contenders for leadership of the Pittite Tories – Hawkesbury, Spencer Perceval, Castlereagh, and Canning, 'all roughly the same age and with about the same qualifications and none of them aware of any good reason why he should defer to any of the others'.[1] Instead the choice had fallen on the elderly Duke of Portland as a safe but uninspiring compromise. Canning became Foreign Secretary, where he quite clearly had an eye to making a reputation as a diplomat which he could add to the one he had already acquired for his skills as an orator. Together, these would lead him, he hoped, to succeed to the premiership when Portland became too frail to continue. Canning was then aged 37. Rory Muir suggests that: 'Much of the history of the Portland government can be attributed to the tension between Canning's energy, impatience and perfectionism, and the more staid conservative qualities of his colleagues in the cabinet'.[2] It was this energy and impatience that led to what was a questionable decision when seeking to eliminate the potential danger of the Danish fleet in July 1807.

The Third Coalition of European powers against Napoleon was on the point of final collapse. The battles of Ulm in October 1805 and Austerlitz two months later had eliminated Austria. Victories by Napoleon at Jena and Auerstadt in October 1806 had crushed Prussia and he had entered Berlin, forcing Frederick William III to retreat into East Prussia. Spain was a subservient French ally, having declared war on Britain in 1804, and, despite Trafalgar, her remaining fleet still remained a potential naval threat when added to that of France. Portugal was coming under pressure from Napoleon to close her ports

---

* Dr. Thomas Munch-Petersen's *Defying Napoleon* is an important detailed assessment of the situation in the Baltic immediately prior to Saumarez taking command of the Baltic fleet, largely amplifying and supporting many of the points in this chapter.

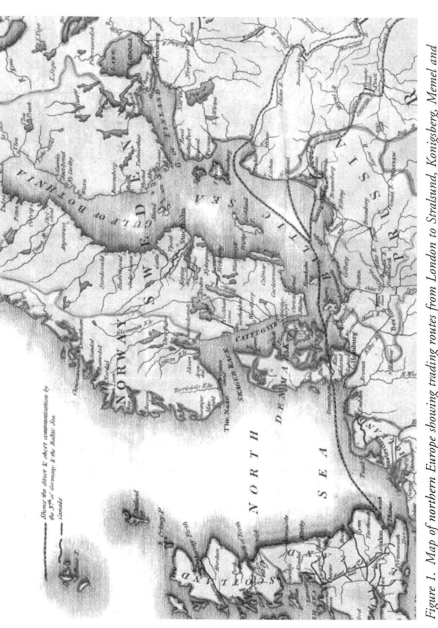

Figure 1. Map of northern Europe showing trading routes from London to Stralsund, Konigsberg, Memel and Riga, accompanying Treatise on European Commerce by J. Jepson Oddy, 11 March 1811 (National Archives, Kew)

to British ships and to seize British goods, leading ultimately in November 1807 to her invasion by Junot's army. France controlled most of Italy, having taken Naples from the corrupt Kingdom of the Two Sicilies whose charms had beguiled Nelson. Sicily, where the King and Queen of Naples had set up court at Palermo, was important to Britain's Mediterranean strategy, as both a supply point and base for the navy and as an entrepôt for British trade;[3] but the Queen, who held the real power since the King preferred hunting, was totally untrustworthy and her army useless, so that it tied up some 15,000 valuable British troops.

All the north European coast from Brest to the Elbe was in French hands, and although Czar Alexander I had a considerable number of troops in the field after the bloody but indecisive battle of Eylau in East Prussia in February 1807, his generals were no match for the military genius of Napoleon. As Lord Hutchinson reported to Canning:

> some serious misfortune must sooner or later happen to the Russian Army – they appear to have no plan of Campaign, no power of Movement in the face of the Enemy, no Science amongst the Officers; in short inferior in everything to the French but in the Courage of the soldiers.[4]

In Scandinavia, Denmark, which at that time included Norway, tried to maintain the neutrality on which her prosperous shipping trade depended. Sweden was Britain's one certain ally, for her king, Gustav IV Adolf, had a religious hatred of Napoleon whom he saw as the Great Beast of Revelations.[5] But he was a capricious and inconsistent leader, often dismissing his best staff in disgrace.[6] Finally, the United States was growing progressively more restive under what she saw as the provocation of the restraints on her shipping under the Orders-in-Council, not helped by HMS *Leopard* firing on the USS *Chesapeake* in June 1807.

In that month, Britain's remaining reserve of 10,000 troops was sent to Stralsund in Swedish Pomerania on the southern coast of the Baltic for a joint operation with Sweden. This was intended to take pressure off the Russians and to maintain Stralsund as one of the few remaining entrepôts for the admission of British goods into continental Europe and as a beachhead for an attack on Napoleon's long line of communications. But it was all too late. On 14 June, the Russians were defeated at Friedland. Alexander almost immediately sought an armistice and on 25 June, the two emperors began their famous meeting on a raft in the middle of the River Niemen at Tilsit, near the border between Russia and East Prussia. The resultant Treaty of Tilsit was completed in its written form on 7 July. In the words of Bennigsen, the Russian General: 'Europe has cause to tremble.'[7] A few days later, a similar but much harsher settlement was made with King Frederick William III of Prussia, who was in a much weaker negotiating position than Alexander.

The treaty saw all Prussia west of the Elbe transformed into a separate Kingdom of Westphalia for Napoleon's brother Jerome and Prussia's Polish provinces made into the Duchy of Warsaw. Russia was encouraged to extend her seizures in Wallachia and Moldavia in eastern Europe from France's former ally, Turkey. In addition, it was agreed that Russia would act as mediator between Britain and France, and that if this offer was not accepted she would declare war on Britain by 1 December 1807 and close her ports to British shipping and trade. The treaty was ratified on 9 July. It was an unlikely partnership that few believed could be long-lasting. It was a political 'time-out' akin to the Nazi–Soviet Non-Aggression pact of August 1939.[8]

Canning had had a report from the British consul at Altona that the French were about to invade Holstein[9] and a further erroneous one that the Danish fleet was preparing for sea.[10] The replacement of the Ministry of All the Talents by a Tory ministry under the Duke of Portland had brought an end to the peace-seeking thoughts championed by Fox (whose death had followed nine months after that of Pitt in January 1806). The cabinet reverted to more aggressive Pittite policies. In the small hours of 22 July Canning received a letter from the Comte d'Antraigues, a French Royalist supporter whom he had inherited as an agent from his predecessor Lord Howick. He claimed that there were 'Secret Articles' in the treaty, involving a naval alliance against Britain by the three Baltic powers.[11] The letter purported to come from an informant in Tilsit whom he would not name, but who, as Thomas Munch-Petersen's extensive research has established, was the Russian General Troubetzkoi who had been in the czar's retinue at Tilsit on 26 June.[12] It came with a 36-page report 'Sur la Russie'. D'Antraigues was well known for his creative imagination as a novelist. It is not unlikely that he had conjured up out of nowhere a story that he knew would be impossible to check and that would put him in good standing with the new British Foreign Secretary. Canning would, he sensed, be ready to believe it and would reward the messenger accordingly.

Thomas Munch-Petersen has found no mention in the three treaties of Tilsit held in Paris of any such 'naval league', nor does it appear to have surfaced elsewhere. The sole evidence of its existence appears to come from d'Antraigues' letter to Canning which was instantly followed by the latter's letters to his newly appointed minister to Denmark, Brook-Taylor, and to Lord Granville Leveson-Gower, who was a close friend and had two spells as Ambassador to Russia. Thereafter, the government steadfastly refused to reveal the source of its information, but equally strongly maintained that 'it appears to rest on good authority'.[13] Much of the confusion appears to stem from the fact that the treaty *did* contain secret articles but they dealt with French acquisition from Russia of Kotor and seven Ionian islands including Corfu, and the Treaty of Alliance, which was also to be kept secret.

Although there may not have been any written documents, it was quite possible that discussions took place during the Tilsit meetings of some form of resurrection of the League of Armed Neutrality of 1800. The Baltic powers, Russia, Denmark/Norway and Sweden, had again banded together then, as they had in 1780, in protest at Britain's exercise of the right she claimed under the Navigation Acts to stop and search neutral ships to ensure that they were not carrying war materials to her enemies. This had been ended by the British navy's attack under Lord Nelson on the Danish fleet defending Copenhagen in 1801 and the virtually simultaneous murder of the Russian Czar Paul. My own belief, in view of the absence of any satisfactory corroboratory evidence, is that this is as far as it went and that the reputed transcript was a fiction, based on an actual letter from Troubetskoi, that d'Antraigues created to achieve his personal financial and career purposes. It has been argued that it does not really matter whether the articles existed or not; they might well have done and this was sufficient reason for Canning to take action. Echoes of the recent situation in Iraq, and whether or not 'weapons of mass destruction' existed there, are curiously loud. Not unlike George W. Bush, Canning used the Secret Articles as an excuse rather than as a reason. As he wrote to the Rev. Leigh: 'Denmark was saucy and we were obliged to take her fleet. Portugal had confidence and we have rescued hers.'[14]

For by the time Canning received d'Antraigues' letter, the decisions had already been taken. Lord Gambier was given command of a fleet to go to the Baltic, and Lord Cathcart was ordered to embark his troops at Stralsund to go to Copenhagen. Both fleet and army were mobilised remarkably quickly and by 2 August Gambier had arrived off Gothenburg with 16 ships, a further six ships arriving with the army transports six days later.[15] Trulsson, in his book *British and Swedish Policies in the Baltic after Tilsit* suggests that Canning panicked and Elizabeth Sparrow agrees.[16] The fears of a French invasion of Ireland from the north were very strong. A Baltic fleet would be well placed to embark Marshal Bernadotte's troops from the north German ports and, in any wind other than a northerly or northwesterly, to sail round Scotland and land in Lough Swilly, Co. Donegal. There was also the danger of the 10,000 men with the King's German Legion at Stralsund being trapped by the Danish closure of the Sound and Great Belt, the only two feasible exits from the Baltic.

Canning had at the same time received a report from Thornton, the chargé d'affaires at Altona, Denmark's seaport neighbouring Hamburg on the Elbe, that Bernadotte had arrived in Hamburg with a major section of his army.[17] This threatened a French invasion of Holstein, where the Danish forces had been withdrawn behind the line of the River Eider. It would have given the French control of both sides of the Elbe, a major trading route. From there they could advance north to Kolding and cross the relatively narrow Little Belt to the large island of Fyn. Thereafter, while the sea remained unfrozen they could be prevented by a British blockade from progressing on to the main island Zealand, containing Copenhagen – the centre of government and of commerce and industry. But from late November the fleet would have to withdraw progressively because of ice, not returning until April, and in hard winters troops would be able to cross over it unimpeded, although in the winter of 1806/07 the Great Belt did not actually freeze.[18] When, in 1808, Napoleon finally agreed to Bernadotte's pleadings to be allowed to pass through Zealand to invade southern Sweden, the April thaw had started and the British navy was blockading the Great Belt.[19] How far the French would have been willing to risk an occupation of Zealand is far from certain. For eight months of the year they would have been exposed to the dangers of a blockade by a British fleet based in Sweden and a hostile population who depended for much of their livelihood on the international trade from which the French would now be preventing them. No consideration appears to have been given to the possibility of the Danish fleet and royal family moving to the safety of Norway in the manner that was achieved in Portugal with its royal family's move to Brazil.

It is difficult to believe that Canning's decision was the result of panic, although this could have been the reason why his proposals were supported by the rest of the cabinet, despite King George III's reluctance, only overcome by a private visit by the Duke of Portland.[20] Having been aggravated by the persistent nagging of the Danish minister in London and by the apparent neglect of his own minister in Copenhagen, it seems more likely that Canning considered a pre-emptive strike by the British fleet – the one weapon in which he could have full confidence – would achieve by terror better and quicker results than tortuous diplomacy. In a letter to George Rose, Treasurer of the Navy, soon after the capitulation was signed in Copenhagen, he said:

> Thank you for your congratulations. Nothing ever was more brilliant, more salutary, or more effectual than the success. The invasion of Ireland prevented – is the first good effect of it. 40 sail of the line saved is another [presumably adding Denmark's 18 to the 11 each of Sweden and Russia]. And it is not a little satisfactory (but let this be for yourself only) as an answer to timid politicians that the report of the firing at Copenhagen has produced at Petersburgh a disavowal of secret articles hostile to England, which no previous entreaties had succeeded in obtaining.[21]

Having set the military forces in motion, his diplomatic actions had been two-fold. He appointed Brook-Taylor as Minister in Copenhagen in place of Garlike who he evidently felt was not to be trusted; in a private letter to Lord Glanville he confessed: 'I wanted him out of the way at Copenhagen, where I thought he had not been doing very well.'[22] He considered he had become too supportive of the Danish claims that their sole objective was to maintain strict neutrality. The truth or otherwise of this claim is at the heart of the question as to the correctness of Canning's decision. He, and his predecessor

Lord Howick, believed that the Danish reaction to Napoleon's Berlin Decree in November 1806 had been muted in relation to their complaints about the orders-in-council of January 1807 that were the British riposte. The withdrawal of the Danish army from Altona to the line of the Eider in November 1806, so as to avoid clashes when France occupied Hamburg and her troops camped close to the border,[23] was seen as another sign of deferment to the French, as were their failure to strengthen the defences of the islands and their stopping the English packet boats via Husum.[24] Moreover, the reported mobilisation of the Danish fleet, in Canning's view, 'could be made in no other contemplation than that of eventual Hostility against Great Britain'.[25] He did not seem to accept that the main role of the Danish fleet was defensive, to protect them from invasion by their inveterate enemies, the Swedes. 'Militarily, she built her defence upon keeping the entire navy as a "fleet in being" in Copenhagen, where the Swedish attack was expected, and by demonstrating a naval strength which was at any time superior to that of the Swedish navy in Karlskrona.'[26] In fact, the Danish government had produced a radical new plan in November 1806, to reduce the navy to 12 ships of the line, 12 frigates, 14 brigs and 300 oared gunboats: this was overtaken by events.[27]

Christian Bernstorff, Danish Foreign Minister, wrote to their minister in Paris in 1806: 'We are lost so soon as we come into hostile relations with England.'[28] Their merchant fleet in 1806 had some 1,200 ships registered in Denmark; there were a further 600 in Schleswig, 300 in Holstein, 900 in Norway, as well as a considerable number based in India (Tranquebar and Serampore) and the Danish West Indies. In all, some 3,500 merchant ships sailed under the Danish flag.[29] Since the British navy controlled the seas, these – and the trade they brought – were likely all to be lost in the event of war with Britain.

The second and more important diplomatic approach was to come through F.J. Jackson. He had been Minister Plenipotentiary in Berlin until diplomatic relations were broken off when Prussia, with French encouragement, occupied Hanover. From Berlin he had been the co-ordinator of British secret service activities across Europe.[30] He was ordered to sail with the fleet to Tonningen in southern Holstein and thence journey across to Kiel to obtain an interview with Bernstorff and the Crown Prince, who ruled the country owing to the incapacity of King Christian. Jackson was given the virtually impossible task of persuading the Danes to enter into a treaty of alliance and mutual defence with Britain, by which a British fleet of 21 ships would be sent to the Baltic and 12,000 infantry and 3,000 cavalry if Denmark were attacked, or a subsidy instead, with Great Britain guaranteeing the restitution of all Danish territories at the end of any war with France. The alternative was for Denmark to put her fleet into protective custody from the French by handing it over to the Commander-in-Chief of the Baltic Fleet. It would be returned in full order to Copenhagen three months after the ratification of peace with France.[31]

It was hardly likely to be well received by Crown Prince Frederik. In 1800, at the time of the Armed Neutrality, he had reacted with anger to the threat posed by Admiral Dickson anchoring off Kullen on the Swedish coast north of Elsinore and wrote to Adjutant General Lindholm:

> I have right on my side and I am leading Danes, which makes me defy everything, especially when the honour and the welfare of this country are threatened ... the British will make so many enemies that they will inevitably be moving towards their fall, which would be a blessing for Europe.[32]

Honour was a significant factor. The Danes knew that if they gave up their neutrality they were probably lost, one way or the other. If they sided with France they would lose their colonies and their trade and the British fleet would destroy their navy. If they sided with Britain, France would invade Holstein and Jutland, and they would lose the vital sources of grain on which they depended, both for themselves and to maintain their hold on Norway. This was probably the lesser of two evils, since grain could be obtained elsewhere with the help of Britain whose blockade would otherwise stifle shipments, and Zealand was where the wealth of Denmark's economy was based. On 31 July, Napoleon ordered Talleyrand to present the Danish minister with an ultimatum: 'ou de faire la guerre à l'Angleterre, ou de me la faire'.[33] Had the French acted more swiftly, Denmark would probably – as she had stated repeatedly – have joined the English side.[34] This was the message that Garlike had been sending to Canning, which he had not been prepared to believe. It is in line with the statement to Gustav IV Adolf of M. de Moltke, Danish Ambassador in Stockholm, that his government would have made common cause with England and with Sweden, even at the expense of all the German provinces, 'if the proposition by England had not been accompanied in the outset with one so offensive [meaning the previous demand of the fleet] as to render it impossible to accede the rest with honour'.[35]

Although an experienced diplomat, Jackson does not appear to have handled the negotiations well, annoying Bernstorff so much at his first meeting on 7 August that he did not even get round to the offer of an alliance and spoke only of the 'custody' of the fleet. He had a history of upsetting people. As minister in Madrid in 1794 he had upset Godoy by his 'vivacité mal placé';[36] he was described as 'only a ninny and pigheaded' when minister in Paris in 1802;[37] and had further problems when envoy to Washington three years later.[38] It is difficult to believe that Canning was not aware of his character, confirming that the negotiations were not meant to succeed, as Jackson himself believed.[39] Jackson asked for his passports, and followed Brook-Taylor who, two days before, had withdrawn the British mission to go on board Gambier's flagship, *Prince of Wales*, north of Copenhagen. Jackson ordered the two military commanders to commence action. The Danes responded with a declaration of war.

The result was never in doubt. Cathcart had 27,000 regular troops, half of them from the experienced German Legion, plus the support of 18 ships of the line, numerous gun brigs, and bombs. The Danish regulars totalled 5,500, many barely trained, and some 7,500 auxiliaries of little military experience.[40] Their gunboats, however, were effective, their long guns outranging the British carronades and forcing Gambier to change to long guns for his own brigs. Nonetheless, Cathcart proceeded cautiously and it was two weeks before he had his batteries in position round the town. He was not by nature a forceful man. A final summons to surrender was rejected and the bombardment started, for three successive nights, using the new Congreve rockets* and red-hot shot – a night attack being chosen to increase the terror effect and the horrors of fire. The naval bombships only joined in on the third night, kept out of range by the harbour defences. By 5 September, one-third of the houses in the city are said to have been destroyed or damaged by fire and some 2,000 Danish civilians to have died.** A capitulation was agreed and signed on 7 September. The Danes gave up their fleet and its naval stores; the British agreed to leave the island of Zealand within six weeks.[41]

Now that they found themselves in possession of Copenhagen and the island of Zealand, thereby controlling both entrances to the Baltic with its access to the north German ports, the British politicians were tempted to hang on to it, despite the terms of the military capitulation. There was even a suggestion that they could meet its strict terms by evacuating the troops to the nearby island of Møn and landing them back again on Zealand 24 hours later. Castlereagh, Secretary for War, wrote to Arthur Wellesley, then a general commanding part of Lord Cathcart's army, of the 'immense control it would give us over all the Baltic powers and interests during the remainder of the war, could we hold Zealand'.[42] Mulgrave, First Lord of the Admiralty, went further, since he believed:

> if we can bring over & fix Russia by retaining Zealand, we shall complete our triumph and secure our fame ... I think a pretence might be set up on the circumstance of the Danish Declaration of War. I think a strong ground, at least of suspension & demur, is furnished by the atrocious treachery of scuttling and piercing the ships of the line in the Danish arsenal. But I am sure we shall have the feelings & the cry of this country with us in any specious ground we may take for retaining Zealand. If Russia is secured, the

---

* The rockets were considered by the fleet to be of dubious value: 'Congreve the rocket maker is become the jest of the whole Fleet.' He was known as 'Commodore Squib' ('Journal of Surgeon Charles Chambers' in Perrin, ed., *Naval Miscellany III*, p. 401).
** Recent Danish research by Mia Lade Krogaard into registers of deaths indicates that these figures are grossly exaggerated and that a figure of 200 deaths is more realistic. I am grateful to Jakob Seerup for this information.

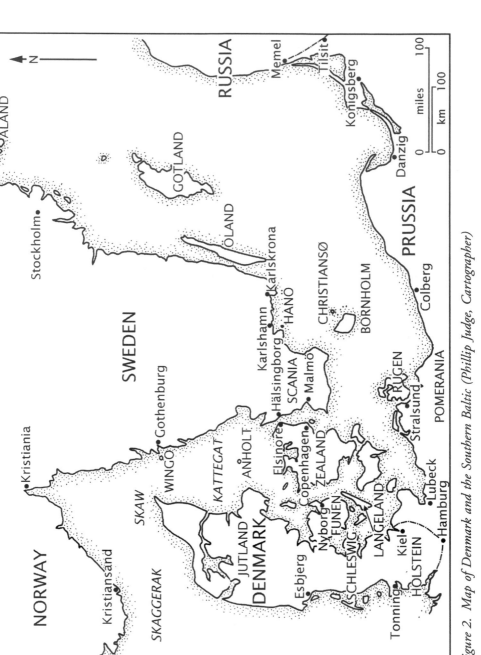

Figure 2. Map of Denmark and the Southern Baltic (Phillip Judge, Cartographer)

manifestos & diatribes of Buonaparte will not signify. Parliamentary attacks we may answer triumphantly by triumph, and if after all any censure for an incorrect exertion of power should attach upon us, I am ready to take my share & more than my share if it can be laid upon me, of responsibility on that score for the attainment of so great an object.[43]

Gambier was told to look at blockade stations in the Belts and the number of troops that would be needed. There were doubts of defending it in winter and it was decided at one stage to invite King Gustav IV Adolf of Sweden to participate with 20,000 men. Canning still believed that the logic of Denmark's situation would force her to make peace with Britain and that: 'A confederacy of Russia, Sweden and Denmark, with Great Britain to support it, I have little doubt might yet save Europe', although he admitted 'I am almost singular in that expectation'.[44]

The military chiefs were much less enthusiastic. Wellesley estimated that a minimum of 30,000 troops would be needed. Where were these to come from, especially if some of the existing expeditionary force were needed to sail the captured Danish ships back to England? The shortage of reserve troops was emphasised by a request from Castlereagh to Cathcart on 27 August to make 10,000 of his men available 'with a view to a particular service',[45] which was later revealed to be Lisbon. This was cancelled in a letter from Canning to Gambier on 4 September,[46] showing the indecision of the government. On 18 September the cabinet agreed to commence evacuation.

Canning, however, still had misgivings. He and Castlereagh appeared to be fairly united in their views at this stage: later, over Moore's expedition to Gothenburg in 1808 and Walcheren in 1809 differences surfaced, leading to their duel in September of that year and resignations from the government. Each saw the other as a rival for the future leadership of the Tories and thence of the government. They now seemed to believe that Denmark might choose neutrality rather than a French alliance and that 'if the neutrality of Denmark can be made the means of excluding the French, it is the best and most natural arrangement'.[47] This was strengthened by a report from Pierrepont, minister in Stockholm, of Gustav IV Adolf's agreement to provide the 20,000 Swedish troops. This was related to Rist, the Danish envoy in London, as a threat 'to quicken negotiations'.[48] Against this, a letter from Wellesley to Castlereagh on 25 September, commented: 'My opinion is that you have overrated the value of the possession of Zealand as much as you have underrated the difficulties attaching the retention of the Island.'[49] Canning later wrote to Gower about the military commanders: 'I am not without any suspicion that the prospect of an uncomfortable service had not something to do in framing their opinions.'[50] The last troops were embarked on 20 October and on the 21st the British fleet sailed with the prizes and transports. Two of the 64s had been destroyed as too old to merit capture, and three ships in the course of building were tumbled off the stocks. The *Neptunos* (80) went aground six miles north of Copenhagen and had to be destroyed, and all the gunboats except three were sunk or abandoned on entering the Kattegat because of bad weather. But 15 ships of the line reached Yarmouth and the Downs in safety, although only four of them proved to be worth the cost of repair. What was of greater benefit was the considerable volume of naval stores – over 20,000 tons being brought off in 92 transports.[51]

Canning saw this as a great victory. Writing to Gower in October on the question of peace with Bonaparte:

> I will fairly state my opinion to you that there never was a moment at which it [peace] was less attainable or less desirable, though I feel a thousand times less objection to it now than I did before the success of the expedition. A peace in the making of which our maritime rights should have been questioned, would have utterly undone this country, stamped with ignominy the characters of those made it. Yet before the Copenhagen operation, could we have hoped to have avoided these questions?

His policy of fighting fear with fear had triumphed:

> With a northern confederacy formed against us, we should have had to contend with fears at home as well as with the enmity of all Europe (for we must not disguise from ourselves – we *are* hated throughout Europe and that hate must be cured by *fear*); not to mention America who will *now* probably listen to reason.[52]

Christopher Hall rejects Hilary Barnes' view that the Danes were not pro-French and the doubt whether 'the whole operation was necessary at all'.[53] He argues that 'when it came to the crunch the Danes would have sided with France' and that 'if the attack gained Britain an enemy, it was one whose teeth had been drawn'. This view appears to be generally accepted by present British historians. However, I doubt whether Saumarez would have agreed with it and I am inclined to accept Tony Ryan's view that

> the policy of terror misfired. It alienated both the Danes and the Russians without doing anything to remove the impression formed in the war of the third coalition that Britain had neither the will nor the means to support effectively continental states that resisted the power of France.[54]

Paul Schroeder also suggests that 'The Danish expedition was thus, if a crime, even more a blunder'.[55] Had Jackson not been rushed over to Denmark and so had arrived after the French ultimatum, his reception in Denmark would have been totally different. The British fleet and troops that by then would have been in the Baltic on their overt mission to assist her ally Sweden, safeguard the British troops in Pomerania and defend trade, would have been looked on as an immediate support for the Danes against any French attack through Holstein. If Canning and Castlereagh were prepared to consider seriously the possibility of retaining Zealand in September, against Danish opposition, how much more practicable and politically advantageous would have been a joint Danish–British defence of Zealand as allies against French aggression. It would have provided encouragement to other continental states, a foothold on mainland Europe perhaps easier to maintain than the tenuous one in Portugal, and an argument for Russia to end Alexander's alliance with Napoleon that had little support within the country.

A joint operation to defend Zealand was something that had been seriously considered by the previous administration in 1806. There were even discussions then that Sweden might provide a force of 25,000 men to assist Denmark in the event of a French invasion of Holstein. But the scheme foundered on the inherent distrust of each other of the two Scandinavian countries. When, in November that year, Denmark withdrew her army into Schleswig behind the Eider, instead of the indefensible Holstein border at Altona, she gave an assurance through Garlike that she would respond to such an invasion by 'the immediate arming of the fleet for the defence of [Zealand] and the adjacent islands'.[56] It would almost certainly have had better results for Denmark, including the retention of her shipping trade and the West Indian islands, and indeed her possession of Norway. In addition, the Danish and Norwegian brigs, gunboats and privateers that were to be such a thorn in Saumarez' side in his task of defending seaborne trade would instead have been assisting him in pursuing French privateers.

Inside and outside Parliament, there was vocal opposition to an attack on a largely defenceless city that had set fire to many of its buildings and was said to have killed a large number of civilians, including women and children. Debates went on well into 1808 but the opposition groups were too weak and divided to be effective. Canning resolutely refused to reveal the source of his secret intelligence on the grounds that it might imperil his agents. Denmark's reaction was to reject all the overtures of peace, ally formally with France in the Treaty of Fontainebleau on 31 October, and in the following year build 150 gunboats.[57] They were built in different ports across Denmark and Norway, with money raised by public subscription from businesses and private individuals, as well as by towns selling their silver. Writing in 1915, C.W. Wandel, a retired Danish admiral, commented:

> The deepest indignation and grief had gripped the whole nation at the loss of its fleet, its pride, its protection, its hope, and reports of ... disgraceful actions that the English in many places on the seas had practised on innocent people,

*Figure 3. Danish rowing/sailing gunboat. Painting by N.C.Dahl (Handel-og-Søfartsmuseet på Kronborg)**

had further created the most irreconcileable hatred against the robbers, the current name for the English in conversation, writings and the Press.[58]

Neither Canning nor Castlereagh had thought out a policy to deal with this. Denmark, through her geographical situation, controlled the two major sea-routes to all the ports along the north German coast and up to St. Petersburg – the Sound and the Great Belt. The Sound, the frontier between Denmark and Sweden, was the easier and more direct of the two for navigation. But there were some awkward shallows, especially for ships of the line, off Malmö at the southern end, making it difficult to defend convoys from determined attacks by squadrons of gunboats. The castle of Kronborg and privateers based in Elsinore were dangers at the northern entrance unless there was effective support and cooperation from the Swedes. The Great Belt too presented considerable navigational difficulties. It was shallow and winding, adding considerably to the distance that the merchant ships needed to be protected, and there were any number of small harbours which were nests of gunboats, within easy rowing distance of the main channel. For in the calms of the Danish summer, the rowing/sailing gunboats were able to manoeuvre while the merchant ships and their escorts were immobile for lack of wind. Seaborne trade closed down in the winter months. Bad weather and the progressive spread of ice often blocked both routes completely, so that ships would aim to be clear by the end of November and not appear again until March or April, depending on the severity of the winter. Much of the Kattegat remained free of ice, but ports such as Gothenburg and Hälsingborg were often frozen in.

---

* The painting dates from the war of 1848–50, but the gunboat design is similar to those of 1807–14.

This, then, was the scenario for the Commander-in-Chief of the substantial fleet that was assembled in 1808 to impose Britain's naval might beyond Copenhagen into the previously tranquil Baltic Sea, to continue the 'policy of fear'. However, despite the government's original intentions, other than a skirmish in the first of the five years 1808–12, the fleet was kept largely as a defender of trade and a 'fleet in being' – a passive diplomatic threat rather than an active military aggressor through the policy of restraint of the admiral chosen to fill that post.

2

Sir James Saumarez' Early Career

When the Admiralty came to consider the Baltic at the start of 1808, it was quite evident that substantial forces would be necessary to meet the needs of a complex and demanding situation. They would also require a commander-in-chief of considerable ability, capable of handling the defensive problems likely to be caused for the important British maritime trade by Danish and Norwegian gunboats and French, Danish and Norwegian privateers; of judging what offensive action might be taken against the Russians; and whether, if Zealand were not to be retaken, there were alternative bases in the Baltic that might be held. In addition, there was the problem of Sweden, Britain's one remaining European ally, whose young king had dreams of military success to match his great forebears which his abilities and finances failed to match. The previous ambassador in Stockholm, Pierrepont, had sent a damning report in June 1807 on his handling of the Swedish troops in Pomerania which had led to their retreat into Stralsund.[1]

Nelson was dead – and it is far from certain, with hindsight, if he would have accepted such a posting or whether he would have been the right man for such a task. Colin White maintains that the two months Nelson had been Commander-in-Chief in the Baltic in 1801, when he superseded Hyde Parker, were 'an important turning point in his professional career' and that he 'displayed a sure hand in dealing with the intricate diplomacy of the Baltic region'.[2] Roger Knight also tends to support this view, commenting that Nelson's sudden departure from Reval 'without the usual courtesies' was 'the only time in the Baltic when his diplomatic dealings carried the stamp of his ill-temper at Naples'.[3] I am hesitant to take issue with such eminent current authorities, but I find it difficult to accept their interpretation of the correspondence and events of that time.

Undoubtedly Nelson possessed high administrative skills of which he made good use in his Mediterranean command and one cannot question his powers of leadership and the inspiration he brought to the fleet. But if we look at his contacts with the three northern powers with whom Britain was in conflict, they are those of a military commander, not those of an ambassador. The negotiation of an armistice with the crown prince of Denmark in the aftermath of the Battle of Copenhagen was, as he himself stressed, 'only intended to be a Military one, and that all Political subjects were left for the discussion of the Ministers of the two Powers'.[4] They were brought to a mutually satisfactory conclusion by the Danes fortuitously hearing of the assassination of Czar Paul in advance of the British and realising it meant that they no longer had to face the almost impossible task of maintaining their honour and keeping both Russia and Britain satisfied in any agreement that they made. It had been Alexander Scott, Hyde Parker's secretary, rather than Nelson who, when a breakdown of negotiations and resumption of fighting appeared likely, had come up with the formula of possible conditions for an armistice. This had extended the talks long enough for the news to come through.[5]

Nelson's contact with Sweden was very limited. One must read from the point of view of the recipient the letter that he wrote to the Swedish Admiral Cronstedt, telling him to stay in harbour or be destroyed, as the British fleet sailed north in May. Roger Knight describes it as one of 'menacing charm', but I am sure that the menace was much more apparent to Cronstedt than the charm.[6] Nelson was, in this threat, carrying out the orders of the Admiralty sent to Hyde Parker, but the abruptness of the letter is military rather than diplomatic.[7] The same is true of letters written to Count Bernstorff and Adjutant-General Lindholm in Denmark.[8] They must have been seen as displaying an aggression and arrogance that were not likely to win hearts and minds, however effective they may have been in achieving short-term military ends. The tone is not surprising when one reads his letter to St Vincent of the same time:

> I hope the reply of the Admiralty to my letter of this day, will be clear and explicit, whether the Commander-in-Chief is at liberty to hold the language becoming a British Admiral which very probably, if I am here, will break the armistice, and set Copenhagen in a blaze. I see everything which is dirty and mean going on, and the Prince Royal at the head of it.[9]

His contact with Russia was his sole one in a diplomatic rather than a military role. His letter to Count Pahlen, Russian Foreign Minister, preparing the way for his entry to Reval (Tallinn) is couched in much more diplomatic terms.[10] But he seems unprepared for the diplomatic rebuff of the Count's reply that 'no negotiation with your Court can take place so long as a naval force is within sight of [our] ports'.[11] Should a good diplomat have responded, as he did, by ordering his ships to weigh anchor and sail in the evening mist into little known waters? At the same time he wrote again to the Admiralty to ask permission to return to England since 'my state of health is such, that I feel at present unable to execute the high trust reposed in me, with either comfort to myself, or benefit to the State'.[12] As Roger Knight has commented, it had all the appearance of a fit of pique and their Lordships expressed regret that 'your endeavours to mark your respect for His Imperial Majesty should not have been attended with success'.[13]

It can be argued that it achieved desirable results in that Admiral Tchitchagov was sent to catch up with him and they had a useful and constructive six-hour meeting. Lord St Helens arrived as ambassador ten days later, was soon on intimate terms with Count Pahlen and on 17 June signed a convention that covered the claim by Britain of her right to search neutral ships, the release of the embargoed British ships, a three-month armistice and an invitation to Nelson to go to St Petersburg.[14] Gunboat diplomacy in the manner of Lord Palmerston may be successful from a position of strength. Would it have been effective when, as in 1808, France, Russia and Denmark were firmly allied and French troops occupied most of the north European coastline? It does make one wonder what role Nelson would have played if he had survived Trafalgar.

Who else might the Admiralty have considered for the command of the Baltic fleet? Studies of other admirals of the period are only slowly appearing as they escape the smothering blanket of Nelson mystique. Le Fevre and Harding's useful symposium[15] of papers on fourteen contemporaries of Nelson – including Saumarez – includes only three others who, to my mind, should have been on a short-list for selection in 1808, if the government of the time had had a clear and sensible policy and the Admiralty had correctly assessed the qualities needed to make a success of it. They were Rainier, Pellew and Collingwood.

Rainier, with his organising skills and 'his appreciation of wider strategic considerations'[16] might have been on the list, but he had retired on his return from the East with vast riches in 1805 and died in April 1808. His successor, Pellew, had found the East equally profitable and would have been reluctant to leave it at that time. After his return in 1809, he spent a short spell as Commander-in-Chief North Sea in 1810 and then moved to the Mediterranean, 'the most complex task falling to a British admiral in the age of sail'.[17] He stayed till the peace of 1814, returning after the escape from Elba and dealt successfully with the Deys and Beys of north Africa by Nelsonian rather than Saumarez diplomacy.

Whether Collingwood would have accepted the post is also most doubtful. He would have had the much longed-for opportunity to be at home during each winter and that might have been sufficient to tempt him to what was a lesser command in status. His role in the Mediterranean was a multi-faceted and multinational one, similar to the Baltic but larger.[18] His reluctance to delegate would have been a disadvantage, but he had shown earlier his ability to establish friendly relations with the Spanish admirals after Trafalgar – 'kind language and strong ships have a very powerful effect in conciliating people' – and Nicholas Rodger considers him a master of strategy and diplomacy.[19] The government's reluctance to move him because it would open the door for the

Duke of Clarence to succeed him in the Mediterranean would, however, have excluded him from selection.

Of the remaining twelve in the symposium, Keats and Hood were too junior and the former showed himself not to have been the right material by his performance in the spring of 1809 as deputy to Saumarez and later at Cadiz. Hood, in the East Indies command, was to prove 'an ideal commander in a war which, as it progressed, demanded ever more versatility from naval officers operating in an ever-greater variety of waters'.[20] Had he not died there of a fever he might have added even more fame to his family name. Troubridge had served as a Lord of Admiralty and was considered an outstanding officer, not just by Nelson until they fell out. However, Pat Crimmin suggests that 'he was not temperamentally fitted for high command'[21] and he had anyway been lost at sea in 1807. Duckworth had returned from his abortive attempt to threaten the Turkish government by taking a squadron through the Dardanelles – a not too dissimilar role to that of the Baltic – but 'though an excellent fighting seaman the admiral was not the obvious choice for subtle diplomacy'.[22] Even Ralfe in his *Naval Biography* found difficulty in resolving the contrary opinions about him. Sainsbury makes a case that Duckworth has been misjudged,[23] but he has a sufficiently chequered history to make one doubt his suitability for the complexities of the Baltic. Duncan was dead. Knowles, having fallen out disastrously with St Vincent, was included in the symposium only as an example of an officer who failed to reach the level of which he was capable, and Sir John Orde never flew his flag again after Nelson's probably unjust criticisms of his actions off Cadiz, prior to Trafalgar. Calder similarly, censured at the court martial for his action before Trafalgar, was confined to the chores of Port Admiral at Plymouth. Hotham was over 70 and had not been employed since 1796.

That leaves Warren. Like Pellew, he had been an outstanding frigate captain. He even had two years' diplomatic experience as ambassador-extraordinary to Russia from 1802 to 1804. Both St Vincent and Thomas Grenville considered him greedy and untrustworthy: 'good for nothing but fine weather and easy sailing'.[24] He was, however, appointed to the modest role of Commander-in-Chief of the Newfoundland squadron in October 1807 and then of the North American station in 1810. His performance in the war of 1812 was considered 'lethargic and uninspired' by American historians and there was a lack of understanding between him and the Admiralty which led to his recall in November 1813, partly as a result of discussing a possible armistice proposed by a Russian mediator for which he was censured.[25]

Of others, Lord Keith had struck his flag in May 1807 to seek some rest after five years in command of the North Sea Fleet. He had also remarried the following January and went with his bride on a summer tour of Scotland.[26] Cornwallis was equally exhausted and perhaps mentally unbalanced, and had

retired from both service and public life.[27] Berkeley 'had a record of irrespon-
sibility going back to the Keppel-Palliser affair'[28] and had just been recalled as
a result of the *Leopard* firing upon the *Chesapeake*. Cotton was later to succeed
Collingwood in the Mediterranean but seems to have played a rather negative
role there and was recalled after a short time; Paul Krajeski's attempt to bring
him out from under the shadow of Nelson rings a little hollow.[29] Lord Gambier
had commanded in the attack on Copenhagen the previous year, for which he
had received a richly undeserved peerage, but was destined for the Channel
Fleet in March

The rigidity of the system of promotion, strictly in order of seniority from
the date of an officer's elevation to post-captain, meant that by the time he
reached any distance up the ranks of admirals, his health, energy or ability
might often be past its best Thomas Grenville, commenting as First Lord of the
Admiralty in 1806 on possible candidates for the post of second-in-command
of the Channel Fleet, had written:

> When one looks at the very long list of Flag Officers, it is wonderful to see
> how very few there are, especially among the higher classes, that are fitted
> for situations of importance, some incapable through age, and others from
> other causes.[30]

It may be that this view was coloured by politics, but it also clearly reflected the
opinion of Lord St Vincent: 'When one looks at the barren list of admirals a
promotion to the Flag ... suggests itself. Should this not take place, Sir Samuel
Hood & Captain Keats should have broad pendants* and Captains, or they
will be worn out.'[31]

What then of Saumarez? Grenville had gone on to consider him, then aged
50, for the Channel post:

> Saumarez would certainly do extremely well; could not be displeasing to Lord
> St Vincent; would be acceptable to the fleet, and would enjoy the confidence
> of the country; but I should doubt your easily inducing him to quit his quiet
> situation at Guernsey where he has all the advantages of a Commander-in-
> Chief, and little, very little indeed to do.

In this he had misjudged his man. Saumarez had been glad to move to a
position of active service in 1807 and had accepted the position of second-in-
command of the Channel Fleet. With the immediate threat of invasion removed
by the failure of Villeneuve's attempt to shake off Nelson, Guernsey had ceased
to be in the front line, whereas the Channel Fleet had the demanding task of
blockading Brest and of maintaining the critical defensive role of the Western
Squadron. He had taken on the task and to a great extent acted as St Vincent's

---

*   Be made commodore, which entitled them to a captain to serve on board under them.

'Viceroy afloat' while St Vincent stayed firmly ashore. He drew from St Vincent the comment: 'No officer on the Flag List of the Navy is better qualified to command the Squadron before Brest, few so well, as Sir James Saumarez.'[32] On St Vincent's final retirement from the Channel command, he paid this tribute:

> I cannot let slip this opportunity to make my warmest acknowledgements for the ability, zeal and perseverance you have shown in conducting the very critical service you have lately been engaged in, which adds, if possible, to your former highly distinguished conduct upon various occasions.[33]

Saumarez had continued under his successor, Admiral Gardner. The latter then asked for Sir John Duckworth to join the fleet as well, who was senior to Saumarez. To be third-in-command under Gardner could not compare with being second-in-command under St Vincent. Saumarez, always very touchy on points of honour, asked to be superseded and returned to Guernsey.

Saumarez' record of service was as full and as distinguished as any other in the navy, with more than his share of fleet actions. Born in Guernsey in 1757, he had first gone to sea in August 1769, sailing to the Mediterranean in the *Montreal*, under Captain Alms, a friend of his two naval uncles. The next five years he spent in the Mediterranean, showing the flag and protecting trade. His fluent French, as a Channel Islander, was useful during service at Smyrna and was much later to be an asset in his diplomatic role in the Baltic. Like other members of the family in the navy, he dropped both the 'de' and the second 's' in the original de Sausmarez name to make it appear less French. The name originated from the Fief de Sausmares (or saltmarsh) in Jersey, reputedly given to their Norman ancestors by William II in 1096.

Through the interest of Admiral Keppel, who as a young officer had sailed with his uncle Phillip Saumarez on Anson's round-the-world voyage in the *Centurion*, he was appointed to Sir Peter Parker's flagship, the *Bristol* (50), for the expedition to put down the rebellious colonists of New England in the autumn of 1775.[34] His baptism of fire was testing. It took place in the abortive combined operation against the port of Charleston in June 1776. The *Bristol* had 111 killed and wounded, including her captain. But deaths lead to vacancies, as Nelson acknowledged in a letter to his brother in 1782: 'we all rise by deaths. I got my rank by a shot killing a Post-Captain.'[35] Saumarez was appointed acting lieutenant.[36] Even at the age of 18 he evidently stood out from among his fellows. On the particularly stormy trip out to America, his zeal and activity caught the eye of Lord Cornwallis who was travelling on board the flagship to take up his military command there: he offered to make Saumarez his aide-de-camp and it was only the mockery of his messmates about 'turning soldier' that persuaded him to refuse. His appointment to the command of the *Spitfire* galley in the waters off Rhode Island on the fleet's return north, working independently with the army and occasionally in combined operations ashore, gave him experience outside the normal routine of a young officer's life and an unaccustomed freedom of action. His experience widened still further when, after he was ordered to land his stores, guns and crew, and burn his ship on the arrival of a more powerful French force, he joined the crews of the other destroyed ships as part of a shore division of sailors.[37]

On his return to England, chance led to an appointment as lieutenant on board the *Victory*, initially under Sir Charles Hardy, and later as first lieutenant under Admiral Sir Hyde Parker who took Saumarez with him to the *Fortitude* in July 1781 on his appointment to command the North Sea Fleet. This was further evidence that he was considered a young man of ability. There followed the inconclusive but bloody Battle of Dogger Bank with a Dutch fleet under Admiral Zoutman. One Dutch 74 was sunk, but both sides claimed victory as the British ships were severely damaged. One, the *Preston*, was sailed back to the Nore by Saumarez as the captain had lost an arm. He must have continued to impress 'Vinegar' Parker, as he was presented to King George III when the king came down to visit the fleet. Saumarez was promoted to commander and made captain of the *Tisiphone*, a fast fireship.[38] Built in 1781, she was one of the first of a class of nine ships on the lines of the French *Amazon*. They carried fourteen 18-pounders. and because of their speed were often used as despatch ships, though two were expended as fireships at Toulon and one at Dunkirk. Six of the *Thais* class that followed on similar lines from 1805 were reclassified as ship sloops in 1808.[39]

A letter from Saumarez to the Navy Office soon after taking up command illustrates his concern for performance and his readiness, despite his lack of seniority, to demand what he thought necessary:

Saumarez to Commissioners of Navy   29th September 1781

I judge it necessary to inform you that HMS under my command is so extremely crank as to require an additional Quantity of Ballast In a moderate Topgallant breeze she has heeled so much as to require two Reefs in her Topsails, and off the Lizard under close reef'd Topsails & Courses it was often requisite for the safety of the Ship to start all the sheets, her Main Deck ports being then entirely under water. She is notwithstanding a very fine ship and I am convinced must sail very well, but her being fitted as a Fireship occasions so much additional weight aloft and her Boats and Booms being necessarily so very high as must make her more tender than she otherways would be. I flatter myself you will please in consequence of this representation to order twenty or at least 15 Tons of Iron Ballast to be delivered for her use.*[40]

---

*   15 tons were provided.

In late 1781, he joined Kempenfelt's fleet that had been ordered to intercept the French fleet under de Guichen who was suspected to be trying to reinforce de Grasse in the West Indies with both ships and troops. *Tisiphone* was heavily involved in the action that followed and Saumarez must have impressed Kempenfelt since, initially, he was going to appoint him to post-rank in command of a captured French 24 *en flute*.*[41] But as he could not be sure that this appointment would be confirmed on return to Britain, he then decided it was better for Saumarez' future to send him on in *Tisiphone* with despatches for Sir Samuel Hood in Barbados to warn him of the approach of French reinforcements. Hood having moved to St Kitts, Saumarez sailed through the intricate channel between it and Nevis to avoid the French fleet, taking soundings as he went as only smaller vessels had used it before. His seamanship throughout his career was outstanding. He persuaded Hood to let him stay with the fleet and make use of *Tisiphone's* fast speed in harassing the enemy.[42]

Again, this impressed Hood so much that when the captain of the *Russell* (74) sought to return home sick, Hood allowed Saumarez to exchange ships with him, giving him the critical status of post-captain at the age of just 25. Two months later in April 1782, he fought with distinction at the Battle of the Saintes under Admiral Rodney. Despite his youth and Rodney's reputation as a stickler for strict discipline, he had the temerity to break out of the line in a manner that was copied by Nelson 15 years later at Cape St Vincent to enormous effect – both on the course of the battle and on Nelson's own advancement. The two fleets had sailed on parallel but opposing courses, firing as they passed each other; Saumarez had been the tail-end ship of the van squadron. For once, the French had the windward position. When he had passed the final French ship, he luffed up to windward to repair his damaged rigging – 'the Mizen Mast dangerously wounded, struck the Mizen yard, sent the Topgallant Mast and Yard down upon deck, unbent the Mizentopsail and bent a Spritsail topsail and a Jib for a Mizen'. Thirty minutes later he wore ship and headed back towards the French. The rest of his division only followed after a further half hour, having at last received a signal from Rodney. It took the *Russell* over six hours to overtake the French rear and recommence the action. Saumarez then worked his way down what was by then a disorganised French line, until he reached their flagship, the three-decker 100-gun *Ville de Paris*, under whose stern he then ran and raked her. Ten minutes later she struck to Admiral Hood.[43]

This action showed an early willingness to take the initiative, even if it meant risking the wrath of his superiors. He had already incurred Rodney's displeasure ten days before:

---

* Reduced to one deck of great guns.

> Both West and Saumarez had better be in smaller ships ... an instance of which happened, which will shew how little the Young Officers know their Duty, and how much they are wanting in respect ... on the *Conqueror's* coming to an anchor ... the *Russell* following her too close was hailed by Balfour to keep further off as they were coming to an anchor ... The return was '<u>so are we too</u>'. If all respect is lost to Superior Officers, there is an end to discipline ... Wisper [*sic*] him how un officer was the answer.[44]

This may explain why, unlike Nelson, Saumarez got no formal credit for his contribution to the success of the battle although 'Rodney's reaction was to declare with an oath that Saumarez' actions had distinguished him above all others in the fleet', while Hood, writing to Middleton, referred to him as 'that excellent young man'.[45]

The end of the war in 1783 brought a period on the beach in Guernsey. During this time, after a long courtship, he married his cousin Martha Le Marchant linking even more closely two of Guernsey's leading families. He later maintained: 'The pleasantest Part of a Man's Life is that which passes in Courtship'.[46] On the outbreak of the French Revolutionary War, he was appointed to the *Crescent* (36). He fought a successful single-ship action, frigate against frigate, both rated at 36 guns, off his native island of Guernsey in 1793, to capture the French *La Réunion*, killing or wounding 120 of her men against just one man wounded (in an accident) on his own ship.[47] For this he was knighted.[48] His success was largely due to another example of his seamanship: box-hauling. Having lost his fore-topmast, he kept his advantageous position on his opponent's larboard quarter by backing his remaining sails to give his ship sternway and with the helm up wore round on his heel to bring himself under his opponent's stern.[49]

The following year with the *Druid* (32) and *Eurydice* (24) under his wing, he fell in with two large French frigates (74s *en flute*), two smaller ones, a brig and a cutter off Guernsey's north coast Sending the slower *Eurydice* straight inshore, he and the *Druid* drew the enemy away, and then the *Crescent* ran firing down the French line while the *Druid* escaped. His own capture seemed inevitable, but knowing the coast himself and having an experienced local pilot, he bore down through a narrow passage in the rocks which had never before been attempted by a ship of that size. The French stood off, fearing that they were being lured into a trap and he made the anchorage in Guernsey Roads safely, further evidence of his seamanship, his willingness to take risks and his personal bravery in challenging such a superior force so as to enable the rest of his squadron to escape.[50]

His position in command of a small independent squadron of frigates in the Channel with excellent prospects of taking prizes was one that many captains would have given an arm for. Despite this, he pressed to be given a ship of the line since he felt that this was the position of honour which was more important to him than prizes. In March 1795, he was appointed to the *Orion* (74) to serve in the Channel Fleet. He took part in Lord Bridport's fleet action in June that year off Belle-Isle and joined Sir John Jervis in time to take part in the Battle of Cape St Vincent. A period of blockading followed off Cadiz under Earl St Vincent, as Jervis now became, and he replaced Nelson in command of the inshore squadron when the latter went off to Elba. It was here that he first showed a talent for diplomacy in his communications with the Spanish Admiral, Mazarredo, even drawing a letter of compliment from St Vincent: 'You approve [*sic*] yourself so able in the diplomatique that you need no assistance from me.'[51] His was one of Nelson's small squadron of three ships that was sent to watch Toulon and with Captain Ball in the *Alexander* came to the rescue off Corsica when Nelson's *Vanguard* failed to reduce sail in time, was dismasted and nearly wrecked.

> In the refitting of her rigging, the exertions of Sir James Saumarez in the *Orion* have been wonderful: if the *Vanguard* had been in England, months would have been taken to send her to sea; here my operations will not be delayed four days'.[52]

As senior captain, he was second-in-command to Nelson at the Battle of the Nile. No recognition of this was given after the battle. Saumarez had not endeared himself to Nelson on his first visit to the flagship two days after the battle, when both men had sufficiently recovered from the wounds they had received. According to Ross, he started to question Nelson's decision not to follow the leading ships around the inside of the French position but to double on both sides, with its attendant danger of damage from 'friendly fire', but Nelson swiftly cut him short.[53]

Saumarez received enormous public acclaim for his victory over a Franco-Spanish squadron at Algeciras in 1801 which gave rise to his sister-in-law's remarks quoted at the beginning of this book. Here again, it was his exertions after the disasters of the first action, when the wind failed and his six ships were caught in the fire of the shore batteries with one of them, the *Hannibal*, aground and later captured,* that made a second and successful attack possible. Working day and night for five days under his flag captain, Jahleel Brenton, his crews re-rigged and repaired the *Caesar* and three of his four other ships, working with the very limited resources of Gibraltar. By then, the *Superb* (74) and *Thames* frigate had been chased to Gibraltar by six Spanish ships that had come from Cadiz to escort back there the original three French ships at Algeciras.

Saumarez was able to sail just in time to pursue the enemy squadron, five ships against ten. Keats, in the fast-sailing *Superb*, overtook the two Spanish

---

* A story liberally adapted by C.S. Forester in *A Ship of the Line*.

First Rates and in the confusion of a night action, set one of them on fire and left them firing at each other, with the result that they collided and soon after both exploded. Only 300 of the total 2,000 men in the two crews were saved. One of the French 74s was captured, but the 80-gun French *Formidable* escaped when the *Venerable* was dismasted and grounded on a shoal.[54] However, the loss of three ships and the damage done to the others in the two actions had defeated the French objective of putting a joint Franco-Spanish squadron into the Mediterranean, where it might be joined later by the squadron from Brest, and 'was one of several factors which propelled Britain and France to negotiate the Peace of Amiens in October of that year'.[55] Brenton's son, editing his father's memoirs, was inspired to more familial praise:

> Officers who would wish to have around them, in the day of action ... a crew like that of the Caesar, must be known among their people as Sir James Saumarez and Captain Brenton were; must secure affection by showing it, and by kindness and attention win the hearts of those who are to be the means of their success, or the instruments of their preservation.[56]

Both Saumarez and his family had expected that he would receive a peerage. Earl St Vincent and Nelson, in his maiden speech, proposed a vote of thanks in the House of Lords in which the latter also formally acknowledged, too late, that Saumarez had been his second-in-command at the Battle of the Nile. He received the Order of the Bath which, prior to 1815, had a very restricted number of members; he was given the Freedom of the City of London and a 100-guinea sword, and a host of other lesser honours especially on his home island of Guernsey, but no peerage. To add to his discontent, reinforcements were sent out to strengthen the squadron off Cadiz and it was now considered too large for a Rear Admiral as junior as Saumarez to command; Vice Admiral Charles Pole was appointed over him. A surprisingly tactful letter from St Vincent accompanied this news, but an unwise indignant reply from Saumarez drew a stiff rebuke and a letter to Addington: 'What shall I say upon Sir James Saumarez his expectations, which are worked up to a pitch beyond all comparison.'[57] But St Vincent tended to blow hot and cold and 21 months later, the Prime Minister, Henry Addington, at St Vincent's request, wrote to George III: 'the eminent services and scanty income of Rear Admiral Sir James Saumarez have induced Mr. Addington, with the entire concurrence of the Earl of St Vincent, to submit to your Majesty the expediency of making a better provision for that meritorious officer' and the King was pleased to approve an annual pension for life of £1,200.[58]

This then was the man, rather spiky – especially towards his superiors – but able, well-liked by his men, driven by duty and honour, now back flying his flag in the modest post of defending the Channel Islands, to whom the Admiralty turned for the very different command in the Baltic. Lord Mulgrave held him in high standing and, in January 1808, had offered him the post of commander-in-chief of the lucrative East Indies station, in succession to Sir Edward Pellew. This he had rejected, nominally on the grounds of his health. The rich prospects of prize money had to be balanced against the dangers to health, long absence from home, and little likelihood of a major fleet action.[59] However, Mulgrave wrote a month later to say that he was sending a squadron of twelve or thirteen ships into the Baltic to attempt to destroy the Russian fleet and to assist the King of Sweden and 'If your health should be such as to admit of your taking the command of this fleet, I know of no arrangement which I can make that would be so satisfactory to myself.' One is not convinced, however, either that the Admiralty at that stage had a clear idea of the nature of the task that they were setting him or that they selected him because they believed he necessarily had the qualities to enable him to make a success of it. He had a good background of experience in fleet actions, unlike Pellew, as well as in the monotonous grind of blockade, had been successful in everything he had done previously in his career, especially in getting results from the men under his command at whatever level, and had shown particular initiative and leadership at Algeciras. He was still relatively junior as a vice-admiral, having only been promoted a year previously when he became second-in-command to St Vincent in the Channel Squadron. The fact that he remained Commander-in-Chief in the Baltic for five years is in an indication of how successfully he grew into the job.

The prospect of a fleet action against the Russians was a much greater attraction to him than the riches of the East Although his actions at Algeciras had ended in success and brought him great public renown, they had not brought him the peerage that he considered his due. Defeat of the Russian fleet would assuredly achieve this, and as an added incentive Mulgrave had proposed that Sir Samuel Hood and Richard Goodwin Keats, both recently promoted to rear admiral, should assist him. They had both served under him at Algeciras[60] and were the two officers he would have sought had they not already been chosen. Keats had also been in command of the detached squadron of Gambier's fleet in 1807 that had patrolled the Great Belt. This was to prevent troops crossing from Holstein, where the bulk of the Danish army was stationed, into Zealand to strengthen the defences of the capital. This posting had given Keats the opportunity to study the intricate navigation of the Belt. Saumarez' outwardly diffident letter expressed a different tune to the one he sang when offered the East Indies.

I feel most deeply impressed with the very obliging manner in which your lordship has been pleased to offer me the command of the squadron proposed to be sent to the Baltic. Although it is with great diffidence that I undertake a trust of so high and great importance, having ever made it the principle of my life to go upon any service where my exertions for my king and country would be deemed most useful, I cannot for a moment hesitate to comply with the commands of your lordship.[61]

He was appointed in February 1808 to the command of a fleet that initially had 11 ships of the line, five frigates and a considerable number of gun brigs and sloops. His instructions from Lord Mulgrave at the Admiralty ordered him to liaise with Thornton, the British Minister at Stockholm, so as to 'concert with him such a system of co-operation with the Swedish marine as may best combine the united efforts of the two powers against the common enemy'. They required him specifically to prevent the passage of French troops from the continent into Zealand or from Jutland into Norway; to guard Scania (Skåne)* from attack; to see if a lighthouse could be re-established on the island of Anholt in the Kattegat; to evaluate the possible capture of the islands of Bornholm and the Eartholms in the Baltic as bases; to 'cause the motions of the Russians in the higher parts of the Baltic to be observed'; to consider the practicability of an attack on the Russian fleet in Cronstadt if his force could be increased; and

> to consider as one of the principal objects of the service on which you are employed the affording every protection in your power to the trade of His Majesty's subjects by granting convoy from time to time ... to the said trade to and from the different ports of the Baltic, and also to ships and vessels under neutral colours which may be furnished with licences from one of His Majesty's principal Secretaries of State.[62]

In addition, as Commander-in-Chief, he was in many ways as important a representative of the British government as the accredited envoy, Thornton, in Stockholm. His liaison with Swedish naval authorities at the various Swedish ports off which he was anchored at different times, as well as with the Governor of Gothenburg, became more critical as time went on. Once war was formally declared by Sweden on Britain in November 1810 his role became even more that of Britain's diplomatic representative to all the Baltic states with whom the country was technically at war. He was also at the hub of a spying network that spread across northern Europe, bringing back information, both political and military, and disseminating news and propaganda in return. He was aged just 50 – probably a good age for such a demanding and varied role.

Sweden held an important place in British policy. On 8 February 1808, Thornton had signed a subsidy agreement of £100,000 a month to fit out and maintain the Swedish army and navy, and other measures if Sweden were attacked.[63] Some considered that this did not show a satisfactory return since,

---

* The province of southern Sweden facing Copenhagen which had been lost by the Danes in 1660 at the Peace of Copenhagen.

unfortunately, King Gustav IV Adolf, if not actually mad, was highly capricious and autocratic. Although he had been king for 16 years, he was still under 30. Sweden, however, was Britain's only substantial ally against Napoleon. The French controlled the European coast from Cadiz to Konigsberg and the border with Russia, including Hamburg and the Hanseatic towns, with officials in each port whose task was to implement the exclusion of British trade as set out in Napoleon's Berlin and Milan Decrees of 1806 and 1807 – as he later insisted, 'partout où sont mes troupes je ne souffre point de contrabande anglaise'.[64]

In theory, there was a complete blockade. However, two powerful factors ensured that there were sufficiently large holes in the net for a multitude of fishes to swim through. First was the need for producers and traders, crippled by these controls, to find a way round them. At Hamburg, the Collector of Customs reckoned there were 10,000 people employed in contraband activities between the town and Altona, across the border in Denmark.[65] Second was the natural greed of the officials themselves, leading to bribery on a massive scale. Marshall Bernadotte – who was considered modest in relation to Masséna, Brune, and his predecessor Mortier – made vast profits from his command in north Germany, taking Fr. 300,000 at Hanover and 400,000 at Hamburg, which enabled him to make a substantial loan to the Swedish government on becoming crown prince in 1810.[66] Tonningen in Denmark had become a major entrepôt, but the British attack on Copenhagen in 1807 brought this to an end. The trade switched to Gothenburg and the island of Fotö in the archipelago off its entrance became a centre of smuggling with warehouses, markets, offices and auctions set up by English traders and continuing even after the formal outbreak of war.[67] Heligoland, captured from Denmark in September 1807, also progressively developed as a smuggling centre owing to its strategic position off the European mainland.

Canning continued to hanker after the idea of recapturing Zealand. He also believed that 'whenever the true balance of the world comes to be adjusted, we are the natural mediators for them all, and it is only through us alone that they can look for secure and effectual tranquillity'.[68] In April 1808, he wrote to Thornton: 'My own opinion (but strictly my own) would be for a greater effort to regain Zealand, and upon that subject therefore I request you to collect and transmit to me every attainable information.'[69] Two months later, Thornton replied: 'I must own that the plan which you may think visionary of making Copenhagen in our hands an entrepôt and a free port for all the commerce of the Baltic under whatever flag, seems to be growing more and more necessary and more and more practicable.'[70] This was the scene which faced Saumarez when he took up his command, although these thoughts of Canning and Thornton do not appear to have reached him. He had more immediate problems to face.

3

Saumarez takes up his Baltic Command

The *Victory* was ready to sail by 17 March, after extensive repairs to make good the damage at Trafalgar. This was to be both her first and her last seagoing commission after that battle, apart from brief trips in the winters of 1808/9 and 1810/11 to Corunna and Lisbon as a troopship.[1] The Admiralty lingered over giving Saumarez his final instructions and he hung around London, impatiently waiting. The reasons for the delay in his departure became apparent on 21 April. 'The causes of my detention in Town on Monday was in consequence of Ministers having decided to send troops to the Baltic under the Command of Sir John Moore and Lord Castlereagh fixed for seeing us on this Day at one o'clock.'[2] On 21 February 1808, Russia had declared war on Sweden, invading Finland nine days later. This would provide a buffer against an attack on St Petersburg which lay rather exposed at the head of the Gulf of Finland. Czar Alexander also wanted to show some gain from the French alliance to his nobles, who were discontented at the feared loss of trade with Britain that it would bring and contemptuous of Napoleon. He had a low opinion of Sweden's antiquated army and poor generals, and believed that Finland could be captured easily and quickly.[3]

The Swedes retreated westwards and on 6 April Admiral Cronstedt, the Governor of Sveaborg, the major Finnish fortress near where Helsinki now stands, agreed to surrender it if he was not relieved by five ships of the line by 3 May. Since the ice did not clear till after that date there was no way this would have been possible. It is quite probable that the fortress would have fallen anyway and Cronstedt, as an experienced commander, may have seen this and have taken what seemed to be the best way out in terms of avoiding pointless loss of life. However, Carl Nordling makes a strong case supporting the popular belief, reported by Saumarez to his wife Martha, that it was treachery by Cronstedt, and Hans Hansson has found some references in Russian and French sources that bribery was involved.[4] It is also true that the Swedish people as a whole, especially the nobility, did not support the war. Other than in the days of splendour under the first Gustavus Adolphus, when Swedish armies had dominated the north of Europe, Swedes could see no benefit from war – a feeling that continues to the present day. They needed to sell their iron and

Figure 4. HMS Victory (photograph by the author, 2005)

forest products and to buy great quantities of salt, which formed 36 per cent of Swedish imports.[5] Trade and warfare do not usually go well together, and if one can stay neutral there may be trading opportunities, as the burgeoning United States merchant marine was discovering. There was an air of defeatism even in the officer corps although the Finnish peasantry showed 'a decided fighting spirit and patriotism that was lacking in their superiors'.[6]

On 14 March, Denmark too declared war on Sweden, another unfortunate result of the British attack on Copenhagen, which had turned Denmark from a neutral into an active French ally. This threatened a joint Danish–French invasion across the Sound into Scania.[7] There was also the fear of Napoleon's armies crossing from north Germany, now that Stralsund had been taken. The British navy could prevent these seaborne invasions for much of the year but once they were forced to leave the Baltic by the freezing of the sea, Sweden would have to rely on her own resources. Instead of concentrating his forces on Finland as his generals recommended, Gustav now opened a third front and invaded Norway. His father, Gustav III, was reputed to have hoped to capture it from Denmark, recognising that at some stage Sweden was likely to lose Finland and this would be compensation.[8] Pierrepont, then Minister at Stockholm, had reported to London in November 1806 that Bernadotte had told the Swedish Count Mörner, whom he had taken prisoner at Lubeck, that it was unnatural that Norway should belong to Denmark and that in justice it ought to be annexed to the dominions of the King of Sweden.[9] The Norwegians were known to be discontented with their Danish overlords and their army was considered to be the weakest of the three Scandinavian countries. However, Norwegians fighting to defend their homeland and using guerrilla tactics were no mean opponents.[10]

There had been a possibility that a British force might assist. Canning had written to Thornton on 1 April: 'I think a partial diversion on the coast of Norway not impossible. But I have cautiously avoided holding out any promise to Mr. Adlerberg, Swedish Minister in London.'[11] A 'Memo on the Defence of Sweden' in the Castlereagh Archives, undated but probably from May 1808, talks of a Swedish army of 16,000 men being ready by 1 June to commence its operations 'the moment that the English Corps approaches the Coast of Norway to effect its Disembarkation ... to the Westward of Christiania Fiord'.[12] A Military Memoir of 3 May 1808 sets out more details under ten headings, including comments that 'the Norwegians are a very strong, robust and hardy people'. It also warned that 'the Norwegians will be more inclined to enter into Negotiations with the British than with the Swedes, who are not liked in Norway'.[13]

In fact, Britain at that time had available an expeditionary force of 10,000 experienced troops, under the command of the one successful general to whom 'all the authorities around the Duke of York were in the habit of referring any question of practical soldiering'.[14] Sir John Moore had fought successfully under Abercrombie in Egypt, having previously made a reputation in the West Indies. In March 1803, he had been appointed to command the brigade at Sandgate that faced Napoleon's Grande Armée across the water in Boulogne. One of his first actions was to develop the Light Infantry from their tentative beginnings at Swanley in March 1800, into the innovative and effective force that they became. In May 1806, he was sent out to Sicily, but was recalled from there to Gibraltar in October 1807 with 10,000 troops, after the failure of the military expedition to Alexandria, which he had advised against and which walked into a disastrous trap at Rosetta.

His arrival placed the government in a slight quandary as to how to employ this able but potentially embarrassing general who was held in high esteem by the Duke of York and the King. He did not suffer fools gladly and was prepared to be forthright in public about them, creating enemies. At a meeting on 10 February 1807, with General Fox and Mr. Drummond, the British Minister in Sicily of whom he had a low opinion, he recorded in his diary:

> I did as I always shall do on such occasions, gave my opinion fully, both with respect to what he had done and what he should do, without troubling myself

whether it was agreeable to him or not. I consider truth and plain dealing as most fit for public business.[15]

His diary comment on Sir Sidney Smith was typical of his caustic views on those with whom he crossed swords: 'From experience, I know that nothing is too absurd for his folly, nothing too mean or wicked where his interest or vanity is concerned',[16] though, in this instance, there would have been many others who shared that view. The Duke of Portland confessed to Canning at the time of the army retreat to Corunna that

from the first knowledge I had of [Moore] as a Public Man, so long ago as when he was in Corsica under the late Sir Charles Stuart, [I] conceived so unfavourable a notion of him from the disposition to intrigue & duplicity of conduct which I observed in him at that time.

Canning and Mulgrave's views were similar.[17]

When the first rumblings came of revolt in Spain against French rule, some of the cabinet, including probably Canning, appear to have been concerned to avoid having to select Moore to command the expeditionary force there instead of the politically more acceptable and better connected, but junior, Wellesley. Sending Moore to Sweden may have been a way out of this, and a way also of giving direct military aid to one of Britain's allies – something that Britain had largely and significantly failed to do in the past. It is somewhat surprising in the light of Canning's comments to Thornton the previous month:

it is essential that His Majesty's word should remain unpledged until there shall have been an opportunity of fully ascertaining the means which this country may have of furnishing any such aid ... and especially until the object to which it is wished that any military operation should be applied shall have been distinctly and specifically pointed out by the Swedish government. The sending of an army to Scania without previous concert ... would be attended with infinite inconvenience.[18]

It marks a step in the divisions between him and Castlereagh that culminated in their duel the following year and the fall of the Portland ministry.

Adlerberg had been very insistent that King Gustav was keen to receive military aid as well as subsidy and that the troops would be warmly welcomed. In this he had acted beyond his instructions, as later events showed. On 17 April, Moore was told by Lord Castlereagh and the Duke of York that he was to command a force of 10,000 men to go initially to Gothenburg to aid His Swedish Majesty against his enemies. Half of them would be from the King's German Legion. Moore makes quite clear that the government's intentions were vague in the extreme: 'It was plain from the whole of Lord Castlereagh's conversation that government had no specific plan and had come to no determination

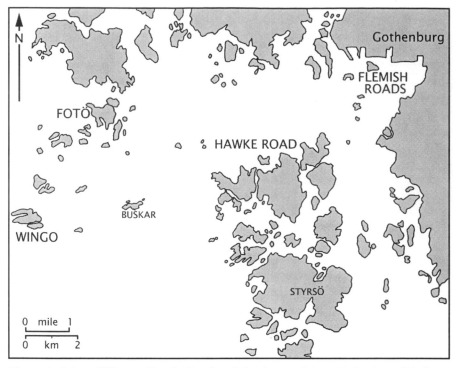

Figure 5. Map of Wingo, Hawke Road and the Approaches to Gothenburg (Phillip Judge, Cartographer)

beyond that of sending a force of 10,000 men to Gothenburg to be ready to act if occasion offered.'[19] This lack of purpose was to bedevil the whole operation and confirm Canning's fears.

Saumarez' understanding of the army's role was certainly a passive one also:

> I presume the Papers are already anticipating, or rather leading, to the expectation of some important expedition – but be assured nothing of that sort is in contemplation, and the most we can expect is that of contributing our aid to the defence of Sweden, in which I trust we shall succeed – but as to any thing further, the Country will I fear be much disappointed. I must once more caution Thee against giving credit to any reports – or believing any accounts however plausible that are not authenticated.[20]

The Times, however, reported that Sir James Saumarez would either: 1. Invade Norway; 2. Attack Cronstadt; 3. Capture Bornholm.[21] Saumarez took on board two army officers for passage to Gothenburg where they were to prepare for the reception of the troops who were to follow. He put to sea on 24 April, was held up by easterlies, and finally arrived in Gothenburg on 7 May.[22] Sir John Moore and the troopships, escorted by Admiral Keats, arrived on 17 May, having been held up for three days outside Gothenburg by fog. They anchored in Flemish Roads at the mouth of the river leading up to the town itself. The unfortunate troops stayed on board for a further six weeks while discussions went on between Sir John Moore and the Swedish King, who would not allow them to land until their future use was agreed, despite Adlerberg's promise that they would be warmly welcomed. Colonel Murray, the quartermaster general, went to Stockholm to assess the situation and then back to London to report.

Gustav IV Adolf objected to three of the conditions that the British government had attached to the troops' employment:

1   *The right to withdraw them if they were needed elsewhere.* He wanted at least a week's notice and a reciprocal right to withdraw his own troops or to order the British out.
2   *That the British troops would act independently and must always be in close connection with the fleet.* This he felt would cramp the operations of both fleet and army.
3   *That they would remain under the immediate orders and disposition of the British general in command.* This was contrary to general custom, 'as the entry of any auxiliary corps into the territory of an independent State necessarily supposes the chief command to be in the sovereign who reigns'.[23]

They were not unreasonable objections, but Moore responded that they clashed with his own instructions and he could only lay them 'before the King, my Master'. One of Moore's first comments in his diary was:

The King of Sweden, from the account of Col. Murray ... is a man of an honourable, upright mind, but without ability, and every now and then proposes measures which prove either derangement or the greatest weakness of mind. He has no Minister, but ... is perfectly despotic.[24]

The King had suggested either an invasion of Zealand or a joint attack on Norway. Neither appealed to Moore:

[Zealand] was defended by 28,000 Danes, and ... 25,000 French, 15,000 Spaniards, 4000 Dutch; total 44,000, were on the island of Funen [Fyn] and on the neighbouring coast. The whole army of Sweden was already fully employed; 6000 under General Armfeldt were opposed to 30,000 Danes and Norwegians on the Norwegian frontier. Ten thousand in Finland were similarly opposed by a superior force of Russians ... the remaining 10,000 Swedes were guarding Stockholm and the southern coast. Threatened as they were by superior numbers on each flank, no point could be weakened to strengthen another without evident risk.[25]

Moore confessed to Castlereagh that he could not offer any better alternatives. If the Swedish plans had been at all possible he would have been happy to arrange an understanding with the King and to have gone ahead immediately, leaving a final decision to be sent afterwards from England. The British fleet would defend Sweden from invasion during the summer, but he could see no sensible use for the British troops and did not expect the Swedes to survive beyond the summer. In his diary, he commented:

> The nobility are adverse to the war and to all resistance, and will be glad to see the King reduced to compromise on any terms, or themselves to become subject to any other Power. The probability is that he is surrounded by persons in the interest and in correspondence with his enemies. In such a state of things we can do him no permanent good; he will not follow our counsels, and our force alone is not sufficient. I am therefore quite satisfied that we should take advantage of the objections he has made to the conditions upon which the force is offered and withdraw it. Zealand should have been kept when we had it last year; it is now fortified and guarded beyond reach of our attack. Cronstadt and the Russian fleet is the only other object worthy of us, but that also has been secured since the Peace of Tilsit. It was within our grasp last autumn. It seems that we left the Baltic when we could have done everything, and we have returned to it when we can do nothing.[26]

The cabinet was slow to make up its mind. Saumarez, too, was fretting at the inaction:

> Our impatience to receive the further directions for the movements of the troops can be easier conceived than described – I only hope if they are continued in this Country it will be to a good purpose, but I am anxious to be left to my own means for the execution of the important service entrusted to me without being shackled as we have so long been from uncertainty of the manner in which the troops are to be employ'd.[27]

He shared Moore's independence of spirit, as later events were to show even more clearly; this will have been one of the reasons why the two men got on so well together. I do not believe that this came from political sympathies. Both were Whigs, but Saumarez had none of Moore's outspoken and aggressive politics. His desire for a peerage was for the honour, not for the opportunity to play his part in the House of Lords, even though his Whig friend Grey championed him in the pursuit of a peerage and ultimately, on coming into power, was able to achieve it for him.

Murray returned from London with instructions that in Moore's view were 'inexplicit and contradictory'. They again showed the lack of purpose of the government. By and large, they accepted the Swedish objections but in a private letter Castlereagh gave Moore permission in the last resort, if given an order by Gustav IV Adolf that he found impossible to accept, to withdraw his troops without further orders from home. On 12 June, Moore decided to go with Murray to Stockholm to see for himself. This proved disastrous. Moore's nature and manner made him the last person one would choose to negotiate with an autocratic and incompetent monarch. He rapidly reached stalemate. 'I soon discovered by his Majesty's answers that reason had no weight with him when opposed to his own opinions. He generally answered either by something which did not apply, or by a simple assertion or repetition of his first observation'.[28] When Moore rejected further wild plans, the King became furious and sent a message that Moore was not to leave Stockholm 'sans la volonté du Roi'. It put Moore in an impossible situation. In the end, after discussion with Thornton, he came to the conclusion that however much it might annoy Gustav, it would give the British government more room to manoeuvre if he were to be out of the country rather than held captive.

There are a number of conflicting stories about Moore's escape, including his dressing up as a peasant to get to Gothenburg undetected. His diary records that Oakely, Secretary of the British Legation, drove him in his curricle two miles beyond the first stage out of town on the Gothenburg road where a courier who had left for Gothenburg an hour later met them in a calèche (an open carriage). Moore drove with the courier to Gothenburg while Oakely returned to Stockholm.[29] This is confirmed by Marianne Ehrenström, wife of the Military Commandant of Gothenburg, to whom Moore presented his courier's pass on arrival. She wrote that he had been helped along in a cart, and the journey had taken four days. He took a ship's boat out to the *Victory* in Flemish Roads and there conferred with Saumarez.[30] The next morning the whole fleet of 200 ships sailed out beyond the Alvsborg fortress to the anchorage at Vinga Sand (or Wingo as the navy called it), a cluster of bleak islands some 14 miles out.* His escape was still not discovered in Stockholm when his military secretary left for Gothenburg two days after him. Moore wrote from Gothenburg to Thornton: 'had I not escaped it was the intention of Sir James Saumarez to have threatened to withdraw his Fleet from the defence of the Sound & Belt if I was not released'. He ended the letter on a gracious note, writing to Thornton: '[I] shall always be happy in the reflection that I had a colleague of so sound judgement ... and who had patience & who made allowance for my exuberance & military impetuosity'.[31]

To Saumarez' great relief the troops were ordered back to Yarmouth. During this time, the *Victory* had been a headquarters ship for both army and navy, with a stream of visitors, so he was relieved when for two days the weather was too rough for contact with the shore. On 3 July, he wrote home:

Sir John Moore has but this moment left me and gone to the Audacious – the transports are all under sail with a fair wind and I hope will get safe

---

* Until 1645, this had been the sole narrow Swedish outlet to the North Sea, squeezed between Danish Scania and Norway.

to Yarmouth before the end of this week. The last has been to me a Week of considerable anxiety and bustle, for exclusive of much official business, great part of it of the highest importance, I have in addition had most of the general Officers to dine with me and yesterday we were not less than twenty at Dinner – I have great satisfaction at saying that the whole time the expedition has been with me the utmost cordiality has prevail'd and no difference whatever has occurred which is saying a great deal considering the sort of people they sometimes are to deal with ... You cannot conceive how pleasant I feel to be disembarrassed from so great a clog as I have been encumbered with, and which I was aware would prove from their first being order'd to this Country. I am only concern'd at the misunderstanding it has created between the two countries and which I think will be very difficult to reconcile.[32]

This was to be his next task, at which he was to prove outstandingly successful. As a measure of his talent in this respect, even Moore wrote to him after his return to England to say that he would be happy to join with Saumarez in any future worthy action – an unusual tribute from a man of his critical nature and further evidence of Saumarez' suitability for his coming diplomatic role.[33] In all this time, there were no fresh instructions from the Admiralty although the weekly packet service ran to Gothenburg from Great Yarmouth on a regular basis that was only checked when there were north-easterly winds or early summer fog. Saumarez complained frequently to Martha of this lack of instructions, but rather than hide behind it, he was prepared to take the necessary decisions himself.

Although Saumarez had been able to send small detachments under Admirals Keats and Hood into the Great Belt and the Baltic respectively to carry out the important work of breaking the French blockade of British ships and goods and maintaining the British counter-blockade of the French, he had had to hold his main force at Wingo in order to protect and co-operate with the army should they finally be permitted to land. Now he was able to take his main force through the Great Belt into the Baltic and by his very presence lend support to the Swedish troops, battling to defend Finland from the Russians, and put pressure on the Russian fleet. There was still just a chance that they might emerge from Cronstadt and give him the opportunity of the fleet action that he craved and which would have been good for British morale at home. In the Peninsula, the Spanish juntas were proving far from the welcome allies that had been hoped. Wellesley's troops were about to land at Montego Bay in Portugal and his victory at Vimeiro was to be followed by public outrage at the unfortunate Convention of Cintra which allowed the defeated French to depart home in British transports and with all their Portuguese plunder. There was need for a public hero to succeed Nelson.

Socially in Gothenburg, it had been a fine time for the officers, both military and naval. The British attack on Denmark the previous year and the state of war that now existed between the two countries meant that Denmark's neutral status had been lost. 1805 had been a peak year for her carrying trade,[34] the Danish flag being at that time acceptable to both French and British authorities, subject to its not being used to shield the carriage of munitions of war. The British Orders-in-Council in response to Napoleon's Berlin and Milan Decrees had seen Tonningen superseded by Gothenburg as the entrepôt for British trade with northern Europe. From there, goods spread to Holland, Prussia and the north German principalities, and as far as Austria and even Italy. Sweden provided the one gap in the northern and western European coastline, otherwise controlled by France from Algeciras as far as the Russian frontier on the River Niemen. It brought a boom time to Gothenburg for its merchants and shipowners in which those of the British officers who were allowed leave ashore, were able to participate.

Marianne Ehrenström, as wife of the military commander, was much involved and wrote in her memoirs: 'Dinners and supper parties followed one another in this trading town, another London, where goods from all over the world were stored because of Napoleon's attempts to blockade the whole continent.'[35] With other local dignitaries, she visited HMS *Victory*. Saumarez took her by the hand to show her where Nelson had died. She considered the officers' cabins very comfortable with, over the door, two or three shelves of books of England and Scotland's best authors. She even tried the seamen's food and considered it 'tasty soup, highly-flavoured and well-cooked meat and good white bread'.[36] Reading between the lines of his correspondence with Martha, it is evident that Saumarez enjoyed the company of ladies and it did him no harm in establishing friendly relations with Swedish dignitaries, aided also by his fluency in French.

In return Marianne Ehrenström had Admiral Saumarez and General Moore to tea. Whether intentionally or by chance, Jacobi-Klöst, the Prussian minister, and Count Axel von Fersen were there too, the latter in his role as a director of the Swedish East India Company.* A few days later there was a ball on board *Victory*. Ships were dressed overall, there was a nine-gun salute, bands and pipers played national anthems as the guests arrived, and the crews cheered ship by ship.[37] After Sir John Moore's escape from Stockholm and the fleet's move to Wingo the partying ceased, a severe blow both to Gothenburg society and to the merchants and shopkeepers.

On the evening of 5 July, two days after Moore had sailed for Great Yarmouth, Saumarez sailed for the Baltic. He had expressed annoyance to Martha at receiving no further instructions prior to Moore's escape from Stockholm and immediate departure for England with the troop transports, despite

---

* Reputedly a former lover of Marie Antoinette, Fersen was shortly to become Marshal of the Realm, but then be beaten to death in a riot in Stockholm (see p. 110).

the frequent packet service and several convoys arriving. He therefore made his own decision to press on.[38] He was beginning to establish his independence as commander-in-chief. He was very conscious of the difficulties that faced him. As he made his way through the Belt, he wrote:

> This Station affords much greater anxiety than the Channel Islands and I may add than any other Station I have hitherto been upon and its being so perfectly novel in all respects makes it the more interesting. I must allow there is very great responsibility attached to it, but so long as I am guided by the best of motives and that I do all in my power for the advancement of the public good, I must commit the rest to the Divine Providence who I trust will endow me with strength of Mind proportionately as the difficulties may increase. I have the satisfaction to say that I never enjoyed greater comfort aboard any Ship than I do in this, the officers being all very estimable characters and most of them of my own selection, particularly Dumaresq* who is everything that can be wished.[39]

David Greenwood, in an unpublished recent biographical work,[40] suggests that the diffidence he had expressed in his formal acceptance letter to Mulgrave[41] indicated personal reservations about his own fitness for high command. My own belief is that it merely expressed conventional modesty and that this letter to his wife more accurately reflects his keenness to take on a demanding and 'interesting' command that would take him into new realms of experience.

His difficulties started with the Swedish king. The day before Saumarez sailed from Gothenburg, he had a letter from Stockholm to say that the King had:

> embarked six days before onboard one of his Yachts and sail'd upon an excursion on the Yacht without any one being informed of his intentions – it is by many supposed he is gone to join his Army in Finland as he appointed a regency to act during his Absence – but he is so strange a character by all accounts that even his Ministers are not appriz'd of his views and as he acts independent of them, it must not be wonder'd at if he acts wrong. With all this he is said to be a good Man and to have upright Principles, but as he imitates Charles the twelfth he may also partake in his eccentricities.[42]

He thought it quite possible that King Gustav had gone to make a separate peace with Russia. The news of the Spanish revolt against Napoleon, instead of making Gustav feel stronger in his alliance with Britain, had made him suspicious and jealous of all the aid that Canning appeared to be giving to Spain in preference to him, desperate for money to fund the Swedish armies since he dared not seek it from the Swedish Diet, the legislative assembly, who would almost certainly refuse. This had been one of his accusations thrown at Moore in their meetings. Another accusation was that Thornton, in the middle

---

* The flagship's captain, another Guernseyman and also a relative.

of discussions of combined operations against Russia, was himself talking in terms of peace. He had asked Baron von Ehrenheim, Sweden's chancellor with responsibility for foreign affairs and no lover of the British alliance, for an audience with the King to 'propose in concert with England Terms of Accommodation with Denmark and with Russia'.[43] Ehrenheim had been on hand at these meetings and was convinced that Britain intended to abandon Sweden in favour of helping Spain and this was the reason behind Moore's inactivity: 'In Spain there are fleets to win, trade to revive, colonies to raise and a mass of power to direct against points far more sensitive to Bonaparte than Russia and Denmark.'[44] Christer Jorgensen suspects that Moore himself, urged to abandon a forlorn expedition by General Brownrigg, his ally at the Horse Guards, might be deliberately provoking a crisis to give him a pretext to return with his troops for more active occupation in Spain.[45]

Saumarez was still very new on the station and did not have the confidence in the good intentions of the Swedes that he was later to acquire. His ships were vulnerably scattered across the whole area from the Skaw to the southern Baltic in defence of the convoys which had been established for British and neutral shipping. He ordered all his ships of the line to rendezvous at the south-eastern end of the Danish islands, and brought on board *Victory* the £200,000 of silver intended for the Swedish subsidy. He would have a force of eight ships of the line, enough to meet either the Swedes or the Russians separately, each of them with 11 ships, 'but if they combine I must find my way back thro' the Great Belt'.[46] In other respects, 'the force is as respectable as I can wish – indeed I could spare one or two Line of Battle Ships in exchange for frigates',[47] a familiar cry of admirals of the time.* In fact, as he knew from Sir John Moore and Thornton's reports, British policy would welcome peace between Sweden and Russia to enable troops and subsidy money to be released to support the Spanish insurrection, as the Swedes suspected. However, it was not impossible that the autocratic and eccentric Swedish king might decide, under Russian pressure in order to please France, to come to terms that imperilled the British naval presence in the Baltic.

The Danish gunboats were extremely active, though only one of the convoys suffered serious losses: off Malmö 13 ships were taken or destroyed as well as the two escorts, *Thunder* and *Piercer*, leading to complaints against the Admiralty by north country merchants being published in the newspapers at Hull. Saumarez' request for a further subordinate admiral to free Keats from the pressures of the Belt was granted and his choice of Admiral Bertie accepted.[48] Saumarez had entered into correspondence with the Danish Admiralty at

---

* An unsigned memorandum to Mulgrave dated 8 April, 1808, concerning a frigate for Lord Strangford, listed a need for a further 36 frigates over the various world-wide stations, not including the additional ones for which Saumarez was asking (WYAS WYL250/8/31).

Copenhagen regarding the exchange of the crews of the two captured Gun Brigs, and had hopes that this might extend to negotiating terms of peace, 'but at present that is impossible'.[49]

His passage through the Belt started well, but light and contrary winds held him up off Sproe (Sprogø), the island that marks the northern limit of the trickiest part of the passage.* Apart from the fickle winds and shallow waters, a major problem of navigation for the deep-draught ships of the line was that they were caught by the undercurrent which, subject to the wind direction, tends to flow out of the Baltic. On 8 July, Saumarez recorded that he was 'proceeding thro' the Great Belt, but such is the contrariety of Currents that with a fresh breeze and favourable, we scarcely make any progress'. One captain later reported: 'The current has been running 6 knots.' Making his way eastward the following May, Saumarez wrote:

> a favourable breeze brought us to the Entrance to the Baltic but here I fear we are likely to be detain'd by the adverse Currents which are so strong that even with a fresh Breeze we can make no way against them, and we have been oblig'd to anchor at different times – it is very trying to our Patience, anxious as I have [been] for some time to join the Ships within the Baltic; a large Convoy is following us under the same predicament, and I only wish a few of the wealthy Merchants were onboard to witness the causes of the delay to their Trade – without so unreasonably ascribing it to the negligence of Officers.[50]

Shipowners wanted the security of convoys, but were ever critical of any delays that might arise: these they would almost invariably attribute to the navy. Naval escorts were equally critical of the behaviour of merchant captains, their failure often to respond to signals and straggling away from the body of the convoy, making them more easily subject to capture.

By 15 July, ten days after sailing from Gothenburg, Saumarez was off Møn – the easternmost of the southern Danish islands – where he was joined by Sir Samuel Hood's detached force. He also received dispatches from England to 27 June. These included a blast from Pole, Secretary to the Admiralty, about the loss of the *Thunder*'s convoy, asking him for a detailed statement of the circumstances, 'which statement their lordships trust will show that the force under your command has been distributed in the most judicious manner as well for the protection of the Baltic trade as for affording assistance to the king's ally'.[51] This reflected pressure on the government from members of parliament representing the major ports, anxious to look after their constituents' interests. Saumarez' reply was forceful:

---

* In recent years, the island formed a useful half-way stage for the bridge and tunnel that now crosses the Great Belt from Nyborg to Korsør.

when it is considered that above three hundred sail of vessels have gone under convoy to the Baltic in the face of the immense flotilla which the enemy have collected in Zealand, it cannot be matter of surprise that 16 of that number should have fallen in their hands'.[52]

The political nature of his command was becoming increasingly clear to Saumarez. He had just sent Keats off to Stralsund on the eastern Baltic coast in response to a report on 21 July from a Swedish cutter keeping watch there, that the French had embarked 9,000 troops with artillery for an invasion of Sweden. If they had, in fact, sailed and Keats could intercept them, it would enable him to strike a severe blow at the French and help restore good relations with Sweden. To add to his worries and call on his diplomatic skills, he had to spend much of two days dealing with the French royal family who were trying to make their way to safety as Napoleon's troops moved further north. In fact they were in no danger; Napoleon later wrote to Davout saying that he had no interest in pursuing the former king 'who could only inspire pity for his stupidity' and tore a strip off his Minister of Police for setting a spy to keep an eye on him in Switzerland.[53] The queen with the Duke and Duchess of Angouleme had been brought from north Germany by the frigate *Euryalus* to Karlskrona, on Sweden's east coast, to proceed by land to Gothenburg, avoiding the dangers of the passage by sea through the Sound or Belt. There the *Euryalus* was to collect them again for their journey to safety in England. The government had restricted to 20 the number of their attendants for whom passage would be provided, although they totalled over a hundred, most of whom had been attached to the royal family for over 20 years. They included the Duke d'Havré whom Saumarez had brought to Britain in 1798 and who sent several long letters to plead his cause, and the queen herself also wrote to him. As Saumarez said to Martha: 'judge then how hard it must be to separate them and leave those excluded without any Azylum whatever or the means of any subsistence.' He used his discretion to include the duke and his family extra to the total, another instance of his willingness to go against orders when it seemed right.[54]

There was also a messenger with dispatches for Sir John Moore to 30 June, which he opened. They asked Moore to assist if he could in the evacuation of Spanish troops on Funen, the large central Danish island which formed the western side of the Great Belt. This confirmed an earlier letter from Thornton. He had considered Castlereagh's plan:

as far as it depends upon the co-operation of our land forces or upon the immediate furnishing of transport, must be regarded as impracticable; but His Majesty's government dwell with so much earnestness upon the importance of any attempt to attain the object of bringing away the Spanish troops, that I cannot forbear impressing it upon your Excellency's attention.[55]

He himself had found it impossible to communicate with either Denmark or the continent owing to Swedish restrictions and he hoped that the navy might be able to spy out the situation.

The Spanish army was one of some 15,000 men, under the command of the Marques de la Romana, and formed the major part of Marshal Bernadotte's multinational force in northern Germany.[56] They had been sent north to Denmark to join with French and Danish troops in the projected invasion of Scania. But because of delays and hesitation by Napoleon, by the time they had reached Nyborg in order to cross the Great Belt, the ice had broken up and two ships of the North Sea Fleet under Captain Parker were in control of the sea crossing, having destroyed the *Prins Christian Frederik* (74), Denmark's sole remaining ship of the line which had been sent from Norway to assist the invasion.[57] One of the bodies of the crew, washed up on the coast of Zealand, was that of Lieutenant Peter Willemoes, who was to become posthumously famous in Denmark for his heroic conduct as the 17-year-old commander of Fleet Battery No.1 against Nelson's fleet at the Battle of Copenhagen in 1801. His friend, the distinguished Danish poet N.F.S. Grundtvig, wrote an elegy on his death.[58] Professor Feldbaek has questioned whether Willemoes was the real hero of the Danish fleet. Sub-Lieutenant Jochum Müller of the artillery barge *Hajen* was the last to strike and it was he who was taken to Nelson's cabin on the *Elephant* and congratulated on his bravery.[59] But he was Norwegian and so later was to serve under the Swedish flag when Sweden acquired Norway. The patriotic myth-makers needed a Dane and Willemoes, having died in action a few years later, filled that billing.

It is possible that Napoleon had delayed the invasion deliberately, wishing to see Russia fully committed to the attack on Sweden so as to protect his back while he turned his attention to Spain. Too swift a Swedish collapse might have shifted the balance of power. But with his blindness to naval matters, he had not appreciated the critical timing of the melting of the sea-ice and now persisted in demanding that Bernadotte's next dispatch came from Stockholm despite the presence of the British fleet. The troops had stayed on Funen and there was a further Spanish regiment in Copenhagen and some in Jutland.[60]

Relations between the French and Spanish had not been good. The Spaniards claimed they always had the worst quarters and although they were well-clothed, many of them were sick. A report to Charles Fenwick, the former British Consul at Elsinore who had now moved for safety across the Sound to Hälsingborg, spoke of them hating and despising each other.[61] The Funen contingent had refused to sign an oath of allegiance to Napoleon's brother, Joseph, whom he had placed on the Spanish throne after forcing the exile and abdication of the former royal family. Riots in Madrid on 2 May had been savagely put down by the French but further risings followed, province by province, in Spain, and on 8 June a deputation from the junta of Asturias, a small province in northern Spain, arrived in London. They were received with enormous enthusiasm.

Canning had actually started to work on detaching the Spanish troops as early as 1 April, *before* the Madrid uprising. He had written to Thornton, sending him a copy of a proclamation to the Spanish troops in Denmark and Pomerania, 'the object of which is to induce them to make their way to Sweden, with promise of being well received and entertained there. The commander of their troops is in good principles.'[62] On 19 May, boats from Hood's squadron had captured a Danish postboat with, amongst other correspondence, a letter in English from one Niemeyer to a Mr. Winckelheim asking him to find a reliable agent to distribute posters to the Spanish troops for £1,000.[63] These were false names used by Edward Nicholas, in charge of Heligoland, when corresponding with his contacts.[64] Keats, too, captured a Danish postboat which carried a letter, which he forwarded to Saumarez, from the Commissioner General of Police at Antwerp to Bernadotte commenting that 'the Marquis de Romana needs to be watched because of the high opinion of him in London'.[65] On 30 June, Canning wrote to Thornton:

> Keep the King of Sweden in good humour till you hear from me again. Disseminate the Spanish news – you cannot exaggerate it. Seek out all opportunities of letting Denmark know that we are still most unwillingly her enemies. Above all things, urge and aid all you can the attempt to rescue the Spanish Army.[66]

Although there is no record that this had been passed to Saumarez, either directly or through Thornton, it is evident that he had been told of it, since he had written to Martha of attempts 'to disperse Proclamations in the Spanish language, in order to make known to these unfortunate people the devastation Bonaparte has been making in their Country'.

News of the risings were believed to have been fed to the troops in Denmark through Father James Robertson, a Benedictine monk, who had been recommended to Canning as a secret agent by Sir Arthur Wellesley.[67] A number of distinguished historians accept Robertson's dramatic account, written many years after the event. However, it now seems likely that the Marques had already been informed by his aide-de-camp Llano on his return from Spain on 24 June[68] and, from Robertson's own account, he was arrested and had to talk his way out to escape when he tried to contact the British ships.[69] Keats' correspondence confirms that his own first contact came from Don Antonio Fabregues, a lieutenant in the Catalonian regiment, stationed on the nearby island of Langeland and bringing details of the number and situation of the Spanish troops. He had been taken on board the *Edgar* by a fishing boat on 5 August.[70]

Keats had got back from Stralsund by 29 July, to report that although the French troops there had indeed been embarked, 'the Vessels [were] not in a state of readiness to put to Sea and it is thought to be more for exercising than any other purpose; they however require to be watched'.[71] Saumarez waited two more days in the hope of receiving dispatches from England. When nothing came, he decided to press on to Karlskrona and thence to Stockholm. Thornton was keen that Saumarez should meet Gustav IV Adolf and was actively supported in this by Ehrenheim.[72] The *Victory* also had on board the subsidy in specie that was urgently awaited by the Swedes. Saumarez suggested meeting at Dalarö to save the *Victory* having to work her way through the channels that led to Stockholm through the off-lying islands: 'we shall be about thirty miles from the City – the Envoy has promised to pay me a Visit onboard – and if the King is return'd I shall probably see him, but be assured I shall take care he does not serve [me as] he did Sir J. Moore.'[73]

Meanwhile, Keats was sent off to Langeland to make contact if he could with the Spanish troops. There he had the good fortune to be joined by the *Mosquito* which had on board Don Raphael Lobo y Campo,* sent by the Admiralty to assist in making contact with his fellow-countrymen. Keats also received a duplicate set of the Admiralty instructions and acted swiftly. He agreed with de la Romana that the Spaniards should take control of Nyborg, the chief town on the Great Belt, on 9 August, and he used threats to force the Danish governor into making transports available to move all the Spaniards from Funen on to the more easily defensible Langeland, until transports were ready to move them back to England via Gothenburg.[74] They would join the 2,000 troops already there, with a further 1,000 from Jutland.

Saumarez reached Karlskrona on 4 August, visited the dockyard, introduced himself to the Swedish heads of department and had the captains to dine with him. He also called on Admiral Cederström who had just been dismissed from his command of the Swedish fleet by the King: 'I should observe Adml. Cederstrom was dismissed his Command because some Russian Frigates got into Finland, when he could not prevent it. He is a very worthy Man and much respected, but the King is very capricious and headstrong.'[75]

On 9 August, Saumarez received a report from a vessel coming from the Great Belt with news that contact had been made with the Spanish troops and confirming that about 12,000 men were looking for means to get back to Spain. 'Knowing it to be the intention of Government that every effort should be made to extricate them from their situation, I decided on returning to the Great Belt for that purpose, and to order Sir S. Hood with a detachment up the Baltic.'[76] It was a difficult decision for him. The temptation to press on towards Russia and the possible scene of a fleet action that was also in line with his overall instructions must have been great. The rescue of the

---

* A Spanish naval officer who had come to London as secretary to the deputation from Seville (see Ryan, Saumarez Papers, p. 36, n. 3).

Spanish troops would be a tricky, complex task of a predominantly administrative nature: his subordinate admiral, Keats was already on the spot and in the event had virtually completed most of the work by the time Saumarez was able to get back. However, duty prevailed over possible glory. He was encouraged to find, a day or two later, when a report from Keats reached him via the *Mosquito* enclosing the official instructions, 'the measures I was pursuing were exactly what was pointed out in my instructions from Government'.[77] The Admiralty letter stressed the importance of their evacuation for both political and military reasons and both the firepower and the carrying capacity of *Victory* could have been critically important.

Having doubted whether the Russian fleet would emerge from Cronstadt in the presence of a combined Anglo-Swedish fleet, Saumarez' decision to turn back to the Belt had been less difficult, although it meant rejecting a Swedish request for joint action.[78] A letter from King Gustav IV convinced him of the continuing support of Sweden. Reporting that the Russian fleet had indeed ventured out and driven the small Swedish observation squadron from Hangö Udd, it asked him to bring all the ships of the line that he could spare for a pincer attack that would cut off their retreat. However, Saumarez judged it more important

> to exert my utmost efforts in extricating the Spanish troops ... and if possible to furnish them the means to unite with their brave countrymen in Spain in extricating their country from the atrocious tyranny of the Usurper Bonaparte. A cause in which humanity is so much interested and which in its consequences may tend to the welfare of all Europe cannot but be sanctioned by your Majesty who has so uniformly displayed such eminent proofs of magnanimity and zeal in the defence of the laws and rights of nations.[79]

The diplomat was beginning to predominate over the post-captain who would dearly have liked to lead his squadron into action against the Russian fleet. He must have been aware also that he was possibly sacrificing his chances of achieving the barony that he felt was already his due. He may have considered that the rescue of the Spanish troops might be considered so important by government that its success would also bring such an honour. Saumarez saw the Spanish rebellion as one of the first signs of hope in the overall conduct of the war against Napoleon. 'The Peace with that country will relieve England from a great part of the burthen of the war – and extend the market for our manufactures', providing alternatives to the Baltic trade route. His comment illustrates his appreciation both of the wider national concerns beyond his own command, and also of the impact that the opening up of new trading possibilities would have upon the Baltic situation. His only regret was a religious one, displaying the anti-Catholicism of many of his contemporaries:

if they [the Spanish people] could only divest themselves of that spirit of idol-
atry and gross superstition which even their late Proclamations too strongly
evince, we might hope to see them emancipated from the grasp of Bonaparte
– but while their Clergy preserve their ascendancy over the minds of the
unfortunate inhabitants, they will always remain an enslaved people.[80]

His views were fully shared by Martha and might have been well received
in Lutheran Sweden. She had much earlier commended him to read a book
that:

proves that Voltaire and the old King of Prussia had entered into a League
to undermine Christianity and that they discovered the most effective way
to promote irreligion was by corrupting the morals of women, as when that
was effected their influence in Society would soon bring the men over to their
side. What a lesson this is to every Woman.[81]

Head winds had held up Saumarez so the Spanish troops had all been moved
across to Langeland by the time he arrived on 18 August. A formal parade
was held with gun salutes to the national flags. The Spaniards were finally all
embarked and sailed from Langeland for Gothenburg on 21 August.[82] There
were still to be considerable delays before they left these unfriendly northern
lands for the sunshine of Spain. Baron Toll, Governor-General of Scania, refused
to allow them to land at Gothenburg since they were foreign troops, and the
merchants of Gothenburg sought exorbitant rates for transporting them elsewhere, so transports were sent from Britain to collect them from Sweden.[83] On
a happier note, Keats wrote to Pole, Secretary of the Admiralty, asking that the
ships' officers should be recompensed for the hospitality they had extended to
the Spanish officers and Pole's recommendation was that their Lordships should
make 'a liberal allowance'.[84]

Although fiercely jealous of his own honour and standing, Saumarez was
never one to play down his subordinates' achievements to his own advantage.
He wrote to Martha: 'Admiral Keats has been indefatigable in the management
of this intricate business, which will add greatly to his well earned fame, and
I hope will draw upon him some mark of Royal favour, which he so justly
merits.'[85] It was Keats' dispatches that were sent to the Admiralty and published
at length in *The Naval Chronicle*.[86] Nelson, as Commander-in-Chief, would
doubtless have made sure that it was his own report rather than that of his
subordinate that took the news of the successful evacuation back to England.
Lord Mulgrave reported to the king:

The dispatches of Rear-Admiral Keats are at once so full & concise that Lord
Mulgrave most humbly conceives that he could not submit a précis for your
Majesty's perusal without omitting some interesting or important circum-
stance of a transaction the beneficial influence of which may be expected

to extend far beyond its more immediate impression in Great Britain & in Spain.[87]

Keats duly got his knighthood and the 'Red Ribband' of the Order of the Bath, although Saumarez was later to write, when on his way back to England:

> I am glad to find Admiral Keats has the Red Ribband. Sir Samuel Hood is created a Bart. It is a happy circumstance Sir Jas. S. sets himself above worldly Honours and is satisfied with those he has obtained – he would otherwise feel mortified at those serving and doing his Orders being thus noticed whilst he remains apparently neglected.[88]

Martha would have understood the irony in his words.

The Danes were furious and complained to Napoleon on 11 August. He replied with a remarkably apologetic letter to 'my brother, the King of Denmark', expressing his sorrow at the imprudence of putting suspect troops in such an important post and promising to replace them.[89] Marshal Bernadotte, in command of all the armies of northern Germany, wrote an emotive appeal – soldier to soldier – pouring abuse on the Marques de la Romana whom he accused of 'treachery unknown even among Tartars' and offering to send any who wished back to their families where they would be able to 'convince themselves of the Jubilee of all Spain for the Brother of the Great Napoleon'.[90] But by then it was too late.

4

The Crisis of Rogervik

Cederström's replacement in command of the Swedish fleet was Admiral Nauckhoff who had written Saumarez 'a very handsome letter, expressing his great desire to serve with me against l'Ennemi Commun – but if this last has kept in his lurking Den, he will scarce venture out in the presence of the two Squadrons'.[1] Nauckhoff was to write again seven days later from off Örö, at the entrance to the Gulf of Finland, with the amazing news that 20 ships of the Russian fleet had indeed come out of Cronstadt on 5 August to chase away the three Swedish ships of the line and two frigates keeping watch at Hangö Udd – the point where the Gulf of Bothnia and the Gulf of Finland could be said to join – and were now themselves cruising off there.[2] This was where shipping, both merchant ships and the *skärgård* (inshore) fleet of shallow-draught galleys, had to leave the protection of the screen of islands and narrow passages in order to round the headland and were vulnerable to attack from ships of the line too deep-draught to enter the shallower waters on either side. It was where naval battles in the Baltic had usually taken place. Nauckhoff urgently sought British help.

Had he known this in time, Saumarez would probably have changed his decision to return to the Belt to rescue the Spanish troops, for this would have given him the chance of the fleet action which he craved but which he had feared the Russians would be too timid to offer him. Indeed, he wrote to Martha on 14 August:

> I fell in with Sir Saml. Hood last Friday who has proceeded towards the Gulph of Finland to re-inforce the Swedish Fleet with three Sail of the Line until I can send a stronger detachment, but I much doubt if it will be required as from ev'ry account the Russian Squadron have no intention to leave their Port of Cronstadt.[3]

He could have brought Hood's four ships – *Centaur*, *Implacable*, *Mars* and *Dictator* – together with *Victory* and *Superb*, and possibly *Goliath* also, who was on her way back from Danzig.[4] These, with the nine Swedish ships of the

Figure 6. Map of Hangö Udd, Rogervik and the Entrance to the Gulf of Finland (Phillip Judge, Cartographer)

line, however uncertain their quality,* would have been more than enough to challenge the Russian fleet of eleven ships of the line. *Goliath* had actually made her way up the Baltic to Hangö Udd and, on 15 August, was the first British ship to see the Russians. She had turned south to report this to Saumarez as soon as possible but the news only reached him on 27 August.[5]

Just two ships, *Centaur* and *Implacable* (Captain Byam Martin), had therefore sailed north to join the Swedes at Örö, arriving on 20 August. The Swedes were still not ready to put to sea; the crews, formed mostly of conscripts, were sickly and inefficient to a degree that astonished Byam Martin. On 24 August, the Russian fleet advanced as if to attack but the entrance was blocked by the two British ships, anchored with springs to enable them to present their broadsides to their attackers. Early the next morning the whole Anglo-Swedish fleet of 13 ships sailed. The two coppered† British ships slowly overhauled the Russians who were well to windward, but the chase continued all night. Frequent tacks in the restricted waters enabled the *Implacable*, who outsailed the *Centaur*, to

---

* In fact, Captain Pipon had returned from a visit to the Swedish fleet on 2 August and brought 'a very good account of them' (Shrubland, Sir James to Lady Saumarez, 2 August, 1808). This proved quite erroneous.
† British ships' hulls were sheathed in copper and so cleaner and faster through the water.

close on the Russians at each tack by better seamanship and by 4 a.m. on the 26th she engaged the rearmost Russian ship, *Sevolod*, which could not match the *Implacable*'s gunnery and before long struck. However, the *Centaur* was still two miles off and the Swedish fleet a further ten miles adrift, so when the rest of the Russian fleet bore down to the rescue, Hood felt compelled to signal Byam Martin to bear away and leave his prize to be retaken. She was then towed by a Russian frigate towards Rogervik (also known as Baltic or Baltiski Port*) where the rest of the Russians took refuge. The *Sevolod*, however, could not make it to windward and anchored outside, waiting for boats to tow her in. The *Centaur* went in to board her, but as she did so, both ships went aground. The *Implacable*, close behind, anchored just in time and, with difficulty, was able to haul her off. They then set the *Sevolod* on fire, having taken off the remaining crew as prisoners.[6]

The superiority of firepower and sailing ability of the two British ships show quite clearly what would have been the probable result of a fleet action but for the distraction of rescuing the Spanish troops. As Saumarez wrote to Martha, if the Swedes could have sailed better, they would have captured the whole Russian fleet: 'I cannot too much lament not to have arrived a few days sooner, but it was impossible, and not a moment was lost in making the best of our way to join the Swedish fleet.'[7] The diversion to Langeland, important though it may have been and have seemed to be to Saumarez at the time, made him just four days late to have the fleet action against the Russians for which he had given up hoping. The British public would have had the naval victory that their morale needed and which they had almost come to expect of their admirals. Saumarez would have won the peerage to which he had considered himself entitled ever since 1801 and the Russian alliance with France would have come under even more pressure.

George Canning was still Foreign Secretary. As has been shown in Chapter 1, he strongly believed that success against Napoleon would only be achieved by a policy that created among the smaller nations a greater fear of Britain than their fear of France. His close friend, Lord Granville Leveson Gower, while he was still ambassador in St Petersburg, had written recommending that he 'send a fleet immediately to Cronstadt, with the view of forcing this court into renouncing her new connection with France'.[8] This view will have coloured Saumarez' instructions in April 1808, which included a requirement to 'cause the motions of the Russians in the higher parts of the Baltic to be observed' and to 'consider the practicability of an attack on the Russian fleet in Cronstadt if his force could be increased'.[9] For as Lord Hutchinson reported to Canning in September 1807:

---

*   Its present Estonian name is Paldiski.

The Alliance between Russia and France is in itself so preposterous and unnatural that it cannot be a lasting one – unless Passion, and circumstances of momentary irritation, induce Russia and England to enter into hostilities, which may be ultimately fatal to the real and permanent interests of both those powers.[10]

However, there were two opposing ways in which Britain might help to bring it to an end. They are well set out in a letter from Thornton to Saumarez as he sat blockading the Russian fleet in Rogervik under whose guns they had taken refuge. One, doubtless supported by Canning in the light of his actions against the Danes, was that Russia

has been driven into hostilities against us by the superior terror which France has inspired in her ... and that nothing but a greater or at least more immediate dread, acting near at home and threatening the internal safety and tranquillity of the country, can make her change her line of conduct.[11]

There was a misguided belief that the destructive bombardment of Copenhagen could be repeated at Cronstadt or Gothenburg, overlooking the fact that the bombardment had not been by the fleet but by the land forces, against a numerically inferior and ill-prepared opposition – circumstances that were unlikely to be repeated elsewhere. The fleet's role had been to blockade and prevent reinforcements being brought in.

The other approach, Thornton suggested, was that

the war itself is an unnatural one and is condemned as such by the most thinking and the soundest part of the nation [and] nothing ought to be done by us which should offend this portion of the Russians, or which should appear to affect the dignity and honour of the country.

This echoed what Hutchinson had gone on to say in his report:

Thinking people here, and indeed the Nation at large, incline very much to a connection with England. The appearance of our Fleet before Cronstadt, any attack upon the Capital, would change these good dispositions, irritate the whole Empire against us, and induce the Government to make efforts against our empire in India.[12]

The Russophobia – linked to a fear of losing the riches of India – that can be seen in the policies of Palmerston in the 1830s[13] had not yet come to feature in British foreign policy. Russia was still an important potential ally in the battle against Napoleon. There was an alternative view in a lengthy report on the political situation sent from the *Goliath* off Danzig on 1 July after some Russian deserters had joined *Goliath*.[14] It maintained that the English were popular with the Russians and that if Britain were to attack them the Russian people would force the government to make peace, because of the hunger and distress caused by the war.

There is little doubt that the Russian aristocracy were seriously affected by the loss of income from their trade in timber, hemp and other products that they had supplied to the British navy for many years. British contractors also had given long-term credits to both merchants and gentry in Russia which made them largely dependent on trading with Britain.[15] Savary, the French minister in St Petersburg, had reported it most unlikely that France could take England's place for imports to Russia and 'what is more, I fear that if measures are taken against England, the Emperor Alexander will have to take severe measures to silence the dissatisfied'.[16] There was a low opinion of the Czar for embracing and dining at Tilsit with Napoleon who a few days before had been hailed as the most detestable enemy of all religion and good order.[17] Both the Russian alliance with France and the Swedish one with Britain were at the wishes of their respective monarchs rather than of the people as a whole, particularly the nobility. The Swedes were dependent on trade, similarly to the Russians; they were tired of a war for which they could see no good purpose and of the taxes that went with it. This should have been true also of Denmark, whose merchant marine had been devastated by the English blockade and her retention of Norway threatened. By 1814 the country was bankrupt. But she remained almost to the end a faithful ally of France since the king, certainly, and the country, probably, were constant in their hatred of Britain as a result of the events of 1807 – further evidence that Canning's attack was misguided.

Thornton suggested that Rogervik was an ideal place to 'try the validity of these opinions'. The destruction of the Russian fleet there would be 'a salutary lesson of terror', while it should not upset those who favoured forbearance since the Russians could hardly expect a British fleet not to attack an enemy fleet that had come out to menace that of its ally. His own view was:

> that Russia must not be spared in any way, but must be made to feel as near home as possible the consequences of the war with us. I think Sir James Saumarez will go nearer to decide which of these two opinions is most correct than can be done by any other: and it will be quite right to wait the issue of his experiment before any thing farther should be done.[18]

A few days later he wrote again: 'It appears to me so important to impress upon Russia a sentiment of dread of what we are able to do, if we set seriously to work, that I shall endeavour tonight in my letter to the Admiral to put this consideration in its proper point of view.'[19]

Although there were some doubts of the value of the relationship with Sweden, Britain was at that time firmly allied to her and was subsidising her to fund the equipment and maintenance of her fleet and army. Denmark/Norway was another matter. Canning still misguidedly hoped that Denmark would return to neutrality.[20] Prussia and Austria, each in a distressed condition after the defeats of their armies by Napoleon, did not particularly enter into the reckoning, but Canning maintained contact with the different courts. In a cabinet note he stated that he had allowed a member of both the Austrian and the Russian missions to remain in Britain as private people and Baron Jacobi of Prussia 'to keep open correspondence with Sir Francis D'Ivernois'.[21] Britain's policy was thus relatively clear during 1808 and Saumarez implemented it vigorously.

The post-captain in him came out strongly again as, after sailing rapidly north from the Belt, he reached the Russian fleet, blockaded by Hood in Rogervik. His first reaction on arrival on the evening of 30 August had been to attack at once. Byam Martin wrote to his brother:

> It is impossible for me to find any language capable of conveying to you the admiration I have of Sir James Saumarez's zeal and anxiety to get at the enemy, and he has once or twice nearly determined to hazard, or rather (as it would inevitably be) to sacrifice, his fleet in order to have the glory of destroying the Russians; the universal opinion of the impracticability of doing so has alone induced him to abandon so rash an enterprise.[22]

He was persuaded by Hood and Byam Martin, two experienced, aggressive and decisive officers, to delay in order to review the situation. They were supported by the Swedish Admiral Nauckhoff. Both Hood and Saumarez would have had vivid memories of the first Battle of Algeciras in 1801 when the wind had failed and a promising attack crumbled, leaving HMS *Hannibal* (74) becalmed, helpless and in enemy hands, battered by the combined guns of the anchored French squadron and its protecting Spanish fortresses.[23]

The decision to delay was one over which Saumarez would retain a lurking anxiety, feeling that a Nelson would have gone straight in, as at the Nile. As he wrote to Martha:

> I assure Thee it gives me sincere regret not to have had it in my power to attack them but I had so many discouraging circumstances to encounter, particularly in the decided opinions of those in whom I had most to confide, meaning Sir Saml. Hood and Captain Martin (as well as I believe all the other Officers) that I felt myself obliged most reluctantly to resign my intentions. I only fear that I shall always retain the unpleasant reflexion that if I had follow'd my opinion, things would have been better, but this *entre nous* only.[24]

If Saumarez had attacked immediately on his arrival, it is quite probable, with hindsight and knowing that a change of wind actually took place, Rogervik could have been another Aboukir. The Russian fleet was demoralised after the events of the previous days. They had already shown the weakness of their gunnery in the action against the *Sevolod* and they were huddled in a shallow anchorage from which there was no escape. But it could equally have been like the first Battle of Algeciras.

The opinion of Sir John Ross, who was serving as a lieutenant on board the flagship HMS *Victory* at the time, was very positive:

> There can be no doubt that, if Sir James had been authorised to take command of the Swedish fleet, he would, even against the opinion of Sir Samuel [Hood], have attacked the enemy's fleet on the 31 August; and, as the wind changed on the following morning, he would have been able to carry off all his prizes without difficulty. We have ever since lamented that the attempt, as planned by Sir James, was not promptly made.[25]

According to Ross, Saumarez' doubts about his performance were shared by the Duke of Clarence. It was only in 1834 that Ross explained the causes to the Duke, now on the throne as William IV, who had always been under the impression that it was Sir James, and not the Swedish Admiral and Sir Samuel Hood, who objected to the attack, rather than the reverse. This could well have been one of the reasons why Saumarez did not receive the peerage that he felt was his due. Much later, it led to Mahan's view that Saumarez lacked genius and was merely 'an accomplished and resolute division or corps commander'.[26] Keats, on the other hand, wrote expressing his support for the decision; Saumarez, in his reply, hoped that 'the Country at large are actuated by the same candid and liberal sentiments'.[27] Thornton's view was 'that the whole might have been taken or destroyed, if all the English ships had been present at the chase, and if the attack had been made in the first day. I am equally sure that the Admiral will endeavour to do it still, if there is any prospect of success.'[28] But he doubted whether the troops promised by Sweden would arrive before the entrance had been additionally fortified by the Russians to prevent any attack. Thornton was a diplomat rather than a military man and may not have appreciated the dangers for ships of the line of having to beat out of the confined entrance under the guns of the fortress against the northwesterly that had brought them in, a much more dangerous test of seamanship even than Algeciras Bay.*

Was 'the object in view adequate to the risk and danger'? Unlike Nelson at Aboukir, only one of Saumarez' tasks was the destruction of the Russian fleet. The loss of several of his ships would have been an enormous blow to the reputation of the navy and that 'fear' which Canning believed was the diplomatic answer. The important thing was to maintain his 'fleet in being' to assist his Swedish allies and prevent a Russian invasion from Finland or a French invasion from Zealand, and to keep the convoys flowing to and from the Baltic against

---

* Paldiski later became a major USSR nuclear submarine base and since its evacuation after Estonian independence has become a considerable merchant port. I went there under sail in the summer of 2006 and can now fully understand Saumarez' fear of getting embayed.

the aggression of the Danish gunboats and the depredations of privateers. The established naval practice of blockade would be as effective and much less risky and the autumn storms might do as much damage to the Russian fleet as British guns. In the event, only one of their frigates was wrecked on the beach, but as soon as Saumarez was forced by the weather to head south out of the Baltic, the Russians scrambled back to Cronstadt, from which they only emerged in 1812 to sail under British guidance to the safety of the Thames, away from the advancing French army.

Byam Martin and Hood were asked to give their opinions in writing. Neither of them was lacking in bravery and spirit of adventure. The following year Saumarez was to rebuke Byam Martin for authorising a boat attack on a Russian flotilla of eight gunboats. Although successful, it led to a number of deaths, including that of an outstanding young officer, Lieutenant Hawkey. While giving credit to the bravery and skill displayed, which he promised to represent in the strongest terms to the Admiralty, he expressed his concern that the attack has been made, not deeming the object in view to have been adequate to the risk and danger attending so hazardous an enterprise. As a result, Byam Martin was with difficulty dissuaded from seeking a court-martial to clear his name.[29]

Byam Martin's succinct reply was:

> I have no hesitation in giving a decided opinion that the Russian fleet in Rogerwick cannot be attacked with any reasonable hope of success, or without the risk of losing some of his Majesty's ships. It would be a hazardous thing with a powerful squadron of British ships to attack an enemy so strongly situated; but with a force composed principally of Swedish ships, I am confident it would end in disappointment – if not in disgrace. Under favourable circumstances I think fire-vessels may be used with a probability of success, fully sufficient to justify the attempt.[30]

In private remarks he sent home to his wife Kitty on 23 September, he made the point that it was actually preferable for the Russians to escape to Cronstadt. The ice at Rogervik opened six weeks earlier than there, enabling them, if they stayed, to attack Stockholm before the British fleet could again come to the rescue.[31] Hood wrote from the *Centaur*, 'If there had been with us about two or three thousand troops the island might have been carried, and the whole fleet destroyed, for there were only the batteries on it for the defence of the port'. But he, too, thought the only chance now would be by a *coup de main* or fireships.[32]

The delay in Saumarez' arrival had been critical. It gave the Russians time to bring up troops, build a boom and to strengthen their position. A report on the guns and forts at Rogervik from Byam Martin to Saumarez, undated but evidently early in September 1808, listed:

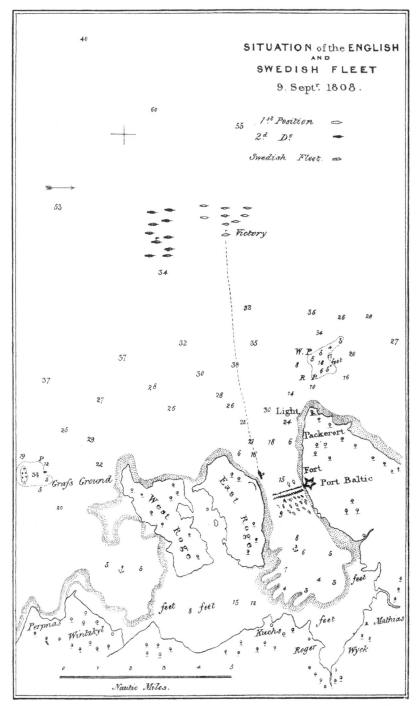

Figure 7. Rogervik. Drawing by Ross depicting Russian boom and fort (Ross II, p. 115)

14 guns on Flanking Point with a large party of men at work there
24 embrasures on with the Church and East of it
4 embrasures in Inner Battery
3 embrasures a little east of above
8 sail of the line, 9 frigates, some very large, 4 corvettes, 2 cutters
Observed a regiment of Horse pass out of the Town on to the Beach
A party of infantry under arms above the Flanking Point.[33]

The Russians had formed a line close under the batteries and the bombs were unable to get close enough to reach them. Without troops, or a sufficient body of marines, fireships were the only sound military way to proceed. Although it was in Saumarez' view a 'mode of warfare which should never be resorted to except in cases of extremity' – a similar view to that of Admiral Gambier at Aix Road the following year[34] – a couple of fireships were quickly fitted out.

But Saumarez instead turned from military force to diplomacy. His first action, on 3 September, was to propose terms to the Russian Admiral Hanickoff under a flag of truce, 'to spare the effusion of blood and as far as lays in my power to assuage the horrors of war betwixt nations that ought to be in perpetual amity'. When he received a polite but non-committal response, he suggested that Byam Martin might present the terms personally: 'he is perfectly informed of the purity of the motives by which I am actuated and the conditions to which I mean to adhere, although subject to any alterations your excellency may wish to propose, founded on the same basis'. This proved unacceptable. Instead, Hanickoff's deputy, Commodore Moller, came on board *Victory* to hear the terms, but they too were found unacceptable since they would have involved the surrender of half the Russian fleet, although the flagship and the remainder would be permitted safe passage to Cronstadt.[35] The reply was that the admiral would rather burn his whole fleet. No final reply to the surrender proposal had been received from the Russians before the deadline, so the short truce came to an end at sunset on 4 September. Saumarez sent copies of the correspondence to the Admiralty and reported that he was fitting out fireships – 'it being repugnant to my feelings to have recourse to this mode of warfare without previously apprising the Russian Admiral of the perilous danger of his fleet and the inevitable destruction that must await the town of Baltic Port'.[36]

The Admiralty severely disapproved of such a negotiation. Saumarez was forced to eat humble pie in response to a letter from Pole:

their Lordships considering that the offering terms to an enemy's fleet has seldom, if ever, been practised in our maritime warfare; and being unwilling to establish such a principle, or to give their sanction to any arrangement with an hostile fleet (unless under their express instructions) short of unconditional surrender; had directed the same to be signified to me for the guidance of my conduct in any future operations.[37]

Saumarez forbore to point out that if the Russians had accepted his offer, the capture of half the enemy fleet without loss might have been considered a considerable victory and that, as recently as 1801 in the same waters, Nelson had agreed an armistice with the Danes in the middle of a battle. He and Hyde Parker had then, after several days of negotiations, agreed terms that were far short of unconditional surrender and that failed to achieve the specific objective in the original orders – that Denmark should be made to withdraw from the League of Armed Neutrality and form an alliance with Britain.[38] It might also have provided an answer to Thornton's questioning, expressed earlier to Canning, as to whether a policy of inspiring fear on the part of the Russians or one of friendship would be more effective.

Despite 15 years of almost continuous bloody fighting – or perhaps because of it – Saumarez was very conscious of the waste and the horrors of war. After a Danish postboat had been captured that May, he wrote:

> all the Letters describe Copenhagen and the whole Island of Zealand in a deplorable state from the loss of their Commerce and the want of Provisions. This evil will increase upon them and it is really lamentable that so many innocent People should be the victims of the measures to which we are obliged to resort in this horrid state of warfare.[39]

On 7 September, he sent the Russian admiral a parcel of English newspapers just received from Thornton 'knowing how much they are kept in the dark in this Country respecting the affairs of Spain and other countries'. When the Russian responded with a present of fruit and vegetables, Saumarez reciprocated with some English porter and a quarter-hundredweight of coffee. Martha commented: 'I am delighted with the reciprocal courtesy that has passed betwixt Thee and the Russian Admiral, it affords a pleasing contrast to the horrors of War, and also the savage barbarity of the French method.'[40] Two years later, he wrote at greater length:

> the ravages of the present campaign has exceeded every former War, and is described as greater than was ever before known – it is indeed too melancholy to dwell upon, and nothing but the prospect of the Austrian Army being at last successful, can any way reconcile the feelings to the sufferings of that unhappy Country, where so many principal Towns and Villages have been laid waste, and the extreme misery it has brought on upon its wretched inhabitants – how fervently it is to be wished that these deplorable calamities may cease and that the seven headed monster Bonaparte may fall the victim of his cruelty and ambition.[41]

His present command will have brought him more into contact with its impact on the civilian population than the fleet actions in which he had been engaged. It will have brought back memories of his earliest service as a teenage lieutenant in the American War of Independence which held more of the bitterness of a civil war than a war between nations, through the antagonism of rebels and loyalists and the destruction of innocent lives and property that went with it. He would have been conscious of the feelings of horror, not just in Denmark, at the British terror bombardment of Copenhagen the previous year. There was a gulf then, as there is today, between the politicians or monarchs who declare war and the men in the services who actually wage it, especially those in the front line. The immediacy of death and destruction made them keener to see an end to it. Canning wrote bitterly to the Earl of Chatham after the news of the Convention of Cintra: 'though the King may disavow an accredited Minister and refuse to ratify a treaty, he cannot undo a Convention however ruinous and discreditable, if signed by a man who has a sword at his side'.[42]

The Admiralty did, however, support Saumarez in his decision to blockade rather than to press on with a fleet attack. As Sir Richard Bickerton, a lord of the Admiralty, wrote:

> none of your friends have wished more ardently than I have done for the success of your operations against the Enemy. I had not however much expectation of your being able to do material injury to Hannikoff in his strong position & I have taken care to promulgate that opinion in all companies, that, if you do succeed in destroying any Ships, you may have the more credit with those that were not taught to expect any attempt to be made for that purpose. I must however here observe that no man ever placed in the high & honorable station you hold, has stood in higher estimation with the Publick. Whatever you do will in their eyes be right, the most brilliant achievement will not surprize, for they know you equal to every practicable attempt, & if you do nothing, the world will be satisfied, it was only because nothing could be done.[43]

Gustav IV Adolf, as ever out of touch with reality, was still insisting on the total capitulation of the Russian fleet.[44]

Strong onshore winds now obliged Saumarez to anchor further offshore: 'We must now confine ourselves to keeping them closely blockaded as long as the Season will admit, in hopes that a strong Gale will drive some of them ashore'.[45] The fireships made their attempt when at last the weather appeared favourable on 13 September, led by *Erebus* and covered by *Salsette*, *Magnet*, *Alaart*, and the *Swan* cutter. But the long daylight hours were a disadvantage, the weather not ideal and the Russian boom across the entrance too strong. The rather half-hearted attack was aborted, with the loss of one of the fireships – a Russian prize brig.[46]

A further problem was the sickly state of the Swedish squadron. Scurvy was rife, more because many of the Swedish recruits had come aboard with incipient scurvy,* than because they had spent too long at sea.[47] Saumarez had before sailing ordered all his captains to 'pay the strictest attention to cause the supplies allowed to the surgeons for the Care and comfort of the Sick to be completed previous to their sailing from England, viz: Medicines, Necessaries, Portable soups, Lemon Juice, Bedding, Fumigating Materials and Apparatus etc'.[48] The British supplied the Swedes with lime juice and sugar, and the *Victory*'s surgeon, Valentine Duke, did what he could to assist. Even those who were considered most healthy, he found to be 'labouring under the latent symptoms of scurvy'.[49] Over the period, more than 4,000 sick were landed at Karlskrona from the 11 Swedish ships of the line. Dr. Jamison, the fleet physician, found their disease to be 'scurvy, dysentery, low fever, catarrhal complaints, all the latter depending on the former'. He recommended that all the patients should be 'exposed to the air, and caused to take all possible exercise, with a nourishing diet, and a plentiful use of fresh vegetables ... with the necessary assistance of Port wine to recruit their strength and support their spirits'.[50]

Saumarez himself had been a sick man for some time. There is a lengthy report by Duke, on a matter about which not only those on board the flagship, but Hood and Keats expressed considerable sympathy and concern. 'Soon after the arrival of the *Victory* at Gothenburg [he] had complained of an obstruction in his bowel which he conceived was brought on in consequence of eating cherries, a fruit that has ever disagreed with him'. This came and went, mitigated by 'the most active and powerful opening medicines', until the beginning of August when he had a severe and continuous chest pain.

> He passed sleepless nights, his countenance betokened much distress ... together with a high state of nervous irritability. Under such unfavourable circumstances the *Victory* arrived off Port Baltic where a variety of anxious occurrences connected with the important situation of Commander in Chief have contributed not a little to both prolong and aggravate his disease.[51]

Stress cannot have been good for his physical condition and vice versa. This may be behind Byam Martin's disparaging remarks quoted in the Biographical Note (see p. 232). There is no evidence of any further problems of this nature during the rest of Saumarez time in the Baltic, often similarly stressful, so this may indeed have simply been triggered by the unfortunate choice of cherries. Nicholas Gold, a retired army doctor in Guernsey who has studied the reports, sees it as a clear case of irritable bowel syndrome.

---

* This may have been combined with dysentery of which there was a severe outbreak in Karlskrona in the summer of 1808, bringing to an end the long life of Sweden's distinguished naval architect F.H. af Chapman (Harris, *F.H. Chapman*, p. 198).

Consultations with the other surgeons in the fleet followed, a blister was successfully administered, Admiral Hood supplied him with 'plenty of Arrow Root' and 'it is not possible to receive on all occasions more attention than is shown me by Sir Saml. Hood and all the Captains'. Saumarez would not confess the seriousness of the situation to Martha, admitting only to a heavy cold and soon after claiming to be 'fully restored'.[52] Duke's report concluded: 'we have this day procured a patent machine for the purpose of evacuating and giving energy to the intestines … I feel the highest confidence and hope of the speedy reestablishment of his health.'

On 15 September Saumarez wrote to his brother Richard: 'I am happy to tell you that I have continued to get considerably better and tho' the pain in my chest is not quite gone it has been much abated'.[53] On the 19th, however, he wrote to Keats, now covering the Belt:

> You will I am sure be concerned to hear that the illness of which I so much complained when I saw you last has increased to so great a degree as to give me serious apprehensions of even being deprived before the severe Season setts in of the benefit of my native air to restore it. I have been fortunate in having the assistance of Captain Martin without which I should scarcely have been enabled for the last fortnight to have gone thro' the fatigues of the Service.[54]

He admitted later to Richard:

> I can assure that all the illnesses I can recollect from my first coming to sea except on one important occasion, has not been equal to what I have suffered in this late attack even for forty eight hours only. I was for a considerable time in great doubt if I should recover.[55]

Saumarez had originally been reluctant to accept Martin as Captain of the Fleet to replace Captain Hope, who had returned home to a sick wife, even though it created a possible promotion for Saumarez' relative, Captain Pipon. But by 10 September he was writing to Martha: 'Captain Martin is everything that I can wish – he is a most excellent worthy man and I am now very glad to have consented to the arrangement, altho' I was at first rather averse to it.'[56] Sleepless nights and the stress of command, combined with the problems of blockading a shallowing lee shore and the monotony of inaction will have done nothing for his temper. It was fortunate that Samuel Hood and his other subordinates were so supportive, but that must be a tribute to the relationship he had built up with them.

On 26 September he wrote to Sir Richard Bickerton: 'I have wished as long as it lay in my power to conceal from my friends the very ill state of my health, but it has of late become so much impaired as to render it indispensable for me to return to England as soon as the Service will permit.' Unless forced by his health to leave the command to one of his subordinate admirals, 'which if possible I wish to have avoided', Saumarez intended to continue off Rogervik as long as the weather permitted, return down the Baltic in the *Salsette*, make the final arrangements for the squadron, and then come home to England.[57] His reticence and determination to carry on make an interesting comparison with Nelson's letters to Davison and St Vincent in the aftermath of his victory at Copenhagen in 1801.[58]

Spared routine duties, free from instructions from London, Saumarez was able to spend time thinking. Two letters from Martha, just over a month old, gave him enormous pleasure: 'never since our blessed Union have I yet derived greater happiness than these precious letters have yielded to me' and, mercifully, none arrived from King Gustav.[59] He admitted to Martha: 'I have fretted very much at not having been able to attack the Russian Fleet and I found the longer I remained off their Port the greater was the impression.'[60] He also had a visit from Thornton with whom he was able to strike up a good relationship. It was a time for reflection; a change in his feelings, that had probably been brewing since his frustrating days off Wingo, became increasingly evident. The diplomat was coming more strongly to the surface and he considered introducing another peace proposal. This was to lead him into dangerous waters in the eyes of both the Admiralty and Foreign Secretary Canning.

Saumarez had kept Thornton informed of his surrender proposal to the Russian admiral and Thornton had reported back to Canning, mentioning that Saumarez

> has requested me to apprise him of any instructions which His Majesty's Government may have given relative to any overtures to a Peace with Russia, having reason, he adds, to believe that in the present situation of the Russian fleet, they would be glad to avail themselves of any opportunity to enter upon a negotiation with Great Britain and her ally.[61]

The fortuitous return of the *Cruizer* to Dalaro, the coastal port most accessible from Stockholm, and the news that the Russian Minister of Marine, Tchichagoff, was expected at Rogervik from St Petersburg, had encouraged Thornton to sail there 'to pay a visit to the Vice Admiral'. He already had instructions from Canning on the essential points of any negotiation:

> The evacuation of His Swedish Majesty's invaded dominions is perhaps the only essential point; for after that the pacification would be almost the natural consequence of the cessation of hostilities. With that evacuation, I have understood that His Majesty's Government would not be unwilling to agree to an absolute neutrality or truce for the rest of the war between England, Sweden and Russia with Denmark. I shall keep this leading point invariably in view, although I have no great hope of even any opening of a

negotiation. Perhaps I may have the good fortune to lay the groundwork of a future opening.

Saumarez' letter to Czar Alexander I was simple and straightforward. It tells the Czar of the happenings in Spain and Wellesley's defeat of Junot at Vimeiro on 21 August, and how Portugal had now 'been extricated from the baneful hands of the enemy of all independent States'. It went on:

> It is to be hoped that these events will induce the Powers on the Continent to unite with Great Britain in restoring that peace so highly to be desired for the welfare of mankind. Knowing it to be the object most at heart of my gracious and beloved Sovereign as also of His Majesty's ally the King of Sweden, should your Imperial Majesty be impressed by the same sentiments nothing can afford me greater happiness than to have the honour of imparting them to my Government; and to desist from further hostile operations upon condition that Your Majesty will give orders to your forces to desist from all hostilities against England and his ally and withdraw your troops from Swedish Finland.[62]

It was dated 17 September. There are two copies of this letter in the archives, which differ. The original draft in Saumarez' hand includes references to Austria and Denmark which are omitted from what appears to be the final copy in his clerk's hand.

Thornton had reached *Victory* on the evening of the 13th and stayed four days. He reported to Canning:

> Vice-Admiral Sir James Saumarez having a few days before my arrival thought of addressing a letter to the Emperor Alexander (a copy of which is enclosed) availed himself of this opportunity of conveying it through the Russian Admiral after a trifling alteration or two, which I took the liberty of suggesting.[63]

This would explain the difference between the two copies held at the Suffolk Record Office. Thornton also agreed with Saumarez that he himself should send a separate letter on similar lines to Tchichagoff. Unfortunately, Saumarez' letter arrived a few days after Tchichagoff, through whom it was addressed, had left Rogervik[64] and by the time it reached him the Czar had left for a summit meeting with Napoleon at Erfurt, to review and amend, if necessary, the Treaty of Tilsit. This meeting took place from 27 September to 14 October. The letter was treated by the two emperors as a formal overture for peace. The two emperors wrote to King George III, offering to send plenipotentiaries to whichever city on the continent he chose to send his own plenipotentiaries: 'In respect to the bases of the Negotiation, their Imperial Majesties see no difficulty in adopting all those formerly proposed by England, namely the *uti possidetis*,* and every other basis founded upon the reciprocity and equality which ought to prevail between all great nations'.[65]

Canning was dismissive of this since it would have confirmed both the seizures of territory by the two emperors agreed at Tilsit and the usurpation of the Spanish throne in favour of Joseph Bonaparte. George III confirmed that he could not accept the principle of *uti possidetis* as Napoleon had usurped so many states; the restoration of the Portuguese and Spanish monarchies was another essential condition.[66] Mulgrave commented in a letter to Canning:

> The management of the strong and popular grounds on which either to decline the invitation of the two Emperors; or to require previous conditions which they cannot admit, I can leave with perfect confidence to the department in which those grounds are to receive their official shape.[67]

Canning chose the latter option and insisted on the inclusion of representatives of the old Spanish regime and of Sweden, which he knew would be unacceptable. And it was.

It is difficult to believe that Napoleon's peace feelers were in any way genuine. He had written to George III as far back as January 1805, immediately after his own coronation as emperor, appealing to the King's known pacific sentiments. This was far too soon after the renewal of fighting at the end of the Peace of Amiens to be productive and George III sent a stalling reply, indicating that he would need to discuss this with his allies, especially Russia. Fox, the Foreign Secretary at that time, had then made an approach to Talleyrand in February 1806, at the same time that he reported his own rejection in horror of an offer to kill Napoleon by a mysterious would-be assassin.[68] Fox's approach had been welcomed by Talleyrand and he suggested that England should send a plenipotentiary to Lille, for which he attached passports. However, Napoleon was not quite ready for peace yet. He wanted to consolidate his hold over Holland, and present it as a *fait accompli* at the negotiations, and also confirm the Confederation of the Rhine, the league of smaller German states that he had set up after Austerlitz in 1806 on the dissolution of the Holy Roman Empire. He played for time by refusing to let Russia join in the talks. It was a pattern that he followed again in 1808 and 1810, blowing hot and cold, not wanting to be seen to be the person responsible for continuing the war. The French historian Coquelle sees him wanting 'to throw back on his adversary the opprobrium of which he was the sole culprit'.[69] It was a tactic he employed right up to his invasion of Russia in June 1812.

Saumarez continued the blockade until the end of September and then, a

---

* A principle in international law that territory and other property remains with its possessor at the end of a conflict, unless provided for by treaty.

southeasterly wind setting in, sailed the fleet south to Karlskrona, leaving three ships and two frigates to guard the northern Baltic and prevent the Russian fleet following. Four days later the severe onshore norwesterly gale that he had feared arrived: in the harbour, one of the Russian frigates was driven ashore and wrecked.[70] It is doubtful whether anything would have been gained by keeping them bottled up in Rogervik. If they had survived afloat until the ice came to protect them, as Byam Martin had commented, they would have been able to get to sea much earlier the following spring from there than from Cronstadt to threaten the Swedish coast again and perhaps cover a landing of a Russo-French force on the Swedish mainland before a British fleet was able to penetrate the Baltic. The demonstration of the speed, seamanship and firepower of the British ships of which they had seen such vivid evidence in Byam Martin's capture of the *Sevolod* made sure that the Russians would not venture to sea in the presence of a British squadron. Saumarez' view was that: 'it is everything that could have been wished as they will not be in a situation to alarm the Swedes during the winter, and I hope in the spring we shall be in good time for them.'[71] He finally sailed from Wingo for England on 3 November, leaving Keats with three ships of the line and a number of cruisers to maintain the overall blockade during the winter from Wingo, Marstrand, or wherever his judgement and the state of the ice determined.

Saumarez' return was not a happy one. He himself was undoubtedly disappointed, having got so near to the major action that he craved. There was still the feeling that so many of his fellow admirals must have had on other occasions, anticipating Mahan – what would Nelson have done had he been here? Would he not in some dashing stroke of genius have gone in hot-foot while the Russians were still unprepared and destroyed the lot? He wrote to Martha:

> altho' it has not terminated equal to my expectations I am well convinced ev'ry thing has been done that could depend upon me – and that the country will be satisfied of it, altho' I know John Bull is disappointed when success does not correspond with expectation. The Swedes who unfortunately are far more concerned, their very existence almost depending upon the reduction of the Russian Navy, are perfectly satisfied that every thing has been done that was practicable, and it [is] what they have upon every occasion testified to me – although their Monarch would hear of nothing short of the destruction or the surrender of their whole force ... I reconcile myself to the disappointment of not having defeated the Russian Fleet from the liberal manner in which my Services have been regarded – nothing can exceed the very handsome terms conveyed in the various Letters I have received upon the subject.[72]

George III wrote to Mulgrave that he was 'satisfied that the escape of the Russian fleet can never be ascribed to any want of zeal or activity on the part of Sir James Saumarez and the officers under his command'.[73] However, instead of receiving a hero's welcome, Saumarez was sent a memorandum from the Admiralty, setting out seven points of complaint and demanding explanations. They covered delays to convoys, why he had left the Baltic before bad weather actually set in, why he sent back three ships the Admiralty had sent out to help, why he had not told them about a letter from the Swedish king and ignored his request to stay on, why he had not used his ships to escort convoys home, and 'by what Instruction he felt himself to have been authorized to write his letter of the 17 September to the Emperor of Russia'.[74]

This last demand was the only one of the seven complaints on which Saumarez was unable to satisfy their Lordships. He had undoubtedly exceeded his instructions. It is difficult to know how far he was aware of Canning's views expressed to Thornton in June:

> A peace such as would satisfy Sweden would be the best end of the war in the North. If the three northern powers were once agreed to desist from worrying and exhausting each other at the instigation and for the sole profit of Bonaparte, such a Pacification might eventually settle into a defensive League – and a League of the North consolidated and protected by the power of Great Britain while the flames continue spreading in the South, from Spain to Italy and thence perhaps to Austria, might yet produce a change in favour of the Liberties and Independence of Mankind, of which but a short time ago all hope seemed to have vanished.[75]

Saumarez evidently discussed the situation closely with Thornton when he came to Rogervik to see him and stayed on board *Victory*, so that it is unlikely that the Foreign Secretary's views were not made known to him. Thornton had written to Canning immediately prior to his visit, saying that he hoped to have a meeting, when at Rogervik, with Admiral Tchichagoff whose sentiments towards Britain he believed had changed: ' if I can speak to him or any other Russian in the sense of our wishes, something may be gained. I believe Admiral Hood's attack has given them a lesson, which they will not like to repeat'.[76]

The meeting cannot have taken place since there is no mention of it and Thornton had written to Tchichagoff instead, in a similar vein to Saumarez, seeking the possibility of a rapprochement between Britain and Russia. But as he told Saumarez after their return to London, 'not a word has been said to me upon the subject of the step which we took in concert before Baltiski Port'. He suggested that Saumarez 'would never have been questioned upon the subject of the Emperor or his Ministers had [Napoleon] not thought proper in his first proposals from Erfurt to allude to your letter'.[77] Canning's own instructions to Leveson-Gower in July 1807 as he travelled to take up his post as Ambassador had been to preserve friendly relations with Russia in the hope that she would soon return to alliance.[78] However, he felt obliged to point out in a letter to the Russian Ambassador in Paris that the overtures made by Admiral Saumarez were 'nullement autorisés par sa Cour'.[79]

The explosion that Saumarez' letter caused in his relations with the Admiralty was largely a matter of timing. Since it only reached the Czar when he had arrived at Erfurt for the conference with Napoleon, they were able to seize on it as evidence that Britain was anxious to make peace and in the joint letters written on behalf of the two emperors to Canning, Admiral Saumarez is specifically mentioned as the author of the overture. This led to Canning disavowing him.[80] The Admiralty had evidently been angered by the fact that a copy of Saumarez' letter had gone via Thornton to the Foreign Office but not to them.[81] In a very lengthy response to the Admiralty memorandum, Saumarez dealt with all the other six complaints. He then made three main points on the letter to the Czar. First, he understood from ministers 'that when an opportunity offered for peace between Great Britain and Russia it would be eagerly embraced and that the arrangements of such a negotiation would neither be difficult or complicated'. Second, he 'considered it a favourable opportunity to inform His Imperial Majesty of the events relative to Spain and Portugal with a view, if possible, to detach Russia from her alliance with the French nation and to return her to her former ties of friendship with Great Britain'. Third, it was written with the knowledge and concurrence of Admiral Nauckhoff, who strongly recommended its being transmitted. Moreover:

> His Majesty's envoy Mr. Thornton, who was at that time on board the *Victory*, having also decided to write to the Russian minister on the same subject, was consulted as to the expediency of sending the letter and expressed his opinion that much good might result from it and that he was not aware of its doing any possible harm.[82]

It does not appear to have been a matter of lack of communication between the Foreign Office and the Admiralty, although Saumarez does not give an explanation of why he did not send a copy to them as well as the one he gave to Thornton. He was usually very good about keeping them informed, despite their failure to communicate with him, and Yorke was later to congratulate him particularly on this when he took over from Mulgrave: 'I take this opportunity for thanking you for keeping me so well informed of what has been passing in your neighbourhood.'[83] Mulgrave was evidently fully in the picture, in the light of his letter to Canning quoted earlier. As Saumarez pointed out, he had got the blessing of both the British Minister in Stockholm and the Swedish admiral, and his proposals were very much in line with current British foreign policy. Thornton himself had already been briefed on what to do and, as he wrote to Canning, his visit to Rogervik was for that very purpose. One has to come to the conclusion that Canning simply felt that it was both premature and inappropriate for it to come out in such a way and from such a source.

He was not averse to expressing his feelings strongly and the mildness of the Admiralty rebuke that followed indicates that Canning had not put them under particular pressure.

It had been a well-intentioned move. It illustrated Saumarez' readiness to act on his own initiative and to look to peaceful ways of carrying out his role. It displayed a good grasp of the diplomatic scene and he had checked with what appeared to be the appropriate other authorities. If successful, it could have brought to a head much earlier the tension and clash, both of interests and personalities, that was just beginning to appear between the French and Russian emperors, portrayed so vividly in Tolstoy's *War and Peace*,[84] precipitating the conflict that was ultimately Napoleon's downfall. If it was premature, there was still no apparent potential harm in it, as Thornton agreed, and diplomatic opportunities had to be grasped as much as military ones. The Czar's departure for Erfurt was an unfortunate coincidence that Saumarez could neither have known about nor expected. Had his letter reached the Czar *after* the Erfurt conference, the result could have been quite different.

It was a relatively mild rap on the knuckles that Saumarez eventually received: 'Their Lordships are of opinion that officers employed on Military Service cannot be justified in stepping beyond the line of their professional duty, by entering into Political Negociations with the Enemy, unless especially directed to do so by their Instructions.'[85] Nonetheless, during the ensuing four years, it was exactly this quasi diplomatic/political role that Saumarez – without any such directions or even on occasion in contradiction of those he did receive – was to pursue and to execute brilliantly, with considerable independence and despite the doubts at the Admiralty and Foreign Office of the wisdom and appropriateness of his conciliatory policies.

5

The Conversion to Peacemaker

The blockade of Rogervik and the capture and destruction of the *Sevolod* beforehand were significant turning points in both the military and the political situation in the Baltic. Good relations were restored between Britain and King Gustav, aided by the recall to London of Thornton who had never got on as well with the King as Pierrepont and who, after the Moore affair, had become *persona non grata*.[1] With his usual blindness to reality, King Gustav told Saumarez that he had given orders to his fleet at Karlskrona to resume the blockade and requested 'that you will help with as many ships as you can the operations of my squadron, to make the result more decisive'.[2] In fact, the Swedish ships were so short of crew because of scurvy and infectious disease that they were unable to sail and Saumarez was able to plead the bad weather for removing to Gothenburg all his ships except two 'as the advanced season of the year must prevent the possibility of further naval operations in these seas'.[3] Having escaped back to Cronstadt, the Russian fleet henceforward would take on a purely defensive role so long as there was a substantial British squadron abroad in the Baltic. The port defences had been strengthened, both to defend the fleet from bombardment and nearby St Petersburg from attack. Moreover, Thornton, announcing his recall to London, had given news of an armistice between Sweden and Russia in the north of Finland, at the request of the Russian commander, which he hoped would spread to the whole of Finland.[4] There is a note on the manuscript in Ross's handwriting: 'The Armistice took place in consequence of the letter addressed to the Emperor of Russia by Admiral Sir James Saumarez.' This would appear to be wishful thinking on Ross's part since the tightness of the timing makes it extremely unlikely.

It had also seen a change in attitude on the part of Saumarez himself. The ardent commander, keen to do battle and destroy the Russian fleet is becoming the peacemaker, as we have seen in Chapter 4, writing to his immediate naval opponent, the Russian Admiral Hanickhof, and to the Czar himself to propose the opening of negotiations. Thereafter Saumarez had little contact with Russia, either diplomatically or from a military standpoint. In the summer of 1809, he took his fleet up to the Gulf of Finland to add weight to the limited Swedish forces guarding against a possible Russian invasion of the Swedish mainland

and expressed a hope to Admiral Keats that the Russians 'will afford us an opportunity to attack them'.[5] In a private letter he told Martha earlier that month 'from every account I receive of the state of the Russian fleet at Cronstadt, particularly yesterday by the vessels from Riga, they remain in an inactive state and no appearance of their moving this summer', and ten days later:

> As to the Russian Fleet, it is scarcely worth my while to attempt at removing thy more than womanly fears – be assured they are more intent to defend themselves in Cronstadt, than of coming out to meet this fleet. All the accounts agree that they are not even half manned, and we anxiously wish for the arrival of the seamen belonging to Admiral Senyavin to remove that pretext.[6]

The aggressive instincts of the post-captain have not yet entirely disappeared.

However, he expressed in the same letter his concern at Sweden's weak situation. Not only were her army and navy much weaker than the Russian forces opposing them, but 'they have not the means to defray the expenses of the war even but for a few weeks longer'. For Gustav IV Adolf had been overthrown by a bloodless military coup on 13 March 1809. Sweden – in a period of 37 years – had suffered three *coups d'état* (1772, 1789, and 1809), one regicide (1792) and one dethronement (1809). Gustav III had re-established royal absolutism in 1772 after fifty years of the 'Age of Liberty'.[7] The impact of his father's assassination in 1792 on Gustav IV was to encourage him to introduce an even more severe and repressive system in which he trusted nobody and by the same token had no natural body of supporters. During 13 years of rule, by depending on foreign subsidies, he only once called the Diet. There was a substantial core of Francophiles among his ministers and the nobility resented his concessions to the peasantry and disliked his war policy. As Merry, who had taken over from Thornton as British minister in Stockholm, reported to Canning in December 1808:

> the general wish of the people of this country, particularly of the nobles, for peace, of their having been always averse to the war, of their attributing all their distresses and misfortunes to Great Britain, and of his Swedish Majesty himself being almost the only person in his dominions by whose absolute will and authority the war has been prosecuted.[8]

Canning had appeared to be aware of the dangers to King Gustav for some while. He had asked Thornton, if he got a chance in casual conversation with the king, to warn him to be on his guard in Stockholm 'after the Garrison have quitted that place'.[9] However, owing to the Moore fiasco, it is unlikely that the opportunity arose or, if it did, that King Gustav would be inclined to listen. Two final matters had turned discontent into revolution. In October 1808, King Gustav had downgraded three guards regiments and 120 of their officers, on the reputed grounds of cowardice and fraternisation with the enemy. These officers came from most of the leading aristocratic families who could not quietly accept such public humiliation.[10] The final straw was the introduction of a new tax, *bevillning*, in February 1809 at five times the rate of 1800.[11]

Admiral Keats had remained off Gothenburg when the rest of the fleet sailed for home in November and was senior naval officer on the station. Merry, according to Malmesbury, was 'a very worthy but nervous man'.[12] In accepting the appointment, much against his will, he had expressed also 'my horror of the Sea, at all times, and the particular dangers attending the Northern Navigation at this season of the year', asking that he should not be conveyed in any ship of war less than a frigate.[13] He wrote to Keats in December 1808, after a stormy private audience with King Gustav, 'not to allow the ships under his commands to be frozen up in a Swedish port, though it is much to be wished that this could be done without the appearance of any distrust of the friendly dispositions of this Court'.[14]

Keats picked up some of this nervousness and on Christmas Day he ordered all his ships and victuallers from Marstrand back to Hawke Road off Gothenburg:

> because, except with favourable winds, it is not possible to get out of the port should it become necessary; because I could not command a supply of water – and that the fortification, the garrison of which I find it reported was ordered to be strengthened, commands the harbour and both its entrances, and is of a nature not to be taken by a *coup de main*, should it be necessary to occupy it. In Hawke Road I believe I can make sure of a supply of water, there is no fortification that commands it; it is preferable for communications, and seldom frozen up, in a situation in which I am certain of my supplies, and from which, in the case of a reverse I should have perhaps less difficulty to extricate myself than from Marstrand.[15]

He was anxious to get instructions and further information from London, and was also concerned about sickness in his ships apparently similar to that which the Swedish fleet had suffered. A report from Karlskrona showed it still continuing there: 'At the close of the year, 69 Officers including 2 Commodores and 14 Captains of ships of the line, and 5,300 Seaman had died.' Dr. Jamison, Physician to the Fleet, had recommended that 'because of the peculiar disposition this climate and its bad water has to induce Sea Scurvy', the squadron should either receive vegetables from England or else be relieved by fresh healthy ships. The Admiralty took until April to reply, rejecting the request as 'they will in a short time be supplied on their station with what may be necessary'.[16] Lord Mulgrave, in the light of Keats' reports, had suggested that the squadron should return to Great Yarmouth, but George III had expressed concern at the impact that would have on relations with Sweden.[17]

Keats' other concern was over ice. Its dangers were emphasised when the *Salsette* and the whole of the final 12-ship homeward bound convoy and seven further escorts, including three Swedish men-of-war, appeared to have been driven ashore near the Malmö Channel by the drifting ice and wrecked, although some of them were later found to have escaped.[18] He was again tempted to leave the station for the winter and run back to the Downs, whither he had already despatched Admiral Bertie's squadron and Captain Graves with the *Lynx* and four smaller escorts, but he 'deemed it proper' to work his way into Gothenburg:

> The *Superb* has been since cut by her own means (having purchased a few necessary materials for ice-cutting)* for more than three miles into Hawke Road ... the frost which has continued to the 25th with unremitting severity, has not only shut every harbour on the coast, but extended the solid ice, apparently as far as the eye could reach into the Kattegat, both from hence and Marstrand, and thickened the ice to an extent from all accounts uninstanced at this season.[19]

It was to be a particularly severe winter:

> The unfortunate loss of the *Crescent* with the winter supply of slops [clothing] has been the more severely felt from the remains of her crew together with those of the *Magnet*, *Sacorman*, & *Fama* having joined the squadron destitute or much in want of cloaths [sic]. In this situation, having found some Guernsey frocks and coarse stockings, one thousand of the former and eleven hundred pairs of the latter, have been purchased by my direction – the former at 7s and the latter at 1s.3d. a pair. And leather and materials for making shoes have been purchased, and all the shoemakers of the Squadron employed in making shoes.

The shoemakers were given 6d per day extra and the two foremen 1s 6d, making a total cost of 6s 6d per pair for 258 pairs. In addition, 41 pairs of trousers were made for the 300 prisoners from Danish prizes, and 60 guernseys, 100 shirts and five casks of soap distributed to them.[20]

HM brig *Constant*, left in the Great Belt to look after the *Jenny* transport when the rest of the squadron had left on 4 January, had been forced to weigh anchor and sail to escape the ice there and 'experienced a most dreadful night between that Island [Anholt] and the Lyse ground on the 6th Inst. The Brig was a mass of ice almost unmanageable, the water above the casks in the hold, pumping and boiling at the same time.' She managed to escape and reach Harwich whence, nothing daunted, her captain wrote: 'The above Sir are my

---

* 10 Ice Saws, 6 Hatchets, plus materials for 16 more saws to be made on board – cost £25–12–3d. (NA, Kew, ADM 80/146, Keats to Navy Board, 2 February 1809).

reasons for returning to England without orders which I trust will meet with your approbation and I take the liberty to observe that I hope I shall have the satisfaction of remaining under your command.'[21]

The ice raised another danger. The Danes might use it to cross the Sound and invade Scania. Consul Fenwick at Halsingborg had convinced Keats that this was intended, because of pressure from the French, and reported the seeming indifference of the Swedes to the threat.[22] A British prisoner released from Copenhagen reported that: 'I saw 480 harrows ... carried into Cronborg Castle on the 9th or 10th January and many more were to follow. They are intended as *chevaux de frise* against cavalry.'[23] This view was strengthened by a meeting Keats had with John M. Johnson, a government confidential agent who covered the Baltic area generally in countries where there was no normal diplomatic representation. He supported Fenwick's opinion, and believed that the invasion would take place if the Sound remained frozen, but thought that Denmark generally would be glad if it were to be prevented by a thaw or any other circumstance – not so much from fear of military difficulties, but from a jealousy of French power and authority.[24]

Denmark had had no great territorial ambitions since the Northern Peace of 1720. Hers was basically a defensive foreign policy, seeking to preserve the link with Norway, to avoid political isolation, and to maintain a 'fleet in being' large enough to resist a Swedish attack.[25] Absolutism was much less entrenched in Denmark than it had become in Sweden. David Kirby suggests that:

> From 1784, when the sixteen-year-old Crown Prince Frederick managed to overthrow the conservative regime which had prevailed since the downfall of the Struensee faction in 1772, the system was run by enlightened members of distinguished families, whose reforming enthusiasm helped transform rural society ... The outward benevolent calm of Denmark was in sharp contrast to the mood of disillusionment and discontent which descended on Sweden in the 1780s.[26]

The Danes were fiercely patriotic and the revolutionary ideas of Jacobinism were more popular in society circles than in the field. By the Peace of Fontainebleau in 1807 they agreed to make common cause with France. Napoleon promised to get compensation for Denmark for her war losses and Denmark undertook to help force Sweden into the Continental System.[27]

Canning still had hopes of persuading Denmark into neutrality. His instructions to Merry in November 1808, following the armistice between Sweden and Russia, were that:

> If proposals from Russia should be the consequence of the armistice, and they should appear likely to lead to any result acceptable to Sweden, H. M[aje]sty would willingly release the King of Sweden from the obligations of the treaty on the conditions already specified of not closing his ports against

the military or commercial marine of Great Britain ... if the overtures now made should appear likely to lead to negotiation, powers will be sent to you to conclude and sign, jointly with Sweden, a secret treaty with Denmark for her neutrality during the remainder of the war.[28]

King Gustav had, in fact, sent a special envoy, Colonel Borgenstjerna, to Copenhagen to negotiate an armistice which would enable him to reinforce his army in Finland in the coming spring.[29] The negotiations got nowhere. However, the food situation in Norway, dependent on shipments of corn from Denmark, was so bad because of the British blockade that in February 1809 Prince Christian August proposed an armistice to the young Colonel Adlersparre, who had taken over command of the Western Army, fighting on the Norwegian front, when General Armfelt was dismissed by King Gustav. The Prince headed the government commission set up in August 1807 to act for King Frederick VI in Norway to overcome the breakdown in communications with Denmark which was another effect of the blockade. The Norwegian troops were starving and in no state to fight.[30] Christer Jorgensen suggests that Christian August knew of Adlersparre's conspiracy with a group of other discontented young officers to remove King Gustav from power and that the armistice might also have been intended to safeguard Adlersparre's rear if he proceeded with his plans to march a contingent of his Western Army troops on Stockholm against the King.[31] Merry certainly believed this. In a series of reports to Canning he went further and concluded that both the truce with the Norwegian army and the agreement with the Russians had been 'concerted with the enemy'.[32] The Russian truce was even more surprising than the Norwegian one since the Russians had been on the point of crossing from the Åland Islands to capture Stockholm.

King Gustav had replaced Adlerberg as ambassador in London with Baron Gustav von Brinkman in October 1808. Brinkman had a brief to persuade Canning to double the subsidy that Sweden had been receiving. This he soon discovered was a thankless and impossible task. As Canning pointed out at their meeting on 13 December, even if the ministry were to agree to such an increase, they would undoubtedly be defeated in the House of Commons and the ministry would then probably fall.[33] He reported this to Chancellor Ehrenheim who, under pressure from Lagerheim, the Finance Minister and a firm opponent of the British connection, had been highly critical of his failure to produce results. Ehrenheim, as we have seen in the Moore affair, felt that Britain was pouring into Spain the money that might have come to Sweden, partly because of the opening-up that it promised of trade with the Mediterranean and South America. This view was adopted also by King Gustav, who meanwhile had turned to intimidate Merry.

At their first meeting on 6 December, Gustav demanded that the subsidy be increased to at least £1,700,000 and that he must receive £300,000 in specie within six days. Otherwise, he would not renew the treaty, which expired at the end of the year, and he would close his ports to British ships. It was blackmail. Merry had been instructed before leaving Britain that he was not to discuss the subsidy at all and that any future subsidies could not be paid in specie because it was all needed for the insurgents in Spain. However, he felt that the amount involved was so much less than the potential cost of the seizure of British ships and property that he agreed to make the payment as an advance of the original subsidy. Canning excused Merry but threatened that the King would recall him 'in disgrace', breaking off diplomatic relations,[34] to show his displeasure to the Swedish King. In the end King Gustav, who had also sought a guarantee from Britain to support Sweden in regaining Finland, was forced by his desperate financial and political position to accept the existing level of subsidy without any further conditions.[35]

However, within days he had fallen from power, with remarkably little disturbance. Colonel Adlersparre had marched his army eastwards towards Stockholm, gathering strength on the way. In the capital, King Gustav had tried to seize the reserves of silver and with his guards escape to the country, but was forestalled by a group of officers, led by General Adlercreutz, former commander of the army in Finland and himself a Finn, breaking into the palace early in the morning of 9 March. A gathering of 'the principal persons of the Government' endeavoured to persuade the King to desist and to publish a proclamation 'annulling the late edict for levying so great a contribution on his subjects, and declaring his intention to summon a Diet forthwith'. When he refused, Adlercreutz arrested him. Lieutenant John Ross was among those present and describes the events at first-hand. Also involved, behind the scenes, was Comte d'Antraigues who was a friend of General Armfelt and had tried unsuccessfully to involve Canning in the plans; his contact in Sweden had reported that Armfelt was Anglophile but needed £4,000–£5,000 to clear his debts. Merry had refused to become involved, but sent frequent reports at length to Canning.[36]

It was far from certain in whose hands the power of the new government would lie and what would be their attitude towards England and France. There was a belief in London that the rebels were predominantly Francophile, but even Baron Lagerbjelke, no lover of England, insisted to Merry that relations would remain the same: he had been Secretary to King Gustav but was now, temporarily, a not very competent Foreign Secretary. The new government would certainly need both the subsidy and the military assistance of the British fleet until peace could be made with Russia. There was no practicable alternative within the existing royal family to Charles, Duke of Sodermania, uncle of King Gustav (initially as Regent and then as King Charles XIII) even though he was elderly and was really only a figurehead: later that year he was to have a stroke. As Merry wrote: 'The Duke of Sodermania is guided by the last person who happens to give advice to his Royal Highness', though Ross placed confidence in his character, 'more perhaps than in that of his ministers'. He was, in Merry's view, a great improvement on Gustav, but he still felt that British money would be far better spent in Spain, as Ehrenheim had suspected.[37]

Meanwhile, Keats was nervously trying to clear all British shipping from the country:

> In this state of things the most urgent necessity in my mind is to remove with the least possible delay all British property from Sweden, for notwithstanding the assurances which the new government hold out of a desire to maintain friendly relations with England, still with a powerful Russian Army within 35 leagues of the capital, it is not to be expected it will be able even to preserve its neutrality to the period fixed for the meeting of the Diet, the 1st of next May.[38]

Ice was still blocking the passage between Sweden and Bornholm, preventing the withdrawal of trade from Karlskrona, and there were 13 ships frozen into Stockholm. Keats expressed his willingness 'to support and defend His Majesty [Gustav] and government as well against rebels as his declared enemies', but he also asked Hood for a squadron strong enough to deal with the Swedish fleet if they became hostile. The ice stretched from Rugen across to the Swedish shore and with easterly winds was threatening to force him back through the Belt. On April 20 he sought Hood's approval to retire from the Baltic as he was still concerned that he had too few ships to protect the trade.[39]

Brilliant though Keats was as a post-captain and renowned for his fighting ability and seamanship, making him much sought after by Saumarez and other admirals for their squadrons, it seems that he may not have had the same self-confidence in the decision-making necessary at higher levels of authority. His handling of the rescue of the Spanish troops from Denmark was masterly and he thoroughly deserved the 'Red Ribband' he won from it. But that was a straightforward military mission, working on clear instructions from the Admiralty as to its objective and under a commander-in-chief whom he knew well and trusted. Christopher Hall, in his book *Wellington's Navy*, points out Keats' indecision two years later at Cadiz, over sending Fleming with the *Bulwark* to Lima, when '[for] eight weeks letters passed back and forth as the two civilians tried to persuade the reluctant admiral to send Fleming'. Keats lamented to the Admiralty Secretary:

> Nothing, Sir, can be more unpleasant to me than the situation in which at this moment I find myself. Feeling that by a Departure from their Lordships' Instructions, I subject myself to their Disapprobation and by a rigid adherence to them, to an Imperfect and unsatisfactory accomplishment of the Service in Question.[40]

A rather peevish letter to Hood prior to Saumarez' arrival in May 1809 to take up his command off Gothenburg, complains: 'I am uninformed both of the Commander-in-Chief's arrangements and of the Naval force appropriate to escort convoys and for the general protection of the trade in this sea.'[41] Colin White quotes Nelson's use of the phrase 'I desire you will not fret upon the occasion' in a letter reassuring Keats who was worried that the *Superb* by then was so slow. He suggests that the use of the word 'fret' was possibly significant in view of Keats' known touchiness regarding his professional reputation.[42] St Vincent's general criticism of flag officers may be relevant:

> There is such a deficiency of nerves under responsibility that I see officers of the greatest promise and acquired character sink beneath its weight. Lord Gardner, and Vice Admiral Thornborough, brave as lions in the presence of an enemy, are instances in point, and the present order of cruising before Brest, requires that the Fleet should be tacked or wore once at least in the night during an easterly wind, which very few Flag Officers can endure.[43]

One of those select few in St Vincent's words quoted earlier* was Sir James Saumarez, although like many other of St Vincent's 'favourites' he went in and out of favour. It is noticeable how the atmosphere changed with Saumarez' arrival off Gothenburg at the beginning of May. He immediately sent a detachment to take possession of Anholt, a small Danish island in the middle of the Kattegat: 'which in case of our being excluded from the Ports of Sweden will be a convenient situation to obtain supplies of water and for the Convoys occasionally to resort to: in other respects it can be of little use being a low sandy island with scarcely any vegetation whatever.'[44] This was something that had evidently been discussed before his departure and for which he had Mulgrave's approval.[45]

Keats, having borne the weight through the winter and prior to joining the fleet for the invasion of Walcheren, was relieved in June by Admiral Dixon. He proved a dependable and efficient operator of the system of convoy defence that Keats had developed to meet the challenge of the Danish gunboats in the Belt. Hood had already sailed for home on 7 May, 'considerably shook by his late illness'.[46] His successor, Admiral Pickmore, was due to bring out a further four ships of the line, to bring the total force up to 20, although probably only nine of these would be available to meet any sortie by the Russian fleet. Saumarez' instructions from the Admiralty, issued when he sailed, were to protect British trade and those neutral ships that had licences issued in London, 'to watch the motions of the Russians in the Baltic' and to attack their fleet should it emerge from Cronstadt, and to ensure his own ships were kept fully supplied with

* p. 25 above.

water in case they could not use Swedish ports. No precise instructions were given for his dealings with Sweden because of the political uncertainty, but he was to keep in touch with the British minister in Stockholm and to preserve an amicable intercourse with Sweden and encourage trade. Their Lordships were also very concerned that he should prevent from spreading to his ships the contagious fever which had decimated the Swedish forces the previous autumn and was still prevalent. They prohibited any unnecessary communication with the shore or Swedish ships.[47]

Merry had requested leave of absence on grounds of health, which may not have been entirely a diplomatic pretext although it did suit Canning.[48] He hung on until the end of April when he finally achieved a private audience with the Duke of Sodermania to take his leave formally and to introduce Foster, the lega-tion secretary, as chargé d'affaires. Merry did not actually sail from Gothenburg until 10 May. This enabled him to have a meeting with Saumarez to brief him on the situation in Stockholm. By then the two governments had exchanged assurances that even in the event of war breaking out between them, the ships, property and persons of each country would be mutually respected.[49] Saumarez' initial impression of Foster was that 'he seems very exact in his correspondence and to judge from it a very well disposed man'.[50]

Saumarez received a warm welcome from his Swedish connections. A flowery letter from Admiral Krusenstjerna attested that 'the noble and disinterested disposition of your excellency to employ the forces committed to your orders for the defence of this country and maintenance of its independence excites in me the warmest sense of gratitude'.[51] Admiral Nauckhoff reported that:

> We are obliged, through the remarkable revolution in Sweden, to remain strictly on the defensive with regard to our neighbours until peace is made. Russia is unwilling to make peace unless we give up Finland and declare that our ports will always be closed to England; it is necessary therefore to continue the war.

He asked Saumarez to send some small gunboats to help defend the passage between Åland and the Swedish coast. He added that the Royal Duke had written to the British government to commend the promotion of John Ross to captain and that Surgeon Duke had been given two Swedish medical honours and a gold medal in recognition of his services.[52] Admiral Puke, writing in English for help with gunboats to defend the Swedish coasts, stated:

> It is only in your excellency I may fix my *confiance*, convinced as I am that, by the good intelligence that subsists between the both nations and His Britannic Majesty's benevolence towards Sweden, your excellency will not omit to protect, as far as possible, the trade from Gothenburg and through the Belts upwards, and retain all hostile enterprises.[53]

Finally, in June, Baron von Platen announced that the King of Sweden had directed him to deliver personally to Saumarez the decoration of Commander Grand Croix of the Order of the Sword.[54]

Saumarez wrote two letters to Foster on 18 May – one public, one private – in response to a messenger from him with details of a conference he had had with Lagerbjelke, stating Sweden's desire to remain in amity with Britain. He set out his proposals for his employing the fleet in the defence of Sweden by stationing a squadron in the Sound to intimidate the Danes, and another in the Baltic to guard against a Russian invasion from Finland, although he had no instructions from the government – 'I trust to be right in using my efforts for that purpose; and I hope to receive the sanction of ministers on the measures I am adopting'.[55] He sent instructions to that effect to Keats, to pass on to his successor Admiral Dixon on his arrival, and orders for Admiral Bertie with the *Stately* and *Africa* to lie off Hälsingborg and protect convoys through the Sound. In London, Canning refused to be the first nation in Europe to recognise the new government. He told Brinkman, the new Swedish ambassador in London, that he was welcome to stay as its unofficial representative, but he would not recognise King Charles XIII. For five months he had no official contact with Brinkman and it was not until mid-August that he told him that he would authorise Saumarez' fleet to support a Swedish offensive against Russia.[56] In fact, as late as 22 August, Mulgrave wrote privately to Saumarez to say that His Majesty could not yet give him permission to wear the Swedish Order of the Sword since it would imply recognition of the Duke of Sodermania as King of Sweden.[57]

I have found no record of political or diplomatic instructions being sent to Saumarez during this period. On 24 May, he wrote to Martha:

> I wish I could speak as favourably of my public correspondents – but they pursue their former plan of leaving me without instructions in the present critical state of Affairs and what is worse without sending the Force* I was given to expect would have followed to join me – it almost appears that my departure from England was the Signal for them to discontinue their Exertions – before I left Gothenburg I wrote to them very fully on the subject – and recapitulated the remonstrance in subsequent Letters. If not speedily attended to, my expectations of success this Campaign will be annihilated and Sweden left to its fate and become a Prey to the Russian Forces from Finland.[58]

In a long letter on 15 July, he said:

---

* It was this force of ships and marines that he had planned to use in an attack on the Eartholms (see Chapter 6).

Sir Richard B[ickerton] preserves his accustom'd silence altho' I have written to him repeatedly. I believe my strong representations on the inadequacy of the Force has offended both L[ord] M[ulgrave] and him, but I should have fail'd in my Duty not to have done it, and I should have been reduced to the mortification of being on the defensive instead of being enabled as I now am to attack the Enemy's Fleet should they have come out of their Port, a circumstance there was every reason at that time to expect.[59]

He therefore continued to make his own decisions and to support the Swedes, and found Foster to be thinking on the same lines.

An undated, unsigned memorandum on 'The Strategic Situation in the Baltic' in the Suffolk Record Office archive is almost certainly a fair copy of Saumarez' proposals, possibly as a basis for discussion with Mulgrave before his departure since, amongst other matters, it deals with the storing of his fleet ready for sea. It goes into considerable detail on the political situation and on the number and stationing of the ships and men that might be needed and gives a comprehensive and intelligent grasp of the needs and duties of the Commander-in-Chief Baltic. I feel, therefore, that it ought to be quoted in full. Professor Rodger believes that strategy was not a word used in the navy at that time[60] and the title of the document – 'The Strategic Situation in the Baltic' – is that given by the archivist rather than by its author. However, it does show that Saumarez was fully capable of strategic thinking and prepared to put forward his own strategy to their Lordships without, apparently, being asked – which would explain why it is unaddressed, undated and unsigned.

THE STRATEGIC SITUATION IN THE BALTIC

The Naval operations in the Baltic for the ensuring summer must greatly depend on the state of Sweden as an ally, a neutral power, or an enemy.

First – supposing Sweden to continue the ally of Great Britain and Ministers should wish to grant licences & encourage the Baltic trade in the same manner in which it was done last year – the protection of the convoys thro' the Sound and the blockade of the Russian fleet will be the two principal objects to attend to. To effect which the following plan of operations is proposed:

Gothenburg to be the general rendezvous for all convoys both outwards & homeward bound, and an Admiral to be stationed there to make the necessary arrangements and give the proper instructions for their further proceedings who can have constant communication by land with the officer commanding in the Sound, and if necessary give him regular notice of the sailing of the convoys from Gothenburg.

Off Helsingborg it will be necessary to have two sail of the line with three or four small vessels to meet the convoys off the Koll [Kullen] and pass them safe thro' the narrows. Sixty fours will do for this service but they ought to have extra boats allowed them and all calculated & well fitted for carrying carronades. The small vessels ought to be well manned & fitted with long guns.

Off Malmo two ships such as the *Madras* & *Agincourt* ought to lay as receiving ships for the crews of the gunboats, and fitted with long guns for their protection as also that of the convoys which may be obliged to anchor in Malmo Roads. And as this will be the grand point of attack from the enemy, it ought to be the only station for our gunboats, which should be as numerous as possible, each under the direction of a Lieut. & the whole under two Captains. The ships boats to be fitted for carronades and an extra proportion allowed.

Off Drago, a sixty four with two small vessels should be stationed to protect the convoys after they have passed the Malmo Channel until they are clear of the enemy's gun boats, and also to afford protection for the convoys coming down the Baltic, which are often prevented for several days by contrary winds from getting thro' the Channel.

For the protection of the convoys from Gothenburg until clear of the Malmo Channel, there ought to be a sufficient number of frigates & small vessels with long guns, so as not to interfere with the vessels appointed to bring backwards & forwards the convoys from the Nore, Humber etc, or to make it necessary for the ships of war in the Baltic to come lower down than Drago.

The Russian fleet consisting of ten sail of the line, three of which are three deckers, a sufficient force to blockade them will be required in the Gulf of Finland, besides frigates & smaller vessels to collect the convoys & to keep the Baltic clear of privateers.

The Eartholmes being the principal nest for the enemy's privateers in the Baltic, ought to be immediately taken possession of. Five line of battle ships carrying two flat boats and one hundred extra marines each with a couple of frigates & two or three bombs would effect this service, and without distressing themselves be enabled to leave a garrison of 500 marines. This would always be a safe depot for the store ships and victuallers, as also (in the event of the Swedish ports being shut) a rendezvous for the convoys, and a place where the fleet might water.

The Belt with this plan of operations would only be used as a passage for the fleet going in & out of the Baltic which the enemy cannot hinder. Except therefore with a view of preventing the enemy fortifying the island of Sproe, there would be no occasion to keep any ships on this part of the station, particularly as it has been found totally impossible to cut off the communication between Zealand and the Continent.

Secondly – supposing Sweden to become an enemy, or a neutral power & shutting her ports against our ships of war & making them unsafe for our convoys to rendezvous at – Anholt ought to be taken possession of which in summer would serve as a point of rendezvous for the outward bound convoys and where ships of war might meet them with the necessary instructions for their further proceedings, and to see them safe into the Belt. Having a light house it will be of great use during the fall of the year.

The Belt in this case will be the only safe entrance into the Baltic, and a very considerable force of frigates & small vessels with their boats well fitted with carronades will be required to pass the convoys thro', where an admiral with two sixty fours ought also to be stationed to superintend the whole.

Convoys in this case ought not be too frequent but regular, so that one convoy should if possible get thro' before another one enters the Belt. The Eartholmes in this point of view will become absolutely necessary as a rendez-vous for the convoys in the Baltic.

No ships will be required in the Sound, but what may be necessary off the Koll to keep in check their force at Copenhagen & prevent their coming into the Cattegat to annoy our convoys.

Thirdly – should Sweden become our enemy or should it be found neces-sary to annihilate their navy:–

Karlskrona in its <u>present</u> state may certainly be attacked, her whole fleet captured and dock yard destroyed, and this service performed with a <u>naval</u> force only.

N.B. All the ships ordered for the Baltic ought to be stored for six months & take as much provisions as they can possibly store. And in the line of battle ships ought to be distributed a proportion of cables, anchors, sails and small cordage for the sloops and gun brigs, which they are always in want of & which it is impossible for them to carry.[61]

Both Keats and Bertie had, like Canning and Merry, remained suspicious of Swedish intentions and Saumarez had forwarded their comments to Foster, at the same time as the reputed news of an Austrian victory over Bonaparte on 21/22 May. Foster's response, thanking him for the news of the victory, was much more encouraging: 'It is complete and glorious indeed and will add to the other reasons I shall entertain for thinking that this government cannot mean to deceive us'. Saumarez concurred and explained: 'although I was before perfectly convinced of the good disposition of the present govern-ment of Sweden towards our country … I could not do otherwise than make you acquainted with the surmises of the two officers next in rank to me in the fleet.'[62] This demonstrates how Saumarez was beginning to diverge from both his superiors and his subordinates in his view of the Swedish connection. It also illustrates how he was willing to pass on the views of those under him even when he disagreed with them. It was at this time that he received news of the award of the Order of the Sword and he wrote to Martha that it showed the Swedish government 'well satisfied at the determination I took to support them without waiting for orders from my Government'. He went on, however:

I believe I shall decline it, unless I should be the means of obtaining better terms from Russia than they at first expected – Peace they must have, for however capable they may be with our assistance to defend their Country, they have not the means to defray the expenses of the War even but for a few weeks longer. I however hope they will not comply with the demands of Russia to exclude our Trade from their Ports.[63]

There were several reasons for Saumarez' evident ability to strike up a happy relationship with his Swedish opposite numbers. First, his excellent command of French, the language of diplomacy. It certainly came more easily to an educated Guernseyman than to the average British admiral, and he had also made use of it when stationed off Smyrna as a midshipman and on a visit to Cherbourg to see the new harbour while unemployed at home during the period of peace between the American and French Revolutionary Wars.[64] Again, a number of Swedish naval officers had served for a time with the French navy and Ross mentions the delight with which, on their return to Karlskrona from Rogervik in October, 1808, Admiral Nauckhoff and three other officers had discovered that Saumarez had been on the opposing side at the Battle of the Saintes, 26 years before. Captain Tornquist had leapt from his chair to shake Sir James' hand, with the words: '*Mon Dieu! Monsieur l'Amiral*, we burnt powder together, let's drink a bumper', which they proceeded to do, 'fighting the battle over again'.[65] There was also a formality to Saumarez' manner which I believe even today would be in tune with Swedish manners and customs.

He extended the same friendly politeness to the Russians, believing that the state of warfare between the two countries was an unnatural one that could not, and should not, last. The courtesies of life continued, even between countries at war, making curious reading for modern eyes. The Russian commander-in-chief at Reval (Tallinn), returning an English seaman under a flag of truce, added a present of melons, green peas and other vegetables, to which Saumarez responded with some English porter. 'They have a disposition to be as friendly as a state of warfare will admit, in which they will meet with a reciprocity on the part of the British Commander.' It was followed by an exchange of 'a further supply of melons, cucumbers, green peas, potatoes, turnips and carrots' for 'a Cheshire cheese, two loaves of sugar and some coffee'. 'Our correspondence is most friendly and he expresses his concern with much feeling at the circumstance that separates the two Nations'. This, however, was coupled on Saumarez' part with the view that:

> It is more to be regretted than ever that we have not long before this declared the ports of Russia in a state of Blockade as it must have changed the Politics of that Country. My opinion has been confirmed by that of Persons whose interest militates against the measure but are obliged to avow it. Our Ministers will see their Error when it's too late.[66]

This echoed the view of Louis Drusina, former British consul in Memel who operated as a secret agent in Prussia under the name Heinrich Hahn:

It was ever my decided opinion that the Russian ports should have been strictly blockaded last year. The dissatisfaction in the country was very great upon the prospect of not having any trade; and if they had not been allowed any, I am convinced the government must have changed their system, and then there would have been a free trade this year.[67]

There was indeed considerable discontent in Russia with the French alliance and the resultant disruption of trade. The Russians had more to lose from a rigid blockade by both French and British, than either France or Britain. But the pressures of vocal English shipping and manufacturing interests, the war-weariness after 15 years' almost continuous warfare, and a Whig opposition which however fragmented and weak could still create uproar, made it most unlikely that any British government would have the courage to take such a step. It was easier to hope for a change of heart on the part of the Russian emperor, though this would be slower. British ministers would not have known the remark that Alexander made in a letter to his Foreign Secretary Rumiantsev in December, 1808: 'since the most enlightened and wise men of France themselves suspect and disapprove the imperial policy, is it for me to approve an ambition which knows no limits and to help it to break all obstacles?'[68] Nor would they have heard Talleyrand's famous question to him at Erfurt that inspired this comment:

Sire, what are you going to do here? It rests with you to save Europe, and you can only accomplish this by resisting Napoleon. The French people are civilized, its sovereign is not; the Sovereign of Russia is civilized, and his people are not; it is therefore for the Sovereign of Russia to be allied to the French people.[69]

But, like Saumarez, they would have been aware that it was a fragile and temporary relationship.

The political confusion in Sweden that followed the dethronement of King Gustav was beginning to be resolved. On 12 May, the Swedish Diet had formally declared that he and his son had lost all right to the throne for ever. There were rumours of plots to restore them and Merry had been unsuccessfully approached before his departure by two men seeking British aid for this purpose.[70] The King and his son had been removed to a castle in the country, but to everyone's relief they left for Germany in December, where they spent several months travelling before settling temporarily for exile in Russia, without the Queen who, after a fierce domestic row, returned to her homeland of Baden.[71] The hoped-for financial assistance to Sweden from France failed to materialise: there was little advantage to come from it for France and Napoleon had no wish to antagonise Russia at a time when Austria had turned to fight him again and invaded Bavaria. Lagerbjelke was replaced as Foreign Minister in

June by Engeström – also Francophile but less committed and more canny. But his overtures to Canning were no more successful than his predecessor's.

This left Sweden friendless, at war with France and Russia, penniless, and under threat of invasion by a superior Russian army. Interpreting his original instructions in the broadest way and lacking any fresh ones, Saumarez took a powerful squadron of ten ships of the line up into the entrance of the Gulf of Finland to besiege the Russian fleet lying at Cronstadt, now that he was reinforced by the arrival on 16 June of Admiral Pickmore with four ships. By 9 July he was anchored off Nargan Island, about eight miles from Reval. Here he had found not only water and wood for his ships, but trees to be cut down for spars.[72] He had already established a good working relationship with Foster in Stockholm. He sent Captain Mansell in the *Rose* to Stockholm at Foster's suggestion to invite Baron von Platen on board *Victory* to discuss ways that some of the British squadron might be stationed off the Åland Islands to protect the projected Swedish reinforcement at Vasa which planned to encircle and capture the Russian army in East Bothnia. Platen was reckoned one of the ablest ministers. He had been dismissed from his post by King Gustav but reappointed as a councillor of state after the revolution.[73]

It was a successful meeting, and Saumarez sent Captain Reynolds in the *Tribune* (36) to assist the Swedes. Platen was very keen to have an English presence. He was aware of the desire of the English government that Sweden and Russia should agree peace terms and was 'confident that the only [*sic*] appearance of an English squadron in those quarters, who are a principal point of contest, would give more weight to the negociation than any other blockade in the Gulf of Finlandia'.[74] Unfortunately, the Swedish attack was not well handled, the Russian troops were allowed to escape, and a subsequent Swedish defeat led to peace negotiations with the Russians holding the upper hand. The Treaty of Frederikshamn on 17 September gave Russia the whole of Finland including the Åland Islands and a strip in the far north. Sweden agreed to join the Continental System, although exceptions were made to allow the import of salt, 'colonial goods',* and a range of other manufactured goods and materials such as leather and tin.[75] Nonetheless, Platen was moved to write, despite having theoretically joined the Continental System:

> At the conclusion of the peace, hard as it is, we cannot yet deny that in an high degree we are indebted to you for our existing as a state ... our ports are open to so brave an ally, to so successful a protector, for so many sails as your excellency judges fit to send in into them for the remaining of the harvest, confident that a man [such] as Sir James is incapable to make other than proper and amical use of it.[76]

---

* *Denrées coloniales* (colonial goods) is a term that appears frequently in Napoleon's instructions and covers products such as cotton, coffee, indigo, pepper, sugar.

Even when the formal Proclamation was made by Charles XIII on 27 October, 1809, closing Swedish ports to all British ships of war and merchant ships, coming into effect on 15 November,[77] it was agreed that any ships already in port would be free to sail and that even warships would be able to put into port if damaged by severe weather. By that date anyway, the weather was closing down, and both trade and navy were anxious to sail for home.

6

The Pea Islands

One of the running problems that Saumarez had to face almost throughout his five years as Commander-in-Chief, Baltic, was the Eartholms. Their possible capture was a controversial issue and shows the degree of discretion given to Saumarez to make his own judgement. The events highlight the way in which a commander-in-chief can avoid taking action when he has doubts about its viability by throwing the decision back to the Admiralty or by procrastination and show differences between the Danish and the British reports of the action.

The Eartholms are a cluster of four small islands lying some ten nautical miles to the north-east of the island of Bornholm in the southern part of the Baltic. The two main islands lie close and parallel to each other. They form between them a natural deep-water harbour, divided into north and south, formerly by a connecting floating walkway but nowadays by a pedestrian bridge. One or other is accessible to sailing vessels under most wind conditions. Frederiksholm is some 300 yards long by 40 wide and Christiansø 400 yards by 155. The largest of the islands, Christiansø, is also the name by which they are generally called, but the official name is Ertholmene (from the Danish word *ært* [pea] which is what they are said to look like on a chart). There is only a thin covering of soil over the granite rock of which they are composed. Much of this was brought by ship from Bornholm, as today are the provisions and even, in a dry summer, the drinking water. Of the other two islands, one is little more than a large bare rocky outcrop; the second, Græsholm, was originally quite grassy, as the name implies. The commandant of the islands kept a cow there which, in good weather swam the narrow channel morning and evening over to the two main islands to be milked.[1] Now Græsholm is a bird sanctuary and their droppings kill most of the vegetation.

Until the middle of the seventeenth century, nobody lived on the Eartholms: a few fishermen used them as a base for herring fishing in the late summer. However, in 1684, King Christian V of Denmark started to create a fortress there to defend the natural harbour, as a protection against the Swedish navy. Bornholm and Ertholmene had been surrendered to Sweden in 1658 together with Scania, but the independent islanders had rebelled and rejoined Denmark

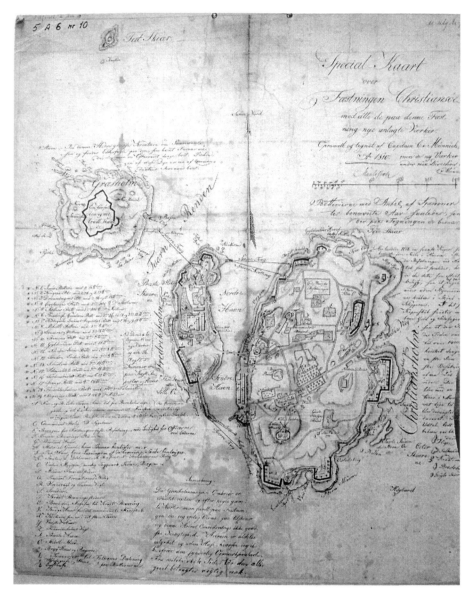

Figure 8. Map of Christiansø fortifications in 1810 by Captain Carl Münnich of the garrison (Jakob Seerup, Royal Danish Naval Museum)

a few years later. For nearly sixty years, from 1725 to 1782, Christiansø was also used as a place of exile and prisoners worked in chain gangs in the granite quarries.[2]

When Denmark responded to Canning's pre-emptive terror attack on Copenhagen and seizure of her fleet in August 1807 by declaring war on Britain, the islands became a base for privateers attacking the trade to the north German and Russian ports. The 'Pea Islands' were ideally placed. The standing instructions to the escorts of the regular Baltic convoys were to escort the merchant ships in their care, usually about 100–200 ships in number, to a point '50 leagues east of Bornholm'.[3] At this point the convoys split up. Individual merchant ships continued to their ports of destination and the escorts normally sailed to Hanö Bay where, from 1810, there was a regular British naval base established for eight months of the year to organise the return convoys until ice prevented the movement of shipping. It was important for any ship going to a port under French control to avoid any evidence of having been part of a British convoy, for its cargo would be liable to confiscation. Ships under whatever ownership – and they mostly went under neutral flags – would carry two sets of papers: one showing that they had touched at a British port, obtained a licence for their journey and cargo and paid duty there, which would satisfy the British escorts and cruisers; the other showing that they came from a French or neutral port, to be presented to the customs officers in north German ports under French control, or to Danish and French privateers, eager for any chance to snap up prizes.[4]

Bribery and corruption were rife. The lower ranks of the customs hierarchy were paid late and badly, and depended on the continuance of smuggling for both their legal and their illegal incomes – as Silvia Marzagalli quotes in her authoritative book on the blockade: 'pour cueillir un fruit ce serait folie de couper l'arbre par le pied'.[5] Bourrienne, Mortier, Michaud, Brune and Bernadotte (the succession of French marshals in command in northern Europe) all reduced the impact of the Berlin and Milan Decrees by their readiness to accept money or favours in return for a blind eye. One proposal to Saumarez by Steen Bille, a Danish lawyer living in Gothenburg, was that his colleagues in England would send out ships to Gothenburg under Prussian colours with British licences for cargoes of British manufactures and colonial produce. He would have a further ship there with a licence to go to Russia in ballast. If Saumarez would allow these ships to join a Baltic convoy, the ship in ballast would 'capture' the laden ships on the journey south from Gothenburg to the Belt, and take them into a Danish port as prizes. Their goods could then be sold legally in Denmark, avoiding some of the duty and escaping the depredations of the customs officers. Britain would benefit by expanding her trade in Denmark.[6] There is no record of a reply and as this was Bille's second attempt at proposing the scheme it is unlikely he received one, but there is no doubt that this practice was occurring, to the detriment of the insurers. A report to the Privy Council by a committee of underwriters at Lloyds said that 'the demands upon the underwriters in London have become in a National point of view alarming'. Consul Smith in Gothenburg was instructed that 'these fraudulent practices hitherto chiefly carried into effect in the ports of Sweden and Prussia but intended as it is stated to be pushed still further in Sweden', should be detected and as much information as possible reported back to the Marquess Wellesley.[7]

Lord Mulgrave, First Lord of the Admiralty, was receiving complaints about the Eartholms, as they came to be called in England, as early as January 1808. These generally concluded by proposing that the islands should be captured and turned into a base both for British warships defending the merchant fleet and for small craft which could smuggle goods from there into ports in the Baltic, suggesting that only a 'modest' force would be needed for this.[8] The cry was taken up by Lord Castlereagh as Secretary of State for War in April 1808, asking Lord Mulgrave to 'give directions to the naval officer commanding in the Baltic to report his opinion on the value of these islands either as commercial or naval stations, and on their means of defence and subsistence'. He enclosed an unsigned, undated paper from Baltic merchants which sets out their viewpoint very clearly:

> It has been recommended by several merchants in the Baltic, and it is also our opinion, that this government should take possession of the islands of Bornholm and Eartholm as considerable trade may be carried on from those islands to the ports of Mecklenburg, Prussia and Russia. The Eartholms are slightly fortified and have a good harbour. A few months ago there was only a small garrison and, it is presumed, not capable of making any great resistance; but, if well provisioned and in our hands, it might easily be rendered impregnable. The island is barren and contains but few inhabitants. Bornholm, which is close adjoining, is a large fruitful island incapable of resistance. The privateers of the enemy have carried away many valuable prizes into Eartholm, which may all be retaken with their cargoes, consisting principally of hemp and other naval stores. The island is a receptacle for privateers from whence they can annoy our trade to the Baltic more than from any other place. In our hands it would be of the greatest utility as it may be made the rendezvous for all our vessels bound to and from the ports in the Baltic. A great smuggling trade may also be carried on with the ports under the control of the French. The French generals, after some short residence, are in the habit of giving permission to the merchants to import goods from England, but it is the policy of Bonaparte to change the generals very often, by which means the permission granted is of little avail on account of the length of the voyage to and from Britain. If we were in possession of these islands, this inconvenience would be remedied as the merchants would suffer the vessels to remain there until they could go into port with safety.[9]

The Admiralty duly passed on Castlereagh's direction as part of their overall Instructions to Saumarez when he first sailed to the Baltic in 1808.[10]

As we have seen, Saumarez was more than fully occupied in his first six months on station. There was the delay at Gothenburg over the role of Sir John Moore's expeditionary force, the need to turn back from Karlskrona in August, just after he had reached the Baltic, in order to support Keats in his evacuation of the Spanish regiments, and then the blockade of the Russian fleet in Rogervik. In his absence further north, the Admiralty had written again about the Eartholms, this time to Admiral Keats, instructing him that: 'If you should find that the islands of Eartholms are of the consequence that has been represented, or if you should consider them to be important objects of capture', he should attack and capture them forthwith providing he felt that his force was adequate and that it did not interfere materially with his other duties.[11] Keats was probably more than occupied with his duties in the Belt safeguarding the passage of convoys against the Danish rowing/sailing gunboats that harassed them continually, and would have had insufficient ships for an attack on the islands. A copy was sent to Saumarez who would probably have received it about the middle of October as he was waiting at Karlskrona for a favourable wind to take the squadron south to the Belt and then on to Gothenburg at what he considered to be the end of the campaigning season.

It was a modest detour for part of Saumarez' returning squadron and Captain William Lukin in *Mars* (74) sailed from Karlskrona on 20 October with the bomb ships *Aetna*, *Hound*[12] and *Devastation*, and the frigate *Salsette*, to be joined shortly by *Orion* (74) and later by the sloop *Magnet* and cutter *Swan*. One assumes that Captain Lukin, a post-captain of 13 years' standing and the senior officer, was given his instructions at that time, but it is unfortunate that there is no record yet found of their exact nature and extent. Curiously, there appears to be no mention of an attack on the Eartholms in either the official correspondence at Kew and in the Suffolk Record Office, or in the Shrubland archive of Saumarez' private correspondence with his wife. Nor does it feature at all in William James' six-volume *Naval History of Great Britain*, published in 1837, which details so many other actions, large and small. This was possibly because what took place was an inconclusive bombardment of no credit to the navy and with no enemy ships involved; but it may simply reflect the lack of written records other than the ships' logs.

The captains' logs record that they were in company with the *Victory* for the following two days, before heading west towards the Eartholms on 23 October.[13] It is probable, therefore, that Lukin received oral instructions in person from Saumarez on board *Victory* and that the absence of any written instructions indicates the lack of serious purpose behind the attack. The three bombs anchored in about 45 fathoms, east by south of the islands, at between 1 and 1½ miles off: a Danish report records the distance as 2,000 metres.[14]

This is one of the deeper parts of the Baltic. The ships commenced firing their shells at 0700 and continued until 1100, receiving a few shots from the Danes in return about 1030. The rest of the squadron, which had been standing further off, then slowly sailed between the bomb ships and the islands, firing several broadsides as they went, at a range, according to the *Mars* log, of 1/3 mile. These, they say, were returned by the Danes. There were no reports of any damage on either side. Lukin records that the bombs ceased firing at 1115 on his signal to weigh anchor. The squadron then went their separate ways, the *Aetna* returning to Karlskrona whence she escorted a homeward-bound convoy on 8 November. Her log records firing 100 shells from her two mortars, but it does appear to have been rather a half-hearted attack.

The memoirs of a young Danish artillery officer, M.C. Bech, in command of the batteries confirm this impression.[15] The two islands had small forts at various points round them, each with four to six cannons, but these were very elderly, and worn-out. There was a small round tower fort on Frederiksholm, and a larger one on Christiansø but neither mounted cannons any longer. The only weapons of any size were two aged 100-pounder mortars placed on the highest point of the island. While Bech was away on a trip to Bornholm, the Commandant had insisted on firing one of the mortars at an English frigate in the offing: as Bech had expected, the mortar burst on the first shot, fortunately injuring only one of its guncrew. In addition to the regular garrison, 200 untrained Bornholmers came over for a month at a time, being relieved in their turn by others.[16]

When the British squadron was spotted, Bech ordered home-made mines to be loaded with gunpowder. These were wooden coffers, placed on the edge of creeks that were possible landing places. They were covered in stones and the barrel of a loaded gun was placed in a hole in them, its trigger connected to a cord that was led behind a breastwork. The hope was that the stones would sink any boat trying to land. The whistling noise of the British shells terrified the Bornholmers, but for the first half-hour the shells nearly all overshot the island and landed in the sea. This was signalled to the bomb ships by one of the rest of the squadron, lying to the south, yet even when the range was dropped Bech claims that very little damage was done. The only deaths were six captured Swedish seamen from one of the Prussian prizes in the harbour, who were playing cards in a temporary prison house when it suffered a direct hit, killing all of them. According to Bech, he did not reply with any of the 12-pounders since they could do no damage to the enemy, but the Commandant insisted that he try the remaining mortar. He laid a long fuse and sheltered with the crew behind a building, and no one was hurt when the mortar duly burst. This was the extent of the Danish response, except for the small batteries firing when the British squadron sailed closer in to fire their broadsides, having started, in Bech's reckoning, at 4,000 yards. Again the British got the range wrong, the shots ricocheting over the eastern batteries, but fragments wounded 15 men in the western batteries on Frederiksholm. The British ships sailed on and, as Bech put it, 'we saw no more of them'.[17]

Another unsigned, undated report, gives a slightly different story. There were 10–15 dead, including one elderly lady, the Commandant was wounded in the leg and 'many houses were hit and much damage done'. It also said that 'in the afternoon a large frigate* came back and this time came so near that the fortress' cannons could hit it. After a few well-judged shots, it turned round and sailed away.'[18] The ships' logs contradict this, but the *Orion*'s log shows that she wore ship and parted company from the others at 2.30 p.m., though there is no record of her firing again. It is also possible that the *Salsette*, whose log is missing, might have returned there. Both Danish versions suggest that it was the wind strengthening that persuaded the British squadron to quit, and the *Mars* log confirms that after a calm morning there were strong winds in the afternoon.

With hindsight, it is easy to believe that a determined landing could have been successful against such weak defences. Lukins' efforts appear to have been neither the forerunner of a landing nor a close reconnoitre of the defences. He wrote to Mulgrave two weeks later asking to be relieved, having been ill all summer from dysentery[19] and he had admitted to Captain Byam Martin when off Rogervik: 'Covering bombs is very stomacky work in a 74 close into a bight full of batteries.'[20] He was probably not the best choice for senior officer, but by then both Hood and Keats were elsewhere. It is arguable that Saumarez himself should have taken charge and used the whole squadron. A letter from Pole instructed him, if Keats had gone ahead with his attack, to garrison the Eartholms with marines from the fleet, but it is most unlikely that this had reached him in time.[21] He too had not been well. It had been a long and demanding campaign, with political and diplomatic pressures as well as military ones, in his first major post as Commander-in-Chief.

Did he, as a result, fail to give the Eartholms the attention that they needed? Or was this an instance of the military leader on the spot rejecting the speculative proposals of ministers at home, driven by pressure from trading interests which carried political weight? And how important was their possible possession to the success of British policies in the Baltic?

Thomas Wilson, chairman of Lloyds Continental Committee sent the Foreign Office in August 1811 a two-page letter he had received from a merchant, Edward Nicholls, setting out six reasons for capturing the islands, together with a long, unsigned and undated, treatise on the benefits of a Malta-like colony in

---

*   Most of the Danish army reports described all the ships, including the bombs, as 'frigates'.

the Baltic.[22] The letter can be taken as a summary of the points made by various other 'projectors' of the scheme. These were:

1   If they were an entrepôt, goods could be taken there in British ships rather than by neutrals who secretly left the convoys and whose crews could be bribed to reveal that they came from a British port, leading to confiscation.

2   They were a secure refuge for privateers and would be used to smuggle goods into Baltic ports between the British fleet's departure and return.

3   A squadron of men-of-war could be left there in the winter to prevent this smuggling and protect our own trade.

4   They could be a recruiting centre for German and Prussian troops.

5   If the islands had been captured by the British, the 'calamity of 'Carlshamn'* might have been prevented.

6   The capture of the islands would forestall the French who had eyes on them.

The entrepôt proposal had most to recommend it. Until the attack on Copenhagen in 1807, Tonningen at the mouth of the River Eider, which connected the North Sea to the forerunner of the Kiel Canal, had been a major entrepôt for British manufactures and colonial goods. This trade had switched to the island of Fotö off Gothenburg[23] and to Heligoland, captured by the *Majestic* in September 1807.[24] Transhipment to the Baltic ports in neutral craft from the Eartholms would have made the French task of maintaining the Continental System of Napoleon's Berlin and Milan Decrees even harder than it already was. It might have prevented 'the calamity of Carlshamn', since merchant ships would not have needed to use Swedish ports when weather or hostile activities prevented them reaching their destination ports.

Against this, the small size of the Eartholms, both for space in its twin harbours and for handling cargoes ashore might have meant smaller more frequent convoys, putting even more pressure on the naval escorts. Feeding and watering the men required to run the entrepôt, in addition to the garrison, would have been a further problem since the water came only from limited rainwater catchments and during the peak trading of the summer there was little rainfall. There seems to have been misleading information about the availability of water on Christiansø, the only one of the four islands with any supplies. Roger Knight quotes Admiral Hyde Parker in 1801 informing Nelson that he was more likely to obtain water there than from Bornholm for the six ships of the line to be stationed there to keep watch on the Swedish navy at Karlskrona.[25] Mansell's report of 5 October 1811 to Saumarez spoke of a spring in addition to the catchment reservoirs and added: 'I have not heard

---

*   See Chapter 8.

that there is a scarcity or in what quantity in might be obtained'.[26] However, Jakob Seerup of the Danish Maritime Museum, who lives on Bornholm, has confirmed in conversation and by e-mail my own impression when visiting the island in 2006 that the rainwater catchment would be quite inadequate for a squadron of men-of-war and that access to the only underground water supply on the island was only recently drilled. Nelson's ships actually drew their water supplies from north Germany.

There were 25 prizes in the harbour when the October attack took place.[27] These were probably waiting for the British fleet to depart, in order to sail in greater safety to Copenhagen for disposal, and so would have been an abnormally high number. Nonetheless, this indicates a considerable level of activity in the summer of 1808. By 1811, counter-measures by Saumarez' cruisers had had their effect. Consul Fenwick at Hälsingborg in May 1810 recorded 87 merchant ships having been captured by privateers[28] and in April 1811 he reported that the Danes had fitted out double the number of privateers that they had had at sea the previous season. Yet by July that year he wrote to Saumarez:

> The vigilance of your cruisers and the formidable convoys sent thro' the Belt have completely disheartened the Danish privateers who making few or no prizes now will be all ruined. The government is also thereby deprived of the large revenue which it last year obtained from the amount of the goods condemned.[29]

The privateer *Bornholm*, three weeks out from Copenhagen when captured off the Eartholms in November 1810, had taken only one Swedish galliot which was recaptured with her.[30] The dangers to shipping lurking in the Eartholms therefore proved less damaging than had been feared, but this might not have been foreseen in 1808.

Points 3 and 6 of Nicholls' letter to Lloyds have little validity. The sea regularly froze over (Bech reports hares coming across the ice from Bornholm[31]) so any men-of-war would be harbour-bound in the winter and the trade anyway ceased with the coming of ice. It is extremely doubtful whether the Danes would have accepted French possession of their island fortress or, if they had, whether the French would have considered tying up and keeping supplied a sufficient garrison to hold the islands in the summer months against a British fleet. It is outside the scope of this work to evaluate the validity of point 4, their use as a recruiting centre.

Although no one denied that their possession would be invaluable to both trade and defence, the other doubts were what force would be needed to capture and hold them without unacceptable loss. In spring 1809, Saumarez was re-appointed to the Baltic command and was ordered 'with as little delay as possible [to] state for their Lordships' consideration, whether you think it practicable to take the Eartholms, and if so, what force and plan you would recommend to be employed on that service'.[32] His answer came in two days. It reflects what must have been Lukins' report (possibly oral) in justification of the failure of his attack in October. Saumarez considered that 'the possession of the Eartholms would be highly desirable'. He gave as a further reason: that in the case of war with Sweden, which was a distinct possibility and later occurred in November 1810: 'It would afford protection to His Majesty's Cruisers in bad weather, when supplies of water could always be maintained'. He estimated that at least 1,000 troops including engineers and artillery would be necessary:

> The position of the Eartholms is naturally very strong and its defence is made more formidable to any attack by a strong wall erected in such parts as are accessible to the landing of troops, with a great number of heavy artillery mounted in various parts, [and] considerable loss must be expected before the landing can be effected; and which must be made under the cover of Line of Battle ships.

He threw the onus on their Lordships 'to determine if the object is in their consideration adequate to the loss that must be expected in an attack upon them, particularly with the doubt of such attack proving successful'.[33]

The misinformation about the water supply would have been disastrous unless Bornholm also had been captured, making it altogether a different proposition to attack and then defend. Saumarez' meetings at the Admiralty before departure again for the Baltic must have changed his mind, for the review of the strategic situation in the Baltic already quoted recommends their capture. He had no hesitation about taking possession of Anholt in May 1809 for the same purpose, as well as to maintain the lighthouse there. The garrison was only 130 troops and some militia, and the low-lying, sandy island was much harder to defend against a naval attack.[34] In fact, it might have been recaptured by a Danish attack in March 1810, but for the arrival of two British men-of-war, forewarned by a message from Consul Fenwick in Hälsingborg,[35] and for the sandy nature of the soil making it hard to haul cannon from the beach under fire. The underlying sandstone did, however, give a good supply of water, unlike the granite of the Eartholms.

Fenwick, who had formerly been posted in Elsinore, Denmark, and who still had good Danish connections, maintained quite erroneously that 'had the [October] attack continued half an hour longer the fort must have surrendered as there was only a very small quantity of ammunition left there'.[36] This error was repeated later in Edward Nicholls' letter when he claimed that the ships of the line 'in twenty minutes completely silenced every [Danish] gun. The Danes were about to haul down their Colours when the Squadron stood out to sea.' Castlereagh in 1809 sent a Royal Engineer, Captain Squire, to report on the practicability of an attack and agreed to hold a corps of troops in readiness 'should it be deemed expedient', adding that the navy could go ahead on their

own if they thought they could capture the islands. But Admiral Keats, holding
the command pending Saumarez' arrival, met Squire on his return to the Belt
and they jointly agreed that Keats did not have sufficient forces. Saumarez
concurred, since his promised reinforcements had not arrived.[37]

Then in August 1809 a report came from Foster, minister in Stockholm, that
there had been a mutiny on the islands:

> The whole Garrison consisted of 200 Germans of the Danish Marine Corps
> and 400 of the Militia of Bornholm. The former who were unopposed by
> the Militia spiked all the guns that they could not carry away, burned two
> privateers, carried off two trading vessels and what stores they could stow in
> them, which they have sold in Sweden, and threw water on the gunpowder
> that was left behind. Two English Frigates who had been with a convoy near
> Karlskrona are reported to have sailed there, in the hopes of surprising the
> castle in its reduced state.[38]

The previous winter had been particularly hard on the islands. Ross relates that:
'The thermometer in January, 1809, sank to forty-five degrees below zero; the
Sound and Belt were completely frozen over, and many passed between Sweden
and Denmark on horseback over the ice'.[39] Two hundred German mercenaries
had been brought over to improve the defences after the October attack,
working in the quarries to provide stone for the perimeter walls under hard
conditions and fierce discipline, which continued into the summer. Discontent
brewed. As a precaution, the governor ordered the mercenaries to relinquish
their guns each time they came off watch. This triggered the mutiny, led by a
Dane, with a Swede and a Saxon in close support. They all intended to sail to
Stralsund to join the forces of the Prussian resistance leader, Major Schill. But
the wind being against them they sailed instead to Sweden where they enrolled
in the Queen's Regiment. Later, they deserted again; many were condemned
and shot, and seven others who came to Copenhagen in 1812 were recognised
and hanged.[40]

HMS *Dictator* was sent forthwith to the islands but went aground on the way
and had to return for repairs to Karlskrona. Saumarez then ordered the *Edgar*
to take the *Dictator* when repaired and a bomb ship 'to take possession of the
Eartholms, summoning the garrison to surrender or attacking them, according
to circumstances'. By the time they were ready, the two frigates already on
station had been driven off the islands by September gales. Ryan confuses this
attack with the one in October 1808, but his conclusion remains valid – that
'the general opinion of naval officers [was] that the place could not be reduced
without the aid of an army'.[41] 'From the corroborating accounts I have received
of the great strength and apparent preparation for defence of that fortress and
not having that description of force under my command to assure ultimate
success without running the greatest risque', Captain Macnamara decided not

to pursue the attack.[42] He was probably correct in his assessment. The improvements made to the defences in the winter had been supplemented by the introduction of seven new Swedish 36-pounders and five 100-pound mortars, and there had been a rapid reinforcement of men from Bornholm whom Bech trained as gun crew. Overall there were now 80 guns in both new and old batteries and a strong magazine had been built. There were also four gunboats that had been built there in 1809 following the lines of the Swedish naval architect Fredrik af Chapman which had come into Danish hands through the Swedish Lieutenant Dahleman in 1799.[43] They were manned by 24 men of whom 18 were oarsmen, and they carried an 18-pounder in the stern which they shot along the line of the boat's length.[44]

The Eartholms continued be a matter for concern in London. Barrow wrote to Saumarez again in September 1811, asking for his opinion 'as to the importance or utility of those islands provided they were in His Majesty's possession, and what force and number of men would be required to defend them during the winter'.[45] Saumarez rather petulantly sent him a copy of his report of 1809, saying it would require at least 1,000 men, but also asked Captain Mansell in the *Rose* to look at it again. A very detailed but not conclusive report came back, speedily. Mansell had had a problem getting up-to-date information, 'the Danish Government having forbidden all correspondence from these Islands with any of the British Cruizers'. Even the boat bringing him this message under a flag of truce stood out far from the shore. His count of guns was remarkably accurate, as was his assessment that the harbours could hold 80 to 90 merchantmen moored in tiers. He made a drawing from each of four quarters, took soundings and reported on what he could see of the fortifications. He evidently gained a little information from the Danish officer who came out, but the Dane was very reluctant to talk. Mansell 'felt too diffident to attempt hazarding an opinion opposed to your judgement as to the force required, or best mode of attack', although he did say that the east side was the only possible place for a landing.[46] Saumarez simply forwarded the report to the Admiralty without apparently adding any further comments. It was put before their Lordships and gave rise to no further instructions. It has the air of a hot potato that Saumarez was hesitant to try to pull out of the fire despite his assertion in 1809 that the Eartholms should be captured.

This seems rather out of character for someone who had shown a readiness to take decisions without waiting for instructions. There is no record of his thoughts about it, which again is rather unusual. There are ten surviving letters between Sir James and Martha from 11 September to 18 October 1811, although one from him that she mentions, dated 1 October, is missing from the archive. On 29 September he gives her a lengthy summary of the squadron's activities and the political situation, with no mention of the Eartholms.[47] I am therefore inclined to think that, rather than giving the Eartholms insufficient attention, he had come to the conclusion that the success of his other policies and the rising possibility of peace with both Sweden and Russia no longer justi-fied either the risks of an attack on what was now a well-prepared and defended island or the dangers and anxieties of maintaining a force of marines there through the winter. He was ready for the end of what had been a demanding season with the uncertainties of the 'Carlshamn cargoes', and his thoughts had turned to home – and also to the splendours of the Great Comet of 1811 whose continuing appearance fascinated both him and Martha to judge from their letters.[48] He was happy to leave any decision on the Eartholms to their Lordships, being himself sufficiently remote from the pressures of commercial interests.

There is a further unsigned report in the Foreign Office files in October that year which recommends capture, saying that senior naval officers have told the writer that it could be done.[49] However the Prime Minister, Lord Liverpool, had the last word. After a conference with First Lord Charles Yorke, Admiral Dommett and Sir Joseph Yorke, he gave the Prince Regent 'the opinion of the professional men that at the late season of the year an attack could not be made upon the Eartholms with any reasonable prospect of success'[50] Sweden had already entered into negotiations with Russia to form an alliance against France and on 17 October Edward Thornton, the former ambassador to Sweden, arrived on board *Victory* secretly, on his way to meet Swedish and Russian plenipotentiaries to make the alliance tripartite.[51] In 1812 the Baltic would cease to be a hostile sea and the Eartholms would lose their significance: the trading battle was won. It provided a reason for Napoleon to invade Russia.

7

Marshal 'Belle-Jambe' Declares War*

A new French chargé d'affaires, Desaugiers, arrived in Stockholm on 8 April, 1810, to ensure the complete extension of the Continental Blockade to the Swedish ports. The Swedish Ambassador Brinkman was recalled from London, although his departure was delayed until May by the dilatoriness of the new Foreign Secretary, Lord Wellesley. Whether this was deliberate or just his natural behaviour it is difficult to say since he soon became notorious for his reluctance to make use of his considerable intellect. A letter between his two brothers in March complained '[that] he hardly does any business at his Office, that nobody can procure access to him, and that his whole time is passed with Moll [a well-known courtesan]'.[1] His clerk took advantage of a period when he was away sick to reduce the pressure on him by destroying all except six of 70 boxes awaiting attention since they were by then too outdated to require any action.[2] Wellington's comment on his elder brother was 'I wish that Wellesley was *castrated*; or that he would like other people attend to his business and perform too. It is lamentable to see Talents and character and advantages such as he possesses thrown away upon Whoring.'[3]

In Stockholm on 6 June, the Swedish government asked Foster, the British chargé d'affaires, to depart at 40 hours' notice to meet French objections.[4] Saumarez was now the sole official British personage in the Baltic. George Foy, an English businessman resident in Sweden, remained as an unofficial link, and the two consuls – Fenwick in Hälsingborg and Smith in Gothenburg – stayed on in their private capacity, as did the agent Heinrich Hahn (Louis Drusina) until his death later that year. For Sweden, the former ambassador Rehausen, who had married an English woman and lived in London, performed a similar unofficial link role.[5]

Saumarez had 19 ships of the line under his command when he sailed from England on 8 May 1810. His instructions from Barrow for the Admiralty dealt only with the immediate military concerns. He was to protect British trade and those neutral ships with British government licences; to keep cruisers off

---

* Bernadotte was nicknamed 'Sergeant Belle-Jambe' early in his army career because of his aspirations towards elegance.

Gotland, Danzig and the southern coast of the Baltic, and to interrupt any trade between enemy ports; to watch the Russians and attack their fleet if an opportunity offered; to observe the Swedish fleet similarly; and to 'transmit without delay to our secretary, for our information, all the intelligence you may be able to obtain on these subjects'. Finally, he was to ensure that his ships kept an ample supply of water. His diplomatic instructions from Wellesley, typically, were not ready and would be sent on by a 'fast sailing vessel' that Admiral Douglas had been ordered to have ready at Yarmouth.[6]

The instructions followed three days later and contained four major points. First, ports from which British ships were excluded, e.g. Swedish ones, were to be treated as enemy ones for the purpose of the blockade and no coasting trade was to be permitted between them except by London-issued licences. Second, Saumarez had authority to pursue enemy ships of war or privateers, and any prizes they had made, into neutral ports or ones from which British ships were excluded that were offering them protection. Third, the order putting Copenhagen and all the Zealand ports under rigorous blockade, which had been suspended during the winter, was no longer in force and they were to be treated simply as any other hostile port. And finally:

> that though His Majesty has been induced by a sense of what is due, as well to the protection of the trade of His Subjects as to the honor of the British Flag, to authorize you to resent any injury or indignity which may be offered to either, His Majesty will feel the most sincere regret, if the determination of the Swedish government to adopt and pursue measures inconsistent with His Majesty's just rights, and contrary as well to the real interests of Sweden, as to the ancient and admitted laws of nations, shall oblige you to take any step of immediate or eventual hostility; and we are further to express to you our reliance not more in your zeal in the execution of any measures which the hostile conduct of Sweden may oblige you to pursue, than in your moderation and temper in abstaining from such measures till they shall become absolutely necessary for the protection of our trade, in avoiding as far as possible all occasions of disagreement and difference, and in conducting any discussions that may arise, in the manner most likely to bring them to an amicable and satisfactory termination.[7]

That is to say, Saumarez had the authority to commence hostilities, but only as a last resort. It was very much left to his judgement and discretion. This was to be the pattern for the rest of his command and shows the degree of trust and respect in which he was now held by ministers.

A further note from Barrow on 24 May told him that Wellesley had instructed that a strict blockade of Elsinore should be enforced. This was accompanied by a private note from Croker, explaining that this was to give neutral ships an excuse not to have to go there to pay Sound dues, thereby damaging the Danish economy. However, it raised considerable difficulties for the ships carrying out the blockade to determine which ships were bound for Elsinore and which were genuinely sailing down the Sound since the course for each, owing to the narrowness of the Sound entrance, was virtually identical.[8] As Fenwick later commented: 'I am however totally at a loss to conjecture what motive Government can have for declaring Elsinore blockaded and at the same time making it next to impossible to enforce it'.[9] It was finally lifted on Admiralty instructions in November 1810.[10] The king of Denmark had also withdrawn his ban on the operations of Danish privateers and authorised them to capture all vessels of whatever nation sailing under British convoy and enacting that all such vessels should be considered lawful prizes without further proof of their being enemy property.[11]

When Saumarez arrived at Hawke Road on 14 May, he found:

> everything much in the same state as when I left last year – the Swedes as disposed to be friendly to us as ever, but apprehensive that we will not let them preserve their neutrality much longer ... [I am] concerned to find that these Northern States are more than ever attached to the French Alliance and I can see no prospect of detaching them from it.[12]

The new governor of Gothenburg, Count von Rosen, had instructed his military commanders on 13 January that, except in extraordinary circumstances, 'Ships flying the English flag are not allowed, unless suffering from substantial damage at sea and needing assistance, to enter a major port or to pass or lie under the guns of the fortress that commands its entrance.'[13] Admiral Pickmore had already realised the loophole of the phrase about needing assistance and in November 1809 had written to Saumarez saying that:

> I shall (upon their representation and not otherwise) state the entrance of men of war as a matter of necessity approaching to distress from the danger of anchoring in the open road at this boisterous season of the year, their entrance being only for the purpose of taking away our trade from their ports under convoy, and not for any other sort of convenience for ourselves. I shall endeavour to conciliate, and assure them of our friendly purpose and avoid any possible cause of offence.[14]

The other loophole, of which von Rosen was well aware, was the wording 'major port'. Fotö, a small island just north of Wingo, had become a massive smuggling centre. There were shops, offices, and warehouses with regular auctions and markets, managed and staffed by Britons and protected by the guns of Saumarez' fleet. From there English and colonial goods went out in vast quantities to Swedish Pomerania and north Germany and to the small harbours on the Swedish coast 'while the local commissioners turned a blind eye'.[15]

Saumarez was aware that to treat Swedish ports as enemy ones and therefore prohibit Swedish coastal trading would have a disastrous impact on the Swedish economy and life:

> They are under the greatest alarm at the measures I have been ordered to adopt against their trade – and which alone would have been a subject of the greatest distress to Sweden, but when added to their other disastrous events, must involve them in the deepest ruin.[16]

He therefore decided to give the Swedes advance warning and then to 'go slow' on its implementation. He covered himself by reporting to Yorke, the new First Lord, that he had:

> acted upon the instructions I received with the utmost possible moderation consistent with the tenor of those instructions – they were not acted upon until I had an opportunity of communicating with the Consul at Gothenburg and some of the principal merchants, who appeared perfectly satisfied with the indulgence I allowed to the trade of Sweden under the existing circumstances and the same has been signified to me by the Swedish Government who have expressed themselves satisfied with the mildness and consideration I have uniformly acted to the country.

Yorke's response was surprisingly supportive of a subordinate evading instructions:

> it seems evident that your first instructions warranted what you are said to have done and that they required explanation. That which they have now received will, I trust, postpone, if not prevent, an *actual* rupture with Sweden which it is very desirable to avoid if possible. At the same time I feel for all your difficulties. With every wish for your glory and success, I remain etc.[17]

But by then, Wellesley had changed his mind and instructed that Swedish vessels in the coasting trade with Swedish produce or in harbour were not to be captured and any already captured should be released.[18] Thanks to Saumarez' deliberate procrastination there were none. His independent line was proving successful. Foster reported: 'the Cabinet of Stockholm seemed to be convinced that you had executed your orders with as much mildness and consideration for this country as could possibly be expected' and Admiral Krusenstjerna wrote of his 'noble and disinterested moderation'.[19]

However, the sudden death of Crown Prince Karl August of Augustenborg[20] threw Sweden into further turmoil. He had only been in Stockholm since January 1810, but had made himself extremely popular and raised hopes in Sweden that he would prove an able monarch in the future. Consul Fenwick had written as early as February 21:

> The new Prince Royal of Sweden is said to be gaining many friends since his arrival at Stockholm. His more solid qualifications seem to prevail over the

want of that exterior show and etiquette to which the Swedes have always been so much attached. His popularity will however chiefly depend on the maintenance of Peace with England, for the Swedes would ill bear to be deprived of Trade, to which they are now so accustomed

A cousin of Charles XIII, Karl August had been elected crown prince of Sweden after the deposition of Gustav IV Adolf. He had previously been acting since 1808 as regent in Norway for the king of Denmark because the British blockade had made communications difficult and a royal representative in Norway was necessary. Although his farewell proclamation to Norway had said he would be maintaining his links with Denmark, he had fallen out with the king over his armistice with Colonel Adlersparre in the spring of 1809. This had helped his standing among Swedes, who had no love of the Danes.[21]

There were strong rumours that he had been poisoned, his death being so sudden and unexpected in one still quite young and healthy. The Danes were extremely suspicious that his death might have been a Russian plot to restore King Gustav's son as crown prince. Von Rosen, in a private letter to the Swedish Foreign Minister, Baron von Engeström· reported:

The conviction that the death of the Prince was not natural is impossible to eradicate. This opinion gets new converts daily, and I can assure you that not 1/10th of the inhabitants of this province and city believe or will ever be convinced of the opposite.[22]

At the funeral, a drunken mob was roused by agitators, attacked Count Fersen, who was leading the parade as Marshal of the Realm and was reputedly a Gustavian supporter, and beat him to death, believing that he was involved in the suspected poisoning. Saumarez shared their suspicion but shuddered at their barbarity: 'but if he was accessory to the death of the Prince Royal we are not to wonder at Providence having permitted his suffering a violent death.'[23] The question now was who would be chosen as future successor to Charles XIII?

There was a considerable feeling that a powerful military figure would be desirable after the vacillations both of Gustav IV and of the army leaders who had toppled him. There was anxiety over the attitude of the Russians and also of Napoleon and the French, now such a dominant force in the area. Significantly, no attempt was made to ascertain the British views, despite their economic importance and the very present threat of the fleet. A visit on board *Victory* from Admiral Krusenstjerna, now in command of the Swedish navy, took place on 21 August, the day that the Diet was to meet to approve the choice of the king and so too late for Saumarez to have any influence. Until then, he had assumed that the late prince's brother would succeed.[24] When he heard the choice was Marshal Bernadotte, he protested in vain that:

the election of a general officer in the service of the most inveterate enemy that England had to oppose would be highly obnoxious to His Majesty's Government, and I earnestly urged him to entreat the King of Sweden to delay the election until I could receive a return of the letters I would immediately send to England by an express.[25]

Foster had reported to Bathurst as early as the previous October, after the election of Augustenborg, that some people were saying then that it would have been the best policy for Sweden to have chosen Bernadotte instead, if he had been willing, since the only refuge open to Sweden from the intrigues of Russia would be in the arms of France.[26]

There had been four candidates: Karl August's brother and successor as Duke of Augustenborg; Frederik VI, King of Denmark; the Prince of Oldenbourg; and Bernadotte. Oldenbourg was ruled out because he was too closely related by marriage to the Russian royal family. Frederik VI appears to have been very keen to unite the two crowns and initially was under the impression that he had French support, but Napoleon was hesitant to see too strong a Scandinavian combination and, after appearing at first indifferent to what seemed a matter of fringe importance, decided to support Bernadotte, 'as an honourable monument to my reign and an extension of my glory.'[27] As he wrote to Metternich:

> I do not see in him any talent for kingship; he is a fine soldier, that's all. For the rest, I am glad to be quit of him and would like nothing better than to see him distanced from France; he is one of those Jacobins with his head askew like all of them, and that is no way to maintain oneself on a throne.[28]

He would come to regret this when Bernadotte from the start showed himself to be a talented ruler, well able to hold his own in the difficult circumstances in which he and Sweden were placed. As it turned out, Sweden could not have picked a better leader for her survival as an independent nation, nor a worse one from the French point of view. General de Suremain,* who devotes a chapter of his *Mémoires* to the election, claiming in his private conversations with King Charles XIII to have tipped the balance in his choice, concludes that although Europe believed that this had been determined by Napoleon, 'this influence was passive and in that way involuntary'.[29]

At the initial Riksdag committee meeting on 8 August, only one member favoured Bernadotte and 11 were for Augustenborg. Two days later Fournier, a Grenobloise importer based in Gothenburg, created the impression that he was acting in line with Napoleon's secret wishes in promoting Bernadotte's election.

---

* An émigré from the French Revolution, he had gone via Prussia to serve in Sweden. Gaining the favour of Charles XIII, he had become inspector general of artillery in 1812 and was a close confidant of the king.

Bernadotte was well favoured by the military and by Count Mörner who was acting as intermediary. His friendly treatment of the Swedish prisoners after his capture of Lubeck was remembered and his cessation of hostilities on the dethronement of Gustav IV Adolf. His rule of the north German territories as Napoleon's marshal had been much less harsh and grasping than many of his fellow marshals. 'Instead of pressurising the conquered territory, he tried instead to lighten their burdens by spreading the occupation taxes, reducing the number of troops to be maintained, curbing plunder and pillage with the same severity as of old'.[30]

Perhaps because of that, Von Rosen's view was that '... If Prince Ponte Corvo* will be a successor to the throne we will get a good man', but he was concerned about whether it would upset the English. However, after the election result was announced, he reported that 'The news about the election of the successor to the throne has not had the good effect down here that was expected; the merchants are not prepared to believe that P[onte] Corvo will be a benefactor of trade.'[31] Ross states that on 16 August, the committee swung right round and supported Bernadotte by ten votes against two for Augustenborg, and on 21 August the Diet's four estates unanimously endorsed him. He maintains that their decisions were aided by Bernadotte sending wagons loaded with specie which he himself saw on the road from Ystad to Stockholm on 15 August, but the timing makes this seem rather unlikely.[32]

There is an interesting letter from Fenwick, whose informants in Copenhagen were usually well placed. This explains the course of the manoeuvring – in particular, that Napoleon had virtually simultaneously assured Frederik VI that he would send a courier with his full support, so that the king relaxed his efforts, and secretly despatched another courier to counteract the first one's operations and persuade Count Wrede, president of the secret committee, to change to Bernadotte as the French choice. Fenwick reported:

> The disappointment and rage of the Danes at this choice is as great as their hopes were sanguine. They now see their situation in its proper point of view, and feel indignant not only at the manner in which they have been deceived by Bonaparte, but also at the evident plan that is formed to swallow them up. Their apprehensions of this subject are certainly well founded, and as the situation of Denmark becomes more critical every day, and she will want a powerful hand to prevent the impending destruction, I should hope that she will not much longer delay renewing her connexion with England and putting herself in a posture to resist the violence and wiles of Bonaparte.[33]

The perpetual hope, both on Fenwick's part and in London, that Denmark would return to the fold, possibly reflected the views of Danish traders rather

---

* Bernadotte had been created prince of this petty papal state after Austerlitz in 1805.

than those of King Frederik who virtually throughout the war and despite both temptation and provocation remained loyal to Napoleon.[34]

The news of Bernadotte's probable election as crown prince reached Consul Smith at Gothenburg on 20 August. He went immediately to von Rosen for confirmation that this was true. Smith told him that he had already written two days before both to Saumarez and to an unnamed senior individual in England, saying that Bernadotte was likely to take a full set of measures against England. Von Rosen 'objected that it was careless of him as a good Swede to write alarming letters about a matter which could only have come to his knowledge [early] through idle talk'. Smith answered that it was his own belief and that he had not learnt about it from idle rumours but from a courier to the Russian consul whom von Rosen suspected of being in cahoots with both Smith and the English government.[35] The next day Smith wrote to Wellesley giving a very detailed account of the election (which was what Engeström had wanted), relating some adverse stories about King Frederik of Denmark being furious at the choice of Bernadotte rather than the Duke of Augustenborg, and stressing the advantages for England of the way it had turned out. He also mentioned the reputed coldness between Bernadotte and Napoleon which was likely to benefit relations with England.[36]

Krusenstjerna had tried to reassure Saumarez that the choice was the only one that was politically possible and that the Prince of Ponte Corvo 'had professed his firm intentions, as far as depended on him, to maintain the relative situations between England and Sweden, and that his proposing himself was without the participation of Bonaparte'. Krusenstjerna also argued that Bernadotte 'was, of all the others, the person who would have the firmness to oppose the intentions of Bonaparte or his agents and ministers in the intercourse with other countries'.[37]

Saumarez was initially very doubtful: 'I very much apprehend that the election of a French general to the Heir Apparent to the Crown of Sweden must be with a view of detaching the country from all intercourse with England.' Fenwick suggested that he post ships off Nyborg and Omø, on either side of the Great Belt, to prevent Bernadotte crossing and Saumarez gave instructions to that effect. On 27 August he reported: 'If I can form any opinion from the host of reports I have received, the Government will studiously avoid a rupture with England, and they are in great dread of an attack from Russia.' Krusenstjerna continued to stress that, in his private opinion, Bernadotte was the only man who could 'maintain the independence and promote the true interest of the Swedish nation'.[38] Saumarez had evidently formed a close relationship with Krusenstjerna which was to prove advantageous to both of them.

At this period of intense political concern, there occurred several of the sort of petty incidents that can so often trigger escalations out of all proportion. Captain Newman of the *Hero* had sent one of his boats into the Swedish

*Figure 9. Jean Baptiste Bernadotte. Portrait by Francois Gérard, 1811
(Royal Collections, Stockholm)*

harbour of Marstrand to attack a Danish privateer that was threatening strag-
glers from the *Hero*'s convoy, including some Swedish ships. They captured her
but were forced to surrender when the Swedish fortress and troops opened fire
on them, and a midshipman was killed. Newman sent a fairly high-handed
letter to the Governor, demanding the return of his officers and men and their
boat, and also their prize – the Danish cutter.[39] Krusentjerna's formal letter of
complaint was quite restrained suggesting that these 'atrocities' were 'contrary
to the intentions of the British government and to the orders they might have
received from your Excellency'. It ended: 'His [Swedish] Majesty earnestly wish
[*sic*] that your excellency, of whose candour and goodwill for maintaining good
harmony His Majesty are plainly confident, would take such efficacious measures, as will be judged necessary, to prevent every future unpleasant accident
of this nature.' Saumarez countered by pointing out that Sweden should not
be allowing foreign privateers to shelter in her ports, threatening depredations
on peaceful traders, some of them Swedish. Further incidents took place about
the same time further south, in the Baltic itself. Captain Acklom, one of the
most experienced and active cruiser captains in the Baltic fleet, had boarded
and spiked the guns of a Swedish warship *Celeritas*, and a French privateer
Wagram had been taken in the port of Stralsund, recently restored to Sweden
by Napoleon.[40]

Von Rosen was extremely concerned lest the effects of the Marstrand incident might escalate:

> The whole Merchant Society is greatly distressed and awaits in fear the conse-
> quences of whether Saumarez is in a good or hostile mood. In case his orders
> should be stamped with the latter emotion, I humbly request to be informed
> in advance, if any sequestration of English property should be made on first
> hearing of any sequestration of Swedish ships. This would be rough justice,
> but if the King finds such means necessary, it would be most convenient to
> have the orders in advance, because if we have to ask then, those involved
> will have time to hide away their possessions.[41]

All he felt he could do was to delay Norris, acting as consul in the temporary
absence of Smith, in sending a report to Saumarez. This would give von Rosen
time both to prepare for any hostile action and to brief the admiral with, in his
view, a true report. A weakness of the British stance was that, to the surprise
of the other British captains and in direct contradiction of orders, Newman
had fired first. For the Swedes, there was a problem that the responsibilities of
the provincial governor and the military commander overlapped. Von Rosen
suggested to the Foreign Secretary that:

> The relations between Sweden and England are so delicate that Gothenburg,
> as the most exposed point of contact for relations between the nations, seems

to need a military commandant, who has enough wisdom and delicacy to be able to make concessions when unavoidable, but on the other hand, [with] reason would support the interests and [honour] of the nation when necessary, and also to act in an open and co-operative way with the commercial controller of the port, the provincial governor, [provided] he deserves it.[42]

He proposed that an adjutant-general should be appointed as supreme commander. On both sides the criticisms were only lightly barbed and an exchange of peacemaking letters followed shortly. Krusenstjerna stressed that Saumarez' supportive actions 'intitle [sic] your Excellency to that gratitude of the Swedish nation and the most distinguished regard from its sovereign'.[43] By 26 September, von Rosen was reporting: 'Thank God, that the Marstrand incident turned out so well. I have really been worried about sequestration measures, which thus are no more to be feared.'[44]

To Krusenstjerna's embarrassment, a complaint that he had forwarded from the military commandant of Gothenburg that the British officers at Wingo had landed on the islands and 'given themselves the cruel amusement really to hunt upon the poor and defenceless fishermen with such fatal effect that one has been mortally and two others less dangerously wounded', proved to be totally unfounded. Eighteen days later he had to send a letter of profuse apologies, ending:

> I shall never cease to offer to the Almighty God my constant prayers for the preservation of your health and prosperity. My wife and family and every honest Swede will join herein with me and our well [sic] wishes will follow you in every corner of the earth as long as we live.[45]

The feelings of goodwill were increased by Saumarez seeking and obtaining Admiralty approval for Swedish ships to be allowed to trade timber for grain from Swedish Pomerania. It was such actions, understanding the difficulties of the Swedish situation, that won him their respect and trust.

It still remained difficult to decide what future actions to expect from Bernadotte and whether to seek to prevent him from crossing into his new country. Yorke was apprehensive. He congratulated Saumarez over his 'prudent and proper manner' with Krusenstjerna over the election and later again on his handling of the Marstrand and Acklom affairs. But he feared that 'their weak and absurd conduct in electing Bernadotte successor to the Crown will probably drive them *malgré* to different measures whenever he has joined and is in possession of his situation in Sweden'.[46] On 21 September, Saumarez reported to Yorke that 'I have taken all the means in my power for his being intercepted should he attempt to come from the Continent, either by Stralsund or across the Belts'. However, he did not expect him to cross until after the British squadron had left the Baltic.[47] On 10 October Saumarez left Hanö Bay to pass back through the Belt, having earlier despatched three ships of the line back to England. A threat that the Russian Archangel fleet might sail round to the Baltic had disappeared.[48]

He was greeted on the way by a request that a Swedish yacht might pass unmolested across the Belt from Nyborg to Korsør with Bernadotte on board. I cannot find any trace of new instructions from the Admiralty, and time would not really have permitted them – although it would have been possible for a less decisive man than Saumarez to delay an answer until he had obtained instructions from his superiors in London. It is difficult also to judge whether the simultaneous arrival at Sproe in mid-Belt of two homeward-bound convoys and a massive fleet of over 600 outward ships (of which more anon), held up at Gothenburg by a westerly wind and because of severe threats of French confiscation at their destination ports in the Baltic, was a determining factor; or whether, indeed, it was deliberately contrived rather than by chance. For whatever reason, Saumarez granted free passage, which took place on 14 October. Ross describes dramatically how the yacht, flying the Swedish flag, passed within a mile of *Victory*, surrounded by six ships of the line and six frigates and sloops, protecting over 1,000 merchant ships under a multitude of national flags.[49] The Swedish Royal Journal recorded the meeting but played down the actual numbers.[50] However, there could have been no better way of impressing on Bernadotte both Britain's maritime power and the importance to Sweden and all the Baltic states of the trade that the ships carried. Von Rosen had reported the previous month that:

> since the Creation, the outer roads of Gothenburg have probably not looked as now. The continuing westerly wind has gathered two convoys there, so the number of ships there yesterday rose to 19 men-of-war and 1124 merchant vessels which present the most delightful* view you can imagine.[51]

Ross comments that 'contrary to the expectation of every officer on board the fleet, excepting Sir James, [Bernadotte] gave manifest proofs of his independence of French influence, and of his intentions to cultivate the friendship of Great Britain'.[52] He adopted the Lutheran religion[53] of his new country** and the historic name Karl Johan, lent eight million francs of his newly acquired wealth to the Bank of Sweden to ease the country's economic problems, but

---

* The Swedish word *raraste* can mean either rarest or nicest. The translator, Commodore Bring, chose 'delightful' as it expresses the evident pleasure that von Rosen showed at this mass of shipping.

** Bernadotte's public adoption of the Lutheran religion is reminiscent (in reverse) of his Gascon predecessor Henri of Navarre for whom Paris had been 'worth a Mass'. In truth, he had been required to do this under the terms of his election as crown prince. He had also been required to resign all his former titles and employments and his principality of Ponte Corvo was passed on to Marshal Murat in 1812.

because of his difficulties in learning Swedish tended to stay close to his Franco-phone advisers.[54] His manly presence and great charm rapidly won over a hesitant court. His wife Desirée, on the other hand, when she arrived in December, disliked Sweden's winter, its customs and its people, and became universally unpopular within a week, as did her disdainful entourage.[55]

Bernadotte had landed in Hälsingborg on 19 October after a brief visit to see King Frederik in Copenhagen en route. Napoleon had greeted the news of Bernadotte's election with friendship and a helping hand to sort out the legal complexities: 'My cousin, I have instructed the *grand juge* to draw up letters patent authorising you to accept the new dignity to which you are called by the king and diet of Sweden. I wish success and happiness to you and the Swedes.'[56]

He had even instructed his treasurer to send Bernadotte a million francs.[57] However, within a month of Bernadotte's arrival Napoleon was insisting, according to von Rosen, that Sweden adopt 'the same system against the commerce of England as the other powers on the continent in alliance with France, and that all British and colonial produce shall be forthwith confiscated, also that measures of hostility shall be immediately pursued towards England'.[58] He had decided that with the arrival of Bernadotte in Sweden he would make sure that the Berlin and Milan Decrees enforcing the Continental System would be firmly applied. He was to find that Bernadotte was both skilful and devious in his responses.

The French had been without a consul in Gothenburg for several months. Von Rosen had commented on the large packets of letters building up for him in the post office. When M. Ranchoup arrived as the replacement in October 1810 he was to prove an aggravating thorn in von Rosen's side: 'since the arrival of Ranchoup my situation is really delicate'.[59] Napoleon had also appointed Baron Alquier as his official representative in Stockholm a month after the ratification of the peace treaty with Sweden in January 1810. Alquier had not arrived there until September of that year, having spent some time in Denmark on the way. His instructions were that all previous agreements were annulled: maintaining peace and friendship should be the objectives, but at the same time he should ensure that English manufactures and colonial goods were not landed.[60]

Napoleon's official correspondence of that time is full of letters, mostly to his then Foreign Minister Champagny, instructing him – country by country – to implement his intention that 'wherever my troops are, I will not permit any English contraband'.[61] He spells out the details very clearly to the ineffective Eugène, Viceroy in Italy:

> there are no longer neutral flags, since all pay a contribution to the English to be allowed to sail … no colonial goods must arrive in ports controlled by

me, even with certificates of origin, which are valueless. Sugar, coffee, cotton cannot even be landed under French flags, unless they come from prizes taken by Italian or French privateers.[62]

He firmly believed that the only way now to attack his principal enemy, the English, was through their economy: 'I have no other means of waging war on England.'[63] He assured Champagny that British commerce, which six months before wanted war, was now crying out for peace.[64]

On 19 October 1810, he had issued a decree from Amsterdam, reinforcing the Berlin Decree of 1806:

> Art.1. All goods of whatever sort that originate from English manufacture and being prohibited, now exist in France, whether in actual entrepôts, or in the magazines of our Customs, of what name soever, shall be burnt.
> Art.2. For the future all prohibited goods of English manufacture proceeding from seizures of our Customs or otherwise, shall be publicly burnt.

Articles 3–7 listed all the countries to which this applied, and Article 8 covered any omissions by adding all those towns within reach of his troops.[65]

He wrote directly to Prince Lebrun ordering him to burn immediately all English-made goods in Dutch warehouses or shops[66] and wrote to Alexander I:

> Six hundred English ships wandering round the Baltic have been kept out by Mecklenberg and Prussia, and are heading for your lands. If you admit them, the war continues; if you seize them and confiscate their cargoes ... the blow that this will strike England will be fearful.[67]

Another long letter, two weeks later, ordered Champagny to tell the Russian ambassador, very politely and softly, some home truths: that all the colonial goods at the Leipzig Fair had come on 700 wagons from Russia; that if Russia wanted to have peace with Britain, she must confiscate the 1.200 ships escorted by 20 English men-of-war that he now maintained had landed part of their cargoes in Russia, and join with France to demand that Sweden confiscates the immense quantity of merchandise the English have landed at Gothenburg; that there were no longer any neutrals since the English did not allow passage to any ship not loaded with their goods.[68]

Champagny's *Report to the Emperor* in December 1810, duly vetted by Napoleon before being printed, had seven pages of justification of the emperor's actions from the Peace of Amiens up to the present, but particularly attacked the Orders-in-Council: 'as long as England persists in her Orders-in-Council, His Majesty will persist in his Decrees, setting against the blockade of the coasts a blockade of the continent, and against pillage on the high seas confiscation of English merchandise on the land.'[69] If Napoleon's letters are to be believed, he considered that he could win the economic war, just as he had won the land war, if only his allies and his officials would enforce his policies. This view lingered among his supporters even in the years after Waterloo. Bail, in the introduction to his edition of of *La Correspondance de Bernadotte avec Napoléon* (1819), maintained: 'The continental system was a great and sublime concept; it would free civilized Europe for ever from an English monopoly; it was the only way to defeat England and assure the peace of the world.'[70]

These, therefore, were the pressures on Alquier when he arrived in Stockholm and they were duly passed on to Ranchoup as his subordinate in Gothenburg. The latter's first report was that on 8 October 1810, 1,700 American ships were in harbour, of these 900 had sailed the day after for the Baltic with colonial goods, and on the 10th, 800 had sailed for England with Swedish goods – iron, timber and hemp. All were escorted by English ships. Packet boats regularly sailed with letters and passengers between Swedish ports and Gothenburg.[71] Alquier presented this information to Bernadotte at his first meeting with the Crown Prince whose reaction, expressed in a letter to Napoleon, was threefold. First, there were indeed smugglers but 'these are for the most part Jews established in neighbouring countries'. Second, that these reports were exaggerated and came from Sweden's enemies, seeking to discredit her. Third, that he wanted to discover the truth and so would send a reliable person to Gothenburg to investigate. He commented that Alquier had evidently received 'very strict instructions relative to English commerce'.[72]

The investigation gave rise to an indignant letter from von Rosen to Engeström. Against the allegations that the 1,200 to 1,300 ships that had arrived in Gothenburg were loaded with colonial products, he maintained that 300 were American, 300 in ballast, and the rest 'have [been] only Germans, Russians, and Danes, all nations with which we live in friendly relations'. The major culprit was Russia 'whither at least 3000 ships have sailed directly from England [and] Denmark ... The Thames is dressed with ships from their nation and currently, according to all travellers, 400 such ships are there.'[73] This, he suggested, was where Napoleon should be turning his attention. Von Rosen 'trusted that sometime, when everything is clear, the Emperor Napoleon will realise the [exaggerations] in the reports now in the papers, which so shamefully cast a shadow on those Swedish officials'. It was a performance worthy of the glib tongue of his royal master Bernadotte.

Alquier went on to complain to Engeström about the *Wagram* affair and the release of the *Hero*'s crew, but the response on that was that the crew were so few in number that they were not worth worrying about. Engeström then relayed von Rosen's comments about the 3,000 ships going direct to Russia. He admitted that some of the Gothenburg ships 'perhaps contained some colonial goods, but one was not certain on this'. In the words of Coquelle: 'Alquier had to content himself with these specious explanations, but they convinced neither him nor Napoleon.'[74] What is strange is that Coquelle, from his study of the French archives, was convinced that at this stage Bernadotte was fully behind the French cause and wanted to wage war seriously against England, and that Alquier had no doubts about it.[75] It was perhaps a not unreasonable expectation that a former French Marshall, brother-in-law of the Emperor's own brother, who had just received from him a gift of a million francs and whose adopted country was nearly bankrupt, with an inadequate and demoralised army, would do other than follow closely the wishes of the most powerful man on mainland Europe.[76]

The von Rosen letters reveal that Bernadotte went in quite the opposite direction although he hid it under the cover of a skilful presentation to Napoleon of his personal situation and that of Sweden. Bernadotte commenced his letter by suggesting that the reported trading in English goods at Gothenburg of which Napoleon's envoy, Baron Alquier, had complained was 'not tolerated at all there'. A week later he wrote that Charles XIII had been about to take action to stop this trade and 'the minister was busy preparing a very strict order on this matter' when news came of the King's illness. He had had a stroke and thenceforward played little active part in affairs. Bernadotte maintained that this illness was the result of Napoleon's prejudice against the Swedes in giving them only five days to respond to his demand that they ban all trade with England, treating them as though they were an enemy nation. It left Sweden with unpleasing alterna-tives: either to break the bonds that united her to France or to declare war on England without any means to combat such a formidable enemy.[77]

He went on in the second letter to say how, when he accepted becoming heir to the throne, he had hoped to be able to reconcile the interests of the country that he had served faithfully for 30 years, with those of the country that had just adopted him:

> I had scarcely arrived when I saw this hope compromised. The King [Charles XIII] had seen how my heart was grievously divided between its attachment to Your Majesty and its feeling for its new loyalties. In such a dire situation, I could only abandon everything to the decision of the King and abstain from taking part in the deliberations of the Council of State.

He argued that the council was not dissimulating when it maintained that war with Britain would lead to the loss of all the ships carrying iron to America, that both money and matériel for war were totally lacking, that they could not afford to repair either Karlskrona's fortifications or the warships lying there, a tax to raise the money for an army would have to be approved by the states-general and, finally, salt was absolutely vital for Sweden; it formed over a third of Sweden's imports and could only be provided by England. It was 'uniquely through deference for your Majesty', that the King had ignored the distress of his people and now declared war on England, and he hoped that Napoleon, for his part, would offer some evidence of his own goodwill.

Three weeks later he argued that Sweden could raise the troops but not equip or pay them without French help: she needed 'the means that nature has denied us'. It was a masterly counter that seems to have taken Napoleon aback. And it set the tone for an intriguing game of demands, offers and deceit between three of the nations most closely involved, the outcome of which was to reflect the nature and impact of the players operating in the field.[78]

Russia, the fourth country, sat on the sidelines. As we have seen above, von Rosen rightly but hypocritically complained that trade with Russia in British manufactures and colonial goods, after a brief token sequestration, had continued with little check through the medium of 'neutral' ships. Napoleon also well knew this and for better reason complained. Then, by a ukase (decree) of 31 December 1810, Russia increased taxes on goods coming by land (predominantly French) but reduced them on those coming by sea (mostly British and colonial goods, albeit under American, Prussian or other neutral flags), damaging French interests to the benefit of the English. The Russian fleet stayed peacefully within the protection of Cronstadt, and Alexander bided his time. As Russia was at war with Britain there was no official diplomatic contact, so when Thornton was sent late in 1811 to open peace negotiations it was in conditions of strict secrecy.

The policy of the 'soft answer turning away wrath' appears to have suited Bernadotte temperamentally; it certainly was the only hope for Sweden in her defenceless state, faced with invasion by a Russian army or bombardment by a British fleet and economic collapse. His officials evidently learnt to adopt the same defensive line.[79] It is difficult to know why Napoleon, so forthright and tough in other instances, allowed Bernadotte to get away with it. An undated, unsigned report in French of Bernadotte's election, copied by Saumarez, had quoted Napoleon as saying in his support for Bernadotte 'Il faut que les Suédois soient gouvernés par un bras de fer couvert de velour' [Sweden needs to be governed by an iron fist in a velvet glove].[80] These words might come back to haunt him.

Napoleon earlier had refused to write direct to Bernadotte since he did not deign to correspond with crown princes.[81] But there is a letter in March 1811 to Bernadotte where he takes the trouble to explain at great length his reasons for his Berlin Decree in response to 'the right of blockade that England has assumed for itself', rather than simply ordering Bernadotte to observe what had been agreed in the peace treaty a year earlier. Although he maintains that his Continental System is more in the interests of Sweden and of Europe than of France, he admits it is the only way he can defeat England: 'I have ships, but I have no sailors; I cannot battle with England, I can only force her to make peace through the Continental System'. His shortage of sailors had come up in the previous December when he promised supplies of corn and permission for Swedish goods to enter French ports if Sweden would provide 2,000 sailors to man four ships; he would even pay for their travel to France. Baron von Engeström had replied on behalf of Bernadotte, very politely, saying that Sweden had more corn than it needed and the war with England was stopping all exports, while constitutionally he could not provide the sailors of whom they too were very short. Anyway, under a southern sun they would only long for home and not want to fight. Officers, however, could go, many of whom had served in the French navy already.[82] Napoleon wrote again in April 1811 to congratulate Bernadotte on becoming regent: 'I trust that your efforts will be crowned with success. I renew with pleasure my assurances of respect and friendship.'[83]

When the official Swedish Declaration of War on Britain was published on 17 November 1810, it insisted that 'all Navigation, Commerce and Communication by Posts as well as all Correspondence under whatever name soever, to and from all the Provinces, Ports, Towns and Places in the United Kingdom of Great Britain and Ireland, shall from this day cease under the penalties of the Laws'.[84] However, Count von Rosen had a meeting with John Mordaunt Johnson, an Irish businessman who was regarded as the most capable and discreet of British agents,[85] to show him a letter from Stockholm accompanying the declaration. 'As far as I can judge from the translation, somewhat confused and imperfect, of the governor, the relations between England and Sweden will continue nearly the same as they have been for the last six months', reported Johnson. Any British merchant ships would be detained but not sequestrated, colonial produce would not be allowed in for the present but a large loophole was left for the future, and even the packet boats might continue to and from England – but discreetly, landing at parts of the coast to be pointed out to Consul Smith. British merchants, because of the earlier warning, were unlikely to suffer any loss; massive amounts of goods had been withdrawn from the king's warehouses and duty paid to avoid sequestration.[86] Count von Rosen 'was instructed by his government to give the strongest assurances ... that it was by no means the intention of the Swedish government to follow up its declaration by any act of hostility'. Von Rosen also wrote confidentially to Saumarez to say that the Declaration's measures 'are perfectly contrary to the sentiments of the Swedish government, and particularly those of the Crown Prince'.[87]

This challenge, coming so late in the season when he would normally have been bringing the fleet home to England, presented Saumarez with a dilemma. Should he accept the Swedish reassurances and carry on with his plans for return, trusting that there would be no hostile action to which he ought to respond and that he would not be giving the appearance of retreating from danger? Or should he commence retaliatory measures against Swedish trade and stay on, risking the dangers of the oncoming winter? He was also conscious of 'the immense property belonging to our merchants in the other ports of Sweden which in all probability would be confiscated did I adopt any measures of retaliation'. For he had responded to reports from the north German ports during the late summer of French preparations to seize all incoming ships, by holding them first at Wingo and then advising them to go no further than the Swedish Baltic ports, in particular Hanö Bay, until it appeared safe. It was this massive number of ships that Bernadotte had viewed on his passage across the Belt, together with the ships that were escaping for home in the other direction. This defensive move had been very successful and, according to Fenwick, the French were 'highly enraged that these ships have been prevented by your cruisers from going into Danzig etc when confiscation was prepared for them'.[88] However, it created a diplomatic rather than a military problem in the following year, one that came to be called the 'Carlshamn cargoes' and is the subject of the next chapter.

In the meanwhile, Saumarez wrote to Yorke expressing:

> the great perplexity this unfortunate and unexpected turn in the state of affairs has caused to me – and my embarrassment has been much increased from there being no person accredited, or in whom I could confide to derive benefit from their opinion or advice, or from whom I could receive authentic information ... [Nonetheless] the very considerate manner in which Sweden appears to put in force the decree against colonial produce and other merchandize, has decided me against taking measures relative to the Swedish trade which I should otherwise have been justified in.[89]

Two days later he sailed from Gothenburg and arrived in the Downs on 3 December. Once again, having weighed up the situation – showing his own doubts as to whether or not the Swedes could be trusted – he had made up his own mind and decided that they could. He had then taken the appropriate action, or rather, as was to be the case more than once during his command, decided to leave offensive military action as a hanging threat rather than a reality.

A much later letter from von Rosen gives an interesting slant on the decision:

> What is most intriguing about this story, is that your Excellency acted without orders, in agreeing to what I was requesting also without authority; for I had an official order from our Minister of Foreign Affairs Count Engeström to act quite differently, and only a private letter* which indicated to me the secret wishes of the then Prince Royal, now our beloved King. Your Excellency thereby sacrificed for the good cause a great fortune – for the 130 Swedish merchant ships lying under your guns and loaded with English manufactures and colonial goods, would have put a mass of prize money into your pocket – and as for me, I risked my position should the Francophile party come out on top in Sweden.[90]

---

* Attempts to find this note in the three Royal archives in Stockholm were unsuccessful.

One of the Admiralty's running apprehensions was that the substantial squadron of line of battle ships that Napoleon had built up in the Scheldt might escape the blockading fleet and find its way through the Sleeve* and Kattegat to Copenhagen and combine with the Swedish and Russian fleets – and such ships as the Danes might still be able to raise – threatening a foray to land troops in Scotland or Ireland, the same fear that had been expressed by Canning in 1807. It was something that Napoleon raised with his Minister of Marine, Decrès, from time to time, just as he kept up the idea of an invasion of Britain from Boulogne, whether as a feint or in reality, in order to pin down British defence forces both afloat and ashore.[91] It seems quite possible that the 'Invasion of Britain' was never more than this. Even if the French fleet gained control of the Channel for long enough for the invasion fleet to cross and land its initial troops, the problem of continuing supplies of men and materials with the British fleet still undefeated and concentrated in home waters would seem an insuperable one.

Napoleon also wanted plans of a 74 that would draw only 19ft 6in so that it could get out of the Texel, and would be as fast as their present 74s.[92] A further project was an attack on Heligoland by three frigates and some gunboats from Cuxhaven plus 3,000 troops.[93] The minister must have dreaded the arrival of a courier with yet another despatch that demanded action, if only a report, on some scheme of dubious viability. The breadth and depth of Napoleon's involvement in everything that was happening in his empire and the constant pressure on his staff call to mind Winston Churchill in the Second World War.

While in England, Saumarez will doubtless have discussed with Yorke a suggestion he had put in writing shortly before his departure from the Baltic: 'If it were possible for us to go on without any trade to the Baltic, I am convinced it would soon reduce Russia to the necessity of making peace and also prevent Sweden having it in her power to annoy us'.[94] He evidently discussed this with Johnson for letters by each of them are phrased in very similar terms. Saumarez' letter antedates that of Johnson by three weeks and it seems probable that he was the first to suggest it; in July 1809 he had written to Martha: 'It is more to be regretted than ever that we have not long before this declared the Ports of Russia in a state of Blockade as it must have changed the Politics of that country.'[95] This demonstrates his readiness to look at the broader picture in a way of which few admirals other than Collingwood were capable. Johnson went further:

For either we are independent of the trade with the northern nations, or it is indispensably necessary to us; if the former be the case, we ought to act a part

---

* The name then given to the waters of the North Sea that lie between the Jutland coast and Norway, now known as the Skagerrak.

worthy of a nation like ours, and if the latter, we can command commerce, and render it ultimately secure and profitable, by withholding it altogether for a time; that this system would produce the desired effect is evident to all those who give themselves the trouble to examine the state of the finances of the different governments in the north of Europe. But whatever diversity of opinion may exist on this subject, I believe it will be generally acknowledged that the active interference of the British Govt. is now become absolutely necessary, as the late measures of the Russian & Prussian governments have rendered the Baltic trade ruinous in the extreme to those British merchants who were concerned in it.[96]

One of the prime concerns was the supply of naval stores, especially hemp for which there was no satisfactory alternative source to Russia, who supplied well over 90 per cent of the navy's requirements. In fact, a report to Yorke at this time, of which Saumarez would not have known, showed that stocks of hemp in store for the navy were 20,249 tons against an annual consumption of 12,000 tons, giving one year and eight months of stock, so that it would have been possible to do without Russian imports for a whole year in that respect. The merchant service required double that amount; there is no mention in the report of what their stocks were, but on economic grounds they are likely to have been rather less than for the navy, so stopping hemp imports might have caused problems for merchant shipping. Efforts were being made to grow hemp in India and in Malta and a committee of the Board of Agriculture in 1811 resolved that a paper be drawn up 'on the publick advantage of employing 90,000 acres in the growth of Hemp, compared with the growth of corn and other articles and stating the policy of a maritime power importing corn rather than hemp in cases where it cannot produce enough of both for its own consumption'.[97]

The Admiralty instructed the Navy Board in June, 1811, to pay £80,000 as commission to the directors of the East India Company for providing 20,000 tons of hemp from India.[98] Sir Samuel Hood's instructions on taking up command of the India Station had three pages of information about the different qualities of hemp available there which, it was hoped, would at least meet the needs of his squadron for the smaller items of cordage.[99]

However, it seems most unlikely that the government would have had the courage to defy both the Lancashire millowners and their workers, and the very vocal shipping interests whose representatives were continually agitating about the effect of the Orders-in-Council. Although the Spanish rebellion against French domination had to a certain extent opened up a market there for English and colonial goods, the Baltic remained the chief outlet through which they could be introduced into Europe generally. To close that by a blockade of Russia would have had a very damaging effect on the British economy, unless the impact on Russia was so severe that a change of alliance followed rapidly. Saumarez' suggestion does not appear to have been given serious consideration.

Instead, when he returned to the Baltic, he had to deal with the problem of Sweden's confiscation of the cargoes of the large number of nominally neutral ships that had gathered in Hanö Bay and overwintered in Carlshamn as a result of his warnings.

8

The Affair of the Carlshamn Cargoes

Captain Barrett of HMS *Minotaur* had written, in November 1810, of the seizure of merchant ships at Pillau (Baltysk) and forwarded a plea from the masters of 13 ships there, unsigned but giving their own names and those of their ships:

> To all or any Commanders of His Majesty's ships of War cruising in the Baltic.
>
> We beg leave to inform you that all ships & goods lying here or coming from Great Britain have been put under sequestration, and the most rigorous measures have been taken that no ship should escape confiscation, that every ship lying in Pillau Road have been taken possession of by Prussian soldiers. I have no doubt but these measures will be adopted in all Prussian Ports. We therefore request you'll dispatch sufficient force that may protect & prevent any vessels from entering any Prussian ports, which will be the saving of ours as well as immense property of Great Britain.
>
> We beg particularly in case you should fall in with any of the undermentioned vessels that you'll inform them of the above and request them to wait at Carlshamn or any other place of safety, that you may think proper until further orders, as in case they should come here they are lost, the spot that requires your particular attention is Pillau Road where there are upwards of fifty vessels all under sequestration, but as the wind blows strong N.E. they are not able to bring their prizes into port, if you can therefore afford us your protection soon, you will be the saving of them, & for your information there are many privateers & small boats fitting out from Danzick.
>
> ... We hope you'll excuse the liberty we have taken in addressing you, but we think it our duty as true Englishmen to do it.
>
> We are your obdt. servts.   Englishmen who have property at stake.[1]

At the end of the 1810 season, Barrett had sailed on 16 November for England from Matvick through the Belt with 63 merchant ships. Saumarez followed on the 28th from Wingo, leaving Captain Honeyman in the *Ardent* as Commodore 'with directions not to permit entry to Gothenburg of any ships or vessels that may arrive from England with English manufactures or colonial produce on account of British merchants'.[2] However, this left a considerable number of ships under neutral flags at Carlshamn, where Saumarez' precautionary measures had gathered them, with goods of that nature on board. A letter from Smith to Honeyman illustrates another factor in the complex situation – the separation between the interests of the shippers and those of the merchants and their insurers:

> My advices from Carlshamn are not at all pleasing; a great number of that unfortunate convoy must winter there and be subjected to the Swedish *ordonnances* whatever they may be. Had this convoy been in the hands of people of good faith and honesty, they would have endeavoured when they saw the improbability of reaching their destination to have put themselves again under British protection. But these brutes, provided they can secure their freights are perfectly regardless of the property, or into whose hands it falls.[3]

There was a further complication:

> It having been represented to the Lords of the Committee of Council for Trade, on behalf of the Underwriters of Lloyds Coffee House, that frauds to a considerable extent have been committed by persons insuring vessels and cargoes in this kingdom and afterwards voluntarily and purposely delivering them up for seizure, to His Majesty's enemies, and privately sharing in the plunder; whereby the policies of insurance ought in justice to become void – that in consequence of such seizures, the demands upon the underwriters in London have become in a national point of view, alarming; and it appearing to this Committee to be highly expedient that the fraudulent practices on the continent, particularly in the Swedish and Prussian ports, where such practices appear to have been most prevalent, should if possible be detected, I am thereupon directed to transmit to you for the information of the Marquis Wellesley copies of the statements which have been made to this Committee on this subject, and I am to request that you will move his Lordship to direct every investigation to be made thro' His Majesty's Ministers, Agents, & Consuls, in foreign ports, or through any other channel which may appear to be calculated to procure information on this highly important subject.[4]

As the Secretary of Lloyds pointed out to Lord Bathurst at the Board of Trade:

> The certain knowledge that the property under sequestration is insured here gives an indifference to the party as to the ultimate results, whether such be confiscated or not. Where markets have not answered to pay the original cost of the goods and expected profits, advantages have been taken; and in some instances, it is supposed, confiscation has been pretended.

A few days later he gave details of a specific instance:

> I send your Lordships copy of a letter from Mr. Peterson to Sir James Saumarez requesting that the fourteen ships named in the within List might

be permitted to go into the Prussian ports of Stettin, Pillau, & Rügenwalde. Mr. Champion, the Admiral's Secretary who furnishes us with this letter, adds that he informed Mr. Peterson the Agent of the danger which existed and the absolute sacrifice which would be made & that if he persisted in sending in those ships he should consider it his duty to communicate the same to the Underwriters.

The Committee have had an opportunity of enquiring as to the fate of these ships and they have been able to ascertain that six of the ships have been seized in port and three captured in proceeding thereto'.[5]

He enclosed an extract of a further letter from an unnamed correspondent in Memel who stated:

that the cargoes are sold only one at a time at the ports where they are confiscated but offered at a certain price to the consignee which price is just sufficient to cover Buonaparte's duties & a small compensation to the Prussian Government. These sales are declared good and the goods so purchased are suffered to pass to any part of the Continent. In consideration of the duties thus paid, copies of the condemnation are granted to the consigned to enable them to recover of the English underwriters.

Samuel Champion, as the Admiral's Secretary, had very largely taken on the role of dealing with convoy reports and shipping information generally, and the issue of licences on his own initiative. This is one respect where Saumarez, so much like Collingwood in many ways in carrying out a diverse role as both Commander-in-Chief and diplomat, differed from him. He was very ready to delegate, whereas Collingwood was well known for keeping everything within his own hands, refusing to have a Captain of the Fleet and even tolerating a Flag Captain, Rotherham, who was incompetent. One of his midshipmen, Hercules Robinson, recalled

his calling across the deck his fat, stupid captain ... when he had seen him commit some monstrous blunder, and after the usual bowing and formality – which the excellent old chief never omitted – he said: 'Captain, I have been thinking whilst I looked at you, how strange it is that a man should grow so big and know so little'.[6]

In the aftermath of Trafalgar, Collingwood appointed Rotherham to *Bellero-phon* which was bound for home,* but his incompetence must have accentuated Collingwood's habit of doing everything himself and the extra burden of work will have contributed not a little to his death.

---

* Rotherham was later court martialled for unofficerlike conduct to his lieutenants and chaplain, reprimanded, and never served again. (Owen, 'Letters from Vice Admiral Lord Collingwood', in *Naval Miscellany VI*, p. 181).

Champion's reports to Lloyds were to cause an unintended storm at a General Meeting of Lloyds in 1811 at the height of the controversy over the Carlshamn cargoes. In the words of the historian of Lloyds in 1928, 'he expressed himself with great freedom as regards political prospects and the action of the Baltic Powers'. These comments were not circulated generally to Subscribers by the Committee that received them, being considered to be 'of a private nature'. The Committee confined itself to publishing extracts of such information as it considered material to underwriters' assessment of Baltic risks. However, a number of Champion's letters came into the hands of the Chairman of the Baltic committee, Thomas Rowcroft, who read out extracts at the first general meeting of the year on 29 March. They fell as a bombshell since Subscribers felt that they had been deprived of important intelligence. A Committee of Subscribers was set up to investigate and, although it was concluded that nothing had been suppressed that would have seriously affected the judgement of risks, a further committee of 21 Subscribers was appointed 'To consider and recommend such Regulations, as in their opinion will tend to the future good management of the Concerns of this House'. It proved to be a turning point in the development of Lloyds.[7]

Once the British fleet had departed at the end of November, von Rosen was particularly concerned to keep the French authorities happy. On the day he received the Royal Proclamation announcing war with Britain, he strongly denied that Gothenburg had been breaking the Continental System. He maintained that the Swedish officials had 'conscientiously performed their duties … when the ships' crews take their oath on the truth of their log-book and their statements, is it then possible to go any further?'[8] Napoleon's view, however, expressed to the French minister, Baron Alquier, the following summer, was that he must persuade the Swedish court, in the disastrous state of their finances, to change their ways so that 'the Swedes conduct themselves as their circumstances demand, without vigour and without passion'.[9] William Berg, the packet agent for Gothenburg, commented to Freeling, his superior at the General Post Office, that '[since] the charges against the Custom House have proved totally unfounded; this has enabled the governor to assume a higher tone in reply'.[10]

Berg was an important part of the intelligence service, as well as carrying out the task of landing the mails as secretly as possible at anchorages in the offshore islands which Consul Smith had been instructed would be free from Swedish military pickets. In January, 1811, he was told by the Consul that he was being spied on by the French. Von Rosen confirmed this and feared that he might have to be arrested and any mail seized, as the Declaration of War had forbidden all intercourse with England. Even he, von Rosen, might be unable to prevent this, especially as he was about to go to Stockholm. Ranchoup, the French consul, had his own network of spies, both Swedish – such as Per Backman, a prominent Gothenburg resident – and 'a number of persons arrived here with passports as merchants from the continent. They sneak everywhere and [illegible] so that you cannot talk to each other in public without noticing someone listening.'[11] Berg bravely asked Consul Smith to tell von Rosen that he was prepared to be arrested 'rather than quit my station without the orders of my own government or that of Sweden'.[12] The liaison of both of them with von Rosen was evidently very close. Reporting to Freeling that all foreigners resident for less than a year in Sweden now had to report to the magistrates and give security for their good conduct, Berg continued: 'In regard to passengers coming by the Packets, Count Rosen has desired to be furnished with a List of their names a sufficient time before they disembark, to allow of his taking measures with the police to obviate the difficulties to which they would other-wise be exposed.'[13] Von Rosen's particular problem was that 'if I arrest a person who has come over with the packet, I acknowledge the use of the packet and consequently our relation with England. If I let the suspect pass, he will let on about it on the continent and compromise both the government and me.'[14]

Saumarez had been given leave of absence during the winter while *Victory*, having been fitted out as a troopship, took reinforcements out to Wellington in Lisbon with seven sail of the line under Rear-Admiral Sir Joseph Yorke.[15] He hoisted his flag again on board her for a fourth year on 2 April 1811. Ross makes the point that it was unusual for an admiral to spend more than three years on a station and that Saumarez might have expected a move to the Mediterranean where Collingwood's successor, Cotton, was shortly to transfer to command of the Channel Fleet. He attributes Saumarez' continuing in the Baltic to the importance of Britain benefiting from the confidence and personal goodwill that he had built up with the Swedes, especially with Bernadotte – an unknown factor – at their head.[16] Yorke, certainly, had a very high opinion of Saumarez. When returning Saumarez' memorial of services in March, 1811, he commented:

> Few men have seen & done so much real service for the state in the course of their professional careers, & yours I trust has yet a long time to run, & will afford you fresh opportunities of adding fresh laurels & honours to those unfading ones which you have already so gloriously acquired.[17]

Yorke had earlier thanked Saumarez for keeping him so well informed of 'what has been passing in your neighbourhood'.[18]

It is difficult to see what reason the Admiralty might have had for moving Saumarez. After all, they kept Collingwood in post in the Mediterranean until it killed him. Saumarez expressed no wish in his private letters to be relieved until the very end of his command, when his eldest daughter died suddenly and also the diplomatic demands virtually ceased with the French invasion of Russia and Britain's re-alliance with both Russia and Sweden. The unique situation of the command in permitting an extended winter leave period during which he was able to be reunited with his much-loved family meant that any other sea-going command would probably not have been acceptable to him.

The one significant event of the long winter had been a Danish attack on 26 March 1811 on HMS *Anholt*, the island base in the Kattegat, classified as a 4th Rate, whose supplies of water and lighthouse were so important both to the British fleet and to the convoys of merchant ships, and would become even more so should Sweden close her coasts as the French were demanding.[19] The Danes had chosen their time well, when better weather permitted a landing force to be transported there by Danish gunboats, without too much surf on the beaches but before the clearing of the Baltic ice had given opportunity for the main British fleet to take up station. Fortunately, Consul Fenwick's strong Danish connections had enabled him to give advance warning to Captain Maurice at Anholt. Fenwick's report to the Admiralty led to the frigate *Tartar* and brig *Sheldrake* being sent to the island.[20] They arrived just in time to support the modest garrison of some 400 men against the 1,600 Danish troops that had landed, and by driving off the gunboats, forced a Danish surrender.[21] Providing there was naval support, Anholt was in some ways easier to defend than the Eartholms. The approaches to the lighthouse fortress were soft sand into which one sank 'more than half leg deep', making it almost impossible to haul cannon when under fire, and a long siege would not be possible with the British navy at hand.[22]

Saumarez reached Wingo on 2 May. His initial soundings led him to believe that 'we are not likely to find the Swedes less friendly than they shewed them-selves last year'.[23] This was echoed in Martha's response:

> I am not surprised at the friendly disposition of the Nation towards the English, but the independent spirit of Bernadotte cannot but excite admira-tion – I could almost say esteem. It is the only one of Bonaparte's Satellites who had dared to act independent of him & shake off his yoke, and I hope he will be able to maintain his freedom with thy assistance.[24]

Two days later Saumarez heard that the governor of Karlskrona had sequestered the Carlshamn ships and ordered their cargoes to be discharged and conveyed up country.[25] The ships themselves, as their owners had hoped, were later released after the cargoes had been landed, although three of the larger ones were converted into blockships for the defence of Karlskrona.[26] According to Consul Smith the sequestration was in retaliation for the Prussian sequestra-tion of Swedish cargoes and 'it is merely a demonstration to appear as having adopted the Continental System but on no account to confiscate the Property which is equally safe in our possession as on board the ships, and which most likely will be returned in a very short time.'[27]

It is not easy to be sure where the loyalties of Smith (or Schmidt as he was called in Gothenburg) lay. There are repeated references in the von Rosen private correspondence to his having been shown by Smith letters to or from Saumarez and Wellesley. At times, this would appear to have been simple indiscretion on Smith's part – von Rosen mentions that one morning soon after Saumarez' arrival in May 1810, Smith denied that he had anything in writing from Saumarez, 'but in the afternoon the old man is not as discreet'.[28] It might, however, have been von Rosen playing the double agent. We know that he was promised £2,000 by Smith in Ross' presence when the war should end, to look after British interests, both in supplying fresh provisions for the fleet and in terms of opening 'a secret communication' which Ross claims led to Sweden's eventually rejoining Great Britain and her allies against France.[29]

Smith was a naturalised Swede who had lived and traded for a long time in Gothenburg and he used the word 'our' in writing both of the interests of Britain and those of Sweden. His exchanges with von Rosen after the election of Bernadotte have been discussed in Chapter 7, p. 113. When, during his temporary absence, Vice-Consul Norris took his place over the Marstrand affair and showed von Rosen a letter from Saumarez, asking him not to tell Smith, who had forbidden it, von Rosen concluded '[Smith] (as I have long believed) is a less good Swede than he ought to be'.[30] Later, Thornton was to write to Saumarez in June 1812 about the proposed treaty of peace with Sweden:

> I need to beg you, my dear Sir, to keep what I write a secret from Gothenburg and I not even except our good Consul, who with the best intentions can hardly preserve upon some points the necessary discretion. The whole race of Gothenburg is *babillard* [loose-tongued] and do mischief by their correspondence.[31]

Fenwick, like Saumarez, believed that Bernadotte was not hostile to Britain. In a very guarded letter, evidently fearful of its being intercepted, he reported that:

> the newcomer has entirely devoted himself to his adopted country and the treatment which he has received in that which he has left, makes it likely that he will still more firmly attach himself to where he is now. It is said that he is very popular there, owing to his having embraced the beforementioned line of conduct.[32]

However, he feared that the loss for Lloyds would be substantial,[33] whereas Foy in Stockholm maintained that it would only be small and that 'the speculators and insurers had only themselves to blame for sending them to Carlshamn after the Swedish government publicly announced that this was forbidden'.[34] He made the interesting point that the action of the Swedish government had saved British property, 'for had the cargoes gone forward, they would have been lost by confiscation at the ports of Prussia after the strong measures which that

Government had taken'.[35] Yorke on the other hand continued to distrust Bernadotte. When Saumarez forwarded a suggestion from a former British prisoner in Norway for an attack on Christiansand, he ruled out any joint projects with Sweden:

> My own opinion is that Bernadotte is playing us false, and at any rate I for one should dread to see a consolidation of the Swedish and Norwegian power, such as it is, in his, or indeed in any hands. Since the arrival of the accounts of the landing [of] the cargoes at Carlshamn and the accompanying measures considerable distrust appears to prevail here about the ultimate views of the Swedish Government – a little more time will develop their plans in all probability.[36]

This was in line with the views of the Marquess of Wellesley and appears to have been the general view in England. A report forwarded to Culling Smith, Foreign Under-Secretary, coming from a 'most respectable merchant in Gothenburg', maintained that the English view of Bernadotte was:

> very erroneous ... I am well assured by some good authority that on every important question he has given his sentiments, as an independent Swede, with the views of the Government & the independence of his country its conscience in his eye & you may rely that but for his services things would have taken a worse turn than they have & that no further concessions will be made.[37]

The Marquess, for once, had responded very promptly to the crisis. He instructed the Admiralty to direct Saumarez:

> to remonstrate strongly against measures so deeply affecting the interests of His Majesty's subjects and that should the Swedish government persevere in acts of this injurious nature, after such remonstrances shall have been made, you should declare to the Swedish government that you cannot permit proceedings which (under whatever pretext they may be disguised) are calculated to injure the interests of His Majesty's subjects in the most serious manner, and that you should be empowered to exercise your discretion in determining on the spot, whether the conduct of Sweden may now require an alteration of that indulgent course, which is now pursued by the British forces in the Baltic.[38]

Saumarez faithfully echoed this in his formal note to Baron Tawast, the military commander-in-chief of Gothenburg and the surrounding province, on 30 May,[39] but he already believed that:

> the decided manner in which I insisted upon indemnification being made for the property landed at Carlshamn from the vessels under the Prussian Flag,

belonging to British Merchants, have been attended with due effect, Baron
Tawast having signified to the Consul that he had agreed to it.[40]

Both Consul Smith and von Rosen, however, were anxious lest Bernadotte
'having from his own disposition and inclination, done every thing in his power
to continue the friendly relations with Great Britain, he will nonetheless not
submit himself to be dictated to'.[41]

Tawast had come aboard *Victory* a week earlier under a flag of truce, nominally to discuss a cartel for the exchange of prisoners. The discussion ranged
much more widely and he stated that

> he was instructed to communicate to me [Saumarez] in the most confidential
> manner that it was the earnest wish of the Swedish Government to keep upon
> the most amicable terms with Great Britain and that it was not intended
> under any circumstances to commit any acts of hostility whatever; that the
> supplies of water and fresh provisions for the use of the Squadron should be
> facilitated both at Hano Bay and Gottenburg; for which purpose the picquets
> should be withdrawn from the points the most convenient for those articles
> to be received. That the correspondence both by Post and by Couriers, should
> be continued unmolested; and that in the event of any British subjects being
> made prisoners on any part of the coast, they would be immediately liberated,
> for which purpose the Cartel intended to be ratified had been proposed. That
> the appearance of any hostile measures was only intended for demonstration,
> and in order to elude the vigilance of French spies who might be dispersed
> in the Country.

Tawast had gone on to assure him that:

> With respect to the late transactions at Carlshamn ... the measure was not
> intended to operate against merchandize belonging to British Merchants
> under any other Flag, the whole of which would be secured, and the Under-
> writers *secrètement* indemnified for the value of the cargoes that were insured
> in England.[42]

Ross maintains that Saumarez was the only person who did not consider it to
be 'an act of hostility, and that a retaliation on our part would speedily take
place'.[43] However, even Saumarez may have retained his suspicions, for he sent
Ross confidentially to obtain written confirmation of Tawast's reassurances and,
being dissatisfied with the document he obtained, wrote formally to Consul
Smith that he should report to Tawast 'that Government will naturally expect
that the British merchants will be indemnified for whatever property belongs
to them which has been landed from vessels in Sweden, trading under [British]
licences' and sent copies of the correspondence to London.[44] It is possible that
he simply wanted something in writing from the Swedish government to send
to London. His comments to Martha were:

while I have the satisfaction to learn that my proceedings are approved by the Government, the situation of this country is critical. They well know they can do us no injury, and that we have much in our power, and yet they are adopting measures against our mercantile interests that they know must fall upon their own heads ... whatever may be their wishes they must soon enter into all the views of Bonaparte who will not rest till Russia and this Country join in destroying our commerce in these seas.[45]

As she said in her response: 'they stand between two fires either of which is likely to consume them'.[46]

Simultaneously, Saumarez suggested on the one hand that representatives of the British merchants and underwriters should go to Stockholm to assert their claims, and on the other, that the two bomb ships intended to join his fleet should be sent as soon as possible. 'Their appearance alone would have the best effect in intimidating the Swedes to a compliance with our just demands.'[47] He was further encouraged in this policy of firmness combined with moderation by a visit from Count Rosen on 26 June. He 'came on board in the most private manner and earnestly requested that his visit and the communication he had been directed to make to me should be kept secret'. Saumarez reported to Yorke:

If I could have any further doubts upon my mind relative to the sincerity of the intentions of this Government, they have been perfectly removed by the conversation I had yesterday with Count Rosen, who came on board the *Victory*, by desire of the Crown Prince, in consequence of my remonstrance upon the affair at Carlshamn.

Von Rosen assured him that Sweden wanted to break with France but dared not do so in case France and Russia settled their differences and Russia then was persuaded to act against Sweden. Saumarez replied that so long as Sweden kept to her assurances, he 'had every reason to believe that his Majesty's Government would be satisfied with it; but that if it should be deviated from, I had the authority, and they might be assured I would exert the utmost in my power to resent any aggression on the part of Sweden'.[48] This was the iron fist in the velvet glove, the quality that Napoleon had attributed also to Bernadotte, so they were well matched. Von Rosen was satisfied with this and promised to convey it to Bernadotte.[49]

Saumarez reported to Croker and Yorke what he was doing – or rather what he was *not* doing –and received remarkably little interference from them. They seemed still to be more concerned about the possibility of the French squadron in the Scheldt escaping and reaching Copenhagen. There was a confidential report from a highly placed medical contact of Dr. Jamison that the Walcheren Fleet was expected at Karlskrona with troops on board to man the forts 'with which and the Russians united you were, or are, to be driven from our shores'.[50] Yorke repeated his original instructions that Saumarez was to keep the bulk of his fleet in the Sleeve.[51] The Carlshamn cargoes affair had undoubtedly had its impact on merchants' and shippers' confidence. 'The trade is very much fallen off to what it has been in former years – most of the ships returning from England without cargoes either of British merchandise or Colonial products'.[52] On top of this, Napoleon was demanding of his marshals that they should step up their efforts to prevent breaches of the continental system: 'all colonial goods, from wherever they come must be confiscated, for they come from England'.[53]

It is difficult to judge whether it was Yorke's respect for Saumarez' ability and a willingness to accept his views as 'the man on the spot', or whether it was the latter's persistence in deferring any overt hostile action (he had insisted both to his own subordinates and to the Swedes that he would not fire the first shot), that allowed Saumarez gradually to prevail. On 16 August, Yorke admitted that:

> the affair of the Carlshamn cargoes is considered here a matter of much more nicety and difficulty than at first appeared ... altho' we cannot altogether entertain (at least to the same extent) the favourable opinion you appear to possess of the fair and amicable intentions of the Swedish government.[54]

Yorke accepted that it was desirable to play for time and avoid coming to any rupture with Sweden as long as there was a chance of a favourable turn of affairs. He still expected the Swedes to 'restore all that could be proved to be British property'. This was probably reflecting the view of the Marquess of Wellesley who was one stage removed from Saumarez' influence and quite possibly, with his known idleness, did not bother to read his reports – his 'negligence and sloth' necessitated a reorganisation of the Foreign Office when Castlereagh succeeded him in 1812.[55] The Lords Commissioners forwarded to Saumarez the following day Wellesley's instructions, signifying HRH the Prince Regent's pleasure that

> you should be directed immediately to address a note to the Swedish government, desiring that all British property detained under those sequestrations may be restored to the owners, with permission either to dispose of the said property in Sweden, or to export it from Sweden to England.[56]

However, as Wellesley should have been aware, this would have been self-defeating. It would also have been totally unacceptable to the Swedes. George Foy in a lengthy letter the previous month had set out very clearly the arguments of Baron von Engeström:

1 Denmark, Prussia and the other countries had violated Swedish ships and the King 'owed it to his dignity to make reprisals'.

2 All the ships other than the Danish had been allowed to go free, but because these states had joined Napoleon's Continental System, the cargoes would be liable to confiscation and their value would go to France.

3 As the claimants, who were mostly British using false papers, would therefore get nothing, they must join in any secret plan to get round this.

4 The slightest suspicion of the goods being claimed on British account would lead to their irrecoverable confiscation.

5 Since, under the Continental System, the cargoes could not go forward to any Baltic or other ports where the system operated, they must remain in Sweden for sale or in transit. 'On this point the determination of the Swedish Government is fixed and unalterable'.

6 If they went to Prussian or other ports, or were re-embarked for England, the loss would be immense, whereas in Sweden prices might be obtained nearer the value of the goods, though they would be subject to an extra duty as part of the deal.

7 Secrecy was vital. 'The Minister for the Home Department is gone to Gothenburg to investigate the reports of too open communication between the fleet under your Excellency's command and Gothenburg.'[57]

As was the case with Bernadotte's earlier deceptive response to the complaint by Napoleon on smuggling, this was not necessarily a serious investigation. Johnson reported to Saumarez: 'Count von Rosen desires me to request most particularly that you will not mention to Mr. Smith or to any person at Gothenburg that you have received any confidential communication from him thro' my medium.'[58]

Every letter from Foy mentioned that Engeström was pressing him for a response over the Carlshamn cargoes[59] and on 9 September, the Swedish Foreign Minister suggested that the only acceptable solution was for the goods to be sold in Sweden on behalf of the Swedish government who would then reimburse the claimants by a payment to the British government. The latter could then divide this amongst them. But it had to be done quickly as the attention of the French and Danes was now focused on the cargoes.[60] This was the proposal that Saumarez had agreed with von Rosen soon after his arrival in May. Foy set out the arguments again on 27 September, adding: 'This country could not enter upon offensive war for want of money as well as men, and however desirable for Sweden to regain Finland and however she might be prompted thereto by France, the government firmly intends to preserve neutrality.'[61] All that Saumarez heard from London, however, was a belated reply from Croker on 10 August to his letter of 29 June, saying that the matter was 'under consideration'.[62]

The secretary of Lloyds was also gravely concerned. He forwarded a paper from an unnamed Carlshamn merchant which pointed out that the adjudication committee in Sweden was guided solely by the documents:

> As most of these documents contain fictitious names, as well from the places where they profess to come from, as at the ports where they were bound to, it is of course out of the power of the agents of Carlshamn to do any thing to save the property of their correspondents, as they cannot bring in Court any proofs or documents corresponding with the simulated papers and dare not officially declare that the papers are not authentic, tho' their not being so seems to be pretty well understood by the Committee. The only possibility therefore for rescuing any part of the property is a direct reclamation from the British to the Swedish Government.

The paper went on to make clear that under any circumstances the underwriters:

> are liable to pay the insured a total loss, against abandonment of the goods, and the law stands so clear in that respect that I am fully satisfied that even Governments tho' they might be inclined to favour the resistance of the underwriters, cannot protect them as they cannot pervert the tendency of the Marine Law as it stands.[63]

It is hardly surprising that Lloyds should be worried. A paper from Lord Chetwynd at the Privy Council to Culling Smith at the Foreign Office enclosed a list of ships and their insured values:

	Ships	£
Carlshamn	60	759,003
Gothenburg	12	72,420
Ystad	7	80,227
Other Swedish ports	3	<u>11,725</u>
Total	82	£923,375[64]

9

The Von Rosen Letters

'If I could have any further doubts upon my mind relative to the sincerity of the intentions of this Government, they have been perfectly removed by the conversation I had yesterday with Count Rosen'. Saumarez' comment at the height of anxieties over the Carlshamn cargoes incident encapsulates the relationship that had built up between Saumarez and his Swedish counterpart, von Rosen.

Saumarez' cordial relationships with both von Rosen and Admiral Krusenstjerna were fundamental to his judgement of the correct line of action to follow. They encouraged him to follow his own line regardless of the anxieties of London. Just after his final return from the Baltic, he wrote a Secret letter at the request of von Rosen to certify that it was the latter's clarifications and assurances of Bernadotte's friendly intentions and his independence of Bonaparte that persuaded Saumarez to continue to act peacefully towards the Swedes before he received instructions from government, and that those instructions when they arrived were based on the discussions that he, Saumarez, had had with von Rosen. He was delighted to verify von Rosen's zeal in serving the Prince Royal and the cause 'of all people who detest the Tyrant's system which has inflicted such misery on so great a part of the Continent under his oppressive yoke'.[1]

In a later letter to Ross, Krusenstjerna makes the sardonic comment that:

> Our friends the French and Danes express their friendship to us with unremitted zeal in capturing and robbing from us our merchant vessels, whilst our enemies the English let them pass unmolested from one port to another. We did not suffer by one hundred times as much from these two nations, the time we were at war against them, as we do now when they call themselves our friends and allies.[2]

Saumarez, Alquier, and von Rosen and Bernadotte were the lead players for their three respective countries in the Baltic in the three campaigning years 1810–12. Their personal relationships and the ways they went about achieving their objectives were critical to the events there of July 1812. The outcome was the destruction of the Continental System, the failure of Napoleon's attempt to defeat Britain by economic warfare, and his fatal march against Moscow. It is worth looking at each of these characters more closely before moving on to the narrative of the final events. If another person had taken the place of any one of them, the timing and even the end result could have been quite different.

Born in 1773, von Rosen fought in the Swedish–Russian war, 1788–90, as a lieutenant in the Life Guards. Promoted to major in 1796, he later left the army and went into local government. By 1808 he was Landshövding (Governor) in Värmlands Lan, but refused to take part in Adlersparre's coup and was arrested. Shortly beforehand, he had been appointed Landshövding of Gothenburg and Bohus, and on his release he took up this appointment where he was to continue, apart from a short period as Governor of Trondheims Lan in Norway after its acquisition by Sweden, until his death while actively battling against the 1834 cholera epidemic.

I have not yet discovered the exact date of his arrival in Gothenburg, but the first of his private letters to the Foreign Secretary, Baron Lars von Engeström, in the Royal Library archive is dated 1 November 1809. It refers to an earlier report, and it would be interesting to know whether his arrival predates or follows Engeström's own appointment in June of that year; but it does not look as though von Rosen was especially picked for what was to become, in his hands, a most important office. There was little to show from his past career that he was the right person for what he himself described the following year as 'the most exposed point of contact for the relations between the nations [Sweden and Britain] at a very delicate time'.[3] He also admitted that 'Quite unfamiliar with managing virtually diplomatic [matters] I fear making mistakes'.[4] But he was young (36), active, and came with a good record from his time in Värmland. He is described as 'good-humoured, high-spirited and worldly-wise',[5] not necessarily the ideal qualities for a diplomat. The Swedish economic historian Heckscher writes of him as 'the most original, humorous, and energetic Swedish actor on the stage of the Continental System in this exciting time'.[6] However, it was the relationship that he built up with Admiral Saumarez that effectively determined British policy in the ensuing three years.

Saumarez' formality seems to have blended well with von Rosen's youthful liveliness, despite a difference of 16 years in their ages. The latter uses the word *gubben* (old man) quite frequently in his letters to Engeström when referring to Saumarez, but it would seem to be more a word of affection than comparison. When they first met, Saumarez, at 52, was relatively young for a commander-in-chief. After the declaration of war, their meetings were unofficial, and held on board HMS *Victory* to keep them secret from the French. Once Napoleon had invaded Russia and there was no further need for secrecy, there was a succession of parties at von Rosen's house, often with return visits of other guests on board *Victory*. The parties will have been a welcome relaxation from the cares of a commander-in-chief, cooped up in a ship at anchor 10 miles offshore for six months at a time.

The letters from von Rosen to Engeström show that contact in the early days was normally through the British consul, John Smith. There is only one letter for 1809, which is of no great significance. The first one for 1810 establishes what was to be the relationship between von Rosen and Saumarez for the rest of that season – a fairly formal channel of communication through the consul. A long report from von Rosen to Engeström on 22 May relays a string of information on the orders that Saumarez had received before his departure from England, the numbers of his ships, the fact that there were no troops with them this time and that therefore there was no likelihood of an attack on Gotland, but that Bornholm had been under consideration (which presumably included the Eartholms). This had been passed on by Smith who had gathered the information while he was forced by head winds to stay out with the squadron at Wingo. In addition, a despatch ship from Yarmouth had brought orders to seize all Swedish ships, coming from or going to any port, unless they had an English licence. 'However, Admiral Saumarez has promised not to act on these orders until he arrives in Östersiön [the Baltic*], where he will sail on the first Wind.'⁷ It was von Rosen's first experience of Saumarez softening the impact of the instructions that he received from the Admiralty.

His letters to Engeström appear as those of a slightly anxious young man trying to keep a new boss informed in a frank way of everything of significance happening on his patch, but ready to take the blame for any errors that might arise through his inexperience. A letter in June reported that the commander of the Elfsborg fortress guarding the entrance to Gothenburg, who came under the Military Commandant rather than the governor, refused entry to the English packet boat. This put von Rosen in difficulty since he had promised Smith that this would not happen until news of the suspension of the packet boats' permission to land could reach England. He was able to sort it out and arrange that both the passengers and the mail came ashore, winning points for this from Smith. 'This has been done without compromising the government in the least, but only myself.' But he was bold enough to continue:

> I hope that you are gracious enough not to be dissatisfied with this incident, in which I am innocent, where the commander of Elfsborg has shown that he prefers to obey the orders given by the Board of the Postal Service in the form of advice, than the instruction given by me on the orders of the King, communicated through the Supreme Commander. Moreover, the man

---

* The term Baltic refers here to the waters beyond the Danish Islands (Sweden's 'East Sea') and does not include the Kattegat and Skagerrak which also fell within the Baltic Command.

is Major of the Fortifications Corps von Henschen, widely notorious from the Finnish War.[8]

For the first part of the summer Gothenburg was less concerned with the presence of the English fleet, now for the third year, than with the sudden death of the then Crown Prince, Karl August.* Civil unrest leading to disturbances was quite possible and von Rosen had the dual task of watching likely ringleaders and making sure 'that arrangements were made for the military, at five minutes' notice, to nip disturbances in the bud.'[9]

The major irritation with the English was their bringing postal bags ashore in broad daylight rather than discreetly, now that the packet boats were officially excluded. Von Rosen warned Smith that he would seize the bags and write to the government if it occurred again.[10] On a lighter note, he had a complaint from a pastor who had gone out to one of the uninhabited islands to cut and collect the hay to which he was entitled as part of his stipend. When he arrived there with his family and servants, he discovered that not only was the island dug over and planted with salad and root crops by the crews of the English warships, but tents had been set up as a brothel. There was a large number of men there, including a ship's chaplain, and they were 'shameless enough to invite him to join in their sinful pleasures'. In the absence of a senior officer who could respond to his claim for compensation for the loss of his hay, one of the young officers stated that it was an extension of the Continental System. The pastor's letter to von Rosen on his return was more concerned with the wicked practices now being followed on church land than with the loss of the hay, but Consul Smith undertook to deal with the matter in cash, which von Rosen hoped would settle it.[11]

Von Rosen asked how he should respond to demands from the French consul, of whose impending arrival he had just been informed: 'If the merchants behave sensibly (which I doubt) the French and Danish consuls should settle matters immediately on their arrival here, but if this is not done, disputes will naturally arise daily.'[12] Shortly afterwards he heard of Napoleon's relaxation of the Continental System; this was the new authorisation of licences entitling the shipper to bring into French ports any quantity of sugar, coffee, pepper, etc., provided he then exported French merchandise to the same value, two-thirds of which must be wine and brandy, and one-third hardware, silks, and other French manufactures.[13] This had upset the Gothenburg merchants, who were enjoying the benefits of the smuggling trade that the Continental System had brought them and, as von Rosen commented, if the relaxation only applied to France, it was very chauvinistic.[14]

When, in September 1810, the incident described over the *Hero* and the

---

*   See Chapter 7, pp. 109–10.

Danish privateer at Marstrand took place,* von Rosen at this stage did not know Saumarez well enough to be able either to anticipate his reaction or to contact him direct. He was greatly relieved when Vice-Consul Norris, in the absence of Smith, showed him the letter he had received from Saumarez, asking Norris to thank General Silfverschöld and von Rosen 'for our way of treating this matter'.[15]

Although there is no official record of von Rosen having met Bernadotte, it is evident from a letter to Engeström in November 1810 that such a meeting took place in Hälsingborg not long after Bernadotte's arrival in Sweden. In the letter von Rosen says that he expects to receive a sharp note from the French Consul because of the publication of a letter from a merchant claiming that the steps taken by Sweden against England were feigned: 'according to what his Royal Highness the Crown Prince ordered me in Hälsingborg, I intend to give him an evasive answer and refer him to his minister in Stockholm.'[16] This is confirmed by Consul Fenwick who had himself moved to live in Hälsingborg. He reported to Saumarez on 29 October that von Rosen had gone there to pay his court to the new Crown Prince. Von Rosen told Bernadotte of the French consul's complaints, said that he had given 'an evasive but civil reply' and asked for his advice. The response was that Bernadotte thought von Rosen had been too good to give the consul any reply at all. Fenwick had heard the story from 'two distinct persons who assured me that they had it from Count Rosen himself'.[17] It is a clear indication that Bernadotte had even at this early stage embarked on a policy of dissimulation towards the French.

There is another revealing letter in June 1812. Von Rosen, commenting on the incident at Marstrand two years earlier, mentioned that he had a reliable spy on board the English fleet.[18] The spy is mentioned again several times, but never by name. It originally seemed that this spy must be the packet ship agent, William Berg, whose letters to Freeling at the GPO in London showed that he played an active part in intelligence work in Gothenburg and had regular meetings with von Rosen.[19] However, von Rosen reported on 1 June 1811 that his informant had left for England 'and thus cannot influence the present Squadron Commander any more'.[20] Berg was still in post at Gothenburg in October 1811, so the spy cannot have been him.[21] It all came out on 17 June 1812 after von Rosen had carelessly put a letter to his contact in the wrong envelope and sent it to Engeström instead. He evidently received a response asking some awkward questions, for his own reply was a four-page full confession: 'sincerely wishing to win forgiveness, and humbly requesting it'. He went on to explain in detail how he had come to be writing, unknown to his superiors, to a contact in England:

---

* See Chapter 7, pp. 113–15.

When I got Your order in October 1810 to try to play down with Admiral Saumarez any undesirable effects of the unexpected declaration of war, I had no other alternative than to find some individual who could give a good [presentation] of what I had to tell the Admiral, especially as at that time I was little, or rather not at all, personally known by Saumarez.* My choice fell on Parisch, who was acquainted to the Crown Prince since Hamburg, and also had relations with Sir James. The outcome proved that I had judged my man correctly, and luck was added in that I then through Parisch got to know Johnstone [sic], who then and there also contributed to the satisfactory outcome. Johnstone on that occasion informed me that Parisch was highly regarded by Marquis Wellesley. Soon afterwards the former went to England. Should I not then as a good Swede making use of his friendship, request that he should talk well about us and praise the qualities of the prince? I did that, and dare to presume that Parisch and Saumarez have greatly contributed to the good opinion they have there about the sincerity of the Prince.[22]

Three things stand out from this section of the letter. First, that Engeström had, immediately following the declaration of war, sought to pacify Saumarez, now England's senior local spokesman. F.D. Scott describes Engeström, who was Chancellor of the University of Lund, as 'more scholar than politician'.[23] He was also at this stage Francophile[24] and as he was unlikely to take such a step towards Saumarez without the authority of the newly arrived Crown Prince, it is almost certain that this was on the instructions of Bernadotte. Second, that even after a year in post, von Rosen admits that he had not got to know Saumarez and establish closer relations with him. Third, that by June 1812, von Rosen believed that the British government now accepted the sincerity of Bernadotte and that this was due to the influence of his spy Parisch and Saumarez. Parisch (Parish in English correspondence) is described by Saumarez as 'an eminent merchant of Hamburg' when reporting to Yorke that he came on board *Victory* with Johnson in November 1810.[25] He had been introduced to Saumarez by letter 'at the request of Miss Mellish' in July.[26]

Encouraged by von Rosen's assurances, Saumarez had sailed home with the major portion of the fleet on 22 November 1810. Von Rosen was able to report in December that 'nothing new has happened'.[27] But he was still concerned that the French Minister's secretary had sailed for France and that 'he will probably not have neglected to collect all the truths and untruths that are to be had down here'. He expressed the hope that Ranchoup might now be more accommodating 'under the pressure of money'. Whether this money was coming through his consular fees, bribery, or von Rosen's secret service expenditure, or whether it referred to Ranchoup's personal lack of funds is not clear.[28] It evidently was

---

* In fact, from von Rosen's letter of 17 September, it seems that Parisch had already been acting as his spy more than a month before Sweden's declaration of war.

wishful thinking, for a month later there is an eight-page diatribe from von Rosen to Engeström against 'the ridiculous and also dangerous remarks of the French consul Ranchoup' and his 'ignorance about trade matters that would not be forgiven in a clerk of one month's experience'. He promises a formal report the following Saturday, where he will call for official action against Ranchoup since he himself cannot take any revenge because of the consul's official position. He sought also Engeström's permission to come to Stockholm for 10–12 days since the sea was now frozen all the way out to Wingo, bringing the port of Gothenburg to a standstill. He suggested that in an hour's conversation, he could 'give you more information, and excuse myself for failure to observe the Continental System, better than in a full year of correspondence'.[29]

The English cruisers were still operating on the edge of the ice and von Rosen persuaded Vice-Consul Norris to visit an English privateer which had captured a Danish ship in order to discover what instructions he had been given by Saumarez. They were to the effect that Swedish coastal trade was allowed, but any ships bound for enemy ports must hold a licence. The packets were also now coming again from Yarmouth. One of them had brought a suspected French spy, which presented the problem mentioned earlier that if von Rosen were to arrest him he would acknowledge that the packets were still operating. He maintained his innocence of allowing any colonial goods to enter Gothenburg. Stories contradicting this were circulating in Stockholm and he feared that they would reach Bernadotte. Should that happen he requested that:

> the Crown Prince can order an inquiry here, the stricter the better, if His Royal Highness is not satisfied by my assurances, and charge me with the character of the lowest human on earth if a single ship with colonial merchandise has entered here since the declaration of war.[30]

It may seem strange that he should make these protestations to his own Swedish superior who knew exactly what was going on and indeed had instructed him. But the letter may well have been written for the purpose of being shown to the French. Technically von Rosen could be said to be speaking the truth. The ships would have unloaded their colonial goods on the offshore island of Fotö rather than entering the port of Gothenburg itself. Once landed and sold there they became Swedish goods and could be loaded again for onward transportation to north German or Russian ports, or to Gothenburg or elsewhere in Sweden.

For that reason, everyone involved found it difficult to believe the first rumours coming through on 2 May of the confiscation of all the colonial merchandise in Carlshamn. It brought confusion on the Exchange, but because von Rosen had no news about it, the merchants comforted themselves by believing that it must therefore be untrue. Smith showed von Rosen a letter from Saumarez, expressing the hope that this was the case, since such a measure would go against what

Wellesley had informed him was to be expected from the Swedish cabinet, and his own mild conduct towards Sweden. When Engeström confirmed that the sequestration had in fact taken place but that it was aimed at Prussian ships in retaliation for their government's actions towards Swedish ships, von Rosen was relieved, but feared that it would be very difficult to convince Saumarez that it was not the result of French demands. He apologised in his letter to Engeström for raising the subject again:

> but firstly, the Prince ordered me at my departure to keep myself well informed about what could be done with regards to England and her fleet, and said that he hoped that England would at least not start an active war; and secondly, your letters to me have always been written on similar principles. This has caused me to be as industrious as possible and to influence Saumarez further through a reliable channel* that I had and still have, <u>and maybe England through him</u>. I believe that I can assure you that we should never want him to be of another turn of mind than he is now. He permits everything to continue as before without insisting that we expose ourselves to France. I have every reason to believe that he, with the least publicity and without compromising us, will support our aim of a union with Norway, without requiring either a quick peace with England, or the import of colonial merchandise etc.[31]

This letter is quoted at length since it shows, at the beginning of the new season and as the biggest trade and diplomatic dispute of the 'phoney war' between Britain and Sweden was breaking out, how von Rosen's attitude towards, and relations with, Saumarez had changed since the previous October. He was doubtless responding to the clear lead given by Bernadotte and echoed by Engeström. But he also had, in the month following the Hälsingborg meeting, established a much closer personal relationship with Saumarez. The latter reported to Yorke a 'confidential communication' on 20 November 1810 in which von Rosen disclosed the latest French demands for the implementation of the Continental System and assured him that they were 'perfectly contrary to the sentiments of the Swedish government' and hoped therefore that he would 'abstain from any offensive measures against Sweden'.[32] Saumarez' acceptance of this and his decision to sail for home without taking any action will have warmed their relationship and led to von Rosen's rather fulsome report of Saumarez' expected support for Sweden in the present year.

One problem was that von Rosen felt he dare not at this stage have any formal meetings with the Admiral because of French pressure. The two countries were after all officially at war, so that the formalities of flags of truce had to be preserved. He took the opportunity of the visit by General Tawast to make a

---

*   Parisch.

cartel for the exchange of prisoners to enlarge the scope of the meeting to cover 'future relations this summer', having briefed the General by a memorandum on what to say about the Carlshamn confiscations. The General was himself made the subject of an official enquiry at the demand of Bernadotte for this visit on board *Victory*, but the wording of Bernadotte's letter indicates again that this was probably done as a smokescreen to allay French suspicion: 'This event could be regarded as a crime of High Treason; but as General Tawast is known to be a good Swede, I will abstain from any decision over him until you have enlightened me about it.'[33] Von Rosen was optimistic enough about Saumarez' reactions to 'assure Engeström in advance that the Admiral will be obliging to us and avoid compromising us while secretly helping'.[34] The meeting was actually very productive and set out the basis of what became the final solution, although it was to take until the following year for London and Stockholm to accept it. Von Rosen sets it out very clearly in his letter of 23 May 1811 to Engeström:

That Swedish coastal trade will run free, without licences,
That the Admiral, who has already written to England about Pomerania, will even more powerfully urge that our trade with the above-mentioned possession on the other side of the sea will be included under the name of permitted coastal trade,
That if Swedish gun sloops are stationed in the Sound, no English ones will go there,
That an expedition to the Gulf of Bothnia has never been intended and certainly will not take place.
In return for this the Admiral requested secret repayment for the losses the English underwriters have suffered through the confiscations in Carlshamn, and he also wanted this to be extended to the seized English cargoes under Prussian flag. The Admiral did not require repayment for such English ships (loaded with textiles), which could be confiscated in accordance with the usual customs statutes.
The memorandum that General Tawast received from me to go by was based on your latest letters and in agreement with the orders the said General had got from His Excellency Essen.
Swedish fishermen are not to be molested.[35]

Saumarez' concession on the English ships with textiles was of no real significance since virtually all of these would have taken the precaution of having Prussian or other safe national papers.

Von Rosen was still not fully confident about his own relations with Stockholm. He received a batch of letters from both Engeström and the Swedish cabinet, evidently critical of his going beyond his authority.* His 'humble

---

* These letters have not yet been found, but his reply gives sufficient evidence.

report' maintains that he had been asked by Baron Toll, Admiral Puke and General Essen, at the beginning of April, to inform them immediately of the arrival of the English fleet and also:

> about the operations and ways of thinking of the English. I could not imagine that such high-ranking officials could express such requests without it being in accordance with the intentions of the Government. I have therefore carefully reported what I knew <u>for certain</u> about Saumarez' turn of mind.

He indignantly assured them that he was not simply acting as a 'news-hound'. He had had a further note from Saumarez to say that he wanted the secret repayments to underwriters to extend to the full amount of the cover and to include even those who were not insured but had cargoes of English origin.[36] Two days later, replying to another Engeström letter, he confessed to being 'between hope and fear, awaiting with impatience either approval or disapproval of what I have done with the best intent'. He was aware that Saumarez was annoyed at his being unwilling to meet him personally. The letter mentioned that Saumarez was poorly and in a bad mood, but still expressed his intention to maintain friendly relations if the English underwriters were reimbursed or the cargoes released. A Prussian merchant reckoned that a great part of the cargoes in the Prussian ships were in fact English property.[37]

Von Rosen was then questioned about General Tawast's meeting. He argued that the General was the appropriate person to negotiate a cartel with the commander of the enemy fleet, and it seemed a good opportunity for someone in whom Saumarez would have confidence to push forward the other matters. They had both agreed that there was a mutual interest in avoiding hostilities and Saumarez had assured Tawast that he had no intention of harming Sweden. Von Rosen then went on to give a remarkable testimony to Saumarez' straight-forward way of dealing and trustworthiness: 'When he has given his word of honour about discretion, Saumarez is too honest a man to expose either our government or those who have been the secret interpreters of it'. As a result, 'Ranchoup ... together with my other enemies' could only suspect what was happening but have no proof. The use of the word enemies in connection with the French Consul shows how the diplomatic balance has shifted. Von Rosen goes on to say he has got used to Ranchoup so often making unpleasant criticisms, especially since he is confident that if Napoleon attributes to him what little he has done to carry out the government's intentions, 'the King will not let a man starve who has worked hard to the best of his ability for the good of the country'.[38]

He further comments that secret agreements and readiness to compromise are possible with a man like Saumarez, but the majority of Englishmen now seem to take the view that whatever the Continent does, 'we will still be able to stand up to Napoleon and we daily find that he is not invincible'. This may be because so much of Von Rosen's contact was with a consistently victorious Royal Navy, but it is an indication of a very different state of mind to the days of Austerlitz and Tilsit both in England and in Europe generally. Part of Saumarez' role was one of propaganda to convince the continental powers that Napoleon would be defeated. To an extent, this fell within his instructions from Yorke that:

> the Swedes should be <u>gently</u> but <u>steadily</u> convinced that it is in our power to resent their ill-usage and to turn the consequences of perfidy on the executors, but the evil day [of Sweden implementing French orders] should be postponed as long as possible.[39]

It was following this that Saumarez, obeying Wellesley's orders, sent his ultimatum to General Tawast, to be passed to the Swedish government: 'I have been directed to remonstrate in the strongest manner ... that if acts of so injurious a tendency are persevered in, I shall be obliged to depart from that indulgent course I have hitherto pursued towards Sweden.'[40] Tawast and von Rosen would have appreciated that he was acting under orders from London, and also that the threat was really rather mild for one that was said to be expressed 'in the strongest manner'. There was still a considerable gulf between Saumarez' own views and those in London, confirmed by Yorke's comment in the letter quoted earlier that 'my own opinion is that Bernadotte is playing us false' (see p. 135). Von Rosen also reported in his long letter of 1 June that it was Saumarez who suggested the solution to the question of damages: 'through an agreement by an experienced merchant from Stockholm on one side, and on the other by an English envoy under the name of a merchant'.[41] This too was an important step on the way to settlement, for which Saumarez does not appear to have been given the credit in the English correspondence.

The Swedish reaction to the ultimatum shows that they were aware of this separation between the local and the London views of the English authorities. Von Rosen reported:

> Admiral Saumarez' ways of thinking and attitude regarding Sweden are quite the same as they so far have been. He protects our trade, lets our ships sail with or without convoys and licences, allows export of colonial merchandise. It would also seem that he expects some more flexible dispatch from England as he has sent the letter to us so late and in a confidential letter asked that it be communicated to the Government through General en chef Essen, who is expected here today or tomorrow.[42]

Von Rosen was instructed to have a meeting with Saumarez.

It was one that he would long remember. Owing to a long series of summer storms, it did not take place until 25 June 1811. For the sake of secrecy, he rowed himself in a boat out to *Victory*. Wind and current were against him both ways and he spent eight hours rowing, ending by landing on the north shore of the entrance at Hisingen and walking back to the city: 'I have never in my life had so tiring a 24 hours, of which my hands, full of blisters, bear witness.' It was a measure not only of his devotion to duty, which later led to his death from cholera, but of his willingness even as a governor to 'dirty his hands' and go beyond the normal role. It also showed his initiative. Saumarez, 'always as honest as he was loyal, received me with the friendship I expected'. He promised to write to Wellesley to support acceptance of the scheme for payment of damages and was not too concerned that this might cause some financial loss. What did concern Saumarez was if the proposals were simply meant to gain time. Von Rosen did all he could to assure him of Swedish sincerity. Saumarez then, in von Rosen's words, promised if that was the case:

> he would stay as ardent an advocate of the Crown Prince and the welfare of Sweden as he so far had been, but if, on the other hand, he ever found out that we had wanted to deceive him, he would, although unwillingly, be forced to inflict all the possible harm upon us, in order to ingratiate himself with his Government, whose confidence he had forfeited through the assurances he all through the last winter had made about Sweden´s friendly ways of thinking towards England.[43]

Von Rosen asked Engeström that no more sales of the goods at Carlshamn should take place 'until the negotiations with England on this sorry matter either reach an agreement or are broken off'.

Another indication of the co-operation that built up between Saumarez and von Rosen was an arrangement that they came to in order to stop the illicit trade from Strömstad near the Norwegian frontier to Scania using Swedish ship's papers. The trade was mostly in Norwegian goods and in many cases the ships went straight to Copenhagen instead of to Scania. Saumarez proposed that any genuine Swedish traders should be given licences by von Rosen which would give them exemption from the attentions of English cruisers. Von Rosen had to clear this with the Swedish government and arranged to have a secret meeting with Saumarez, who would be rowed to one of the islands by officers in a small boat and be disguised.[44] Saumarez had already released all the bigger *skärgård* boats: it is difficult to be sure whether this was for political reasons or from soft-heartedness since von Rosen comments: 'It is almost impossible for the old man to refuse when the poor men come and beg him for mercy. Admiral Durham* again is of a more greedy mind and does not like the generosities of Saumarez very much'.[45]

By contrast, von Rosen was receiving yet more complaints from Ranchoup

---

* Admiral Durham, on the Downs station, would have been operating on the North Sea coasts.

which he forwarded to Engeström, adding, 'from this correspondence you will see what a scoundrel he is and what a burden it is for me to have to deal with such a character'.[46] There is no doubt that both Ranchoup and his superior Alquier damaged the French cause quite seriously by the personal antagonism that their arrogance and lack of courtesy aroused in the Swedes with whom they had dealings, including even the Francophile party which had included many members of the nobility. Coquelle believed that Alquier was so irritated by the Swedish deceit over the 'Blocus' (the French name for the Continental System) that he forgot to be diplomatic. Alquier had also been so impoverished by his sudden forced flights from Naples and Rome that, with only Fr. 9,000 income, he could not carry the style of the representative of a great nation. He held no dinners, kept only one carriage and had a bad reputation for paying.[47]

One of Alquier's complaints was about General Tawast's visit to *Victory* in May. He said that the English consul had been present at the meeting and had signed a contract to provision the English fleet: 'he promised him six hundred cattle, of which one hundred and fifty have been delivered already.' He went on to complain of Consul Smith still living in Gothenburg, of 300 ships, mostly English, gathered off Wingo, of the convoys that came and went between England and Sweden, and of the supplies delivered from Sweden to the English base on Anholt.[48]

Engeström took this up with von Rosen who was able to maintain that it was 'entirely untrue that General Tawast went with Consul Schmidt to the English fleet. Only my nephew, who sailed the sloop, went along on that trip'; he had come aboard *Victory* under a flag of truce soon after Saumarez' arrival in May 1811 and later offered his services as a spy.[49] This enabled von Rosen to avoid answering all the other points, which were indeed true, and to point out, in contrast, that 'Admiral Saumarez has this week captured 2 Swedish ketches and 5 larger inshore boats because they carried merchandise from Norway to Denmark' – to show that he was being hostile towards Sweden. Von Rosen did not expect Engeström to pass on to Alquier his other piece of information: that Saumarez had privately let him know 'that if we wish them [the ships] back, they would be delivered against some reimbursement for the prize masters'. He added that Saumarez had now started to get supplies from Jutland and prayed that this would develop so that 'we could be spared from being the suppliers' and thereby avoid French criticism.[50] A week later von Rosen confiscated 10 oxen which were bound for the fleet and asked that this might appear in the papers, 'so that I, poor sinner, may for once shine with continental acclaim in the annals of Europe'. He had warned Saumarez in advance so he would not be upset.[51]

Alquier's complaint of 20 July 1811 had gone on to say that Sweden was not keeping to her agreements and could not at the same time be a friend of both France and England or the Swedish government would ' find itself in the situation that produced the disaster of the last Gustav'.[52] Engeström answered the detailed points but refused to show Alquier's letter to Bernadotte. He admitted some guilt and said the guilty would be punished, but wanted clearer proof than Alquier had bothered to obtain. In August, von Rosen commented to Ehrenström that Ranchoup

> is very unfavourably disposed towards me, in which I from my heart highly reciprocate, but such private considerations have to be removed for the common good. If the English capture your carriage coming from Russia, Admiral Saumarez will certainly have pleasure in getting it back. God grant that our great allies had as little greed as he and half as much good faith.[53]

10

Diplomatic Intrigues
Napoleon's Fateful Decision

In the winter of 1811/12 relations with France were at breaking point. Princess Desirée had returned to France, which might have improved relations since she was so unpopular, but it represented a further breaking of Bernadotte's bonds with his native country. Coquelle, however, maintains that her influence on Bernadotte was favourable to Napoleon and that he 'was still entirely behind his former master'.[1] These views appear to be too much based on the reports of Alquier who had evidently misread the situation, unlike Saumarez. A more recent biographer, Christian Bazin, also maintains that until 1812, Bernadotte 'was cautiously pro-French' and that 'in Paris Charles Jean was seen as a French viceroy'.[2] On the other hand, Vandal, writing in the 1890s, believed that 'he showed himself more occupied with building up a cheap popularity than with establishing his influence in the royal counsels' – that he missed the opportunity to give Sweden strong leadership, lacking because of the near senility of Charles XIII, and left decisions to a duumvirate of Engeström and Adlercreutz, who themselves lacked any authority.[3] It is a measure of how successfully Bernadotte had dissimulated, if we are to believe the evidence of the von Rosen letters.

In theory, the French position was strong. Despite the rumblings of discontent and future warfare, Russia was still her ally and was placed within easy range of Stockholm from her newly conquered Grand Duchy of Finland. The British fleet with its deep draught ships of the line would be unable to prevent an invasion launched by the extensive Russian *skärgård* fleet of gunboats through the intricate archipelago of the Åland Islands that closed off the southern end of the Gulf of Bothnia. Denmark remained firmly true to her alliance with France despite British destruction of her trade and disruption of the physical links with Norway, which was suffering from starvation as a result.[4] She had so far proved hesitant to allow French troops access to Zealand in any number, but was in no position to resist possible French insistence on using her as a springboard for an invasion of Scania, the former Danish province of southern Sweden. And Swedish Pomerania was wholly at the mercy of the surrounding French troops, as was confirmed when Marshal Davout met no resistance when he invaded in January 1812.

Napoleon's multinational force of troops occupied the whole of the north German Baltic coast from the Russian frontier to the Danish frontier in Holstein. Since France controlled all the ports, the prevention of entry of British manufactures and colonial goods should have been fully possible. There was also a further line of customs posts set up on land.[5] This was supposed to be supported by the Prussians on the barriers of the three great rivers, the Vistula, the Oder and the Elbe.[6] But we have already seen how commercial pressures and corruption made great holes in these controls, and as von Rosen had rightly commented, Russia was as guilty as any of France's allies of failing to implement the Continental System. This was why convoys of reputedly neutral ships continued to flow into the Baltic under the guiding and guarding hand of the British navy.

On the other side of the coin, maintaining French imports of the raw materials or manufactures that France herself could not produce when the British were preventing supply by sea, was a still harder problem. Napoleon spoke in 1810 of creating 'a canal which will be executed within five years and will join the Baltic to the Seine'. Two years later, in January 1812, he proposed a lock-free canal to connect Cuxhaven on the Elbe with the Weser at Bremerlehe and from there to Delfzyl,* protected by a fort like the one at Den Helder: 'Of all connections from the Baltic to the Rhine, the best, shortest, and most economical is the sea. But the sea being closed by superior forces, there comes the idea and the necessity of an interior connection'.[7] But this was for the long term. For the present, he was dependent on sneaking what could escape Saumarez' cruisers through to Kiel and then by the Holstein canal to Tonningen, where they still had a perilous journey on the edge of the North Sea to reach France. Customs receipts fell from Fr. 51 million in 1806 to 11.5 million in 1809.[8]

French exports to countries outside Europe, especially since she had lost most of her colonies, were similarly hard hit. The Napoleonic regime gave priority to foreign policy at the expense of trade – leaving the ports and their hinterland suffering.[9] Napoleon's hope was that the whole of Europe was now a land market where French products could replace the banned British ones. To assist this, he applied heavy duties on other European manufactures and insisted on lower tariffs on French goods so that France could compete, making the real victims of the Continental System the domestic industries in those countries now subject to France.[10] From 1806 onwards the import of textiles, especially Italian silk, was prohibited other than to France. Even so, figures for Italian silk exports to Germany and Switzerland (neither of which had a silk industry, but re-exported the raw material to England) still exceeded those to France in 1812.[11]

---

* A line followed by the present Ems–Jade Kanal.

As for the possibility of France taking England's place for imports into Russia, Savary, the French Ambassador in St Petersburg after Tilsit, commented:

> If we cannot receive special privileges we will not have any trade here. Frankly speaking, at present I consider it impossible to bring the Russian trade under French influence. What is more, I fear that if measures are taken against England, the Emperor Alexander will have to take severe measures to silence the dissatisfied.[12]

On the English side, Saumarez controlled the sea. His military task now was almost entirely the control and protection of trade – escorting convoys, especially through the Great Belt against Danish gunboats, chasing privateers, and taking as prizes enemy merchant shipping endeavouring to break the blockade and neutral ships that avoided or abused the system of licensing. This was largely carried out by a substantial fleet of gun brigs and other small cruisers. There remained, however, the potential threat of carrying out an attack on a Swedish or Russian port, as at Copenhagen in 1807. Early in the Carlshamn Cargoes affair, Saumarez had asked for two bomb ships to be made available. In fact, Gothenburg, Stockholm and Cronstadt would have been extremely difficult to take without a substantial force of troops and artillery. It is often overlooked that the navy played little part in the close attack on Copenhagen in 1807. Saumarez, if the 'Strategic Situation' report of 1809 is correctly attributed to him,* had believed then that Karlskrona could be taken by a purely naval assault, but by 1811 its defences had been considerably improved and the use of three of the sequestered merchant ships as blockships would have made it much harder to attack. Reval (Tallinn) would have been easier to bombard thanks to the wide nature of its bay, which is one reason why its governor in 1801 found the presence of Nelson's fleet undesirable and requested him to leave since the Russian fleet was absent at Cronstadt.[13] But casualties would have been very high, as at Algeciras, if an attack was made without army support when the Russian fleet was there: all the available British troops were fully committed in Spain. We have already seen the difficulties of an attack at Rogervick. A British naval assault was thus extremely unlikely to be anything much more than a token.

Saumarez' real power, therefore, came from his mercantile control and its impact on the Swedish economy. Since Sweden was at least nominally at war with England, her merchant fleet was potentially liable to capture. As Bernadotte had pointed out to Napoleon, she depended on the fleet for her exports of iron to America and her imports of salt for herself, as well as for corn when her own crop failed, and a mass of timber exports and naval materials to pay

*   See pp. 86–88.

for colonial goods and manufactures that she could not produce herself. Fortunately for her, England was as keen as Sweden to maintain this trade for the sake of her own economy and the money to fight the war. More susceptible to pressure was the Swedish coasting trade, for seaborne communications were so much cheaper and quicker than road. Wellesley's order in May 1810 not to permit any coasting trade between ports from which British ships were excluded (thereby including all Swedish ports) unless ships had a British licence for that voyage threw von Rosen into dismay: 'all business here will be destroyed.'[14] Saumarez' procrastination in implementing that order, leading to Wellesley countermanding it a month later, won him enormous support with both the Swedish government and its officers, and the merchant community. It also meant his forgoing the opportunity for a colossal sum in prize money for himself, and his officers and men, something that many other admirals might have been reluctant to sacrifice.

The weakness in his situation came primarily not from military action. The Danish gunboats and French and Danish privateers were a constant but relatively minor danger, and the convoy system and cruiser vigilance kept the losses to a low level. The Russian fleet was extremely unlikely to emerge from Cronstadt for both political and military reasons, nor would the Swedish fleet sortie from Karlskrona, and there were no longer Danish ships of the line, although two of the ships in the Scheldt fleet were manned and officered by Norwegian conscripts.[15] The only threat would come from a sortie of the Scheldt fleet should it escape the blockading squadron of the North Sea fleet and endeavour to reach Copenhagen – a danger of which the Admiralty continued to be nervous as late as the autumn of 1811. Saumarez' chief concern was the supply of water, wood and (ideally) fresh provisions. Wood in an area as well forested as the Baltic would not be a problem, but water would be a major worry without the cooperation of the Swedes. Anholt had a small supply for local needs, but the islands off Gothenburg were largely barren. His basic supplies were brought out from Great Yarmouth by victuallers: the substantial amounts can be seen in his orders to the Victualling Office for three-monthly requirements:[16]

Bread	896,000 lbs	Sugar	51,000 lbs
Wine	39,667 galls	Cocoa for Cheese	38,250 "
Spirits	39,667 "	Vinegar	4,250 galls
Beef	8,500 pieces of 8 lbs	Tobacco	34,000 lbs
Flour	204,000 lbs	Lemon Juice	59,500 "
Raisins	34,000 "	Sugar for do.	59,500 "
Suet	17,000 "	Coals (Chaldrons)	264
Pork	68,000 "	Candles	1,586 doz
Oatmeal	2,125 "	Pease (Bushels)	4,250
Do. for Butter	76,500 "		

Off Wingo, they were 'constantly supplied with the finest fish – Salmon, Turbot & Cod', but not, to their surprise, at Nargan Island in the Gulf of Finland; they did add 'three fine sheep' there to their stock and plenty of poultry. The packets 'usually bring out pease and other vegetables which although not in their prime are acceptable' and 'the Officers have shot abundance of partridges, hares and other game', some of which found their way to Saumarez' table. 'We have had for some time plenty of fine mackerel which we all find a great recreation'. Dumaresq and other captains allowed their officers to cultivate salad crops on the islands, but the flagship's crop of peas was stolen by one of the other ships; Saumarez had hoped it would accompany a haunch of venison sent by a Guernsey friend.[17] A turtle from there also reached him alive and well in the *Gorgon* hospital ship, but much more welcome was the Guernsey cow which after endless delays reached him in the same ship in mid-June 1811: 'the Cow has been these three weeks enjoying the green pastures and the milk is in consequence highly improved'.[18]

The other danger of positive hostile action on the part of the Swedes would be the lack of a convenient convoy assembly anchorage for putting together the return convoys from the Baltic. It was provided over the years 1810–12 by the island of Hanö off Carlshamn; this was only just off the coast of Blekinge and would have been impossible to defend once naval protection was unavailable in the winter. It would have been necessary instead to capture Bornholm and the Eartholms, which were not well suited for the numbers of ships that would be involved, or to consider the larger island of Gotland further up the Baltic. This would have demanded a considerable number of troops both to capture and to defend, as the Russians had discovered in their abortive brief capture of it in 1808.[19] Another possibility was the island of Rügen, off Stralsund in Swedish Pomerania, where the King's German Legion had briefly been stationed in 1807, under Lord Cathcart, before being moved to attack Copenhagen under his leadership. But that too would have been difficult to defend in the winter months, lacking the presence of the British fleet because of ice.

The story of the island of Hanö and its British base is curious.[20] The French remained in doubt of the existence of the base. General Tibell, a Swede who had served in the Cisalpine Republic for some years, had returned home to Sweden in 1811 and was an acquaintance of Alquier. Bernadotte asked him to investigate the stories of Anglo-Swedish connections. He went to Carlshamn, but was prevented from going further along the coast by Swedish hussars, 'because of an epidemic'. He pretended to be a doctor acting for the King and found the English camp on Hanö, with over 2,000 men and several men-of-war, as well as a forest of masts of merchant ships. He told Alquier on his return, who rushed to report it to Napoleon. It was confirmed by Danish reports and a Prussian officer, but when Cabré, Secretary of the French Legation in Stockholm, went there he could find nothing. Tibell went back to France on family business. On

Figure 10. Map of the Blekinge coastline: Bornholm, Christiansø, and Hanö Bay (Phillip Judge, Cartographer)

his return to Sweden he was arrested, but begged for forgiveness, saying that he had fooled Alquier and there was no English camp. Coquelle believed this: 'there was no English camp on the Swedish coast and Tibell, probably at the instigation of the Danish minister, had misled the French minister.'[21]

The British settlement was perfectly well known to Bernadotte and the Swedish authorities. They had issued an order in May 1811, forbidding any strangers to go into the neighbourhood of Carlshamn, in order to conceal any contacts between the British fleet and the shore. George Foy was asked by Engeström in November that year to find out from Saumarez how long

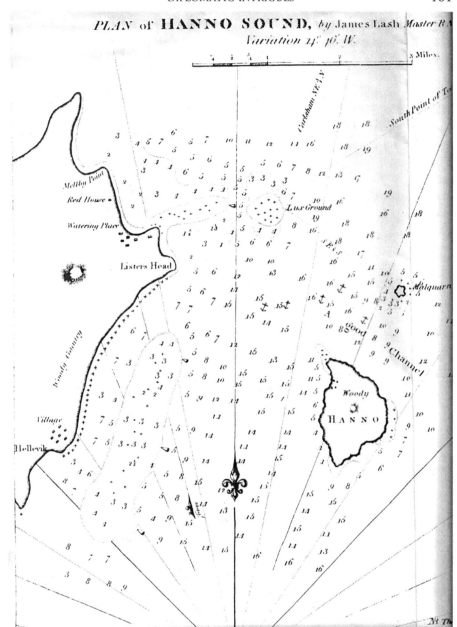

Figure 11. Chart of Hanö Convoy Assembly Anchorage by James Lash, Master R.N, 1809 (in possession of author)

he proposed keeping any part of his fleet at Hanö or in that neighbourhood since numerous business agents wanted to go there to deal with their personal affairs.[22] Not only was there an English camp on the island, but they had put up buildings with the help of local stonemasons, including a slaughterhouse to deal with the supplies of cattle they bought to feed the fleet. They had dug a well for water supplies to avoid having to go to Nogersund on the mainland for this. Contact with the authorities was through a local man from Carlshamn, Duvell, who also dealt with the distribution of licences to masters of ships trading with Swedish Pomerania on the other side of the Baltic. He was under strict instructions from Krusenstjerna, commanding the Swedish fleet at Karlskrona, to be careful over his contacts with the British so as to avoid Danish suspicions over Swedish policy.[23] As we have already seen in his letter complaining about the Marstrand and *Wagram* incidents, Krusenstjerna was extremely well disposed towards Saumarez.

By contrast, Alquier made himself so unpopular in Stockholm by his hostile note over the same *Wagram* incident that the pro-French party there blamed him for the ending of Napoleon's idea of a union between France and Sweden. General de Suremain, in his memoirs, records a conversation with Charles XIII (transcribed literally, he claims):

> 'What do you think', he said to me one day, 'of this villain Alquier, who wants to play the Roman consul here?' I recognised this expression as belonging to the Crown Prince and replied: 'I do not think the emperor could have made a worse choice if he wanted to get himself liked'. 'Alquier', he continued, 'is determined to find fault with us and does so in a manner that is insupportable. Even Engeström, who used to be fully pro-Bonaparte, begins to change his mind. As a result, the Prince's opinion, and it is mine too, is not to let ourselves be led by the nose. The sea stands between France and us; it's a good ally.'[24]

It is interesting that, despite the effects of his stroke and the failings of senility that Bazin, in particular, attributes to him, the old king could have the ability to assess a situation quite shrewdly, in the same way as one can see in the letters of his fellow-monarch, George III, outside his periods of illness. It is clear, too, that Bernadotte knew where the future of Sweden should lie. Two months later, on 2 November 1811, Alquier was appointed by Napoleon to a similar post at Copenhagen and left without the courtesy of leave-taking.[25]

Von Rosen in October had reported a visit to Gothenburg by Cabré. He described him as a '*Chevalier de bonne humeur* ... Schmidt says he has never liked a Frenchman as well as this one, so if he were to stay for long, he would surely be made a member of the Bachelors' Club'. Ranchoup had kept out of the way by staying in the carriage during the meeting. Von Rosen feared Cabré would return to Stockholm with too much information as he had never met a worse man for ferreting around. This makes it surprising that he was so deceived over Hanö. Von Rosen suspected that the French might be thinking of sneaking in some gun sloops at Vinga when the English fleet had sailed. Franco-Swedish relations might have been very different if Cabré had been in the place of Alquier.[26]

Sweden lay uncomfortably between the three great powers of Russia, France and Britain. She had just lost a series of military engagements which had drained her of men, equipment and money. One-third of her population had gone in the surrender of Finland to Russia. She depended for survival on her trade, which would disappear instantly if she took positive action against Britain, from whom she also hoped to receive assistance in acquiring Norway as compensation for the loss of Finland. Yet she knew that either France or Russia could invade at will and reduce her size and importance still further by carving off Scania, Swedish Pomerania or further parts of North Bothnia at the head of the Gulf of Bothnia, to their ally Denmark, Prussia or Russia's new Grand Duchy of Finland respectively. The only card that she held in addition to her usefulness to the British fleet and as a clandestine entrepôt for British and colonial goods was her possible role in the event of war between France and Russia, which everyone knew was likely to take place at some time, probably quite soon. If Russia could rely on Swedish neutrality or even her support, it would release for service against the French all the troops that otherwise were needed to be kept for the defence of Finland and St Petersburg from possible Swedish attack. For that same reason, France was ready to buoy up Swedish hopes of regaining Finland with French assistance as an incentive to stay loyal to France. Neither France nor Russia would therefore welcome the other taking possession of Sweden.

How did Bernadotte deal with this complex situation? He was himself a complex man. He had worked his way up from the ranks. Napoleon, in a letter to the Directory in 1796, introduced him as:

> this excellent general who made his reputation on the banks of the Rhine and is today one of the officers who contribute most to the fame of the Army of Italy ... You see in Gen. Bernadotte one of the foremost champions of the Republic, one whose principles and character make it impossible that he should sacrifice the cause of liberty or the ties of honour.[27]

Fifteen years later, writing to Metternich, he expressed a rather different view, damning him as a Jacobin unfit for kingship,* but by then there had been too many confrontations between them and he was making a political point. An earlier remark by Sieyes, member of the Directory, who disliked Bernadotte's

* See p. 111 above.

cult of popularity, also tried to cut him down to size: 'There goes a thrush that thinks itself an eagle'.[28]

There is no doubt from Bernadotte's career in the army that he was an outstanding military leader, capable by his own personal inspiration and example, as at Wagram in July 1809, of rallying troops that had been put to flight. But he then infuriated Napoleon by issuing a typically Gascon vainglorious Order of the Day, drawing the latter's unreasonable, incorrect, but understandable response in a letter to the Minister of War: 'He is a worn-out man who seeks money and pleasure but does not want to pay for them with the dangers and fatigue of war.'[29] Bernadotte was quick to adapt and quick to learn. Palmer records how at dinner in 1796 he was cross-examined by Napoleon on military science and thereafter spent much more time studying. He had the ability to charm, too, and used it to great effect on his arrival in the Swedish court which might well have been hostile or supercilious towards someone so far removed from royal circles. But Queen Hedvig-Charlotte, wife of Charles XIII, having initially been hostile, wrote in her diary after the formal audience: 'The Prince is splendid; he is big, holds himself well and has a presence so noble and so dignified that he appears born into the rank that he now occupies'.[30]

Bernadotte, by his manner, presence and words, won over all levels of Swedes, including Gustav Armfeldt, an old supporter of Gustav III and violently anti-French. Even the noble friends of Fersen succumbed and the reputation of Fersen himself was restored posthumously at the insistence of Bernadotte over Charles XIII's doubts.[31] Byam Martin too, no lover either of the French or the Swedes, was amazed on his return to the station in May 1812 at how well Bernadotte had captivated his new countrymen: 'It is quite astonishing how Bernadotte has contrived to make himself so popular amongst all classes of the Swedes: they absolutely idolise him'.[32] On the other hand his wife, Desirée, who finally arrived in December 1810, had not hesitated to show her distaste for Sweden and bemoan her absence from France. In June 1811, she had returned to France, seizing the excuse of her sister's move to Spain to be with her husband King Joseph, to everyone's annoyance, including Napoleon's. Bernadotte also lost his military aides who were recalled by Napoleon. His failure to learn Swedish was one evident shortcoming, leading to a reduced circle of close contacts, but perhaps that helped him to see more clearly the way that Sweden needed to go.[33]

It seems strange that such an interesting man, founder of the oldest present reigning house in Europe, should have had so little written about him, especially about his time in Sweden where he reigned from 1818 till his death in 1844 and had effectively been regent for the eight years before becoming King. It may be that his progression from Jacobin revolutionary to ultra-conservative monarch has not been welcomed in such a social democrat stronghold as Sweden. It seems also that military history has no great public following in

*Figure 12. King Karl XIV Johan of Sweden (by kind permission of James Perkins of Aynhoe Park)** *

that peace-loving country. It is perhaps understandable that for French historians, as for most British, the Baltic is considered, rightly or wrongly, to be a fringe area that did not greatly influence the mainstream of European affairs in those times.

Christian Bazin's biography of Bernadotte, published in 2000, quotes a number of letters, but there are no references, save a general mention in the bibliography of the 'Archives Royales Bernadotte' in Riksarkivet in Stockholm.[34] He writes with great élan and enthusiasm and makes some interesting points, but it is difficult to evaluate their soundness. Bazin suggests that Bernadotte was susceptible to flattery, but the Crown Prince seems to have kept too level

* The bust by 'A follower of Frederik Westin' (undated) was cut at some time from the original full-length portrait given by Bernadotte to Saumarez after a long delay in 1834. It has been restored for the purchaser at the Shrubland sale in September, 2006, who acquired with it the rest of the canvas from which it had been cut.

a head and shown too much skill in the tightrope walking that was forced on him by circumstances for this to be a serious weakness.

By summer 1811, the rumblings of war between Russia and France were growing louder. Initially, Saumarez had been dubious, unconvinced by the wishful thinking that had been prevalent in England even in the days of Canning as Foreign Secretary:

> If I was to believe the accounts brought by different Passengers from England, war between Russia and France will soon take place – but I am concerned to say the Letters I receive from the Continent by no means state it so positively – altho' preparations are making in Russia for such an event.[35]

But by September, he had changed his mind, writing to Martha:

> There seems little doubt but that next Year we shall have a friendly power in Russia – it is very probable that by that time, if not even earlier, she will be engaged in a contest with France – the result of which must be always doubtful. Sweden is also menaced with an Attack but as it must be by conveying Troops over Zealand it may be some time before that can be effected. It is no small satisfaction to me that the expectation I always held out of the friendly disposition of the government has been strictly fulfilled. What they may be hereafter drawn to, I cannot be answerable.[36]

The same day, the Admiralty received Wellesley's commands in the name of the Prince Regent to instruct Saumarez 'to afford every practicable aid to the Prussian government or any of its officers in resisting the power of France'. Intelligence had been received that war was probably imminent between them. But Saumarez was warned that no action should 'precede the actual commencement of hostilities' and the Admiralty stressed that he should not commit ships to stay in the area beyond the safe period of navigation.[37] A consignment of arms and powder was despatched in transports in case it would be of use to Prussia. This was in response to a plea from Colonel Gneisenau, one of the leaders of the resistance to France, that they needed arms and ammunition.[38] No definite destination was given, beyond a suggestion that Colberg, considered to be a fortress that the Prussians would be able to defend against French attack, might be the best place when the time was right.

One of many indications of French preparations for a spring attack was a note from Napoleon to General Lacuée asking whether he could get three million bottles of wine and half a million pints of brandy to Danzig for the army, either from Bordeaux with English licences, or in winter via Lubeck and the Baltic.[39] Foy, in a long letter setting out the pros and cons of the Carlshamn deal, stressed that Sweden was in no position economically to engage in any form of warfare. Despite French encouragement to her to endeavour to regain Finland from the Russians, she was resolved on strict neutrality. This would help Russia, enabling her to free the forces which would otherwise have had to be stationed in Finland.[40]

Napoleon still instructed Champagny in April 1811 to inform Alexander how he had told the French Chamber of Commerce he knew all about the huge convoy about to sail for the Baltic and that all the merchandise would be confiscated wherever it arrived, 'in Prussia, or even in Russia', since Alexander had agreed that the war with England must continue as the only way of maintaining peace on the continent. If they did not dissociate themselves from all commercial connection with England, they would lose everything. Even if the smugglers continued to try to find ways to get through and spin their web of deceit, 'I will cut through their conspiracy with my sword if necessary; so far I have been indulgent, but this year I have decided to be rigorous against those who make contreband their business'.[41] In another letter, three days later, he stated he would not declare war on Russia unless she wanted something more than the left bank of the Danube or, tearing up the Treaty of Tilsit, she made peace with England.[42]

To complicate the situation further, the failure of the Swedish harvest led to an urgent need for them to import some of the surplus corn lying at Riga and Liebau (Liepaja). Saumarez had sought authority from the Board of Trade via the Admiralty to allow Swedish ships to be given licences for this purpose and had stipulated that these licences should bear no fees. In addition, he allowed licences for Swedish ships as a humanitarian act to take building materials to the town of Königsberg (Kaliningrad) in Prussia which had suffered a disastrous fire, not uncommon in northern towns that were largely built of wood. The fire had also destroyed substantial stocks of rye and other corn. On 26 September, the Admiralty sent approval for the Swedish government to import grain from Riga and Liebau, and even to clear out with Liverpool salt, of which there was currently a surplus in Sweden, in lieu of ballast. The salt could be sold in Prussia to make the trips more economic.[43]

Thornton, the former minister to Sweden, then made his reappearance. The hopes of a Russian break with France had made the chances of a renewal of the old Anglo-Russian alliance come alive. Wellesley, in a letter to the Prince Regent as early as August 1811, 'had been wondering whether power should be given to Sir James Saumarez or to anyone else to sign preliminaries of peace with Russia' and Perceval, as Prime Minister, had agreed, only suggesting that it might be betraying too much eagerness on their part.[44] Perhaps because of this, the plan was not progressed. It is a measure of how far Saumarez had advanced in government esteem that he should be the first name that was proposed. Less than three years before, he had been officially rebuked for meddling in matters outside his scope by his letter to the Czar.

Instead, in great secrecy, Thornton was sent to enter into negotiations with both Sweden and Russia. He arrived on 17 October, having nearly been lost when his ship went on the rocks north of Wingo, having lost her bearings, and was only saved by hearing the *Victory*'s morning gun. The flagship's boats were sent to the rescue. Saumarez told Martha that he was happy to have Thornton on board and 'I wish his Mission may prove successful, but at present I form no great opinion of it'.[45] After several unsuccessful attempts to get him ashore unnoticed, he was smuggled into the Elvsborg fortress at the entrance to Gothenburg as the servant of John Ross, whose knowledge of Swedish enabled him to pass as a Swedish officer. As Ross put it, 'it was determined to keep up the appearance of war without committing any act of hostility on either side'.[46] Thornton's first actual interview ashore was eight days later.[47]

He and von Rosen had an informal meeting since Thornton was only authorised to deliver the official dispatches to Netzel, the person deputed by the Russian government, but because of its informal nature they were able to speak more freely. Von Rosen came to the conclusion that England wanted closer relations with Sweden and was not as worried as he thought about Carlshamn. The main subject was Sweden's hoped-for acquisition of Norway and Thornton appeared supportive of this. However, he seemed to von Rosen taciturn and, unlike Saumarez, 'the sort of person from whom one should ask the impossible to get something reasonable'. He was travelling as an American merchant under the name Ebenezer Thompson, but despite the attempts to preserve secrecy, the word was soon out that a so-called American was having conferences with a Swedish government official and that there would soon be peace with England.[48]

Thornton was also under instructions from Wellesley 'to negotiate and conclude that perplexing business of the Carlshamn cargoes',[49] although Barrow the previous month had sent Saumarez, by fast ship from Yarmouth, a letter from Culling Smith at the Board of Trade with the relevant papers on Carlshamn, which he was to make use of 'when the moment shall arise for your entering into discussion on the subject with the Swedish government'.[50] It was another mark of the government's growing preparedness to rely on Saumarez over matters normally outside the scope of a naval commander-in-chief. Wellesley, however, still preferred to keep such matters in Foreign Office hands. Thornton made little progress on an overall peace treaty since Sweden was not prepared to move openly until Russia's intentions had become much clearer; but he was evidently more successful over the cargoes. On 11 December 1811, Croker sent Saumarez a copy of a letter from Culling Smith 'stating that Mr. John Atkins and Mr. Isaac Adelbert are about to proceed to Sweden under instructions from the merchants and underwriters of this country upon the subject of the vessels and cargoes detained at Carlshamn and other Swedish Ports'. He was to give them 'every information and assistance in [his] power, in promoting the object of their enquiries, without making His Majesty's Government a Party to their transactions'.[51]

That final phrase indicated that the British government had seen sense and accepted the Swedish arguments that they should keep at arm's length to minimise French suspicions. These remained as strong as ever – justifiably. A note from Napoleon to Maret, Duc de Bassano, now French Foreign Minister, reads:

> I send you a report from a privateer. The same sounds come from all sides. It seems to me proper to demand conclusive explanations about this island.* Question my *chargé d'affaires* on what this is all about. Let him know that, if Sweden should effectively let the English establish themselves on this island, this would be the equivalent of a rupture and, in that case, he should quit Stockholm immediately with his legation.[52]

Foy reported that

> the French party, as I intimated in a former letter, is rapidly in the decline here. Mons. Alquier, the French Minister, was to leave Stockholm today. This may perhaps be more owing to personal pique than to political differences between the two Governments, but I have good authority to say that the Swedish Government [is] gradually recovering its strength and seeing now more clearly who may & who are really inclined to befriend it (to which conviction your Excellency's humane and friendly command in these seas has so conspicuously contributed). The period of French influence is drawing to a close. This may appear extraordinary with a Ruler here of French extraction, but we have daily proofs of his sacrificing all other considerations to the benefit and tranquillity of Sweden.[53]

This was confirmed by Fenwick, reporting that Alquier had crossed from Hälsingborg to Elsinore, to take up the position of French Minister to Denmark, without the usual ceremony of taking leave of the court. Bernadotte had given 'a very peremptory and spirited refusal' to his demand that a cargo of colonial produce seized at Stralsund in Swedish Pomerania should either be burnt or the proceeds of its sale at auction be paid into Napoleon's treasury. Fenwick confirmed that French influence was declining and that 'It is not to be wondered that M. Alquier has left Sweden in bad humour for it is the only country from which he has gone without effecting its ruin'.[54]

Ranchoup also returned to Paris about the same time and did not leave any public substitute.[55] Foy's comments about Saumarez' 'humane and friendly command' were not mere flattery, but a measure of the impact that the difference between his approach and Alquier's arrogance had had on the diplomatic

---

* Fotö, just north of Wingo, which had become virtually a British base (see p. 108). It is interesting that it is Fotö rather than Hanö that is mentioned despite Napoleon's reported fury at Tibell's report.

situation. Coquelle has noted a similar contrast between Alquier and the Russian envoy, Colonel Tzerenicheff: 'France's man stiff, almost abrupt, condescending and demanding the impossible; he of Russia, elegant, hinting and suggesting, flattering the self-esteem of the Crown Prince, not seeking anything that Sweden's economic situation would not permit.'[56]

Saumarez must have been pleased to receive a brief note from Sir Richard Bickerton, now one of the naval Lords of the Admiralty, saying 'Your measures respecting Sweden seem to have been dictated by the soundest policy and must be approved'.[57] It was an acknowledgement that his personal impact on the determination of British policy and its successful outcome was acknowledged and appreciated. However, there was still some time before the Carlshamn Cargoes affair was to be closed. It was not till May 1812 that the Clerk to the Privy Council wrote to Culling Smith's successor at the Board of Trade, Edward Cooke, 'their lordships see no objection to Sir James Saumarez's being authorized to permit vessels bearing any flag except the French to export from Carlshamn the cargoes which have been condemned there'. He had to be satisfied that the cargoes were the condemned ones and that permits should cease after the first day of August.[58]

As to the attacks on the convoys, Consul Fenwick had been anxious at the beginning of the 1811 season that the Danes had fitted out 'more than double the number of privateers that they had at sea last season'. A number of fishing boats had been bought for this purpose from along the Swedish coast as well as in Zealand.[59] But the convoy system worked so well that they had few successes. Watts, captain of the *Woodlark* off Rostock, asked for a move to a less inactive station as he had only seen one Danish privateer in a month.[60] There were still a few French ones active, mostly fairly small. Von Rosen's nephew, Count Ernst Robert von Rosen, who had volunteered his services as a source of intelligence 'which might cause our unworthy enemies any loss', reported three French privateers in the Sound on 2 September 1811.[61] These were capturing American ships as well as Swedish, leading to strong remonstrations by Erwing, American Minister in Copenhagen. It was even reported that two Danish coasters had been taken in Copenhagen Roads on the plea that they had a small quantity of coffee and sugar (colonial goods) on board.[62] In this confusing political scene, it is perhaps not so surprising that the French privateers were chased away by the gunboats of their allies the Danes, who then escorted the American ships to safety down the Sound.

On 5 October 1811, both Croker and Yorke wrote separately to Saumarez. The former's letter gave instructions that 'the last homeward bound convoy from Hanö Bay is on no account whatever to be delayed beyond the 1st of November', the original date agreed with the shippers' representative Emes in March of that year. The ships of the line, other than those allocated to convoy duty, were to proceed to Spithead, but it was left to Saumarez' discretion 'to make such a disposition of the frigates and smaller vessels under your orders as may appear to you most advantageous', with a view to assisting any of the Baltic powers that turned against France. This should include leaving two or three gunboats at Colberg if the governor there so desired and if the benefits warranted the risk, but stressing – with due Admiralty caution – that he should select those which were most suitable for the purpose 'but which at the same time, if any accident were to happen to them, would be of the least loss to the public service'.[63]

Yorke's letter was revealing in another way. He acknowledged receipt of Saumarez' letters of 1, 2, 6, 14, 18 and 28 September, thanking him for 'keeping me so well informed of what is passing within the limits of your command' but indicating what little response he himself had made.[64] This was a running complaint of Saumarez and not unfamiliar amongst other commanders-in-chief of stations which, although outside home waters, had a regular packet service or other potential source of communications. It was particularly true in the first two years on station when he was still feeling his way in a new political/diplomatic world. He expressed it frequently in his letters to Martha:

31.5.08, off Gothenburg. I am anxious to receive the dispatches I expect before I proceed from hence – notwithstanding our Friend [Bickerton]'s promise to convey letters by different opportunities, several have offered without my receiving a single line – no fewer than three Packets have arrived besides different Convoys but the Admiralty have not yet written by the former, although it is the best conveyance.

8.7.08, the Great Belt. the great inattention of the Adm[iral]ty in sending off their dispatches – the inconvenience of which I have strongly represented.

24.5.09, entrance to the Baltic. I wish I could speak as favourably of my public correspondents – but they pursue their former plan of leaving me without instructions in the present critical state of affairs and what is worse without sending the Force I was given to expect would have followed to join me – it almost appears that my departure from England was the Signal for them to discontinue their exertions. Before I left Gothenburg I wrote to them very fully on the subject and recapitulated the remonstrance in subsequent letters.

15.7.09, Nargan Island. it shows them [Sweden] well satisfied at the determination I took to support them without waiting for Orders from my Government ... Sir Richard B[ickerton] preserves his accustomed silence although I have written to him repeatedly.

11.6.10, off Karlskrona. I have not received a single line from our Brothers in Town – nor from Lord M[ulgrave] or Sir Richd. Bickerton. These two

last show the same reluctance as last year to take any share of responsibility
– although with the former particularly I am obliged to enter into private
communication relative to various points not connected with the Board.*

22.7.12, Wingo. *Les Messieurs de l'Amirauté* are as silent as usual and confine
themselves solely to the acknowledgement of my letters – the late events
[Napoleon's invasion of Russia] will probably draw something from them
soon.[65]

It is noticeable that by 1810 Saumarez had become much less concerned
with receiving instructions, since he had gained in confidence and was more
prepared than ever to act on his own initiative. In fact, he complained in June
1810: 'the orders I received were too explicit to admit any other interpretation
than that I gave them although it was with great reluctance I put them in force'.
By 1812, he was happy to write:

I am at present nearly passive – at the same time adopting such measures as
may tend to forward the general good cause, entirely I must add from my
own impulse – as the instructions which were held out to be sent after me
are [not] yet forthcoming, and everything is just as when I left Town – I have
only the satisfaction to be informed that the measures I am pursuing receive
the approbation of Government.[66]

He was also quite prepared to reject Yorke's suggestion that Captain Fanshawe
would be 'a very proper officer to select for this service', if Saumarez decided
to leave gunboats at Colberg over the winter of 1811/12. Fanshawe had
served in the Russian navy up to the age of 20, his father, General Robert
Fanshawe, serving in the Russian army; the son was presently serving in the
Baltic as commander of the 18-gun brig-sloop *Grasshopper*. His Russian experience and family connections appeared to make him, aged 33, eminently
suitable. However, the Commander-in-Chief's reply was: 'Permit me in confidence to observe that Captain Fanshawe appears by no means calculated to be
entrusted with a service of so much importance.' His proposal instead (which
was accepted) was that Captain Acklom of the *Ranger*, who had been on the
station four years and was one of the most able junior officers, should be given
this opportunity to shine.[67] One of the problems that Saumarez faced was that
on a healthy station with very little serious fighting, casualties (and therefore
vacancies) were few, giving little opportunity for him to advance his own men:
'I have an incredible number onboard whom I wish to promote but such is
the limited power of Commanders-in-Chief that few, very few opportunities
offer to advance even their own relations'.[68] In this respect, the Baltic command

---

*   A search of the Mulgrave archive at Normanby Castle failed to reveal what these private
matters were.

rated as a home station which limited the commander-in-chief's authority to promote. The unfortunate Fanshawe was in command of the *Grasshopper* two months later when in company with the *Hero* she was wrecked on the Haake Sand off the Texel. Most of the crew were saved but captured by the Dutch and Fanshawe spent the next three years in prison.[69]

Collingwood in the Mediterranean had similar problems over promotions. In March 1806, he wrote:

> Ever since the Action [Trafalgar] the Adm'ty seem to have cut off all correspondence with me and my fleet ... Not a promotion of any officer in the fleet here. The consequence is that the Senior Officers are in extreme dejection with vexation and disappointment, and the younger ones all desirous of getting home, where they may have a chance of promotion.[70]

He had the added disadvantage in the Mediterranean that 'now that all countries are alike inimical to us there is not a ship on the sea from which any information of the enemy can be collected'.[71] In theory, this should have been true also of the Baltic after Sweden's declaration of war in 1810, but a wide variety of sources continued to provide information to Saumarez, not only on maritime movements but on troop movements too over northern Europe and Russia, and political and diplomatic affairs. As late as November, one of his cruisers, the *Earnest*, had strict instructions to appear off Colberg 'at least once in six days to pick up any dispatches, usually conveyed out by fishermen to avoid suspicion'.[72] In fact, the Admiralty even looked to Saumarez to provide copies of French newspapers such as *Le Moniteur* since they were no longer able to obtain them closer at hand.[73] For his part, Napoleon had likewise instructed Savary, Minister of Police: 'to continue taking steps to ensure I receive all works printed in London, either on politics or current affairs. I draw very important revelations from them.'[74]

The Admiralty's anxieties in 1811 about the onset of winter, expressed in Croker's letter of October and equally felt by Saumarez, were to be borne out by a series of delays and accidents primarily the result of bad weather. The last homeward convoy was held up by nearly ten days of gales followed by light airs and did not finally get under way until 9 November, escorted by Admiral Reynolds in his flagship, *St George* (98). A week later, anchored off Nysted at the southern entrance to the Belt, a further 'furious gale' hit them, driving a large merchant ship athwart the *St George*'s hawse, parting her cable. She was blown into shoal water, lost her rudder and had to cut away her masts. Saumarez, at Wingo, feared for a time she was lost, but she managed to crawl there on 1 December under jury masts and with a makeshift 'Pakenham' rudder.* With

---

* For details, see Griffiths, *Observations on some Points of Seamanship*, p. 238.

the six escorts were 72 of the convoy that had sailed from Matvik, the small port near Hanö whose use the Swedes permitted in bad weather. About 30 of the ships were missing: 'of those some totally lost and others driven on shore on the island of Zealand. This has been an unfortunate season to the Trade from the tempestuous weather the greatest part of the season.'[75]

There was still the problem of the arms sent to the Baltic in case they were needed by the Prussians. Saumarez wrote to Martha:

> the injudicious measure for sending supplies to the Baltic at so late a season of the year, and in the uncertainty of their being required, or required at the present juncture – with the risk and danger to which the transports must be exposed causes me as thou wilt readily suppose no small embarrassment.[76]

An added difficulty was that the bar at Colberg was too shallow for the deeply laden transports, so that the arms would first have to be offloaded into barges, for which weather conditions would need to be right. Dashwood, senior officer now at Hanö, finally gave up on 29 November and sailed for Wingo the next morning, hoping that Saumarez would approve. He had not served long under Saumarez and was not yet fully aware of the degree of discretion that Saumarez gave to those under his command, providing they performed their duties capably.[77] Another rather hesitant private letter followed, hoping 'that my conduct, since I had the honour of being under your command, will meet your approbation. Believe me, I have done everything to the best of my poor judgement.'[78]

In fact, he had brought the transports and the remaining escorts in the Baltic back through the Sound since he considered it would be too dangerous through the Belt, and did this in a gale of wind on a lee shore, without local pilots but led by Captain Acklom in the *Ranger*. The succinct 'turnover'* note by Croker on the back of Admiral Hope's report to Saumarez was: 'Dashwood deserves approbation, Acklom to be promoted to post.'[79] Three of the merchant vessels were so damaged by the gale that they had to put into Landskrona where their papers were seized and sent to Stockholm; but according to Consul Fenwick orders came back that the masters were to be put 'in full possession of their ships with free liberty to proceed whenever they please ... the Swedish government does not consider the circumstance of joining convoy as subjecting ships to capture or detention'.[80]

Both fleet and convoy finally left Wingo on 17 December. But the worst was still to come. It had originally been proposed to leave the *St George* at Gothenburg over the winter. However, Admiral Reynolds was so insistent that she was 'as fit to make her passage with the assistance of another ship of the line as any

---

* The Secretary used to turn over the top right corner of a report to put a note of their Lordship's recommendations.

in the fleet' that Saumarez, after consulting with the ship's captain, gave way
to his entreaties. They were good friends. She was given two 74s, *Defence* and
Cressy, to escort her but it proved an unfortunate decision.[81] The weather was
still very unsettled and Saumarez ordered the convoy back. He was tempted to
return himself but *Victory's* sailing qualities were so good that she continued
with three of the 74s. *St George* pressed slowly on at about five knots. On
23 December yet another northwesterly gale blew up, putting her on a lee shore
and apparently unable to wear ship to clear the Horn Reef north of Esbjerg.
Captain Atkins of the *Defence* stayed by her, unable to help in the storm conditions but not willing to wear ship and escape without orders from Admiral
Reynolds. Captain Pater of the *Cressy* had offered to try to take the *St George*
in tow earlier, but by 2230, seeing no chance otherwise of clearing the land, he
wore ship and 'by carrying a press of sail' – impossible for the *St George* with
her jury masts – managed to escape. Both the other two ships were lost with
only 18 survivors.[82] Fenwick reported to Saumarez that King Frederik had given
orders that they should be treated with the utmost attention and humanity in
response to Saumarez' earlier treatment of Danish prisoners and that the Danes
were 'impressed with the highest personal respect towards you'.[83]

There is now a museum* on the Jutland coast with a mass of finds recovered
by divers from the two wrecks, including the original rudder, discovered quite
recently at its site in the Belt. The body of Admiral Reynolds was never found,
but that of Captain Atkins was. It was buried with military honours by the
Danes, and later taken to Anholt under a flag of truce and returned to Britain.
The convoy, hit by the same storm, was scattered and the *Hero* escorting a
group of 18 vessels was lost further south, off the Texel.[84] Over 2,000 men
were lost in total, the greatest number of Royal Navy officers and men on any
occasion during the wars. Ross relates that *Victory's* squadron reported their
noon positions on the 23rd, all of them showing well to the westward of that
of the flagship, by as much as 84 miles in one case. Saumarez characteristically
stuck to his own ship's reckoning, but for which, in Ross' view, they might
have suffered the same fate as *Hero* – a disaster that would have been even
greater than that of Shovell's fleet on the Scillies in 1704, especially with the
emotive loss of Nelson's flagship.[85] Saumarez had always been both competent
and confident as a navigator as his early passage between St Kitts and Nevis
showed; in more familiar waters off Guernsey, in the frigate *Crescent* in 1794,
he had made a similar escape from a squadron of four French frigates and a
sloop by sailing through a narrow passage between offshore rocks, on that occasion with a local pilot (see pp. 27–28). Despite Mahan's strictures (see p. 2),
his whole career bore witness that he never lacked nerve, whether it was his

---

*   Strandingsmuseum St George og Marinarkaeologist Center, Torsminde.

innovation of taking the Brest Inshore Squadron into Douarnenez Bay to ride out a westerly gale, his attack on the French squadron lying under the guns of Algeciras,or his readiness to attack the Russian fleet in Baltiski Port.*

On the diplomatic front, things had been moving slowly but with a certain degree of optimism. To preserve secrecy, Thornton had met the Russian commissioner Netzel at Åmål, a small town some distance north of Gothenburg and inland, on the edge of Lake Vänern. The secrecy was partially successful as it was only on 26 November that Foy wrote to request that, if the reports in the papers of Thornton's arrival were false, Saumarez could deny them for fear that they might stir up French activity.[86] But the choice of a small town for the meeting was unwise, for local gossip soon grew, hence the newspaper reports, and von Rosen reported that 'the travel of Mr. T from England seems not to have been kept as quiet as wished'. He assured Engeström 'that the gentleman at least passed here unnoticed, which cost me much trouble'.[87] The meeting was on 10 November, nearly four weeks after Thornton had arrived, and he agreed to wait a further six to eight days while Netzel got an answer from the Russian court. What encouraged him was Sweden's refusal of a French demand to allow her troops through to Norway in small groups – a recurring British anxiety. Saumarez' instructions from London regularly included an item covering the need to guard the Norwegian coast against such landings.[88] Thornton believed that the Swedish refusal might help precipitate her into war with France. In this he was not far wrong; a letter from Napoleon to Jerome, King of Westphalia, countermanded sending a present of horses to Bernadotte since Sweden was behaving badly and they might at any moment be at war.[89] Thornton was an experienced diplomat, well versed in the subtleties of diplomacy. He had written of Sweden to Canning in 1808:

> I ought to observe that if you have any statements or opinions to express, indirectly to this government, there is no way more simple than that of directing that the dispatch containing them should be sent by the public post of this county. If the examination of a Foreign Minister's correspondence has its disadvantages, it has also the advantage of enabling him to say to the government where he resideswhat he would not choose to say to themselves. Those who open letters must, like listeners, expect to find something said of themselves.[90]

---

*   See pp. 1, 2 and 29.

11

The Final Year

It seems clear that by the winter of 1811/12, there was little doubt on all sides that the long-threatened war between France and Russia would take place in the coming summer. Both France and Russia were beginning to accumulate forces near the frontier under various pretexts. The Russians sought to release their army of the Danube by a treaty with Turkey, which took place in May 1812, and were rather more assiduous and successful than France in their courtship of Sweden to protect their western flank and St Petersburg. A Swedish–Russian offensive/defensive alliance was formed in April that year.[1]

Through the winter the blockade of Norway was being enforced, leading to severe shortages of food and trading income. Three Swedish masters, whose ships had been chased by English cruisers, said that they were told that Saumarez' orders were that 'all ships of whatever nation shall be captured when approaching the Norwegian coast closer than 5 miles' and von Rosen suggested that this might be to put pressure on the Norwegians to look favourably on union with Sweden as a way out of their distress.[2] Denmark itself was suffering almost as much. Fenwick reported in May 1812 that:

> the poor can scarcely obtain food and the daily applications at the bakers shops are not only very tumultuous but the purchasers are obliged to fight their way to procure the bread … The suffering classes at Copenhagen attribute their misery to the French and do not hesitate to pour their maledictions on them as well as their King for obstinately adhering to their cause.[3]

Nonetheless, Frederick VI had sufficient control of the country to maintain its loyalty to Napoleon right through to January 1814, despite pressure from the allied powers to join them.

In reality, the Franco-Russian alliance had begun to turn sour very soon after it had been signed in 1807. At Erfurt in 1808, Alexander had slightly strengthened his position, encouraged by Talleyrand who, by then, was actively and treasonably working against Napoleon's policies simultaneously with being his special adviser in lieu of Champagny.[4] In January 1811, the Czar had hoped to bring men from the dismembered remnants of Poland into the balance on his side, by proposing a Grand Duchy of Poland on the lines of the new Grand

Duchy of Finland he had created.[5] By some rather optimistic calculations of military strengths, he thought he might have a front-line army of 230,000 with 100,000 in reserve, against a total for Napoleon of 155,000. He approached Prince Czartoryski, a Pole who had not long before been Russia's Foreign Minister; but neither Poles, Vienna nor Berlin were forthcoming in support and his plans for an attack through Germany dissolved. Threats that Napoleon might want to partition Prussia made it more likely that Gneisenau and his supporters there might lead an attempt to throw off the French yoke, but King Frederick William remembered the events of 1805 and 1806 too clearly. Hardenberg, the chancellor, was equally cautious although, having been born in Hanover, he was sympathetic towards Britain. Metternich and Austria, after the defeat of 1809, were extremely hesitant to offend Napoleon.[6] Without Russia, no one was likely to move. Wellesley's views echoing this were set out in his *Notes on the General State of Europe* to a junior diplomat on his way to Spain. In it he also expressed his distrust of Sweden:

> Bernadotte says that as he is now a true Swede, he naturally adopts all the true feelings and interests of his country, and is therefore hostile to the ambitious projects of Bonaparte. But his affectation is so gross and absurd that Lord Wellesley cannot persuade himself to give credit to Bernadotte's protestation.[7]

He ignored, or was not aware of, Bernadotte's own ambitions – that he saw himself as a successor to Napoleon as ruler of France. This became more evident after the French retreat from Russia and the advance of what became Allied armies in pursuit, a great part led by Bernadotte. To that end, French defeat in the short term was necessary, as was his own survival as the effective ruler of Sweden; but his links to the French people had to be maintained also.

The build up to the invasion was long and slow. The Russians by the Czar's ukase of 31 December 1810, had made clear their reluctance to observe in practice the terms of the Continental System.* In December 1811, Napoleon had asked his librarian to provide books on the topography of Russia and especially Lithuania, and details of Charles XII's campaigns there. Bassano, the new Foreign Minister, was ordered to recruit spies to report on roads and fortifications on various routes to St. Petersburg, Moscow and Grodno.[8] By January 1812, Napoleon was ordering Davout, as soon as he could be assured of seizing a large quantity of colonial goods there, to take possession of Swedish Pomerania: 'It is essential that you close all the crossings between Sweden and the Continent hermetically.' Only the Swedish couriers going to France were to be allowed to pass and the route through Denmark was to be similarly closed.[9]

---

*   See p. 122.

Jerome in Westphalia was instructed to prepare his army since the Russians had moved their forces from the Danube.[10] Thereafter, there was sabre-rattling by both sides, balanced by polite letters.

Both Coquelle and Bazin see the French invasion of Swedish Pomerania under Davout, in January 1812, as the moment that Bernadotte made up his mind to side with Russia rather than France and that Napoleon must have been aware that this would be the result. The fact that Davout and Bernadotte were old enemies, as a result of events at Jena and Auerstadt, will not have helped. It is probable that, just as London was hesitant to trust Bernadotte, so Paris felt that the Swedish foothold on the eastern side of the Baltic might provide a threat to the long lines of communication on the roads to Moscow and St Petersburg should Bernadotte forsake his old French loyalties. Coquelle suggests that Napoleon could not bear to depend for help on his former aide, his potential rival, and someone who had been at times a thorn in his flesh and had even married his former fiancée: 'personal feelings dictated this impolitic behaviour and here the head of state gave way to the man'. He argues that if someone other than Bernadotte had been crown prince, Napoleon's treatment of Sweden and the results of the Russian campaign would have been quite different.[11] Bazin quotes a letter from Bernadotte to Napoleon of 11 February 1812, but gives no source: 'Caring little for the glory and power that surround you, Sire, I am much more concerned not to be considered your vassal. Your Majesty commands the greater part of Europe, but his domination does not extend to the country to which I have been called.'[12]

Bazin maintains that Napoleon had believed for some time that Bernadotte would not succeed as a king: that he was no more than a good general. He goes on to argue that Napoleon, as a man of genius, had the power to create events whereas Bernadotte was a creature of circumstances: 'he is the child of destiny'. Nonetheless, he had the skill and intelligence to profit from circumstances, and in the end his was the dynasty that survived.[13] The successful French general, in becoming a Swedish prince, had become a man of peace, for he knew that peace in Europe was essential to Swedish survival – to the recovery of its economy through trade. In this, he found a sympathetic parallel in Saumarez, the successful fighting captain and admiral who now avoided using his naval strength and turned the war between them into a 'phoney war' to preserve that trade and Sweden's independence. Through force of circumstances they never met. Their channel of communication was von Rosen.

The latter's relationship with Saumarez had been put to the test by the Carl-shamn Cargoes affair and had come out of it strengthened. In June 1811 von Rosen had, on Bernadotte's instructions, had a meeting with Saumarez and, as we have seen, had agreed a basis for settling compensation for English property. It had been reported back to Stockholm and his measures were approved on 8 July. However, in September, von Rosen was concerned to receive a letter from Engeström saying that there was no English property in Swedish ports or else it would have been confiscated long since: this appeared to be a complete change of stance. Von Rosen begged that, if Saumarez had to be told of it, someone else would convey the message. He was, however, prepared out of patriotism to take the blame, even though it was not his. He wrote this: 'to an excellently patriotic and honest superior who attaches more value to proper frankness in his subordinates than a quiet acceptance of matters contradictory to their inner opinions'.[14] He was being unduly anxious since nothing more came of it and it is most likely that Engeström's letter once again was written to satisfy the French that nothing was going on between Sweden and Britain in this connection. But it demonstrates the bond that had built up between von Rosen and Saumarez.

As a result, Saumarez, with the persuasive voice of von Rosen singing in his ear and in much closer contact than London with Swedish affairs generally, through his various correspondents and connections there, made the correct judgement. Bernadotte and Sweden's interests were the same and they were both dependent on British success, but this must remain hidden until the military power of France became less dominant. In this, Wellington's victories in the Peninsula were beginning to have political significance. Part of Saumarez' role was to ensure that news of these broke through the French censorship. Almost as important as the gathering of information through the various agents like Johnson, Hahn/Drusina who died in 1810, and Baron von Dornberg, was the outflow of this propaganda.

Thornton was back on board *Victory* by 24 November, and was still there on 14 December, a westerly continuing to blow for the sixth week preventing his departure.[15] He had established a very happy relationship with Saumarez, dating back to his period on board the flagship off Rogervik in 1808 when they jointly discussed their respective letters to the Czar. They had conferred again on their mutual return to London when Saumarez incurred censure for his letter, but Thornton had no come-back from Canning on his own letter. His stay on board *Victory* in October while they tried to smuggle him ashore had gone very well. Saumarez commented to Martha: 'As he has no retinue whatever, with only one servant, I find it rather pleasant having him for a guest.'[16] This changed the following summer and Saumarez was a little less than pleased that September with Thornton's slow passage to Stockholm on account of his wife. Travelling problems due to her pregnancy meant she stayed on board *Victory* much longer than expected, and Saumarez had to move out of his cabin into the one formerly occupied by his son.[17] 'I have at last a letter from Mr. Thornton who since Madame's arrival has been unpardonably remiss in public affairs which I am sorry to say is become too notorious here.'[18] The blip in relations appears not to have lasted for when Mrs. Thornton produced a son two months later and Saumarez was back in England, having hauled down his flag, he received a very touching letter asking him to be godfather. It began: 'I have had too many proofs of your goodness of heart and of the kind interest which it leads you to take in every thing which relates to those who possess a share in your friendship.'[19]

Piers Mackesy in his book *The War in the Mediterranean*, writes 'The relations of the soldiers and seamen with the diplomatists were uniformly bad'.[20] He quotes Nelson's comment: 'Diplomatic men think, of course, they know much better than anyone else.'[21] Collingwood, writing off the record to his sister, said:

> I am sure they are the most zealous and most disinterested, but your diplomatics. God keep me from the diplomatics. I have no idea of any thing more frivolous, more perplexing, than a young Minister, what they call a sucking ambassador. They imagine that the fate of Europe depends on them – and bless them, poor dears, if they would be moderate in the exercise of their talents, Europe would be perhaps the better for it ... I am persuaded from what I have seen that honesty is the best policy, and yet the great art of diplomacy is, that nothing they do should be understood, always to have an object that is not [to] be discovered by the person with whom they treat.[22]

Sir John Moore was equally rude about an encounter with Lord Strangford on his way from the Mediterranean in December 1807 to his abortive expedition to Sweden: 'Lord Strangford is, I understand, a very young man, one of those who upon leaving college without any intermediate intercourse with mankind become statesmen and diplomatists'; but then Moore was rude about almost everyone – except Saumarez.[23]

Saumarez' relations with diplomats of a variety of nations appear to have been consistently good. Certainly Thornton's immediate predecessor Foster had a close and happy relationship with him – Merry had only been there during the winter of 1808 and so had had contact with Keats rather than Saumarez. Of the two consuls, Smith gives little indication of their relationship in his correspondence but Fenwick was more forthcoming. His letters to Saumarez are full of details which assuredly would not have been included if he had not felt well disposed towards the recipient. A letter at the end of the 1810 season said how much he had appreciated the three years working under him and thanked Saumarez for his kind comments on Fenwick's work on provisions – with apologies that the quality of the beef was not all the time as good as he would have wished. However, this should perhaps be somewhat discounted as he was also asking for a good reference to the Marquess of Wellesley in case he needed one in the future.[24]

St Vincent's comment in May 1797 on Saumarez' handling of the diplomatic relations with the Spanish Admiral Mazarredo showed that it was a skill he had acquired quite early. It did not seem to matter whether they were friend

Figure 13. Admiral James, 1st Baron de Saumarez. Mezzotint by W. Say of portrait by Thomas Phillips R. A, 1810 (in the possession of the author)

or foe. His Russian opponent at Baltiski Port responded warmly to his friendly approaches and even the Danes, who looked with hatred at most things British since the attack on Copenhagen in 1807, expressed their respect for him personally as was shown above in connection with the wreck of the *St George*. On his hauling down his flag in 1812, Bornemann, their Auditor-General, wrote: 'You have known, Sir, how to combine your duties as chief of an enemy fleet with humanity and with the magnanimity of a noble warrior.'[25] His relationships in Sweden have already been covered.

Comparing his role as commander-in-chief with that of Collingwood in the Mediterranean after Trafalgar, the Mediterranean command was more diffuse, with many more countries and a greater physical area. There was also a greater prospect of major military action; Collingwood wistfully commenting as he sailed out of Port Mahon in the *Ville de Paris* on the very eve of his death: 'Then I may yet live to meet the French once more',[26] whereas by late 1809 Saumarez was almost certain there would be no fleet actions during his command. His only hope was that Admiralty fears would be realised that the French Scheldt fleet would escape the blockade northwards, sail round the Skaw and attempt to reach Copenhagen. Nonetheless, the two roles involved controlling widely scattered squadrons, defending trade, and above all keeping up relations with all the heads of state, great and small, within the command. Max Adams in his biography of Collingwood asks:

> What had prepared Collingwood for a career as a diplomat? His interest in history and politics, his geographical curiosity, and his natural wisdom; perhaps also the ingenuous honesty and directness of the naval officer. Combining these with his felicity of expression, he now showed that there was more than one weapon available to the navy in its dealings with foreign powers. Where Nelson had threatened, Collingwood deployed enlightened self-interest and flattery.[27]

Although Saumarez was an intelligent, well-educated and well-read man, I do not find that he had a particular interest in either history or geography. His letters certainly show a strong political interest but not one that was attached to any party or philosophy – very much the reverse, for he turned down two offers of an Admiralty-controlled parliamentary seat.[28] His religious belief guided him in his actions probably more strongly than Collingwood, but without the extremes of Gambier. It also gave him confidence: 'We cannot always command success, we can only strive to deserve it and with the divine assistance we cannot fail.'[29] Honesty was a cardinal strength and distinguished him in the view of von Rosen and other Swedes from most other English, as two of his letters to Engeström illustrate: 'the keeping of promises among the Englishmen often depends on how much wine they have with their food' and 'When he has given his word of honour about discretion, Saumarez is too honest a man to expose

either our government or those who have been the secret interpreters for it'.[30]
Moreover, rather than the 'directness of the naval officer' that Adams attributes
as a cause of Collingwood's success, Saumarez was rather old-fashioned and
courteous: 'the civilest man I ever saw' in the words of Betsey Fremantle.[31]

His best-known portrait, by Thomas Phillips, gives him rather a haughty or
even arrogant look, yet he had a capacity for friendliness that belies it. This,
I believe, has led naval historians to misinterpret his nature. For that reason
the later portrait by Samuel Lane has been chosen as the frontispiece to this
volume, and the Phillips one is shown on p. 182 for comparison. Von Rosen
had responded to this hidden warmth: 'Saumarez, always as honest as he was
straightforward, received me with the friendship I had expected.' But he was
also aware of the firm determination that lay behind the friendly manner in
Saumarez' comment over Carlshamn that if he 'ever found out that we had
wanted to deceive him, he would, although unwillingly, be forced to inflict all
the possible harm upon us'.[32]

By the time Saumarez arrived at Wingo on 2 May 1812, at the start of the
campaigning season, the political atmosphere had changed. There was a new
First Lord, Robert Dundas, Lord Melville, who had only taken office on 25
March. Thornton had arrived in Gothenburg at the end of March and gone
on to Örebro, a royal castle and town in central Sweden, to continue peace
negotiations. Saumarez wrote to him saying that he had received no instructions before departure: 'You will therefore judge how anxious I must be to be
apprised of what may be intended with respect to these countries (Russia more
particularly) for I hope we may regard Sweden as favourably inclined'.[33] This
absence of briefing was, he said, due to insufficient reports on which to base
the instructions, but will not have been helped by a new First Lord taking over.
The instructions were still not forthcoming in June when he wrote to Martha:
'I have only the satisfaction to be informed that the measures I am pursuing
receive the approbation of Government.' This displayed the government's readiness to leave it to Saumarez to make decisions on the spot, as Martha was quick
to point out in her reply: 'it is a great proof of their confidence in Thee and the
result I hope will justify them.'[34]

Thornton replied with a lengthy and optimistic report. Russia and Sweden
had signed and ratified a defensive and offensive treaty of alliance which was
made public in the *Naval Chronicle* in May 1812,[35] together with a report that
Bonaparte's offer of Finland and part of Russia as far as Lake Ladoga in return
for 35,000 Swedish troops, had been turned down: 'I regard the peace as made,
though in truth it is not signed for we wait for more from England.' He had
also come round entirely to Saumarez' view of Bernadotte:

> I am extremely satisfied with the prince royal. He is, I am persuaded, perfectly
> sincere, loyal, and is the life of the good cause here and in Russia. His influ-

ence on Alexander is prodigious; and I am sure, he more than any other has brought Russia to the stand where it is.[36]

He told Saumarez that the Swedish government intended to present him with a sword ornamented with precious stones as a mark of their gratitude 'for the distinguished kindness you have on all occasions shown them', adding for his own part, 'these marks so deserved will serve to perpetuate them to your childrens' children'.[37] At the same time, Fenwick reported that Bernadotte's own hold on power in Sweden was continuing to grow and that he had fore-warned Alexander of a conspiracy which had led to the dismissal of the pro-French reforming Russian minister Michael Speransky.[38] Denmark, however, was 'getting daily more deeply into the whirlpool which must inevitably one way or other draw it to destruction', as indeed happened – bankruptcy and the loss of Norway to Sweden in 1814. The government in London still appeared to hope for an alliance of all three northern powers against Napoleon,[39] but despite statements from Bernadotte of the friendly relations of Denmark and Sweden, reports from Stockholm and Copenhagen appeared to contradict this. The historic latent hostility between the two would not easily disappear, what-ever the economic and political logic of their working together. This appears frequently in the letters of von Rosen. A typical sarcastic comment about anon-ymous letters from Copenhagen that had been sent to Gothenburg trading houses in August 1810, ended:

> However pleasant it would be to have their beloved King as the genius, making our country blissful, and also to have our language beautified, which the author among other things promises,* the privateering system still breaks the hearts of the merchants enough to stifle their neighbourliness.[40]

He also later suggested: 'if you want [Thornton] in High Spirit you should talk to him about Danes, because he hates them worse than the dog hates the cat.'[41] Fenwick welcomed Saumarez' return and went out of his way to congratulate him, saying that his conciliatory measures had 'operated powerfully on the resolution which this government has taken to maintain its independence and to shake off the trammels of Bonaparte'.[42]

Von Rosen came out to Wingo to see Saumarez soon after his arrival and spent two days there. He was no longer concerned about secrecy and noted that there were several Swedish merchants on board who would spread news of his visit. However, 'I could achieve very little with the good-humoured Saumarez'. Saumarez promised to ask his cruisers to treat Swedish ships gently, but could not give them written orders to that effect since he still had to consider Russian

---

* Danes readily admit their spoken language is one of the least beautiful in Europe, sometimes claiming it is a disease rather than a language.

ports as hostile. Von Rosen was well aware of the pressures of prize money on cruiser captains: 'as long as the orders are not in writing you can never rely on these ruffians'.[43]

Manifestations of goodwill continued to grow. With the English fleet had come out to Gothenburg an English camp bed and two cases of Seville oranges for the Crown Prince and a further case of oranges for Engeström.[44] Saumarez also sent his surgeon to treat peasants on the outlying islands at Wingo, and von Rosen wrote to thank him in the King's name.[45] The letter was addressed to 'M. le Baron!'* One cannot be sure, but it seems quite probable that the two of them were now on such close terms that von Rosen was aware of Saumarez' feelings about his lack of recognition in England and of the peerage he felt was his due, and von Rosen was suggesting that, just as Sweden was acknowledging his contribution to the successful outcome of Anglo-Swedish relations with a superb sword, so the British government might at last grant him this wish. This appears to be the first time that von Rosen used 'Baron' rather than 'Admiral' or 'Excellency', but not the last. A copy of the letter of tribute in 1813 (see p. 3 above), was similarly addressed, which is one of the reasons for thinking it came from von Rosen rather than from von Platen, as Ross and others have believed. Saumarez asked to be able to pay his respects to Bernadotte to acknowledge the closer relationship between the two countries. The Crown Prince was expected to visit Gothenburg on 15 August, but yet again other things intervened. Saumarez' eldest son James had come out on board *Victory* for the experience and later was Thornton's guest at Örebro, going on afterwards to Åbo in Finland and even St Petersburg. Bernadotte expressed surprise to von Rosen that he was going to become a priest.[46]

In the light of the changed demands, the Baltic fleet had been reduced to ten ships of the line. Hope, the former Captain of the Fleet, had been promoted rear admiral late in 1811 and had briefly flown his flag at Wingo over the rump of the fleet there when Saumarez had sailed for home in *Victory*. In January 1812, Hope had turned down Yorke's offer of a continuing post in the Baltic. Nominally it was in order to go ashore to settle his private affairs, but one gets the impression that tensions had built up between him and Saumarez. Hope had served four years in the same post, except for a brief break to return to England to a sick wife for the month the fleet was off Rogervik in September 1808. By the end of 1811, to judge by a letter from Saumarez to his wife, he and Hope had seen enough of each other:

---

* The use of an exclamation mark is quite common in Swedish and so has less significance than it would in English.

the Party after passing so much of the day together, often become dull *et très ennuyant* particularly when the first Captain or the Commander-in-Chief might not be in the most pleasant mood, which sometimes has happened as well as in the preceding years. Thou wilt easily comprehend we are too great for each other – which is the long and short of the matter.[47]

It is noticeable that this is the only comment, good or bad, on Hope in the whole domestic correspondence, whereas there are several mentions of others serving under him.

The admirals now under his command were James Morris at Hanö in place of Reynolds whom he was sad to have lost, especially in such a tragic way. There were some accusations, roundly dismissed by Ross, that Saumarez was at least in part to blame for having allowed the *St. George* to sail, but Reynolds' insistence, incorrectly, that his ship was in safe order was the prime cause.[48] Morris' father had been killed when Captain of the *Bristol* at the attack on Sullivan's Island, Charleston, in 1776. The son, James, had been on Jervis' list of October 1796 of 22 of the best post-captains.[49] The other admiral was Byam Martin, who had stepped into the breach to relieve Hope as Captain of the Fleet in 1808. Significantly, Saumarez did battle with Melville, newly in office, over a replacement for Hope now that he had been promoted to admiral. Melville had forgotten to discuss this when they had met at the Admiralty before Saumarez' departure for the Baltic. Melville then wrote formally to say that:

such an appointment would be very satisfactory to me & is much wished by the Board ... there must be a variety of subordinate though necessary details that require a large portion of time & attention which may with more benefit to the public interest be devoted to other & more important objects.

He did not suggest any names. Saumarez' immediate reply, for he was then still in London, was that with his reduced fleet and when not more than three or four ships of the line were likely to be collected at any time, there was no need: 'I trust that a measure to which I am decidedly averse will not be pressed upon me.' Melville gave way: 'as you appear to entertain so strong an objection'. But he maintained face by only accepting 'as long as your force does not exceed the number <u>at present</u> destined for the Baltic' and went on to give a warning note of his powers: 'I am not sure that I can include <u>all</u> the names of the young gentlemen whom you have recommended to be inserted in my list for promotion'.[50]

After four years in his command, Saumarez now had confidence that he knew what was best for his own situation and to do battle with the politicians. Collingwood equally refused to have a Captain of the Fleet, but gave rather different reasons: 'I do everything for myself, and never distract my mind with other people's opinions'.[51] Collingwood is well known for his lack of ability or willingness to delegate. He exhausted himself by taking even the smallest matters under his personal control. It was resented by the more able of his subordinates and was bad man-management that could lead to strained relations. It may explain why he was not a popular figure with his subordinate officers, however well-liked he may have been by the ship's companies. It was a strange weakness in someone who took a particular pleasure in training the young. Saumarez, on the other hand, was very prepared to listen to other people when forming his own judgement as he showed clearly at Algeciras and Rogervik, and indeed throughout his Baltic command. He was prepared to allow his subordinates to use their own initiative and to support and commend them. But he was equally prepared to make clear to them when he thought that they had made a mistake, as over the dispute with Byam Martin.

There now followed a waiting game which proved rather frustrating, although the defence of trade still had to go on. Saumarez had a report that the Norwegians had eight brigs and a frigate working in divisions to harass trade on the Norwegian coast of the Sleeve.[52] Early in the year, the newly built Danish frigate, *Najad* (36) had sailed secretly from Copenhagen to Christiansand where she was given six more 18-pounder carronades. An inconclusive action with an English frigate, not identified in the Danish report, let the news out and on 6 July the *Dictator* (64) sailed from Wingo with three gun brigs to hunt her down. They found her with three accompanying brigs off the coast near Arendal. Outgunned, the Danes sought refuge in Lyngøers Havn, through a narrow entrance defended by batteries. Despite two of the British brigs going aground, the *Dictator* forced her way through and after a particularly bloody battle destroyed the *Najad* and sank most of the rest of her squadron.[53]

There were similar actions going on through the command, though on a rather smaller scale. The *Briseis* (10) cut out with her pinnace a captured merchant vessel *Urania* off Pillau, chartered by Solly & Sons, a regular contractor used by the government to import hemp.[54] Later that year, the *Briseis* was disguised as a merchant ship to sail at the head of a large convoy. One of a force of four privateers came alongside her and was easily captured, and the other three, in endeavouring to escape, ran on the rocks and were destroyed.[55] French privateers were continuing to emerge from the canal at Kiel to threaten shipping. This was the original canal that linked the Baltic to the River Eider and reached the North Sea at the then Danish port of Tonningen. In the heyday of 1805 the port had become the chief entrepôt for supplying the Baltic, until Canning's attack on Copenhagen in 1807 made the Danes declare war and Tonningen lose the trade to Gothenburg. The French had been forbidden by the Danes to stop ships in the Sound and so moved more into the Baltic.[56]

Count von Rosen had called on Smith at the time of Saumarez' arrival at Wingo in May, with a letter from Admiral Nauckhoff who was very anxious to see British cruisers in the Sound and Baltic 'for the purpose of keeping in check and destroying the enemies' privateers which are swarming everywhere and committing depredations on the trade'. Smith passed this on to Saumarez, adding:

> the friendly relations between the two countries not being yet ratified or entirely arranged, although the admiral looks on them as if they really were so, this government cannot communicate openly and direct with you ... they are very sensible of the many indulgencies you have granted, and the willingness you have always shewn to do every service in your power to Sweden consistent with times and circumstances'.[57]

Saumarez sent the *Zealous* and *Rose* to patrol off Hälsingborg and asked Croker for more cutters for this purpose.[58]

Thornton sent Saumarez a Russian request that their ships might not be molested by British cruisers if they joined Swedish convoys. This was passed on by Admiral Byam Martin to be observed by the cruisers. Saumarez had given permission for Swedish vessels to bring corn, mostly rye, from Russian ports to Stockholm and other Swedish ports to alleviate the distress caused by the previous year's poor crop. Thornton had persuaded the Russian mission in Sweden to allow this as an exception to the embargo that they had otherwise laid on the export of grain, to prevent its supply to the French army.[59] The Swedes were fitting out eight sail of the line and five frigates at Karlskrona. Consul Smith had passed on to Captain Dashwood of the *Pyramus*, as senior naval officer in the winter absence of admirals, a request from the Swedish government that these ships should not be molested. Dashwood gave instructions to his cruisers 'to treat the Swedish Flag with the respect and attention due to a great and friendly Nation, and on no account whatever to molest them', and informed Admiral Puke so that there should be no misunderstanding. He wrote to Saumarez:

> although I have not received any commands from you on this subject, but considering the importance of a mutual good understanding existing between the two nations, I feel I shall be only anticipating your wishes by venturing to write the enclosed official letter to Admiral Puke, the commander-in-chief at Carlscrona, which I trust will be honoured with your approbation.[60]

It was another instance of subordinates under Saumarez having the confidence to act on their own initiative – Dashwood had soon learnt how Saumarez worked.

Morris, on his arrival at Hanö, was more suspicious of the Swedes, despite a report from Fenwick that Sweden would stay neutral and not enter any alliance until Russian resistance to Napoleon was successful:

> A maritime power equipping its navy can never be considered a mark of neutral intentions; and until I see the Swedish squadrons employed in assisting

our convoys through the Sound or acting in equal numbers in conjunction with us, I cannot help feeling very jealous of their movements.[61]

He spoke with the familiar distrust of Bernadotte that had coloured London's views of the Swedish scene ever since his election as crown prince. He was soon put right by Saumarez who forwarded Thornton's request that any possibility of collision or misunderstanding between the British fleet and the Swedish squadron of eight ships of the line and five frigates should be avoided as they cruised along the southern shore of the Baltic.[62]

Puke's orders from Bernadotte had actually been to fit out four of his ships for war and four *en flute* while he was waiting for the funds to be available. He wanted them to be ready to show themselves in the Baltic by the end of June so that other nations would see that they were prepared to defend their neutrality: 'But since we are not rich, we must be economical in our expenditure.'[63] According to Byam Martin's information, the Swedish Diet had 'unanimously voted an augmentation to their army of 60,000 men, which I understand will give them a total of 140,000; but I don't feel quite satisfied with my information on this point'. He was quite right to doubt, for the figures could have been nowhere near this amount in reality, whatever was said in public. He said they were also asking England to provide a subsidy of £60,000 per month, half to be in articles of British manufacture. It was, however, a measure of the degree of popularity that Bernadotte had built up in his short time as crown prince. Byam Martin wrote that 'this clever fellow has completely renovated the military character of the country, and makes one recognise in the nation that mad spirit of war which we read of in the time of Charles XII'. He much admired his decision to ban the distillation of grain for *akvavit* (schnapps), despite the Swedish love of it, in order to release stocks for bread.[64] Bernadotte had backed his actions with Gascon oratory. His instructions in May 1811 to Admiral Puke to prepare Karlskrona against a sudden attack were followed by this exhortation: 'Assemble your captains forthwith, speak to them in the language of Duty and Honour. They should never surrender and their Glory tells me that they never shall. Whatever the strength of the enemy, triumph or let all your ships go down.'[65]

The disparity between two of Napoleon's letters dated 25 April 1812 illustrates parallel lines of thought proceeding in opposing directions. The first, to his Foreign Minister Bassano, instructed him to ensure that there were good and active men in Kolberg, Elbing, Königsberg, Memel, Riga, Libau, Rostock, Wismar, Stralsund and all the north European coastal ports 'so as to have active communication of everything happening on the coast ... They must write every day'.[66] The second, to Czar Alexander, said that his envoy, Comte Narbonne, was bringing a letter with important messages: 'They will prove to Your Majesty my desire to avoid war and my loyalty to the sentiments of Tilsit and Erfurt.'

But he added a characteristic rider: 'if fate makes war inevitable between us, it will not change in the slightest the feelings that Your Majesty inspires in me and which are sheltered from any vicissitude or alteration'.[67]

At the same time, Bassano wrote to Castlereagh that he was authorised to enter peace discussions. The independence and integrity of both Spain and Portugal would be guaranteed and the Kingdom of Naples restored: if this fourth offer of peace failed, the blood which would flow would fall entirely on England.[68] Castlereagh and the British cabinet believed this was simply an attempt to sow dissension among the allies and allay discontent in France, and their reply simply asked him to be more specific about Spain; this Napoleon failed to answer.[69] Political spin is not a modern invention. It would enable him to proclaim in his first Bulletin to the Grande Armée on 20 June 'every means of conciliation was employed on the part of France: all was in vain'.[70]

Napoleon also asked for copies of any relevant treaties, particularly for Austria, Prussia, and Denmark, together with the Erfurt convention and the latest treaty with Sweden. Despite the French invasion of Swedish Pomerania, for the second time, at the beginning of 1812, Napoleon still hoped to keep Sweden at least neutral, if not an active ally. He instructed Marshal Berthier, Prince de Neuchatel, Minister of War, 'you must continue to treat the Swedes as friends'.[71] Ideally, he would have liked to have Sweden as an ally who, by threatening a recapture of Finland, would draw off Russian forces which might otherwise be available to resist his own attack. The Baltic states would be on the left wing of his route into the heart of Russia, although at that stage, according to Metternich, he maintained: 'I shall open the campaign by crossing the Niemen. It will be concluded at Smolensk or Minsk. There I shall stop.'[72] He sent Berthier a long list of enquiries about the provision of boats to take men or supplies up the Baltic, and ones suitable to navigate the shallow expanse of the Frische-Haff, the long lagoon-like stretch of water along the Gulf of Danzig.[73] He still hoped to persuade Bernadotte of the validity of the argument he had put to him soon after he became Crown Prince:

> You appreciate without doubt the motives of my Decree of 21 November 1806. It in no way prescribes laws for Europe, it simply depicts the road to follow to arrive at the same goal; the treaties I have signed do the rest. The right of blockade that the English have arrogated to themselves harms Swedish commerce just as much and is as contrary to the honour of her flag and maritime power, as it harms the commerce of the French empire and the dignity of her power.
>
> The aspiration to dominate of the English is even more offensive to Sweden. Your commerce is more maritime than continental; Sweden's real strength is as much in the existence of her navy as of her army.[74]

However, Bernadotte knew well that the existence of his merchant marine depended upon friendly relations with Britain, so dominant on the trade routes, just as he accepted that he must balance his actions very carefully while France remained as dominant by land. This is where Saumarez' influence on Bernadotte through von Rosen was so important.

News of the assassination of the Prime Minister, Perceval, reached Saumarez from Byam Martin, the account having reached Deal on 13 May 1812, the morning that the latter sailed in the *Aboukir* for Wingo. It came as a great blow to Saumarez: 'Most sincerely do I deplore an event that has deprived the country of one of the ablest of men – whose loss is irreparable and will long be felt by the whole nation.'[75] Both Thornton and Morris concurred, in letters sent to Saumarez in response to the news, a reaction that would not have been expected when Perceval first took office in 1809.[76] It is a measure of the impact he had made in his quiet way. The Irish politician Grattan's pithy description was 'he is not a ship of the line, but he carries many guns, is tight built, and is out in all weathers'.[77] The only other comments of a similar nature by Saumarez concerning the departure of a politician had been his regret at the resignation of the much more flamboyant Canning.

There was now concern that this might delay the accession of Britain to the Russo-Swedish alliance that had so recently been agreed. Lord Liverpool's failure initially to win sufficient support to carry on the government without recruits led to three weeks of manoeuvring in which Wellesley managed to offend ministers bitterly by a posthumous attack on Perceval, and Canning made a serious political miscalculation in turning down Liverpool's offer of the Foreign Office. Wellesley had already damaged his reputation in February in an unsuccessful attempt to manoeuvre himself into the premiership, when the Prince of Wales had taken full powers as Regent. This led to Wellesley's resignation as Foreign Secretary. He had been replaced by Castlereagh, and Lord Melville – in Muir's view 'a competent but uninspiring administrator' – had become First Lord. Liverpool's second attempt to continue without any new recruits in place of Perceval managed to gain a majority of over a hundred in the resultant vote of confidence.[78] Thornton and Saumarez both waited anxiously for ministers to occupy themselves with the international rather than the domestic scene. In Fenwick's view, 'could the Marquis of Wellesley have come in it would have been a great advantage both at home and abroad, but by what now appears this was quite impracticable',[79] and von Rosen believed Saumarez was of the same mind: 'S[aumarez] believes with certainty that Wellesley will be premier and Canning Sec[re]t[ary]. for the foreign affairs. He supposes that this change will do away with all difficulties which have been in our way.'[80]

Liverpool's accession was a turning point in the political direction of the country, bringing in strong government after a long period of weakness and change, but it came too late to have much impact on the Baltic scene where matters had already moved towards a dénouement. Saumarez had suggested that the new situation might allow a Swedish convoy to pass through the Sound, a shorter route which, with a friendly eastern shore, would avoid many of the dangers of the Great Belt and was subject only to the shallows off Malmö.[81] For the same reasons, Admiral Morris had asked whether he could send ships under Swedish convoy direct to Wingo rather than going to Hanö.[82] Fenwick had recommended some fishermen from south of Hälsingborg as potential pilots. Thornton initially welcomed this. However, he never received an answer from the Swedish government and did not press it since he was confident the whole situation would shortly change. He was also far from certain that:

> we can trust to the entire zeal and activity of the Swedish men of war in protecting our convoys; and if that were even the case I am still less sure whether such a convoy would answer the nature of the engagement subsisting between a shipper and underwriters in England ... English convoy must be understood and a court of law ... would hardly allow that a Swedish convoy meant the same thing.[83]

There was a momentary threat to relations when Saumarez heard that a Swedish frigate in charge of a convoy of merchant ships had been seen by one of his cruisers entering Kiel. She had not been stopped since the captain, Wilkinson, was reluctant to stop a Swedish convoy although his instructions were to prevent supplies going to the French. Saumarez asked Thornton to make a formal complaint to the Swedish government. He was initially told that the convoy contained a ship that was to collect wine, books and other effects of Crown Prince Bernadotte. However, an order from the Crown Prince followed rapidly, that: 'no convoy of Swedish merchant ships must proceed, nor any of his Majesty's warships give convoy, to ports regarded as enemy by the British government, except for the ports of Russia'.[84]

Thornton wrote again to Saumarez, later the same day, to amplify his earlier letter, and it is worth quoting in full as a word picture of the confused state of affairs:

> I have been extremely mortified by the intelligence transmitted to me in your public and private letters, in every account (that of the Public most particularly which at this moment more than all others must have suffered exceedingly if Captain Wilkinson and (I hope) Captain Servell had not conducted themselves with moderation and prudence).
>
> I am writing to attribute much of this untoward circumstance to the negligence and to a forgetfulness which he takes upon himself, of Baron d'Engeström; and as for the Prince Royal and all the persons about him (with some of whom I am on the best terms) I am persuaded they are totally guiltless even of that minor fault; but I am not at all sure, that there has not been a real fault on the part of others, even principal persons, and that, in concert with merchants they have not been capable of conniving at trans-

actions, the result of which might have rendered us, instead of almost friends as we are, open and declared enemies. I do not go so far as to say that this was the object; but you know what is the character of some of these people calling themselves merchants, and of others who seek nothing but gain, who would not scruple for a trifling personal advantage to set two countries in a state of hostility.[85]

This letter was accompanied by a copy of a letter to Thornton from Gyllenskold, Naval ADC to Bernadotte, saying how appreciative the Crown Prince was of the 'delicate and honourable proceedings' of Saumarez and his captains which he would always remember.[86]

It is noticeable from the correspondence that the return of Thornton had changed the balance of relationships as far as the Baltic was concerned, between the Admiralty, the Foreign Office and Saumarez as Commander-in-Chief. Since Yorke's appointment as First Lord, Saumarez had very much been left to run the Baltic as his own fief. Now with Thornton in place, albeit unofficially, foreign policy returned more immediately into the hands of the Foreign Office and Saumarez' diplomatic role was reduced. That is not to say that he did not still have an important part to play in achieving the goal of a renewed northern alliance against Napoleon. However, it did appear to lead to some resentment on the part of Saumarez towards Thornton and the new government which was noted in von Rosen's letters, duly reporting it to Engeström: 'The day after tomorrow I will go out to Saumarez. The old man is in a very irritable mood, angry about our convoy, about the wickedness of the English Ministry, yes I believe even with Mr. Thornton himself.'[87] He confirmed this a month later:

I now have the honour to report that I am fairly certain in supposing that Saumarez and Thornton do not get on very well. They were together here with me for 6 hours and during that time they did not say one word to each other. Before Thornton went out to the fleet he told me, in a sure tone that the Admiral will sail to the Baltic. When I again asked the latter, he answered: 'he may want that, but I will stay here as long as I can, for I believe it is in the interests of Sweden, that if we need to co-operate, it must be I who should direct the operations of my fleet'.*[88]

Saumarez had always been very touchy on points of honour. It is understandable that, having taken the weight of decision-making in the Baltic over the past four years and having brought about its successful completion in the preparations for the signing of peace by his policy of moderation and of understanding the needs of the Swedes, he should resent his usurpation by London and the Foreign Office envoy, however customary and correct it might be for this to

* Saumarez' remark is in French in the original.

happen. He would certainly be upset at his own particular Swedish connection being told by the envoy what the fleet under his command would be doing. He evidently poured out his heart to Martha, but she in her response confirmed, sadly for us, that she had followed his instructions of 'committing it to the flames and locking up its contents in Memory's sacred Repository'.[89]

On 6 June, Thornton revealed he had been sent 'full powers to sign a Treaty of Peace with Russia' which he had sent on by courier to Wilno (Vilnius) where Alexander was, with the main body of the Russian army. He hoped to have a response within ten days and then it would simply be a matter of waiting while copies were made.[90] However, it was not until 17 July that he was able to report that 'I have this day signed a treaty of peace with the Swedish and Russian plenipotentiaries'. On 24 June, the French army had crossed the Russian frontier.[91]

Following the French invasion of Russia, all relationships changed. Thornton was now concerned to get Sweden to play an active part in the struggle against Napoleon. Saumarez, left on the outside of the decision-making circle, began to show his displeasure at the slow manner in which affairs proceeded. When von Rosen made some comments about Thornton, Saumarez 'answered with an expression of impatience 'and, my dear count, do not forget his unprecedented circumspection'. Saumarez went on to accept a Swedish request for licences to ship sugar from Carlshamn across the Baltic which Thornton had just turned down. Von Rosen commented 'I have on this occasion found Saumarez his usual self and the other worse than before ... we were both angry'.[92] One reason is revealed in von Rosen's letter of 2 August: 'Mr. Thornton leaves today with his odious wife, on whom nothing but her teeth are sufficient, in physical and moral terms. Poor man, he has got a vixen. I have had a lot of trouble with her.'[93]

Saumarez had decided to confound Thornton's earlier statement that the fleet would be sailing to the Baltic by staying at Wingo. It was fortunate that he did, for Lord Cathcart arrived at Gothenburg as British Ambassador to Russia and wanted to confer with him: 'when the Ministers found by the Dispatches I sent home that he was most likely to find me here they were quite rejoiced at it'. There was a splendid party at von Rosen's to welcome Cathcart and Saumarez spent the night ashore for the first time that season, but was back in his cabin by 9.30 a.m. and 'soon surrounded by officers who had arrived in the morning'.[94] Cathcart's task was to represent Britain at a meeting between the Emperor Alexander and Bernadotte. It was a meeting that promised great co-operation and a joint attack on Zealand, pursuing Bernadotte's own objective of the acquisition of Norway. However, the Russian troops never materialised since they were too heavily committed at home. The subsequent history is outside the scope of this book.

Once the diplomats had left, Saumarez and von Rosen were both able to relax. There was time for an excursion. Von Rosen took him to the Falls of Trollhättan and on to see the flight of five locks that were the beginning of the Gota Canal, just being built, which was to connect Stockholm via the great lakes in central Sweden to Gothenburg and the Kattegat – thereby by-passing Denmark and the potential dangers of the Great Belt and the Sound, as well as avoiding any payment of Sound dues to Denmark. Baron von Platen, with whom Saumarez had previously been in touch, was the power behind it and had been given leave of absence from the Council of State by Bernadotte in order to supervise this 'epoch in the annals of Sweden'.[95] By a curious chance, while breakfasting at an inn they met the jeweller who had been commissioned to mount Saumarez' presentation sword. He told them the tale of how, when the gold used was tested at Örebro, it was found to be below weight. He had returned to Stockholm and found that his principal workman had been defrauding the customers to the tune of £40,000 over the last five years, which the jeweller then made good.[96]

Soon after their return, a fire broke out in the dockyard which Saumarez helped to fight, 'moving about at the work like a young midshipman'.[97] More importantly, Saumarez complained to Martha:

> I have [no letters] yet from Mr. Thornton which is rather extraordinary as he knows that on the communications I receive from him depends much the proceedings of the Squadron. I cannot describe the ill humour that his delay in arriving at Stockholm has excited in this country. Count R[osen] read to me some letters from the first people full of their remarks on the subject – highly discreditable I am sorry to say to our Minister.[98]

There is a strong undercurrent of resentment in his letters to Martha. He had enjoyed the independence of his command in the previous four years and now felt that he had been shuffled to the sidelines to watch other players take over and apparently prejudice relationships that he had so carefully built up. He was able, however, to busy himself making arrangements for the Russian Archangel squadron which was to be sent to winter in England, together with the Cronstadt squadron which would join them off Wingo.[99] This was in case the French took St Petersburg. That was being made less likely by the efforts of Byam Martin, now promoted to rear-admiral, who was supporting the Russian troops defending Riga against Macdonald's French army. His enterprising efforts are entertainingly described in Byam Martin's letters[100] which formed the basis of the still more entertaining but less accurate Hornblower novel, *The Commodore*, by C.S. Forester.

In the midst of this, on 9 October, Saumarez received news of the sudden death of his eldest daughter Mary. Melville responded immediately to Saumarez' request to be relieved and return home. He appointed Rear-Admiral George Hope who knew the station well and who set out the next day. To Hope's chagrin – there is a testy exchange of letters – Saumarez insisted on staying on briefly until he had received dispatches from Lord Cathcart and finished organising the passage of the Russian fleet, now including the Archangel squadron, through the Belt to Wingo and on to the safety of various ports in Britain for the winter, for fear of the French advance towards St Petersburg.[101] Duty still prevailed over personal distress.

12

Conclusions: the Man or the Situation

In the Introduction, I set out five main questions to be considered in this study:

1 How far did Saumarez create the policy of restraint, as opposed to offensive use of his fleet, or was he simply implementing orders from London?
2 Was the decision not to attack the Russian fleet at Rogervik a sign of weakness and indecision, or of mature judgement and political understanding?
3 Why were his initial suspicions of Swedish constancy replaced by confidence that their actions would remain friendly even under a French marshal and in a state of war?
4 Were there other vice-admirals at the time who might have been equally successful and what difference might another Commander-in-Chief have made?
5 Did the situation produce the man or vice versa and did he have political weight that made it easier for him to take an independent line?

The answers that I have put forward should be evident from the chapters that have gone before. But it may be helpful to look at the questions in turn and set out the conclusions that I suggest may be drawn.

1 *How far was the policy of restraint that of Saumarez rather than London?*

There is little doubt that the Duke of Portland's government in the spring of 1808 had little idea of how it should deal with the problems it had created in the Baltic by the pre-emptive strike on Copenhagen the previous autumn. The influence of the peace-loving Fox within the Ministry of All the Talents had been replaced in 1807 by the Pittite views of Canning 'who moved quickly to signal that the change of ministers was matched by a change of policy'.[1] Subsidies to allies were again to be used as a weapon and the war continued. But the long delay in the departure of Saumarez and his fleet as he waited for instructions, and the lack of a clear purpose behind the sending of the country's only reserve of 10,000 experienced troops to Gothenburg under Sir John Moore are indications of a reaction to circumstances rather than a coherent policy. The Moore expedition ended in a fiasco, having wasted two months of Saumarez' campaigning time for what he had been told were his main tasks. These were to give support against Russia to Britain's remaining ally Sweden, to restrict the Russian fleet and, if possible, attack it and to protect the Baltic trade, reporting on the practicability of establishing bases on Anholt for a lighthouse, and on Bornholm and the Eartholms to create another Heligoland.

The surrender of the fortress of Sveaborg and King Gustav's earlier incompetence in resisting the French invasion of Swedish Pomerania led both government and opposition in England to question whether the subsidy of £100,000 a month was well spent. The riots in Spain, leading to a second front against Napoleon on the Peninsula, looked a more promising affair to support both financially and militarily. Canning still half-believed that Denmark would bow to economic sense and that a northern league of Russia, Sweden and Denmark 'while the flames continue spreading in the South ... might yet produce a change in favour of the Liberties and Independence of mankind'[2] – typical Canning oratory. His belief was that it was only by creating a fear of England greater than the fear of France that this could be brought about.

Saumarez' first real impact on policy came at Rogervik, which was also a critical point in his own evolution. Had he arrived four days earlier and the annihilation of the Russian fleet ensued, Canning's policy of fear would have prevailed and Saumarez would have got his peerage. Whether a palace revolution in St Petersburg would have followed and reversed the Tilsit alliance, as both Leveson Gower and Thornton suggested, cannot be certain. But an attack on Cronstadt would have been made much easier and provided more leverage to change Russian minds. It might have brought an earlier French attack on Russia or it might have brought another peace, perhaps short-lived like that of 1801. As it was, Saumarez, without authority and within days, swung from being the conventional fighting sea-captain to the peacemaker offering negotiations, first to the Russian admiral and then (admittedly after close consultation with Thornton, the remaining British minister in the Baltic) to the Czar himself. Thornton's letters of 4 September, to Canning and to Saumarez, show Thornton supporting the policy of 'dread'. Yet on his visit to *Victory* he endorsed Saumarez' peace proposal and sent his own similar letter to Tchichagoff.[3] Saumarez, it seems, was beginning to sway minds. He took a bold step and he was duly rebuked, twice, but relatively mildly and more for the temerity of intervening in matters outside his proper scope than for any error in what he proposed.

The fall of Gustav IV in spring 1809 left Keats and Merry on the ground, and the government at home, at a loss to know with whom they should deal. George III was adamant that no recognition should be given yet to the new

king Charles XIII. It was thought that the leaders of the coup were predominantly Francophile and Marshal Bernadotte, in command in north Germany,
had immediately ordered a cessation of all French attacks on Swedish posses-
sions. Keats was particularly worried and was trying to clear all British shipping from Sweden, while Merry had evidently given Sweden up as a lost cause
and asked to return home as he was suffering from a nervous complaint. His
successor, the legation secretary Foster, proved much more positive and immediately established contact with Saumarez on his arrival at Gothenburg in May.
Between them, they set up a working arrangement and Saumarez stationed
squadrons in the Sound and the Baltic to hold both Danes and Russians in
check. 'I trust to be right in using my efforts for that purpose; and I hope to
receive the sanction of ministers on the measures I am adopting'. He certainly
received no instructions at the time and as late as August Mulgrave refused him
permission to wear his Swedish Order since it implied recognition of Charles
XIII.

If the supposition is correct that the document described in the SRO archive
as 'Strategic Situation in the Baltic' is by Saumarez (and the fact that I have
found no other copy or mention of it in any other files gives weight to this),
he appears to be the only person who had considered beforehand the necessary
courses of response to the three options before Sweden of alliance, neutrality or
war. He now implemented his second course, tailored to Sweden being neutral,
and as a first step captured Anholt as a base. He then sailed up the Baltic,
arranged a meeting with Baron Platen and sent some smaller ships to assist the
unsuccessful Swedish attack on the Russian forces in Finland. The very presence of his fleet, however, enabled Sweden to make a better peace with Russia
at Frederikshamn in September. Meanwhile Canning and Castlereagh had been
too busy with Portugal and Spain, the disaster of Walcheren, and their own
quarrel and duel that September, to pay any apparent attention to the Baltic.
There is a very touching eve-of-duel letter from Canning to his wife that ends:
'There could be no end of taking leave & of saying how dearly I have loved
you. I hope I have made you sensible of this, dearest, dearest Joan. I hope I
have been good and kind and affectionate towards you. I hope I have made
you happy. If you have been a happy wife & if I leave you a happy mother &
a proud widow, I am content.'[4]

Chapter 6 on the Pea Islands demonstrates the degree of discretion given
to Saumarez even during his first season and the scope for the commander-
in-chief of a distant station to evade instructions, by half-hearted measures or
procrastination. If Saumarez had used the force available to him when he left
Rogervik – for he had just received and actually sent back to England three 74s[5]
which would have replaced the three that he had left guarding the northern
Baltic – he would have had little difficulty capturing the Eartholms and leaving
there enough marines, guns and provisions for a garrison, plus a gun-brig or

sloop, until the fleet returned in the spring. He would also have recaptured the 25 prizes lying there to his own financial advantage. Warned by the failed attack, the Danes were able to strengthen the fortifications during the winter, so that by 1809 the capture of the islands was a much harder proposition. It appears now a missed opportunity: although it may have appeared differently to Saumarez and to Lukin, neither of them fit and Saumarez tired out by a demanding season.

In 1809, the Portland government had fallen and after considerable hesitations been replaced by one under Perceval. Rather to everyone's surprise, he was to prove an effective leader; the government became more positive and by its determination survived several crises, including the Walcheren Enquiry, the collapse of the economy in 1810/11 and the return of the King's porphyria. Wellesley was Foreign Secretary – a man of great intelligence and charm, but evidently paying more attention to affairs of the heart rather than of state. His instructions to Saumarez in spring 1810, typically not available before the fleet sailed, gave Saumarez the authority to commence hostilities, but only as a last resort. They also classed Swedish ports as enemy ones, making their coastal trade open to prizetaking by British cruisers. Saumarez delayed putting this into effect but informed the Swedes so that they could make their plans to circumvent it, at the same time giving Wellesley the time to change his mind, which he duly did. It was an action that won him enormous goodwill in Sweden; Yorke, the new First Lord, was supportive too.

The next test was the election of Marshal Bernadotte as crown prince. The immediate British reaction, including that of Saumarez, was that this would bring Sweden under active French control. However, Saumarez' relationship with leading Swedes, especially Admiral Krusenstjerna, at this time brought a swift change of mind as he listened to their comments and began to put his trust in them. Letting Bernadotte in his Swedish yacht cross the Belt in full view of the British naval and mercantile strength was a brilliant stroke. Whether it was contrived or fortuitous, it was his decision – going against what he had earlier said to Yorke. His two other significant decisions of that period were the instructions to merchant ships not to sail to the eastern coast of the Baltic that was under French control, for fear of almost certain sequestration, and his acceptance of the assurances conveyed by von Rosen that the declaration of war of 17 November would not be followed by any act of hostility. There was not time to seek advice or instructions from London. The decision had to be his and it was to favour restraint – to avoid an escalation of hostility and to save the confiscation of 'the immense property belonging to our merchants in the other ports of Sweden' as well as again forgoing a massive opportunity of prizetaking for his own part.

The affair of the Carlshamn Cargoes offered as great a challenge to the policy of restraint as even the declaration of war the previous year. Yorke and Wellesley both still distrusted Bernadotte. Wellesley's surprisingly speedy response came in his instructions to the Admiralty that Saumarez should 'remonstrate strongly' to the Swedish government that if they 'persevere in acts of this injurious nature' he should exercise his discretion 'in determining on the spot, whether the conduct of Sweden may now require an alteration of that indulgent course which is now pursued by the British forces in the Baltic'.[6] Saumarez carried out this order but was in no hurry, asking for his remonstration to be delivered to Baron von Essen when the Baron arrived some two weeks later, and wording it very mildly for a 'strong remonstration' – a message that was picked up by von Rosen as indicating the different views of Saumarez and London. Ross maintains that Saumarez was the only person who did not expect British retaliation to follow, though Saumarez made it clear that should the Swedes let him down 'he would exert the utmost in his power to resent any aggression' on their part. Agreement on the basis of compensation was a long time coming, but in the end it was on the lines agreed between Saumarez and von Rosen at their meeting soon after the news from Carlshamn became known.

That was the high point of Saumarez' impact on British policy towards Sweden. Nonetheless, as he wrote in a letter supporting Ross' efforts to obtain a payment for von Rosen in 1813, although the instructions thereafter may have come from London, they were based on the reports that he had sent to government founded on the communications that he had with von Rosen, 'in the mutual interest of both countries'.[7] The assassination of Perceval had led to a new prime minister in Lord Liverpool and Wellesley had earlier been replaced by Castlereagh. According to von Rosen, Saumarez had hoped to see Wellesley as Prime Minister with Canning as Foreign Secretary. He had had a high opinion of Perceval who had led the government for the bulk of Saumarez' time in the Baltic, but he evidently thought well too of Canning and Wellesley, who had been the other leading ministers in that time. So, despite the differences in their views, there was no apparent lack of goodwill or respect on Saumarez' part for their abilities. His main complaint was their lack of communication, but as Martha wrote in July 1812, 'it is a great proof of their confidence in thee'.

2 *Was the decision not to attack the Russian fleet at Rogervik a sign of weakness and indecision, or of mature judgement and political understanding?*

The lack of obvious action and success at Rogervik led to Mahan rating Saumarez as no more than a 'division commander', competent but without genius. On past form, there seems little doubt that if it had been Nelson chasing up the Baltic and finding the Russian fleet holed up in Rogervik, he would have attacked instantly. Would it then have been another Aboukir Bay or a Santa Cruz – or, indeed, an Algeciras? The situation was nearer to that of Santa Cruz: it lacked the surf, but a combined sea and land operation would have been necessary to eliminate the fortress that guarded the entrance. Byam Martin's report on the harbour's defences, dated simply September, lists 14 guns on a flanking point with many men working there and seven embrasures within the town: not a massive defence but enough to cripple the rigging of squareriggers beating out of the narrow fjordlike entrance against the prevailing northwesterly. By chance, as Ross records, the wind changed and would have brought them safely out, but a week later there was a week of onshore gales. George III's words after Santa Cruz are relevant:

> I own the attempting Expedition on shore, without Troops seems [sic] hazardous undertakings, and unless there is an almost certainty that the Enemy have no military Force, ought not to be attempted, for I do not wish for empty displays of valour when attended with the loss of many Brave Men and no solid Advantage gained by their exploits.[8]

Lacking Nelson's genius and supreme self-belief, Saumarez was more ready to listen to the views of others. Hood and Byam Martin had been on site and in action over the previous four days. Each of them had a history of gallantry, action, seamanship and initiative. They both expressed their view, confirmed in writing, that an attack would lead to an unjustifiable loss of ships and men, and were supported in this by the Swedish Admiral Nauckhoff. As Byam Martin wrote of Saumarez to his brother: 'the universal opinion of the impracticability of doing so has alone induced him to abandon so rash an enterprise'. Only attack by fireships or with the help of troops could have a chance, and the weather, the Russian boom and their military reinforcements put paid to that.

What 'solid Advantage' would have come from a successful attack? This has been considered under 1 above. An unsuccessful assault, however, with the loss of a ship or worse, would have damaged the reputation for invincibility of the British navy, weakened the relationship with King Gustav that the capture of the *Sevolod* had just restored, and diminished the fear of another attack like that on Copenhagen that supported Canning's policy of terror. As it was, the British 'fleet in being' – dominant but used for defence rather than attack – exerted its power over the Baltic for the next four years and the Russian fleet escaped back to Cronstadt to be locked deeper into the winter ice, never to venture out again.

I doubt if Saumarez foresaw this when he made his decision to blockade rather than attack. Nonetheless, his speedy change to offering surrender terms to the Russian admiral showed that he was capable of looking at the broader picture. Half the Russian fleet captured without loss would have equalled or exceeded most of the naval victories prior to Nelson. It would have achieved the same ends, if less fame than a bloody battle. Mulgrave at the Admiralty was too short-sighted to see this. Hanickoff's refusal to accept may not have come just from pride, but from a knowledge that his defensive situation was too strong to be easily overcome. After fifteen years of almost continuous war, Saumarez was very conscious of its horrors; in letters to Martha he wrote: 'it is really lamentable that so many innocent people should be the victims of the measures to which we are obliged to resort in this horrid state of warfare', and 'how fervently it is to be wished that these deplorable calamities may cease and that the seven headed monster Bonaparte may fall the victim of his cruelty and ambition'.[9] He was also keen to avoid the unnecessary loss or wounding of his own men. He fell out with Byam Martin in 1809 over what he deemed to be a reckless attack and wrote to Martha: 'the Admiralty may probably approve of it, but in my Opinion it was too hazardous a service to order the Boats upon'.[10] He followed up with a memorandum to all captains and commanders banning such attacks unless there were 'very strong grounds for the expectation that the service will be accomplished without too severe a loss' and that the action would be 'materially detrimental to the enemy'.[11] The Admiralty were to copy with a similar instruction a year later.[12]

His offer to Hanickoff was followed by the letter to the Czar. This suggested, in the light of the news from Spain, that if the Czar had the same desire for peace as King George and King Gustav, 'for the welfare of mankind', Saumarez would inform his government and agree locally to a mutual cessation of hostilities. The English papers in October reported that he was 'negotiating a peace' and Martha saw this as 'the highest Triumph to thy humane and beneficent heart'.[13] This would have referred to his peace offer to Hanickoff rather than the letter to the Czar since that would not have been public knowledge so soon, but it obviously came as no surprise to her. Nor was Canning wholly averse to peace, but he wanted the approach to come from Napoleon, not from a British admiral. Napoleon had, in fact, been making indirect approaches, according to Coquelle; how genuine they were is rather doubtful on his past form. But for the timing of the Erfurt conference, Saumarez' approach would have gone only to the Czar and so might have been more influential. He had got the approval of both Thornton and Nauckhoff and it seems a commendable, intelligent and creative action.

3 Why were his initial suspicions of Swedish constancy replaced by confidence that their actions would remain friendly even under a French marshal and in a state of war?

The von Rosen letters have been covered in previous chapters and provide useful evidence of how his relationship with Saumarez grew. In fact, it was Krusen-stjerna's influence at the time of Bernadotte's election that persuaded Saumarez to make his important decision to allow Bernadotte safe passage across the Belt. Further research into the Engeström correspondence with Krusenstjerna would be helpful to reveal the background to this, but the letters from Krusenstjerna to Saumarez in the Suffolk Record Office archive bear out the great goodwill that had built up between them by that time. Baron von Platen was another important contact: a leading member of the Swedish government who was grateful to England for permission to import special tools for work on the Gota Canal, his cherished project. He and Saumarez had a fruitful meeting the previous year off the Gulf of Finland and after the peace with Russia Saumarez had received his tribute: 'we cannot yet deny that in an high degree we are indebted to you for our existing as a state … our ports are open to so brave an ally, to so successful a protector'.[14]

But these personal connections, however warm and pleasing, would have been of little benefit without Saumarez' reading of Sweden's political and economic needs and whether they fitted or clashed with those of England. Canning's policy of fear had driven Denmark into a state of hostility against England that she would not relinquish, even when it was evident that Napoleon's days were numbered, leading inevitably to bankruptcy and the loss of Norway. If Saumarez had carried out Wellesley's instruction to treat the Swedish coastal trade as 'enemy' at the start of the 1811 season, or had retaliated for the Carlshamn Cargoes by using his firepower to retake the sequestrated merchant ships, Sweden would almost certainly have felt bound to respond to Alquier's pressure with action rather than deception, to enforce the Continental System to which she was tied by treaty with France, and to cease providing supplies, shelter and, above all, water to Saumarez' Baltic fleet. She would have found herself in the same situation as Denmark, leading to ruin, crushed by the hammer of British seapower on the anvil of the French and Russian armies.

Saumarez recognised this, and realised that it would not be in Britain's longer-term interest. Britain and Sweden both depended on external trade to and from the Baltic, both for their economies and for particular raw materials – salt for Sweden and naval materials for Britain. A 'phoney war' which allowed trade to continue was the best solution for both of them. Smuggling on a grand scale could still continue in a genuine state of war, but it would never match the volume of regular trade and would be subject to frequent intermissions as special efforts were made to eliminate it. Without the constant presence of a British fleet, privateers would be able to do such damage that insurance rates would become prohibitive.

The Admiralty too had recognised this to a degree in their anxiety that Saumarez' fleet should maintain its stocks of water on board its ships at the time of King Gustav's dethronement. But there is nothing apparent in the records of what action should be taken if Bernadotte's impact on Swedish policy were to turn out as they appeared to fear. Their failure to give more positive instructions on finding 'another Malta' which could provide a secure base in the event of active warfare indicates either a lack of thought or a feeling that the Baltic trade would become impossible to maintain. Efforts were certainly being made to find sources for hemp elsewhere in the world and there were hopes that timber and masts from North America might be the answer, despite Byam Martin's derogatory comments on them.[15] As Wellington's campaign on the Peninsula progressed, the Mediterranean was once again opening up to British trade so that the Baltic was no longer the only channel for the distribution into mainland Europe of English manufactures and colonial goods. Rather than make difficult decisions – hence the long delay in coming to a settlement of the Carlshamn dispute – they were happy to leave it to the man on the spot, Saumarez, which is why they showed no wish to replace him after the normal three-year period of command.

What I have not been able to establish is whether von Rosen was a double agent. A memorandum from Ross in 1834 sought to obtain payment to von Rosen of £600, the balance of an amount of £1,000 authorised by Navy Treasurer Rose in 1810. Von Rosen was a younger son with five children and a modest salary. In July 1810, he had written to Engeström: 'Money to defray secret expenses is indispensable. I have already, in my great poverty, paid 400 riksdaler banco and that is a sum I really cannot afford to be without, as I have to borrow for my daily maintenance'.[16] Ross and Consul Smith had been instructed by Saumarez 'to open a secret communication with some individual who had power to supply the fleet with fresh provisions, vegetables etc'. Since fresh provisions were largely organised through Smith, Fenwick and the other unofficial consuls, did the 'etc'. mean secret information or was this just a sweetener to enable Smith more easily to arrange supplies to Wingo?[17]

4 Were there other vice-admirals at the time who might have been equally successful and what difference might another commander-in-chief have made?

In Chapter 2, I looked briefly at other admirals who might have been both available and suitable in the spring of 1808 and come to the conclusion that there were only three, none of whom would probably have wanted to move from their existing situation, one of them in fact dying at about the time Saumarez hoisted his flag. There may well be others lurking in the shadows and still to be researched who might have had the capacity to grow into the task as Saumarez did. There is still so little known about many of the admirals who were active in the ten years of warfare following Trafalgar, partly the result of the dominance of Nelson's fame and partly because the British public of that time, and many historians of later times, have primarily been interested in fleet actions. In his short time in the Baltic when he progressed from post-captain, via Captain of the Fleet (with a short break as Captain of the Royal Yacht), to an independent role as rear-admiral under Saumarez, with two 74s and a joint gunboat force working with the Russian army to defend Riga from French attack, Thomas Byam Martin matured and developed into a politician capable of persuading Wellington that his criticisms of the navy's performance in support of his Peninsular armies were unjustified. The three volumes of his letters published by the Navy Records Society (Hamilton (ed.), *Letters and Papers of Sir Thomas Byam Martin*) throw light on an interesting, talented officer, too junior to take on Saumarez' role but possibly capable of doing so later if he had been able to overcome his distrust of the Swedes. Samuel Hood was even more able, as his masterly evacuation of Moore's troops from Corunna demonstrated, and deserves greater acknowledgement. Had he had a couple more years of seniority as post-captain, his career could have been transformed.

As the government was uncertain in its policy for the Baltic fleet in 1808, one cannot say that Saumarez was specially tailored for the command. He was a 'safe pair of hands', well-liked in the fleet, and a fine seaman. He had also had some diplomatic experience off Cadiz. He was prepared to use his initiative and had shown at Algeciras that he was capable of responding to initial defeat by a vigorous counter-attack. But there was no particular reason to believe that he would stamp his own views so firmly on the command that the government would stand far back and let him get on with it. There may, therefore, have been other vice-admirals who could have responded similarly to the challenges but history does not yet appear to have revealed them.

There were seven critical points at which Saumarez made decisions where another admiral might have chosen differently:

1 At Rogervik, he took the advice of Hood, Byam Martin, and Nauckhoff and allowed himself to be persuaded not to launch an immediate attack, where a Nelson or a Berkeley would have gone straight in. If successful, it could have brought Russia back into the anti-French fold. Failure, of which the odds were great, would not have been disastrous other than the loss of men and material, but would have been a major diplomatic setback.
2 His failure to make a serious attempt to capture and make a base of the Eartholms missed an opportunity that a Nelson or Collingwood would have seized. Trade would have benefited from the ability to use British-flagged vessels to discharge their cargoes there into warehouses for transhipment by smaller neutral craft, and from the removal of a privateers' lair, though water would have had to be found elsewhere.
3 In 1809, his move up the Baltic to support the new Swedish government, not yet recognised by Britain, was an initiative that many other admirals would have waited for the Admiralty to approve and have had to wait too long.

4 Few other admirals would have turned down the opportunity for prize money offered by Wellesley's order in 1810 to treat Swedish ports as 'enemy'. Such aggression would have destroyed the delicate diplomatic balance that had been established.

5 A less positive admiral would have hesitated to allow Bernadotte safe passage across the Belt without any reference to London. Its impact on Bernadotte in favour of maintaining friendship with Britain was enormous.

6 Similarly, Saumarez' decision to take his fleet home without retaliation on the Swedish declaration of war was made without Admiralty advice. It preserved the status quo.

7 Saumarez was alone in not considering British retaliation essential on the news of the Carlshamn Cargoes in 1811. The two-way trust built up between Saumarez and the Swedish government through the mediation of von Rosen was a very personal one that his subordinate admirals and his successor, Hope, failed to achieve.[18]

5 Did the situation produce the man or vice versa, and did he have political weight that made it easier for him to take an independent line?

The government's actions right up to the tripartite treaty of July 1812 were based on the reports Saumarez had sent, as he rightly claimed 'en suite de ma propre conviction'.[19] This conviction had grown and strengthened his actions as the command continued. But he had never been afraid to use his undoubted intelligence and to act on its conclusions. As a newly promoted post-captain at the Battle of the Saintes he had had the temerity to break out of the line, wear to windward of the end of the French line after repairing his damaged rigging and fight his way back along it till he reached their flagship *Ville de Paris* while the rest of his squadron sailed away waiting for its admiral's instructions.[20]

He had shown at Algeciras his ability to turn defeat into triumph and it had also demonstrated his leadership in getting those under him to work like furies to get his damaged squadron back into fighting order in five days. He had done the same in *Russell* after the Battle of the Saintes[21] and again when his men assisted Nelson after the *Vanguard* was dismasted off Corsica, drawing fulsome praise from Nelson.[22] Although not particularly fortunate with prize money, he had little difficulty in recruiting crew, many of them from Guernsey, and on his appointment to *Orion* (74), the whole crew of officers and men of the *Crescent* sought to transfer with him.[23] One reason may have been his strict but fair discipline: 'One great satisfaction I enjoy, that of having a very quiet well disposed Ship's Company, and that are kept orderly and I flatter myself well regulated without exercising severity or rigour.'[24]

Of his subordinate admirals and captains, Samuel Hood and Keats served happily under him both at Algeciras and in the Baltic, and Byam Martin returned after his time in the Royal Yacht, the row over Saumarez' rebuke to him patched up. Admiral Bertie, accepting his appointment under Saumarez in 1808, wrote: 'I had rather serve under your Command than any other person I know in the Service.'[25] Admiral Hotham in his memoirs describes him as 'formal and ceremonious in his manner, very popular with those who serve under him and modest to a degree of himself'.[26] He did not always get on with Hope, his Captain of the Fleet, but Hope stayed for four years till he was made admiral. Saumarez did fall out with Manley Dixon, one of his subordi- nate admirals: 'after his manner of conducting his late correspondence I can no longer have much confidence in him'. Martha was 'scandalised at the ingrati- tude with which he requites thy kindness', but the earlier letter from Sir James giving the details has not survived. Even so: 'the difference existing between us was made up – I believe I may say cordially on both parts'.[27]

The row was connected to his approving Dixon's appointment of his young son to post-captain of the latter's flagship and probably touched upon his honour. As St. Vincent once said in correspondence with Spencer about Captain Foley's hurt pride: 'The honour of an officer may be compared to the chastity of a woman, and once wounded never can be recovered'.[28] Saumarez' particular concern about honour worked two ways. It made him very determined to do what was right and honourable, which helped him to his good understanding with von Rosen, but it made him very touchy – to say the least – over anything that might be considered to diminish his own; hence his remark to Martha on Keats' Red Ribbon and his continuing efforts to obtain the peerage that he felt he deserved both for Algeciras and for his Baltic command.

In an appeal to Lord Liverpool at the Peace in 1814, he lists the personal thanks or letters of approbation he has received from a great range of eminent people for the particular benefits that they or their countries had received from his services in the Baltic: the Emperor of Russia and King of Prussia, Count Metternich of Austria, Viscount Cathcart and Mr. Thornton, General Suchtelen of Russia and Count von Gneisenau of Prussia. Curiously he does not mention Sweden and Bernadotte. It might be thought, however, that if Sweden had seen fit to a make him a Knight Grand Cross of the Order of the Sword and later for King Charles XIII, at the evident request of Bernadotte, to present him with a magnificent sword, his own country should at least have matched these awards. His only recognition from Britain had been a formal letter from the Admiralty on his hauling down his flag conveying the government's 'marked appreciation' for his period of command. Perhaps it was the result of both government and opposition disenchantment with Bernadotte for pursuing his own goal of the capture of Norway and dream of the leadership of France rather than the final defeat of Napoleon.[29] Saumarez' letter rather forlornly ends:

I trust that these important services which I have here enumerated, as also my services in the Americas, and in the late War, will be found to merit your Lordship's favourable consideration, and that you will do me the honour to lay them before the Prince Regent in furtherance of the Memoire which I shall have the honour of laying at the feet of His Royal Highness.

Your Lordship will, I am persuaded, make due allowance for the great anxiety of my mind upon the present occasion, and that in the high rewards conferred upon Naval Officers for their Services during the late long and arduous Contest, I shall also be found deserving some mark of favour.[30]

Further salt was rubbed into his wound in 1818, giving rise to another letter of complaint to Lord Liverpool, when George Hope was given the plum sinecure of Major-General of Marines that had been promised to Saumarez.[31]

Closely linked to honour was honesty. This was a quality in Saumarez that von Rosen recognised and was a major factor in their ability to trust that each would keep his word, making secret agreements possible. 'Saumarez, always as honest as he was loyal' was his comment after his long row out for a meeting on board *Victory*.[32] It also lay behind his relationships with those serving under him and that he expected, but did not always find, in those above him. Invited to 'dine when [the] situation permits' on board the flagship by St Vincent, when blockading off Ushant, he decided: 'I shall sparingly avail myself – there is too much duplicity and deceit in his composition to suit me; and I believe his Captain, with apparent frankness, possesses as much.'[33] Yet was it dishonesty, a desire to maintain morale, or just the wishful thinking of an unsuccessful attacker that enticed Saumarez to report to the consul at Tangier, the day after he had been driven off in the first battle of Algeciras, that he had 'completely succeeded in disabling the enemy's ships who I trust are rendered entirely useless to the enemy for a considerable time, but I am concerned to add with the loss of His Majesty's Ship *Hannibal* who unfortunately got aground under one of the Spanish batteries'?[34]

Linked to honesty was his religious belief: 'So long as I am guided by the best of motives and that I do all in my power for the advancement of the public good, I must commit the rest to the Divine Providence who I trust will endow me with strength of mind proportionately as the difficulties may increase.'[35] It gave him a confidence in taking difficult decisions when he had no instructions from Admiralty – 'with divine assistance we cannot fail'.[36] Writing in 1810 to his nephew, another Richard Saumarez, who was at an early stage of his naval career, he puts on paper his personal principles and motivation:

I cannot be silent on the satisfaction with which I heard that you had preserved and <u>maintained</u> the religious principles planted in your mind before leaving home. <u>This</u> gave me more pleasure than I can express, because it is what will prove of most importance to you – with them you can be <u>every thing</u>, without them the most brilliant exploits are but vanity & emptiness. Courage without principles is a mere animal instinct – a constitutional impulse which may lead men to 'valiant deeds' but never to <u>Great</u> ones. The <u>Good</u> only can be great because they act from motives which whether the issue be prosperous or adverse will maintain their Hearts unshaken, and led on by duty they will be equally 'sans peur & sans reproche', knowing that though the vessel may be wrecked, there is a Harbour ready to receive them!

Cultivate then these Principles my dear Richard, and may <u>experience</u> teach you how precious they are; may they be your guide, your shield, your comfort amidst the difficulties, perils, & troubles of your profession; and if you are called to a career as arduous & active as your Uncle's may you <u>seek</u> support from the same source and find it as he has done.[37]

He regularly sailed with a chaplain on board and held Sunday services: 'allowing nothing short of the most imperative duties of the ship to interrupt divine service'.[38] He was not a 'blue-light' (evangelical) admiral like Gambier, but both he and Martha had these strong religious convictions. While still a captain, he wrote to Lord Spencer, First Lord: 'We have signals to denote that the ship's companies will have time for dinner or breakfast; why should there not be one to signify that they will have time for the performance of Divine service?'[39] Not unusually at that time and in their class, their Protestantism extended to a detestation of the Roman Catholic Church. Martha even enthused about the French entry into Rome and deposition of the Pope: 'I think we may now say Popery is at an end ... an event which since the Reformation has been expected with ardour and pious zeal by the Reformed Church.'[40] On a lighter note, she later reported 'another Abomination in Israel'; the Grave-digger had planted potatoes in the churchyard – 'it is probably for his own use, and as the Dean cannot but know, for he must see it, who is to find fault? But it is shocking!'[41]

On his return to Guernsey Saumarez gave land and £1,000 for the first English-language church on Guernsey.[42] He was also very involved with the funding of church schools there:

Thy account of the School and its progressive state gives me real pleasure – spare nothing that can be of service for the benefit of the Scolars [sic] of both the Schools. I wish we undertook a similar plan at some of the other Parishes where it is so much wanted, particularly the Vale.

He tells Martha that his prize money for 1807/8 is likely to be £12,000 or more – 'we needed not this addition to require my repeating to Thee not to be sparing of expense'.[43] This extended to other charitable works including donations to individuals ruined by the failure of a local bank: 'It is our part to afford any relief to the industrious and who have familes that may need it and two or three hundred pounds cannot be better applied ... the [fall] in the stocks makes our loss the greater – *mais n'importe*, Providence will always make up to us the deficiency' and 'we cannot apply the superfluity which Providence has entrusted to us [better] than in bestowing it on those who are in need.'[44] Even as a captain, he had been generous in his charitable giving, sending a bill of exchange for £50 to be distributed to the poor of Guernsey because of the adverse weather and cost of food, adding: 'I wish on no consideration it should be known coming from me.'[45]

It may explain why he was prepared twice to forgo the opportunities of taking a great number of Swedish ships as prizes. Not many naval wives will have received such a letter as he wrote in July 1808: 'I wish thy draft had been for 1,500 instead of 150 and must entreat Thee to be a little more lavish of what we have such superabundance.'[46]

In the same way, much of Saumarez' concern over prizes was for those serving under him. When a city bank collapsed, his fear was that 'Mr. Champion [his secretary] may have left a considerable portion of Prize money belonging to the Squadron in Austin Friars'.[47] Another source of reward was freight – a commission of 1 to 2 per cent when a warship carried gold or silver, as a safer transport than a merchant ship. Sweden received substantial subsidies in specie in the first two years of his command which had to be physically transported, not always in ships that were under his flag: 'Dumaresq [his flag-captain] is to receive the Money – £150,000. I was fortunate in having applied for it – as it had been intended for another ship. It will give him near five hundred pounds. Tell Mrs. D. of it but I do not wish these things to be much talked of.'[48] He refused a gift of Madeira wine from an American trader, insisting that 'it will at any time give me pleasure to render service to the ships of the United States so long as I can do it consistently with my Duty' – the diplomat in him then adding 'if a good understanding between both our countries enables me to continue my favourable disposition to the subjects of the United States'.[49] However, with the American declaration of war, by August his views had changed and, like the whole of the Royal Navy, he expected 'to see in England the whole of that insolent Squadron that struck the first blow, and after we have taught them humility by a little chastisement we may hold out the olive branch once more to them'.[50] Pride came before a fall; though doubtless he would have been delighted at his family's link, mentioned on p. 217 below, to Captain Broke of the *Shannon*, who restored the navy's pride in 1813 in his defeat of the USS *Chesapeake*.

A scattered command such as his could only be run satisfactorily with a good degree of delegation. Saumarez established this from the start. His rear-admirals in the Sound, the Belt and the Baltic were very much left to get on with their tasks. Information was exchanged rather than instructions sent. Keats and later Dixon established the convoy routine successfully with amazingly low losses of ships considering the numbers involved and the hostility of the Danish gun-boats. One convoy and its escort were destroyed in 1808, another lost in the ice that winter, but the worst loss was the capture of a complete convoy of 47 ships by five Norwegian gun-brigs off the Skaw in July 1810.[51] Individual officers were expected to use their initiative and, like Captain Dashwood, soon learnt to adapt. A letter to Byam Martin makes it quite clear:

> The very unaccountable neglect of Mr. Champion in having inclosed the orders intended for you by the *Cressy* to Admiral Morris, would have been attended with the greatest inconvenience had it not been for the very judicious manner in which you carried into effect what you considered to have been my instructions and I return you my sincere thanks for preventing the service sustaining any injury from so great a mistake.[52]

In conjunction with this, he was ready to let them take the praise. It was Keats' report on the successful rescue of the Spanish troops that reached the King and the pages of the *Gazette*, not one from Saumarez – something that Nelson is unlikely to have allowed. In the search for the French fleet, Nelson was unwilling even to let a letter from Sir James to Lady Saumarez go with those he was sending to government, 'mais tu sais bien qu'il ne se met guère en peine d'écrire lui-même'.[53] Saumarez had the not uncommon ambivalent way of not wanting to be seen to blow his own trumpet but being upset when other people wouldn't blow it for him.

His awareness of the horrors of war for a civilian population had come as a 20-year-old lieutenant in the War of American Independence: the destructive savagery of a civil war. He had fought in as many fleet actions as any other officer and been successful in a close-quarters action against a French frigate of the same size. More than once men had been killed alongside him and he had appeared unmoved, so he had mastered fear of personal injury, helped both by that greatest of blessings, luck, and by his religious faith. At Cape St Vincent, he was making notes as he climbed up to the poop with the master, who ducked as a roundshot whizzed overhead. Saumarez 'never moved – but said coolly "we are not shot yet" and went on with his scribbling'.[54]

These qualities had carried him through his very active and successful career as post-captain and admiral, and brought him to the Baltic command. His early opportunities had depended on the connection of his two uncles with Keppel during Anson's voyage in the *Centurion*. But he had no other inherited interest, depending simply on the reputation he built for himself by his actions. He twice turned down offers of safe Admiralty seats in Parliament:

> from my coming into the Service I had kept myself perfectly detached from all Party, and under many Administrations I had ever been ready to be employed where my Services were required – my sole and only view being the good of

my Country and I feared I could not accept of a seat in Parliament consistent with these Principles.[55]

Writing to his brother in 1807, when in temporary command of the Channel Fleet, he spoke of a possible seat in Parliament 'at some future period ... but you may rely on it that I never wish to have one without maintaining my independence, and being perfectly free and unbiased by any party'.[56] Both he and Martha were ardent supporters of George III and against Catholic Emancipation. Celebrating the Royal Birthday in 1811, she wrote:

> I fear it is the last any of us will have to celebrate <u>The Day</u>. From every appearance our venerable good King will ere the next arrives have shaken off his earthly Crown for an incorruptible one – blessed exchange for him! What it may prove for the Nation must be left for Time to shew'.[57]

Contrary to St Vincent's belief that when an officer of the navy married, he lost much of his value in his profession,[58] it is clear that it was above all Saumarez' love for his wife Martha, along with his religious principles and sense of duty, that supported him in the difficult times in the Baltic and strengthened him in his willingness to follow what he believed to be the best course without or even against instructions. Their love for each other shines through all their letters. His were normally addressed to 'My Dearest Life' or 'My Dearest Love' and the expression 'Best Beloved' is frequently used by both of them – words that were all deeply meant. They had married on 27 October 1788, when Saumarez was aged 31 and she was 20. An undated commonplace book in his handwriting maintains:

> Those Marriages generally abound most with Love and Constancy that are preceded by a long Courtship. The Passion should strike Root and gather Strength before Marriage be grafted on it. A long Course of Hope and Expectation fixes the Idea in our Minds and habituates us to a Fondness for the Person beloved.
>
> Good Nature and Evenness of Temper will give you an easy Companion for Life. Virtue and good Sense an agreeable Friend; Love and Constancy a good Wife or Husband.
>
> Marriage enlarges the Scene of Happiness and Miseries. A Marriage of Love is pleasant. A Marriage of Interest easy; and a Marriage where both meet, happy. A happy Marriage has in it all the Measures of Friendship, all the Enjoyment of Sense and Reason, and indeed all the Sweets of Life.[59]

From the early days of his marriage, the letters Saumarez received from Martha were of enormous importance to him and he chafed when the post was delayed. On his first absence, two years after his marriage, a plaintive letter to Martha starts: 'My dearest Life, I wait with the utmost solicitude the arrival of the post, and every minute after ten o'clock appears an hour until my expectation is determined.' Twenty-two years later, he writes: 'I cannot tell Thee how often I have perused and reperused the contents of the last precious letter to the 22nd and always with fresh delights.'[60] At Wingo, letters to and from Guernsey took 13–16 days although, to her delight, one of his letters arrived in eight days. When he was up the Baltic, they could take six weeks or more. Off Gotland, in 1808, he wrote:

> It is now six weeks since the date of Thy last letter, as long a privation as I have yet experienced since I came upon the station, and I fear it is what I must still be subject to for some time longer as we are on our way higher up the Baltic.*[61]

It was one reason why from 1810 he made Wingo his base: 'I am in doubt if I shall go up to the Gulf of Finland, this place being more centrical, and admitting easier access to every part of the squadron exclusive of receiving the dispatches more expeditiously', adding (in 1811) 'particularly from the means it affords me of hearing from Thee'.[62] In a long letter written in the turmoil of affairs after the French invasion of Russia, he welcomes the arrival of the packet with her

> thrice precious letter of 22nd which I need not say was my companion and formed the chief occupation of my thoughts during the night – though it did not break in upon my rest having had near four hours good sleep ... Thy dear letter will be my solace and joyful comfort when I can enjoy its precious contents more tranquilly than in the midst of this busy scene.[63]

She shared his craving for letters:

> When thou art gone, what shall I do, perhaps to be a fortnight, three Weeks, a Month without hearing from Thee? What a desolate being I shall become – For Thou art the life of my life, and from thy Letters & the expectation of those Treasures I derive all the comfort I enjoy in Thy absence.

This particular letter, written in January 1795, is a splendid one. It ranges from that heartfelt cry of a young wife (she was 27 at the time), through a motherly entreaty 'to provide Thyself amply with flannel waistcoats and draws [sic], & even with worsted stockings – & let me recommend seriously your taking

---

* They retained the use of the old-fashioned 'Thee' and 'Thou'; I am not sure whether this is an archaism or whether it was the French influence on Guernsey, where French was in many cases not the second but the first language (Saumarez' distinguished naval uncle Philip had been sent to England to learn English at the age of 11 in order to get into the Royal Navy).

our Aunt B's advice of wearing night caps made of the fleecy hosiery';* to the oratory of:

> reflection restores my fortitude & again my breast glows that at a period so critical our Country has such a one as Thee to defend its dearest rights. May the Almighty long preserve Thee such & raise up many like Thee, in the defence of such a Cause. For such a Cause, & in such times, I, even I, feel I could too 'do mighty deeds'. But to descend from Heroics to matter of facts, I shall tell Thee I was last night at Mrs. Nelson's; she is a cheerful, pleasant woman and I passed a cheerful, pleasant evening.[64]

Both Martha and Mrs. Nelson, like many naval officers' wives, were staying in Bath and, after the news of Cape St Vincent, they had: 'seen each other almost every day since these good news & the more I know her the higher she rises in my esteem'. Later, she:

> asked the Nelsons but they excused themselves – the Admiral I do not take to be much of a <u>Ladies Man</u> – Lady N says as much, so that it is something like a wonder his having called with her. Do you know that he accused Thee of <u>spoiling</u> all the wives of Thy brother officers on your station? Yes truly, by thy attention in writing so constantly to thy own that it made all the others murmur. He said till you came among them he thought he was a very punctual correspondent, but that you outdid everybody. Think whether my heart did not thank Thee.[65]

Martha's letters during his Baltic command are wide ranging: a mixture of local news, management of the house and estate, reports of the family, but also comments on the political situation, what she read in the newspapers and his own reports on the situation in the Baltic, and religious matters, as well as anxieties about his health. And many endearments:

> Four weeks this day since I lost sight of Thee, dearest and Best Beloved of my Heart! At this hour I still heard Thy voice, still saw Thy form – but the hour of separation was also in view – and what that hour is none can conceive but those who feel it.[66]

She was very alarmed when the Guernsey packet with long-awaited letters was captured by a French privateer off Alderney 'lest one of Thy precious letters should have fallen in the Enemy's hands', and even have been read 'by the Giant himself' but was relieved to hear that the mailbag was sunk before the packet surrendered.[67]

---

* He responded that he had already provided himself 'with draws of the fleecy hosiery – they are 9 shillings a pair but I think them so well worth the price that I would advise your father to have them'.

However deferential she might seem to his views and wishes, she had a strong mind of her own. When there were rumours of an impending attack on Guernsey, he wrote urging her to cross to England. She in reply made no mention of the French. He tried teasing her: 'I must suppose Thou art determined to repel their whole force with the aid of thy household only, as thou hast not condescended to hint even at their intentions.' But she responded: 'the alarm ceased before I thought it necessary to take my departure – my going would have been the signal for many other families to move also, but while the Admiral's Lady stayed they thought they could stay too.'[68] *Noblesse oblige*!

Sir James, Martha and the children were a close and devoted family and concern over the children was a constant theme of the parents' letters. They had eight: the birthdate of the last, Martha, is not known but their seventh child, John, was born in 1806. His son, the 4th Baron, was to marry in 1882 the granddaughter of Philip Broke, captain of the *Shannon* in her victory over the USS *Chesapeake*. She had inherited the Middleton family estates in Suffolk and London, and five years later they came to live at Shrubland Hall outside Ipswich where the family stayed until 2007, when the 7th Baron moved back to Guernsey.

A great attraction of the Baltic command was that Sir James could return to family life in Guernsey for much of each winter. At the end of a long and worrying period of winter gales, when he was desperately trying to get the last, long-overdue convoy back to Britain, he still found time to write a lengthy letter ending: 'Thou wilt more readily conceive than I can express the happiness I feel at the prospect of so soon embracing Thee with all the precious Group.'[69] This is a rather different view to that of Captain Griffith, a friend of Byam Martin, relating that his wife had added to his family: 'the inevitable tax of my coming on shore: and yet I was in hopes that well stricken in years as we both are, there was an end of all such doings between us – my share of the concern now amounts to 3 boys and 3 girls.'[70]

By 1812, little Amelia Saumarez, aged 12, was being taught by her elder sisters but had 'so little taste for music that it would be wasting time to attempt her learning it'. Sir James was against her learning to draw, for reasons unexplained but accepted by Martha, and was only persuaded to agree since 'in this Age of Talents, a young lady who neither Plays nor Draws will not be supposed to have been educated & it may be as great a disadvantage to her as the evil we wish to avoid'.[71] Martha was surprised to find that the eldest son James played in a cricket match when visiting Guernsey and ranked among the best players. She was relieved that Colonel Le Blanc was there to 'guard against its being a passport to other dissipation'.[72] James had just come down from Christ Church, Oxford, but the next year took deacon's orders and ended safely as a parson in Yorkshire.

Actually, it seems that Martha had not been Saumarez' first choice as wife

Figure 14. James Saumarez and Martha Dobree. Miniatures on ivory by Philip Jean, 1786 (by kind permission of R.R. Jeune of Jersey)

and that he had been turned down earlier by a Miss Pierce. He reported a chance meeting with her in June 1790 at the trial of Warren Hastings. Martha wrote back: 'she claims a portion of my esteem & regard from her having once possessed so great a share of yours – I sincerely wish the new connection she has formed may be equal to her merit, though it can never equal, much less make amends for the happiness she rejected'. Her letters acknowledge that he enjoys the company of the fair sex and, indeed, encourage him in it. When he relates the visit of a German countess on her way from Wingo to England, she writes: 'Mary [their eldest daughter] asked if thou wert not highly delighted to see a female after being so long without the sight of one – I said I doubt it not'; after another visit: '*c'est bien* que Madame la Consule is too antiquated for scandal – or rather the Chief is known to be impregnable, or these frequent visits would, no would not, make me jealous … Badinage apart, I am really glad Thou hast an opportunity of conversing with a sensible <u>female</u> now and then.'[73] Countess von Rosen's parties in Saumarez' final year gave him opportunity for this and there were return visits on board *Victory*: 'The Countess is an amiable well bred woman – without having the least of that laxity of character which most all the Ladies in these countries too much possess.'[74] A long gossipy letter from Martha ends with details of their son James, aged 20, riding with a lady 11 years older:

> Dost thou not recognize <u>Thy</u> son in this <u>penchant</u> for the Sex? – and since it is '<u>safe</u>' can'st Thou lament it? What a barbarous being is he who is insensible

to the influence of those whom God made to be an 'Helpmeet for him' – so that while it is under proper restraint I do not regret at finding him a <u>general</u> admirer and <u>in due time</u> may he find a select one, whom like his Father he may bless, and who like his Mother, may bestow on him an undivided heart, and a love as durable (that is to say eternal) as that which fills the soul of her who hopes to be through the infinite ages of eternity Thine.[75]

If Saumarez enjoyed the company of women throughout his life, it did not in any way diminish his love for Martha or hers for him. He wrote to his brother at the time of his marriage: 'To have the power of making her happy who has ever been the joy and delight of my soul, far surpasses all that I have ever formed of felicity in this world.'[76] Wishing he could find her a gift 'in this desolate country that affords nothing worthy of Thy acceptance', he wrote: 'be assured of the sincerity of <u>that heart</u> which is for ever devoted <u>to Thee</u> and <u>Thee alone</u>'.[77] At the time of their wedding anniversary in 1811, she wrote of:

> Retrospects such as never woman had cause to love as I have ... this was the day – this the hour, when seated on the window seat in our Parlour, and I on a chair adjoining, thou first essayed the pledge that two days after bound us for ever ... Oh my Saumarez, what a pledge of felicity has it proved to thy happy Wife and how many, <u>many</u> grateful sensations does it not excite for thy faithful accomplishment of all that it promised. God reward Thee! Dearest of men.[78]

Unlike St Vincent's belief that when an officer of the navy married, he lost much of his value in his profession, that love combined with Saumarez' religious principles and sense of duty to support him in the difficult times in the Baltic and strengthen him in his willingness to follow what he believed to be the best course without or even against instructions, as he had shown as early as the Battle of the Saintes.

Leo Heaps suggests that the rounding of Cape Horn in the *Tryallon* was the making of Saumarez' uncle Philip.[79] Sir James was older when he came to the Baltic and was already 'made', but his command there enabled him to flower in a way that had not been possible in his earlier appointments and might not have been foreseen. In so doing, he imposed himself upon the situation and created the circumstances in which he was able to continue to flower. 'Cometh the man, cometh the hour', rather than vice versa. The effect was to give substance to a British Baltic policy where there had been none, to preserve the two-way trade that was vital to the British economy, to keep Sweden – in practice, if not in theory – as an ally rather than an enemy, to help bring Russia back into the fold of resistance to France and, by the frustration of Napoleon's attempts to enforce the Continental System, to be at least partly responsible for his fatal error of the invasion of Russia.

As for his opponent Napoleon, if one accepts the arguments of Professor Esdaile on his motives for that invasion, there is 'one explanation and one explanation alone: frustrated by the long war in Spain and Portugal, and the failure of the continental blockade to bring the British to heel, Napoleon was simply bent on flexing his military muscle and winning fresh glory'.[80] Yet beyond and above was there still a more grandiose dream?

> How can I help it if an excess of power leads me to assume the dictatorship of the world? ... My destiny is not yet accomplished: I must finish that which is but as yet sketched. We must have a European code, a European court of appeal, the same coins, the same weights and measures, the same laws: I must amalgamate all the people of Europe into one, and Paris must be the capital of the world.[81]

Against that, Saumarez had played his formidable but quiet part. In a letter of 15 June 1827, von Rosen goes to the heart of the matter:

> The history of this period picks out the names of people who in the cause of that time have shown only bravery, first duty of every military man who fights for his country. I wager that in the biographies of your Excellency the historian will extol as they deserve your high military deeds, but will slide over if not forget your stroke of politics in 1810 which led the way to a change in the very existence of Europe that was better devised than anything that Lord Castlereagh did in all his long ministry.[82]

I hope that this study may have continued the work so ably commenced by Tony Ryan to show Admiral Sir James Saumarez in his full worth.

Epilogue

After his return from the Baltic in November 1812, Saumarez did not serve again afloat. Promotion up the ranks of admirals followed as those ahead of him in seniority died. He flew his flag again as Admiral of the White from April 1824 till 10 May 1827 as Port Admiral, Plymouth, and in 1830 he became Admiral of the Red, the highest rank short of Admiral of the Fleet. He received an Honorary DCL from Oxford in 1814, but it was not until 1 October 1831 that the longed-for reward was announced – his being raised to the peerage as Baron de Saumarez. He was the first native-born Guernseyman so honoured and the island went wild with excitement, greeting his return from England on 25 October, after a passage beset by gales, with cheering crowds and, the next day, a more formal civic address.[1] His journeys to England thereafter were infrequent[2] and his only attendance in the Lords was to vote for the Reform Bill.[3]

Although retired from active naval service other than his time at Plymouth, he became heavily involved in a wide range of other public and charitable services, particularly those concerned with the Church, the Bible and schools. After three years of declining health, he died on 9 October 1836, aged 79. He was buried at his parish church in Castel at what was intended as a private ceremony, but over 1,000 people are said to have attended, all the shops in town closed and minute guns fired from Fort George throughout the day.[4] Sadly, four of his eight children died before him, two in infancy, but he had 84 nephews and nieces and their children living, to each of whom he left £100.[5] He was succeeded as second Baron by his eldest son James, Rector of Huggate in Yorkshire. Martha lived on for 13 years and was buried beside him in 1849. In 1876, a 99-foot-high obelisk in Guernsey granite was erected in his honour on top of his favourite hill in Delancey Park. It was demolished by the German occupation forces in 1943 and a group was set up in 2006 to study the possibility of its replacement on the remaining base of the old one to a new design.

Appendix 1
Glossary of Place Names

I have generally used the place names from *The Times Comprehensive Atlas of the World*, 10th edition (1999), except where the anglicised form is widely used currently or the name used by the navy at that time seems more appropriate. In these instances the Atlas names are shown below:

Name in text	*Atlas name*
Åbo	Turku
Baltic (Baltiski) Port	Paldiski
Colberg	Kolobrzeg
Copenhagen	København
Danzig	Gdańsk
Elbing	Elbląg
Elsinore	Helsingør
Flemish Roads	Ålvsborgsfjorden
Friedland	Pravdinsk
Frische-Haff	Kaliningradskiy Zaliv
Funen	Fyn
Gothenburg	Göteborg
Grodno	Hrodna
Hawke Road	Hakefjord
Jutland	Jylland
Koll	Kullen
Konigsberg	Kaliningrad
Ladoga (lake)	Ladozhskoye Ozero
Liebau	Liepäja
Memel	Klaipėda
Moldavia	Moldova
Nargan Island	Naissaar
Niemen (river)	Nyoman
Pillau	Baltiysk
Pomerania	Mecklenburg-Vorpommern
Reval	Tallinn
Rogervik	Paldiski
Scania	Skåne
Serampore	Shrirampur
Skaw	Skagen
Sleeve	Skagerrak
Sproe	Sprogø

Stettin	Szscecin
Sveaborg	Suomenlinna
Tilsit	Sovetsk
Tonningen	Tönning
Tranquebar	Tharangambadi
Wallachia	(now incorporated in Romania)
Wingo Sound	Vinga Sand
Zealand	Sjaelland

England/English. Since these terms were so widely used at the time instead of Britain/British, I have not corrected them unless there is a danger of confusion.

Appendix 2
Brief notes on some Lesser-known Names

France

Alquier, Baron	Special envoy and minister at Stockholm, 1810–11
Antraigues, Comte d'	French royalist agent in Britain; murdered 1812
Berthier, Prince of Wagram	Marshal, Chief of Staff to Napoleon
Caulaincourt, Duke of Vicenze	Ambassador in Moscow, 1808–11; Foreign Minister 1813
Champagny, Duke of Cadore	Foreign Minister, 1807–11
Davout, Prince of Eckmühl	Marshal; succeeded Bernadotte in northern Germany 1810
Maret, Duke of Bassano	Foreign Minister, 1811–13
Ranchoup	Consul at Gothenburg, 1810–11

Great Britain

Barrow, John	Secretary to the Admiralty, 1804–48
Cathcart, Lord	Commander of British army at Copenhagen, 1807
Champion, Samuel	Secretary to Admiral Saumarez
Croker, John Wilson	Secretary to the Admiralty, 1809–30
Dixon, Rear Admiral Manley	In command in the Great Belt, 1809–12
Drusina, Louis	Consul, then agent, in Memel; alias Heinrich Hahn
Dumaresq, Captain Philip	Flag captain of *Victory*; relative of Saumarez
Fenwick, Charles	Consul in Denmark, moved to Hälsingborg, Sweden, 1808
Foster, Augustus	Secretary/chargé d'affaires in Stockholm 1808–10
Foy, George	British businessman/agent in Stockholm
Hope, Captain George	Captain of the Fleet, later Rear-Admiral, 1808–12
Johnson, John Mordaunt	Irish-born; confidential British agent in northern Europe
Martin, Captain Thomas Byam	Captain of *Implacable* 1808; Rear-Admiral at Riga 1812
Merry, Anthony	Minister at Stockholm, 1808–9
Mulgrave, Sir Henry Phipps	First Lord of the Admiralty, 1807–10

Pole, William Wellesley	Secretary to the Admiralty, 1807–9
Reynolds, Rear-Admiral	In command at Hanö 1810–11; drowned in *St George*
Smith, John	Consul in Gothenburg, 1804–13
Thornton, Edward	Minister at Stockholm, 1808 and 1812–17
Yorke, Charles	First Lord of Admiralty 1810–12

Sweden

Adlerberg, Carl Gustaf	Minister in London, 1807–8
Adlerkreutz, General	Commander, Swedish army in Finland
Adlersparre, Colonel	Leader of rebellion against Gustav IV
Armfelt, General	Commander, Swedish army of the North
Cronsted, Admiral	Commandant, Sveaborg; former Commander-in-Chief of Fleet
Ehrenheim, Baron von	Chancellor 1801 to June 1809
Ehrenström, Colonel	Military Commandant, Gothenburg
Engestrom, Baron von	Chancellor from 1809
Krusenstjerna, Admiral	Flag-Captain, Karlskrona 1808, then Admiral
Lagerbjelke, Baron	Secretary to Gustav IV; briefly Foreign Secretary, 1809
Lagerheim, Baron	Finance Minister
Nauckhoff, Admiral	Commander-in-Chief Swedish Fleet at Rogervik
Platen, Baron von	Former Admiral; important Councillor of State
Puke, Admiral	Commander-in-Chief Karlskrona, 1809; then Admiral of the Fleet
Sodermania, Duke of	Uncle of Gustav IV; succeeded him as Charles XIII
Suremain, General de	French émigré; became inspector general of artillery
Tawast, General	Commander of Swedish West Coast Army
Toll, Field Marshal Baron	Governor-General of Scania

Bibliographical note

The Saumarez letters, both private and public, have provided the core of the research. There are in the Shrubland archive 277 letters between husband and wife from the five years Saumarez was Commander-in-Chief in the Baltic; they wrote to each other, often at length, at least once a week during his months abroad. The official correspondence, catalogued in the Suffolk Record Office through the assistance of the Historical Manuscripts Commission has over 3,600 documents. A number of the latter evidently only came to light after Tony Ryan had completed his edition of Saumarez' official Baltic correspondence for the Navy Records Society. This gives an excellent but relatively concise picture of events in the Baltic from 1808 to 1812. Whether for financial or editorial reasons, Ryan only selected for publication 150 documents – just over 4 per cent – from the archive. A further 100 documents were included by Ryan from other sources. There were also a considerable number of documents added to the Suffolk archive after the publication of the edition. This may explain why the interesting and revealing document which appears to show Saumarez' strategic thoughts prior to the 1809 season was not included.* There are many other interesting and useful unpublished documents in the archive that add substantially to the picture that Ryan drew. However, his two earlier articles on British trade with the Baltic and its defence provide more detail and their conclusions appear as valid today as when he wrote them.[1] Sadly, though I twice made contact with him, Tony Ryan was already restricted by the illness that ended in his death and we were not able to discuss the documents and sources used for this study.

Count Von Rosen acted as the link man between Saumarez and the Swedish government. Efforts to find any archive of his letters in Sweden for a long time proved abortive, until I was told of the Engeström Collection. Efforts to trace the other side of the correspondence – from Engeström to von Rosen – were unsuccessful. Reading and translating handwritten old Swedish was beyond my limited skills in the language and since the letters were in bound volumes they had to be microfilmed rather than photocopied, adding substantially to the time and expense. However, Jan Bring, a retired Royal Swedish Navy Commodore, came to the rescue and transcribed and translated the two-thirds of the letters that I thought looked most relevant. They have been invaluable

* See pp. 86–88 above.

in substantiating Swedish government attitudes and objectives in the difficult and complex diplomatic situation, the other side of the coin to those revealed in Saumarez' domestic letters.

I was disappointed to find that there were apparently no letters to von Rosen in Bernadotteska Arkivet held in the Royal Castle in Stockholm from Bernadotte (later King Karl XIV John) when he was Crown Prince during the period under study. Through the Archivist, I obtained permission from King Gustav to access the letterbooks for 1810–11 which held some useful comments (written in French since Bernadotte always used his native language rather than Swedish), but no direct letters – although von Rosen indicated that he had received some. The main problem was that documents had to be speci-fied in detail and requested a month in advance for transfer to the Riksarkivet, so browsing was impossible. The Gierrta-Pukesta Collection in the National Archive had a few letters from Bernadotte to Admiral Puke.

Until 2006, Sir John Ross's edition of the Saumarez Memoirs formed the only full biography of the Admiral, published in 1838, only two years after his death in Guernsey. Ross, later famous as an Arctic explorer, served under Saumarez in the Baltic: he became the liaison officer between the British and Swedish navies and spoke Swedish fluently. He evidently had full access to the Saumarez correspondence when editing and there are annotations in his hand on a number of the items, including some of the domestic correspondence, though only a few of the latter documents are quoted in the *Memoirs and Corre-spondence of Admiral Lord Saumarez*. Ross also drew from his own experiences in the Baltic, and understandably takes a somewhat hagiographic viewpoint, drawing the bulk of his information from the one source. The Saumarez family were actually not at all happy with Ross' work and the reviews also were bad. Nonetheless, Count von Platen, writing in 1840, felt that the book, despite its weaknesses, displayed: 'the great many noble and exalted qualities that were entered in one man, handing down to posterity the memory of that man as one of the brightest ornaments of his profession, of his country and in fact of the whole mankind'.[2]

The entry for Saumarez in Ralfe's *The Naval Biography of Great Britain* is even more praising, like many others of his entries, and records the events without adding greatly to one's understanding. Ralfe devotes considerable space to deploring the failure of government and monarch to raise Saumarez to the peerage, quoting Lord Grey's speech at the Royal Naval Club, Plymouth, in 1825, when he said: 'if ever name should or would have graced the peerage, it should have been that of Saumarez'. It was a matter on which Saumarez himself felt extremely bitter, which was only remedied five years before his death – by Grey, in October, 1831. William James' six-volume history of 1822–4 predomi-nantly concerns itself with battles, both fleet and single-ship, so it is unsur-prising that his only reference to Saumarez personally in the Baltic is that in

1810 'with five or six sail of the line [he] prevented the Swedish or the Russian fleet from being in any degree troublesome'.[3] I have commented in the Introduction on the works by Mahan (see pp. 2–3).

Happily, the twenty-first century has seen a revival of interest in admirals of the French Revolutionary and Napoleonic Wars other than Nelson, perhaps in reaction to the flood of books and articles arising from the Bicentenary of Trafalgar. Peter Le Fevre and Richard Harding's volume on Nelson's contemporaries, *British Admirals of the Napoleonic Wars*, following on from their similar one on his *Precursors*, contains a sound chapter on Saumarez by David Greenwood. He suggests: 'While on occasions he was tactically unimaginative, his strategic vision was unrivalled, even by Nelson. There were few who achieved as much, and even fewer who achieved more', and he maintains that Saumarez was one of those who contributed to Napoleon's downfall.[4]

David Shayer's recent useful 'chronological narrative' for La Société Guernesiaise deliberately omits footnotes and quotations from primary sources in order to be succinct and readable rather than a work of scholarship. But his conclusion is one with which one would not argue, that Saumarez' Baltic command: 'demanded skills quite different from those normally required of a naval commander confronting the enemy. If Saumarez just missed Nelson's fighting genius, he demonstrated a breadth of ability over a wider range of challenges'.[5]

Lee Bienkowski's similar study, *Admirals in the Age of Nelson*, also has a chapter on Saumarez.[6] It is entertainingly written but not entirely accurate and simply draws its information from Clowes, James, Brenton and Corbett, with just a touch of Ryan. Another recent publication devoted to Saumarez, by A.W. Wilson, also quotes extensively from material already published and does not really add anything new. Its title, *The Happy Warrior*, conveys a rather misleading image of the Admiral.

G.J. Marcus, in *The Age of Nelson*, the second volume of his three-volume history of the British navy, is one of the few earlier historians to pay tribute to Saumarez' role in the Baltic: 'The skilful diplomacy and personal popularity of the Admiral were a major contributory factor in the development of the alliance against Napoleon in 1812. Saumarez, indeed, may be said to have played much the same role in the Baltic that Collingwood played in the Mediterranean'.[7] He does not point out the great advantage Saumarez had over Collingwood: that the coming of the northern winter allowed the commander-in-chief to return to England to recuperate from December to February, unlike the unfortunate Collingwood. Marcus' comments appear to be drawn almost entirely from Ross and Ryan.

Most other works in English do little more than mention Saumarez in passing, as a relatively minor player in a fringe area. His name very often fails to appear even in the index. Of the more recent political histories of the period,

Rory Muir has two paragraphs on the Baltic in his study *Britain and the Defeat of Napoleon 1807–1815*. He is complimentary towards Saumarez, saying that 'he displayed great tact and skill in handling his difficult duties which were as much diplomatic as naval'; but his comments too come from Ross and Ryan and do not add anything new.[8] Similarly, Robert Daly's paper in *The Mariner's Mirror* on the Russian navy of this period draws on Ross, Anderson, Byam Martin and Mahan, again without adding anything. Alistair Horne's *How Far From Austerlitz?* does not mention him at all; nor does Wendy Hinde in her biography *George Canning*. Christopher Hall in *British Strategy in the Napoleonic Wars* mentions that Saumarez' fleet in May, 1810, was the second largest in the Royal Navy and pays considerable attention to the situation in the Baltic without pointing particularly to Saumarez' part in it, other than mentioning the rebuke he received for writing to the Czar.[9] Paul Kennedy in *The Rise and Fall of British Naval Mastery* pays tribute St Vincent, Howe, Hood, Duncan, Cornwallis and Keith, as admirals alongside Nelson and to Broke, Douglas, Troubridge, Darby, Hardy and Foley as captains, as well as to some of the brilliant frigate captains. But Saumarez does not rate a mention and Kennedy's coverage of the Baltic at that time is sketchy and inaccurate as to the part played by Sweden in breaching the Continental System despite French pressure.[10] Oliver Warner's earlier wide-ranging study of the Baltic in history, *The Sea and the Sword*, does acknowledge fully the part that Saumarez played there in 1808–12: 'Saumarez had an extremely difficult task, but his abilities were worthy of it, and for five years his was the master hand in naval affairs of the western and central area.'[11] Michael Lewis in his survey of the distribution of officers by home counties in the British Isles draws attention to the high number (11) relative to population coming from Guernsey and mentions Saumarez as 'one of the war's greatest sailors'.[12]

The section on Saumarez in Ludovic Kennedy's book, *Nelson's Band of Brothers*, draws attention to his correspondence with the Spanish Admiral Mazarredo when in command of the inshore squadron blockading Cadiz in 1797, for which St Vincent wrote to congratulate him on his diplomatic skills[13] – the first mention of him in this light in any correspondence. Otherwise, it does not go into any depth. Fitchett, 70 years earlier, writing also about Nelson's captains, is much more perceptive. He believed that 'Nelson frankly did not like Saumarez' and that there was 'a complete and permanent lack of sympathy'. 'He was apt to offer Nelson not compliments but advice' and 'while both Saumarez and Ball admired their famous admiral, Ball's admiration was of the loudly vocal sort, such as Nelson loved; that of Saumarez was inarticulate'. In a rather delightful phrase, he writes: 'Saumarez might have sat with benevolent countenance and lawn sleeves beside Ball on the bench of bishops, and with as little incongruity', yet he goes on to add: 'for downright fighting

Saumarez was almost the equal of Nelson, and in more technical seamanship, he was probably superior'.[14]

The most recent masterly work by Professor Rodger also acknowledges Saumarez' role and his insistence on 'following his own policy of conciliation, ignoring the fears, and at times the direct orders, of ministers'.[15] But Peter Padfield is the first current naval historian since Ryan to look more closely at the importance of the Royal Navy's presence in the Baltic, devoting a whole chapter to the continental blockade in general and Saumarez' leading part in it in particular. Indeed, he goes further than anyone, maintaining that it was Saumarez who had provoked Napoleon into the occupation of the Baltic coast and led to his disastrous decision to invade Russia.[16] The same thought had come to me when first reading Ryan and had encouraged me to believe that Saumarez deserved deeper study. His masterly control of the complex naval and diplomatic situation was clearly one of the major factors leading to Napoleon's frustration at the failure of his attempts to close the whole of continental Europe to the flow, inward of British manufactures and colonial goods, outward of naval supplies. A much deeper study of French archives than the present work permits would be needed to evaluate it against other factors, pressures and motivation behind the invasion, but Napoleon's voluminous correspondence shows his concern and his frustration at the failure of his officials and of his reputed ally Russia to prevent the Baltic being the great gap in *le blocus*, the French term for the economic blockade designed to cripple the British economy and hence her war effort.[17]

Two of the three leading economic histories of the Continental System are in French. Silvia Marzagalli's excellent study, *Les Boulevards de la Fraude*, concentrates on Bordeaux, Leghorn and Hamburg and so is more concerned with the Atlantic, the Mediterranean and the North Sea rather than the Baltic; it makes no mention of Saumarez and very little of the Baltic. François Crouzet, however, pays considerable attention in his massive work, *L'Economie Britannique et Le Blocus Continental*; but he is concerned with economic matters rather than with the political or personal. The same is true of E.F. Heckscher, the Swedish historian, writing in English in 1922, though he does bring into the picture Count Axel Pontus von Rosen, Governor of Gothenburg from 1809 until his death from cholera in 1834 – 'the most original, humorous and energetic Swedish actor on the stage of the Continental System in this exciting time'.[18] Another personal and detailed commentary on the impact of Saumarez' fleet and the Admiral himself on the Gothenburg community comes in Hans Hansson's engaging book of 1984, *Engelske flottan har siktats vid Vinga*.

P. Coquelle's research at the beginning of the twentieth century into some hitherto neglected French state archives provides an unexpected insight into the series of Anglo-French peace talks between 1805 and 1810.[19] His paper in 1909 on Baron Alquier, French envoy in Stockholm, 1810–12, gives a striking and unchauvinistic picture of counter-productive arrogance on Alquier's part that made Saumarez' task much easier.[20] The brief collection of correspondence between Bernadotte and Napoleon at the outset of the former's move to Sweden in 1810 has also been illuminating.[21]

There are few comments on Saumarez in the writings of his fellow-officers. Thomas Byam Martin is the one with most references. Most of these are complimentary except when the two fell out over Saumarez' criticism of him for what he considered a reckless attack and Byam Martin was with difficulty dissuaded from seeking a court-martial. But there is an early story Byam Martin tells of his first meeting with Saumarez (then aged 28) in Guernsey. He describes him as having a 'wildness of expression' and 'being at times much excited' and that he had recently been confined in a mad-house. If correct, this would have been two years after he returned from his successful time in the West Indies and shortly before he got engaged to his wife, Martha. It seems unlikely. Martin admitted his source's stories 'need be received not with grains but with pounds of allowance'. He added that 'Lord De Saumarez was certainly subject to great depression of spirits, and when labouring under such attacks, which sometimes lasted for weeks, he was hardly a safe man to be entrusted with the direction of duties of great national interest. ' Byam Martin wrote this from memory in 1832/3, when he had been forced out of the comptrollership by the Whig government that had just given Saumarez his peerage and it is in great conflict with everything else that he writes. His editor, Sir Richard Vesey Hamilton, in the introduction to the second volume, writes of Saumarez' 'forbearance, tact and judgement' in the two years that Sweden was theoretically at war with Britain and that 'notwithstanding much difference of opinion ... his conduct was not only politic but generous'.[22]

Notes

Preface and Acknowledgements, pp. ix–xi

1. Ryan, *The Saumarez Papers*, p. xxv.

Introduction, pp. 1–4

1. Ross, II, pp. 3–5, Mrs. Richard Saumarez to Saumarez, 5 August 1801.
2. Ibid., pp. 6–7.
3. Morriss, *Channel Fleet*, pp. 172–3, Warren to Spencer, 30 December 1796; p. 291, Bridport to Spencer, 18 April 1798; pp. 561–2, Knight to St Vincent, 23 September 1800.
4. Ross I, pp. 304–7 and 323; St Vincent to Saumarez, 1 April 1801.
5. Leyland, *Blockade of Brest* I, pp. xlii and 249, Cornwallis to Nepean, 19 January 1804; II, pp. 104–7, Melville to Cornwallis, 26 October 1804; II, pp. 107–13, Captain Hurd's Report.
6. Mahan, 'Admiral Saumarez'.
7. Mahan, *Types of Naval Officers*, p. 409.
8. Shrubland, Saumarez to Lady Saumarez, 22 June 1798, quoted in Ross I, p. 207.
9. Mahan, *The Influence of Sea Power upon the French Revolution*, p. 346.
10. Quoted by Joscelyne Bagot in *George Canning and his Friends*, p. 385.
11. Priaulx Library, Guernsey, Saumarez family file.
12. SRO, HA/93/6/1/2447, Von Rosen to Saumarez, 22 August 1813.
13. Ross II, p. 160.

1 The Baltic in Autumn 1807, pp. 5–19

1. Hinde, *George Canning*, p. 142.
2. Muir, *Britain and the Defeat of Napoleon*, p. 10.
3. Ibid., pp. 166–7.
4. WYAS, WYL250/8/44, Lord Hutchinson to Canning, 9 March 1807.
5. Trulsson, *British and Swedish Policies*, p. 120, quoting Wetterstedt to Ehrenheim, 22 July 1807.
6. Hansson, *Engelske flottan*, p. 111.
7. Rose, 'A British Agent at Tilsit', p. 63.
8. Schroeder, *Transformation of European Politics*, p. 321.
9. WYAS, WYL250/8/44, Thornton to Canning, 1 July 1807.
10. WYAS, WYL250/8/50, Lord Pembroke to Canning, 28 May 1807.
11. WYAS, WYL250/8/59b, D'Antraigues to Canning, 21 July 1807.
12. Munch-Petersen, 'Secret Intelligence', pp. 84–5.
13. NA, Kew, Granville MSS, PRO 30/29/8/4, Canning to Leveson-Gower, 22 July 1807.
14. WYAS, WYL250/8/17, Canning to Rev. Leigh, 19 December 1807.
15. NA, Kew, ADM 50/49, Journal of Admiral Gambier, 2 August 1807.
16. Sparrow, *Secret Service*, p. 343.

17. NA, Kew, FO 353/56, F.J. Jackson Memoirs, p. 2.
18. Trulsson, *British and Swedish Policies*, p. 51.
19. Hansson, *Engelske flottan*, p. 102.
20. Aspinall, *Later Correspondence of George III*, pp. 607–10.
21. BL, Add. MSS 42773, Canning to Rose, 24 September 1807.
22. NA, Kew, PRO 30/29/8/4, Canning to Leveson Gower, 21 July 1807.
23. Feldbaek, 'Denmark in the Napoleonic Wars', p. 90.
24. Andersen, 'Denmark between the Wars with Britain', p. 236.
25. NA, Kew, FO 22/53–4, Canning to F.J. Jackson, 28 July 1807.
26. Feldbaek, 'Denmark in the Napoleonic Wars', p. 90.
27. Feldbaek, 'Denmark and the Baltic', p. 277.
28. Hansson, *Engelske flottan*, p. 108.
29. Feldbaek, *Dansk Søfarts Historie* III, p. 7.
30. Sparrow, *Secret Service*, p. 326.
31. NA, Kew, FO 22/51 (p. 31) Draft Treaty of Defensive Alliance between Britain and Denmark.
32. Feldbaek, *Denmark and the Armed Neutrality*, p. 55.
33. *Napoléon* XV, no.12962, Napoleon to Talleyrand, 31 July 1807.
34. Andersen, 'Denmark between the Wars with Britain', p. 238.
35. WYAS, WYL250/8/43, Thornton to Canning, 15 March 1808.
36. Rigsarkivet, Copenhagen, F.u.A Spanien II Depecher 1795, Dreyer's Despatch No.9, 4 March 1795.
37. NA, Kew, FO 27/70, Secret Intelligence from France, 15 February 1802.
38. Aspinall, *Later Correspondence of George III*, fol. 4058 n.2.
39. NA, Kew, FO 353/56, Jackson memoirs.
40. Ryan, 'The Navy at Copenhagen', p. 201.
41. Hinde, *George Canning*, p. 175; James, *Naval History* IV, p. 291.
42. Castlereagh to Wellesley, 13 September 1807, quoted in Trulsson, *British and Swedish Policies*, p. 46.
43. WYAS WYL250/8/31, Mulgrave to Canning, 20 September 1807.
44. WYAS, WYL250/8/42, Canning to Pierrepont, 10 October 1807.
45. NA, Kew, WO 6/14, Castlereagh to Cathcart, 27 August 1807.
46. WYAS, WYL250/8/42, Canning to Gambier, 4 September 1807.
47. Castlereagh to Cathcart, 22 September 1807, quoted in Trulsson, *British and Swedish Policies*, p. 53.
48. WYAS, WYL250/8/32, 1 October 1807.
49. Wellesley to Castlereagh, 25 September 1807, quoted in Trulsson, *British and Swedish Policies*, p. 50.
50. WYAS, WYL250/8/42, Canning to Leveson-Gower, 5 November 1807.
51. James, *Naval History* IV, pp. 292–5.
52. Ryan, 'Documents Relating to the Copenhagen Operation', p. 324, quoting Canning to Leveson-Gower, 2 October 1807.
53. Hall, *British Strategy*, p. 162; Barnes, 'Canning and the Danes', p. 138.
54. Ryan, *Saumarez Papers*, p. xv.
55. Schroeder, *Transformation of European Politics*, pp. 329–30.
56. Munch-Petersen, 'Prelude to the British Bombardment', p. 52.
57. Anderson, *Naval Wars in the Baltic*, p. 322.
58. Wandel, *Søkrigen*, p. 1.

2 Saumarez' Early Career, pp. 20–33

1. WYAS, WYL250/8/42, Pierrepont to Canning, 15 July 1807.
2. White, *Nelson: The New Letters*, p. 250.
3. Knight, *Pursuit of Victory*, p. 394.
4. Nicolas, *Dispatches and Letters* IV, p. 361, Nelson to Addington, 8 May 1801.
5. Feldbaek, *Battle of Copenhagen*, p. 220.
6. Nicolas, *Dispatches and Letters* IV, p. 363, Nelson to the Swedish Admiral, 8 May 1801; Knight, *Pursuit of Victory*, p. 391.
7. Nicolas, *Dispatches and Letters* IV, p. 379, quoting Clarke and McArthur, *Life of Admiral Lord Nelson* II, p. 286, Secret Orders, 6 May 1801.
8. Nicolas, *Dispatches and Letters* IV, pp. 356–7, Nelson to Bernstorff, 6 May 1801; pp. 385–6, Nelson to Cronstedt, 23 May 1801; p. 405, Nelson to Lindholm, 11 June 1801; pp. 409–11, Nelson to Lindholm, 12 June 1801.
9. Ibid., p. 412, Nelson to St Vincent, 12 June 1801.
10. Ibid., pp. 364–5, Nelson to Count Pahlen, 9 May 1801.
11. Ibid., pp. 371–2, Pahlen to Nelson, 16 May 1801.
12. Ibid., p. 374, Nelson to Nepean, 17 May 1801.
13. NA, Kew, ADM 3/144, draft letter Nepean to Nelson, 31 May 1801.
14. NMM, CRK/11/50, St Helens to Nelson, 20 June 1801.
15. Le Fevre and Harding, *British Admirals of the Napoleonic Wars*.
16. Wilkinson, 'Peter Rainier', p. 111.
17. Lambert, 'William, Lord Hotham', p. 24.
18. Adams, *Admiral Collingwood*, p. 33.
19. Rodger, *Command of the Ocean*, p. 550.
20. Duffy, 'Sir Samuel Hood', p. 345.
21. Crimmin, 'Sir Thomas Troubridge', p. 321.
22. Rodger, *Command of the Ocean*, pp. 550–1.
23. Sainsbury, 'Sir John Duckworth', pp. 164–95.
24. Quoted by Le Fevre in 'Sir John Borlase Warren', p. 237, Grenville to Marquess of Buckingham, 8 November 1806.
25. Ibid., p. 241, Croker to Warren, 17 May 1813.
26. Lavery, 'Lord Keith', p. 396.
27. Lambert, 'Sir William Cornwallis', p. 373.
28. Rodger, *Command of the Ocean*, p. 566.
29. Krajeski, *In the Shadow of Nelson*.
30. Huntington Library, Grenville Collection, STG Box 169 (43), Thomas Grenville to Admiral Sir William Young, 29 November 1806.
31. Lloyd, *Naval Miscellany IV*, pp. 475–6, St Vincent to Grenville, 21 October 1806.
32. Ibid., p. 483, St Vincent to Grenville, 21 November 1806.
33. Shrubland, SA/3/1/3, Lord St Vincent to Admiral Saumarez, undated.
34. Ross I, pp. 19–24.
35. Nicolas, *Dispatches and Letters* I, pp. 57–8, Nelson to Rev. Nelson, 8 February 1782.
36. Shrubland, Saumarez to his family, 8 July 1776.
37. Ross I, pp. 30–42.
38. Ibid., pp. 44–54.
39. Lyon, *Sailing Navy List*.
40. Shrubland, SA/3/2/2/7, *Tisiphone* letterbook.

41. Shrubland, SA/3/2/2/12, Saumarez diaries.
42. Ross I, pp. 55–64.
43. Shrubland, SA /3/2/2/8, Log of HMS *Russell*.
44. Quoted by Dorothy Hood in *The Admirals Hood*, p. 71, Rodney to Sir Samuel Hood, 2 April 1782.
45. Laughton, *Lord Barham* I, Hood to Sir Charles Middleton, 22 May 1782.
46. Shrubland, 'Notes on Love and Marriage', in an undated commonplace book.
47. Ross I, p. 104.
48. James, *Naval History* I, p. 207.
49. Ross I, pp. 101–3.
50. Ibid., pp. 131–8.
51. Ibid., p. 179.
52. Clarke and McArthur, *Life of Admiral Lord Nelson*, quoted in Ross I, p. 194.
53. Ross I, pp. 227–9.
54. James, *Naval History* III, pp. 124–30.
55. Rodger, *Command of the Ocean*, p. 472.
56. Brenton, *Memoirs of Sir Jahleel Brenton*, p. 75.
57. Bonner-Smith, *Letters of the Earl of St Vincent*, pp. 209 and 211, 13 August, 2 October and 2 November 1801.
58. Aspinall, *Later Correspondence of George III*, fol. 2719, 24 March 1803.
59. Ross II, p. 97.
60. James, *Naval History* III, p. 113.
61. Ross II, pp. 99–101.
62. NA, Kew, ADM 2/1365, Instructions to Saumarez, 16 April 1808.
63. Hansson, *Engelske flottan*, p. 110.
64. *Napoléon* XXI, no.16768, Napoleon to Champagny, 7 August 1810.
65. Marzagalli, *Les Boulevards de la Fraude*, p. 196.
66. Kermina, *Bernadotte et Desirée Clary*, pp. 103–4.
67. Tiselius, 'Landshövdingen Axel Von Rosen'.
68. WYAS, WYL250/8/42, Canning to Gower, 2 October 1807.
69. WYAS, WYL250/8/42, Canning to Thornton, 28 April 1808.
70. WYAS, WYL250/8/43, Thornton to Canning, 11 June 1808.

3 Saumarez Takes up his Baltic Command, pp. 34–53

1. Goodwin, *Nelson's Victory*, p. 81
2. Shrubland, Saumarez to Lady Saumarez, 21 April 1808.
3. Jorgensen, *Anglo-Swedish Alliance*, p. 117
4. Shrubland, Saumarez to Lady Saumarez, 14 May 1808; Nordling, 'Capturing the "Gibraltar of the North"', 17; Hansson, *Engelska Flottan*, pp. 115–18.
5. Trulsson, *British and Swedish Policies*, pp. 74–8.
6. Jorgensen, *Anglo-Swedish Alliance*, p. 119.
7. Oakley, 'Trade, Peace and the Balance of Power', pp. 231–2.
8. Kirby, *The Baltic World*, p. 18.
9. NA, Kew, FO 73/36, Pierrepont to Howick, 18 November 1806.
10. Jorgensen, *Anglo-Swedish Alliance*, pp. 132–3.
11. WYAS, WYL250/8/42, Canning to Thornton, 1 April 1808.
12. Trulsson, *British and Swedish Policies*, pp. 147–8.
13. NA, Kew, WO 1/189, military memoir, 3 May 1808.
14. Maurice, *Moore* II, p. 66.

15. Ibid., p. 154.
16. Ibid., p. 138.
17. WYAS, WYL250/8/33, Portland to Canning, 31 December 1808; WYL250/8/31, Canning to Mulgrave, 9 December 1808.
18. Muir and Esdale, 'Strategic Planning', p. 46.
19. Maurice, *Moore* II, pp. 203–4.
20. Shrubland, Saumarez to Lady Saumarez, 24 April 1808.
21. *The Times*, 13 April 1808.
22. Shrubland, Saumarez to Lady Saumarez, 8 May 1808.
23. Maurice, *Moore* II, p. 207.
24. Ibid., p. 209.
25. Ibid., p. 206.
26. Ibid., pp. 210–11.
27. Shrubland, Saumarez to Lady Saumarez, 9 June 1808.
28. Maurice, *Moore* II, pp. 215–20.
29. Ibid., p. 230.
30. Hansson, *Engelske flottan*, pp. 144–5.
31. NA, Kew, FO 933/35, fol. 1227, Moore to Thornton, 1 July 1808.
32. Shrubland, Saumarez to Lady Saumarez, 3 July 1808.
33. SRO, Ipswich, HA 93/6/1/215, Moore to Saumarez, 25 July 1808.
34. Kirby, *The Baltic World*, p. 34.
35. Quoted in Hansson, *Engelske flottan*, p. 107: 'Middagar och supéer avlöste aradra i denna handelsstad, ett andra London, der all handel från jordklotets fyra delar var samlad i följd af Napoleons åtgärder, som blockerade hela kontinenten.'
36. Ibid., pp. 141–2: 'Vilken smaklig soppa, vilket saftigt och väl lagat kött, och vilket präktigt, vitt bröd.'
37. Hansson, *Engelske flottan*, p. 144.
38. Shrubland, Saumarez to Lady Saumarez, 14 and 31 May and 3 July 1808.
39. Shrubland, Saumarez to Lady Saumarez, 8 July 1808.
40. Greenwood, 'A Study of the Life', p. 96.
41. Ross II, p. 100, Saumarez to Mulgrave, 27 February 1808.
42. Shrubland, Saumarez to Lady Saumarez, 5 July 1808.
43. WYAS, WYL250/8/43, Thornton to Canning, 23 June 1808.
44. SRO, HA/93/6/1/203, Thornton to Saumarez, 20 July 1808; Riksarkivet, Stockholm, Anglica/504, Ehrenheim to Adlerberg, 7 July 1808; WYAS, WYL250/8/43, d'Ehrenheim to Thornton, 6 July 1808.
45. Jorgensen, *Anglo-Swedish Alliance*, p. 145.
46. SRO, HA/93/6/1/174, Saumarez to Mulgrave, 6 July 1808.
47. Shrubland, Saumarez to Lady Saumarez, 4 June 1808.
48. Ryan, *Saumarez Papers*, pp. 22–3, Saumarez to Mulgrave, 5 June 1808; SRO HA/93/6/1/154, Mulgrave to Saumarez, 26 June 1808; Shrubland, Saumarez to Lady Saumarez, 12 and 17 June 1808.
49. Shrubland, Saumarez to Lady Saumarez, 27 June 1808.
50. Shrubland, Saumarez to Lady Saumarez, 8 July 1808; NMM, MKH/113, Captain Sir Archibald Dickson to Keats, 29 March 1809; Shrubland, Saumarez to Lady Saumarez, 24 May 1809.
51. Ryan, *Saumarez Papers*, pp. 31–2 and 26–8.
52. SRO, HA/93/6/1/192, Saumarez to Mulgrave, 14 July 1808.

53. *Napoléon* XXII, no.17905, Napoleon to Davout, 11 July 1811 and no.18151, Napoleon to Savary, 26 September 1811.
54. Shrubland, Saumarez to Lady Saumarez, 21 and 27 July 1808.
55. Ryan, *Saumarez Papers*, pp. 29–31; SRO, HA/93/6/1/186, Thornton to Saumarez, 12 July 1808.
56. Muir, *Britain and the Defeat of Napoleon*, p. 33.
57. SRO, HA/93/6/1/3, Parker to Paulett, 9 March 1808; HA 93/6/1/9, Thornton to Parker, 23 February 1808; Ryan, *Saumarez Papers*, pp. 5–6.
58. Mörner, 'Marskalk Bernadotte', pp. 31–2; Andersen, *Orlogskibet Prinds Christian Frederik*.
59. Feldbaek, *Battle of Copenhagen 1801*, pp. 163–4; *Slaget på Reden*, pp. 181–3.
60. Jorgensen, *Anglo-Swedish Alliance*, p. 110.
61. NA, Kew, FO 22/58, Narrative of Mr. Metz's Journey from Hamburg to Copenhagen, 26 August 1808.
62. WYAS, WYL250/8/42, Canning to Thornton, 1 April 1808.
63. NA, Kew, ADM 1/6, Hood to Saumarez, 19 May 1808.
64. NA, Kew, FO 933/35, Nicholas to Thornton, 22 June 1808.
65. SRO, HA/93/6/1/196, Commissioner General of Police at Antwerp to Bernadotte, 16 July 1808.
66. WYAS, WYL250/8/42, Canning to Thornton, 30 June 1808.
67. Ryan, *Saumarez Papers*, p. 31 n.
68. Professor Magnus Mörner, in a letter to the writer, 3 June 2003.
69. Robertson, *Narrative of A Secret Mission*, p. 86; Maffeo, *Most Secret and Confidential*, p. 54; Sparrow, *Secret Service*, p. 315; Rodger, *Command of the Ocean*, p. 553.
70. SRO, HA/93/6/1/232/1, enclosure to letter from Keats to Saumarez, 5 August 1808.
71. Shrubland, Saumarez to Lady Saumarez, 27/29 July 1808.
72. Ryan, *Saumarez Papers*, p. 34 n.
73. Shrubland, Saumarez to Lady Saumarez, 27/29 July 1808.
74. NA, Kew, ADM 1/6 Keats to Governor of Nyborg, August 1808.
75. Shrubland, Saumarez to Lady Saumarez, 2 August 1808.
76. Shrubland, Saumarez to Lady Saumarez, 9 August 1808.
77. Shrubland, Saumarez to Lady Saumarez, 8 July and 9 August 1808.
78. Shrubland, Saumarez to Lady Saumarez, 2 August 1808.
79. SRO, HA/93/6/1/2500, pp. 55–8, Gustav IV to Saumarez, 8 August 1808; pp. 59–63, Saumarez to Gustav IV, 11 August 1808.
80. Shrubland, Saumarez to Lady Saumarez, 21 July 1808.
81. Shrubland, Lady Saumarez to Saumarez, 3 March 1798.
82. SRO, HA/93/6/1/257, Saumarez to Keats, 15 August 1808; Shrubland, Saumarez to Lady Saumarez, 20 August 1808.
83. SRO, HA/93/6/1/253, Saumarez to Mulgrave, 14 August 1808.
84. NA, Kew, ADM 1/7, Keats to Saumarez, 11 August and 10 September 1808.
85. Shrubland, Saumarez to Lady Saumarez, 20/21 August 1808.
86. Tracy, *Naval Chronicle* IV, pp. 183–8.
87. Aspinall, *Later Correspondence of George III* IV, fol. 3704, Mulgrave to King George, 23 August 1808.
88. Shrubland, Saumarez to Lady Saumarez, 24 October 1808.

89. Rigsarkivet, Copenhagen, Deptartement for de Udenlandske Anliggender, 302/1921, 24 September 1808.

90. NA, Kew, FO 22/58, Proclamation by Prince Ponte Corvo, 20 August 1808.

4 The Crisis of Rogervik, pp. 54–74

1. Shrubland, Saumarez to Lady Saumarez, 2 August 1808.
2. Ryan, *Saumarez Papers*, pp. 37–8, Nauckhoff to Saumarez, 7 August 1808.
3. Shrubland, Saumarez to Lady Saumarez, 18 April and 14 August 1808.
4. Ryan, *Saumarez Papers*, p. 32, Draft Letter by Saumarez, 18 July 1808.
5. NA, Kew, ADM 2/1385, Puget to Saumarez, 20 August 1808.
6. *Byam Martin Letters* II, pp. 31–9; Hansson, *Engelske flottan*, p. 159.
7. SRO, HA/93/6/1/288, Saumarez to Lady Saumarez, 30/31 August 1808.
8. WYAS WYL250/8/57, Leveson-Gower to Canning, 1 August 1807.
9. NA, Kew, ADM 2/1365, Instructions to Saumarez, 16 April 1808.
10. WYAS, WYL250/8/44, Hutchinson to Canning, 1 September 1807.
11. Ryan, *Saumarez Papers*, pp. 44–5, Thornton to Saumarez, 4 September 1808.
12. WYAS, WYL250/8/44, Hutchinson to Canning, 1 September 1807.
13. See Hopkirk, *The Great Game*.
14. NA, Kew, ADM 1/6, Intelligence obtained by HMS *Goliath* 26 June–1 July 1808.
15. Niven, *Napoleon and Alexander I*, pp. 59–60.
16. Ibid., p. 61.
17. WYAS, WYL250/8/57, Leveson-Gower to Canning, 1 August 1807.
18. WYAS, WYL250/8/43, Thornton to Canning, 31 August 1808.
19. WYAS, WYL250/8/43, Thornton to Canning, 4 September 1808.
20. WYAS, WYL250/8/42, Canning to Thornton, 10 June 1808.
21. WYAS, WYL250/8/43A, Cabinet Minute, 12 July 1808.
22. *Byam Martin Letters* II, pp. 57–8.
23. Ross I, pp. 341–7.
24. Shrubland, Saumarez to Lady Saumarez, 12 September 1808.
25. Ross II, pp. 124–5.
26. Mahan, *Types of Naval Officers*, p. 409.
27. SRO, HA/93/6/1/345, Saumarez to Keats, 19 September 1808.
28. WYAS WYL250/8/43, Thornton to Canning, 4 September 1808.
29. *Byam Martin Letters* II, pp. 125–36; SRO, HA/93/6/1/988–90, Correspondence dated 13 July 1809; Shrubland, Saumarez to Lady Saumarez, 15 July 1809.
30. *Byam Martin Letters* II, pp. 50–5.
31. BL, Add.MSS 41365–7, Byam Martin to Mrs Byam Martin, 23 September 1808.
32. SRO, HA/93/6/1/289, Hood to Saumarez, 30 August 1808.
33. SRO, HA/93/6/1/364, Byam Martin to Saumarez (undated, probably September 1808).
34. Shrubland, Saumarez to Lady Saumarez, 2 September 1808; Bienkowski, *Admirals in the Age of Nelson*, p. 163.
35. SRO, HA/93/6/1/302, Saumarez to Hanickoff, 3 September 1808; HA 93/6/1/362, proposals to Admiral Hanickoff to be communicated by Captain Martin.
36. SRO, HA/93/6/1/303, 304, 312, 314 and 315, Saumarez to Hanickhoff, 3 and 4 September; Hanickoff to Saumarez, 3 and 4 September; Saumarez to Pole, 5 September 1808.

37. SRO, HA/93/6/1/400, Saumarez to Pole, 26 October 1808.
38. Feldbaek, *Battle of Copenhagen*, pp. 214–25.
39. Shrubland, Saumarez to Lady Saumarez, 31 May 1808.
40. Shrubland, Saumarez to Lady Saumarez, 10 September 1808; Lady Saumarez to Saumarez, 27 September 1808.
41. Shrubland, Saumarez to Lady Saumarez, 11 June 1810.
42. WYAS WYL250/8/31, Canning to Chatham, 17 September 1808.
43. SRO, HA/93/6/1/365, Bickerton to Saumarez, 1 October 1808.
44. SRO, HA/93/6/1/334, Gustav IV to Saumarez, 13 September 1808.
45. Shrubland, Saumarez to Lady Saumarez, 12 September 1808.
46. Ryan, *Saumarez Papers*, p. 47, Saumarez to Pole, 14 September 1808.
47. Shrubland, Saumarez to Richard Saumarez, 15 September 1808.
48. NA, Kew, ADM 80/145, Memo from Saumarez to all Captains, 24 March 1808.
49. Ryan, *Saumarez Papers*, pp. 46–7, Duke to Saumarez, 12 September 1808.
50. SRO, HA/93/6/1/375, Dr. Jamison to Saumarez, 11 October 1808.
51. SRO, HA/93/6/1/348, Report by Valentine Duke, 21 September 1808.
52. Shrublands, Saumarez to Lady Saumarez, 10 and 16 September 1808.
53. Shrublands, Saumarez to Richard Saumarez, 15 September 1808.
54. SRO, HA/93/6/1/345, Saumarez to Keats, 19 September 1808.
55. Shrublands, Saumarez to Richard Saumarez, 8 October 1808.
56. Shrublands, Saumarez to Lady Saumarez, 10 September 1808.
57. SRO, HA/93/6/1/358, Saumarez to Sir Richard Bickerton, 26 September 1808.
58. Nicolas, *Dispatches and Letters* IV, pp. 353–4 and 369–70.
59. Shrubland, Saumarez to Lady Saumarez, 2 September 1808.
60. Shrubland, Saumarez to Lady Saumarez, 6 October 1808.
61. NA, Kew, FO 73/49, Thornton to Canning, 13 September 1808.
62. SRO, HA/93/6/1/339, Saumarez to Alexander I, 17 September 1808.
63. NA, Kew, FO 73/49, Thornton to Canning, 27 September 1808.
64. SRO, HA/93/6/1/347, Hanickoff to Saumarez, 19 September 1808.
65. Cobbett, *Parliamentary History* XII, p. 93.
66. Aspinall, *Later Correspondence of George III* V, p. 143, King George III to Canning, 22 October 1808.
67. WYAS, WYL250/8/31, Mulgrave to Canning, 23 October 1808.
68. Coquelle, *Napoléon*, pp. 86–94.
69. Ibid., pp. 95–100.
70. SRO, HA/93/6/1/383, Saumarez to Gustav IV Adolf, 16 October 1808.
71. Shrubland, Saumarez to Lady Saumarez, 20 October 1808.
72. Shrubland, Saumarez to Lady Saumarez, 20 and 24 October 1808.
73. Aspinall, *Later Correspondence of George III* IV, fol. 3741, George III to Mulgrave, 14 October 1808.
74. SRO, HA/93/6/1/427, 'Memorandum for Vice-Admiral Sir James Saumarez'.
75. WYAS, WYL250/8/42, Canning to Thornton, 10 June 1808.
76. WYAS, WYL250/8/43, Thornton to Canning, 13 September 1808.
77. SRO, HA/93/6/1/449, Thornton to Saumarez, 22 December 1808.
78. NA, Kew, PRO 30/29/84, Canning to Leveson-Gower, 21 July 1807.
79. Bagot, *George Canning and His Friends*, p. 285, Canning to Bagot, 16 January 1809.
80. Cobbett, *Parliamentary History* XII, p. 93, Romanzoff to Canning, 12 October 1808.

81. SRO, HA/93/6/1/427, Memorandum to Saumarez from Pole, 16 November 1808.
82. Ryan, *Saumarez Papers*, pp. 52–8, Saumarez to Pole, 21 November 1808.
83. NMM, YOR/16A, Yorke to Saumarez, 19 October 1810.
84. Tolstoy, *War and Peace*, p. 668.
85. SRO, HA/93/6/1/445, Pole to Saumarez, 15 December 1808.

5 Conversion to Peacemaker, pp. 75–92

1. Jorgensen, *Anglo-Swedish Alliance*, pp. 144–5.
2. SRO, HA/93/6/1/380, Gustavus IV to Saumarez, 15 October 1808.
3. SRO, HA/93/6/1/383, Saumarez to Gustavus IV, 16 October 1808.
4. SRO, HA/93/6/1/378, Thornton to Saumarez, 14 October 1808.
5. Ryan, *Saumarez Papers*, p. 90, Saumarez to Keats, 17 June 1809.
6. Shrubland, Saumarez to Lady Saumarez, 5 June and 15 July 1809.
7. Alm, 'Royalty, Legitimacy and Imagery', p. 20.
8. NA, Kew, FO 189/11, Merry to Canning (Most Secret), 9 December 1808.
9. WYAS, WYL250/8/42, Canning to Thornton, 26 April 1808.
10. Jorgensen, *Anglo-Swedish Alliance*, p. 164.
11. Carr, 'Gustavus IV and the British Government', pp. 64–5; NA, Kew, FO 189/11, Merry to Canning, 3 February 1809.
12. Malmesbury, *Diaries* IV, pp. 400–2.
13. WYAS, WYL250/8/43, Merry to Canning, 26 October 1809.
14. SRO, HA/93/6/1/448/1, Merry to Keats, 6 December 1808.
15. SRO, HA/93/6/1/454, Keats to Saumarez, 25 December 1808.
16. SRO, HA/93/6/1/457 and 487, Keats to Saumarez, 27 December 1808 and 31 January 1809; HA/93/6/1/460/1, Jamison to Keats, 28 December 1808 and 1/628, Barrow to Saumarez, 27 April 1809.
17. Aspinall, *Later Correspondence of George III* V, p. 165.
18. Ryan, *Saumarez Papers*, pp. 59–61.
19. SRO, HA/93/6/1/487, Keats to Saumarez, 31 January 1809.
20. NA, Kew, ADM 80/146, Keats to Navy Board, 30 January and 2 February 1809.
21. NA, Kew, FO 22/60, Lt. John Stoker to Keats, 15 January 1809.
22. NA, Kew, ADM 80/146, Keats to Fenwick, 2 February 1809.
23. NA, Kew, FO 189/11, Report from ex-British prisoner in Copenhagen, 16 January 1809.
24. NA, Kew, ADM 80/146, Keats to Saumarez, 2 February 1809.
25. Feldbaek, *Denmark and the Armed Neutrality*, p. 14.
26. Kirby, *The Baltic World*, p. 14.
27. Feldbaek, 'Denmark in the Napoleonic Wars', p. 94.
28. NA, Kew, FO 73/50, Canning to Merry, 10 November 1808.
29. Jorgensen, *Anglo-Swedish Alliance*, p. 155.
30. Ibid., p. 156.
31. Ibid., pp. 167–8.
32. NA, Kew, FO 73/55, Merry to Canning, 14 April 1809.
33. Jorgensen, *Anglo-Swedish Alliance*, p. 157.
34. NA, Kew, FO 73/50, Canning to Merry, 23 December 1808; NA, Kew, FO 189/11, Canning to Merry, 24 February 1809.
35. NA, Kew, FO 73/54, Canning to Merry, 7 March 1809.

36. NA, Kew, FO 73/55, Merry to Canning, 14 April 1809; Ross II, pp. 131–4; Jorgensen, *Anglo-Swedish Alliance*, p. 165; WYAS, WYL250/8/44, R. Matthews to Canning, 7 February 1809.
37. NA, Kew, FO 73/55, Merry to Canning, 23 March and 21 April 1809; Ross II, p. 152.
38. SRO, HA 93/6/1/548, Keats to Hood, 26 March 1809.
39. NA, Kew, ADM 80/146 Keats to Merry, 11 March 1809; SRO, HA/93/6/1/602, Keats to Hood, 20 April 1809.
40. Hall, *Wellington's Navy*, pp. 135–6.
41. SRO, HA/93/6/1/697, Keats to Hood, 6 May 1809.
42. White, *Contemporaries of Nelson*, pp. 360–1; Nicolas, *Dispatches and Letters* VI, p. 442.
43. Lloyd, *Naval Miscellany IV,* p. 482, St Vincent to Thomas Grenville, 16 November 1806.
44. Shrubland, Saumarez to Lady Saumarez, 19 May 1809.
45. Ross II, pp. 145–7.
46. Shrubland, Saumarez to Lady Saumarez, 6 May 1809.
47. SRO, HA/93/6/1/612, Admiralty to Saumarez, 22 April 1809.
48. NA, Kew, FO 73/55, Canning to Merry, 4 April 1809.
49. SRO, HA/93/6/1/708, Pole to Saumarez, 8 May 1809.
50. Shrubland, Saumarez to Lady Saumarez, 18 May 1809.
51. SRO, HA/93/6/1/848, Krusenstjerna to Saumarez, 4 June 1809.
52. Ryan, *Saumarez Papers*, pp. 77–8, Nauckhoff to Saumarez, 16 May 1809.
53. SRO, HA/93/6/1/867, Puke to Saumarez, 7 June 1809.
54. Ryan, *Saumarez Papers*, p. 91, Saumarez to Mulgrave, 23 June 1809.
55. SRO, HA/93/6/1/753 and Ross II, pp. 143–4, both Saumarez to Foster, 18 May 1809.
56. Jorgensen, *Anglo-Swedish Alliance*, p. 174.
57. SRO, HA/93/6/1/ 1066, Mulgrave to Saumarez, 22 August 1809.
58. Shrubland, Saumarez to Lady Saumarez, 24 May 1809.
59. Shrubland, Saumarez to Lady Saumarez, 15 July 1809.
60. Rodger, 'The Idea of Naval Strategy in Britain in the 18th and 19th Centuries'. I am grateful to Professor Rodger for this reference.
61. SRO, HA/93/6/1/1248, 'The Strategic Situation in the Baltic'.
62. Ross II, pp. 150–4, Saumarez to Foster, 3 June, Foster to Saumarez, 9 June and Saumarez to Foster, 15 June 1809.
63. Shrubland, Saumarez to Lady Saumarez, 15 July 1809.
64. Ross I, pp. 22–3 and 85–6.
65. Ibid., pp. 75–6.
66. Shrubland, Saumarez to Lady Saumarez, 15, 26 and 30 July 1809.
67. Ryan, *Saumarez Papers*, p. 95.
68. Vandal, *Napoléon et Alexandre 1er* I, p. 40.
69. Metternich, *Memoirs* II pp. 289–300, Memorandum in Vienna, quoted in Niven, *Napoleon* and *Alexander I*, p. 21.
70. NA, Kew, FO 73/55, Merry to Canning, 21 April 1809.
71. Jorgensen, *Anglo-Swedish Alliance*, p. 185.
72. Shrubland, Saumarez to Lady Saumarez, 9 July 1809; SRO, HA/93/6/1/1075, Barrow to Saumarez, 26 August 1809.
73. Ross II, pp. 160–1.

74. SRO, HA/93/6/1/1071, Platen to Saumarez, 23 August 1809.
75. Ross II, pp. 172–3.
76. SRO, HA/93/6/1/1129, Platen to Saumarez, 22 September 1809.
77. SRO, HA/93/6/1/1168, Proclamation of Charles XIII, 27 October 1809.

6 The Pea Islands, pp. 93–105

1. Bech, *En Kjøbenhavnsk Grosserers Ungdomserindringer*, p. 120.
2. Tourist information booklet, Christiansø (2006).
3. Ryan, *Saumarez Papers*, p. 66, Pole to Emes, Möller and Emes, 7 March 1809.
4. NA, Kew, ADM 1/8, translation of instructions to captain of a Danish privateer enclosed with Mason's letter to Saumarez of 30 April 1810.
5. Marzagalli, *Les Boulevards de la Fraude*, p. 213, quoting Archives Nationales (Paris), F ⁷8846, dossier 3148, 21 mai 1810.
6. SRO, HA/93/6/1/1972, Steen Bille to Saumarez, 30 November 1811.
7. NA, Kew, FO 73/66, Culling Smith to Consul Smith, 12 January 1811.
8. Mulgrave, Box VII, Bundle 20, fols 180 and 663, William Chapman to Mulgrave, 14 January 1808 and J. Staniforth to Mulgrave, 11 February 1808.
9. SRO, HA/93/6/1/10 and 11, Castlereagh to Mulgrave, 6 April 1808.
10. SRO, HA/93/6/1/43, Admiralty to Saumarez, 16 April 1808.
11. NA, Kew, ADM 2/1366, fols 260–2, Pole to Keats, 30 September 1808.
12. I am grateful to Rasmus Voss for identifying *Hound* as a bombship. She was converted from a 16-gun sloop in 1808.
13. NA, Kew, ADM 51/1813, 1857, 1887 and 1905 (*Mars, Devastation, Aetna* and *Orion*). The log of the *Salsette* for that period is missing, probably owing to her disastrous experiences in the ice that winter – see Ryan, *Saumarez Papers*, pp. 59–61, Keats to Saumarez, 25 January 1809.
14. Tøjhusmuseet, Copenhagen, BON/04, pp. 15–16. I am grateful to Jakob Seerup for this reference.
15. Bech, *En Kjøbenhavnsk Grosserers Ungdomserindringer*, pp. 122–33.
16. Ibid., p. 122, ' yderst slette og medtagne af aelde' and p. 12.
17. Ibid., p. 132, 'saae vi ei senere noget til dem'.
18. Tøjhusmuseet, Copenhagen, BON/04, p. 16: 'om eftermiddagen kom en stor fregat tilbage, og denne gang kom den så near, at faestningens kanoner kunne raekke den. Efter få velrettede skud med 'god effect' vendte den om og sejlede bort.'
19. Mulgrave, Box VII, Bundle 20, fol. 387, Lukin to Mulgrave, 5 November 1808.
20. *Byam Martin Letters*. II, p. 55, Lukin to Martin, 8 September 1808.
21. NA Kew, ADM 2/1366, Pole to Saumarez, 16 October 1808.
22. NA Kew FO 22/63, Nicholls to Wilson, 7 August 1811.
23. Heckscher, *Continental System*, p. 182; Gulin, 'Kriget där inte ett enda skott avlossades'.
24. James, *Naval History* IV, pp. 295–6.
25. Knight, *Pursuit of Victory*, p. 393 n.52.
26. NA, Kew, ADM 1/13, Mansell to Saumarez, 5 October 1811.
27. Lilletårn Museum, Christiansø, official museum guide.
28. SRO, HA/93/6/1/1331, Fenwick to Smith, 17 May 10.
29. SRO, HA/93/6/1/1708 and 1787, Fenwick to Saumarez, 18 April and 12 July 1811.
30. NA, Kew, ADM 1/11, Acklom to Saumarez, 11 November 1810.

31. Bech, *En Kjøbenhavnsk Grosserers Ungdomserindringer*, p. 121.
32. NA, Kew, ADM 2/1367, fol. 316, Barrow to Saumarez, 15 March 1809.
33. NA, Kew, ADM 1/9, Saumarez to Barrow, 17 March 1809.
34. NA, Kew, ADM 1/7, Saumarez to Pole, 20 May 1809.
35. SRO, HA/93/6/1/1270/2, Fenwick to Admiralty, 13 March 1810.
36. NA, Kew, FO 73/55, Merry to Canning, 10 April 1809.
37. SRO, HA/93/6/1/613/1, Castlereagh to Admiralty, 21 April 1809; HA/93/6/1/639, Keats to Saumarez, 29 April 1809; NA, Kew, FO 22/63, Nicholls to Wilson, 7 August 1811.
38. SRO, HA/93/6/1/1149/5, Foster to Canning, 18 August 1809.
39. Ross II, pp. 130–1.
40. Bech, *En Kjøbenhavnsk grosserers ungdomserindringer*, pp. 167–78.
41. Ryan, *Saumarez Papers*, p. 106, n.2.
42. NA, Kew, ADM 1/9, Saumarez to Pole, 22 August 1809 and deposition; Macnamara to Saumarez, 2 October 1809.
43. Harris, *F.H. Chapman*, p. 45 and *passim*. F.H. af Chapman (1721–1808) was the son of an English naval officer who joined the Swedish navy. His designs transformed Swedish naval shipbuilding and he was behind the creation of the inshore (*skärgård*) fleet that had won the second Battle of Svenskund in 1790, bringing the war with Russia and Denmark to a successful end.
44. Tøjhusmuseet, Copenhagen, BON/04, p. 17.
45. NA, Kew, ADM 2/1373, Barrow to Saumarez, 10 September 1811.
46. NA, Kew, ADM 1/13, Mansell's Report on Eartholms, 5 October 1811.
47. Shrubland, Saumarez to Lady Saumarez, 29 September 1811.
48. Shrubland, Saumarez to Lady Saumarez, 15 and 23 September; Lady Saumarez to Saumarez, 11 September 1811.
49. NA, Kew, FO 22/63, unknown writer, London, 12 October 1811.
50. Aspinall, *The Correspondence of George, Prince of Wales* VII, fol. 3212, Liverpool to Prince Regent, 17 October 1811.
51. Shrubland, Saumarez to Lady Saumarez, 18 October 1811.

7 Marshal 'Belle-Jambe' Declares War, pp. 106–127

1. Raglan MS 101, Wellesley-Pole to Wellington, 7 March 1810, quoted in Muir, *Britain and the Defeat of Napoleon*, p. 123.
2. Aspinall, *Later Correspondence of George III* IV, fol. 4234 n.2.
3. Quoted in Muir, *Britain and the Defeat of Napoleon* pp. 123–4, Wellington to Wellesley-Pole, 6 April 1810.
4. SRO, HA/93/6/1/1388, Foster to Saumarez, 14 June 1810.
5. Ryan, 'Ambassador Afloat', p. 251.
6. NA, Kew, ADM 2/1370, Barrow to Saumarez and Croker to Saumarez, both 8 May 1810.
7. Ibid., Croker to Saumarez, 11 May 1810.
8. Ibid., Barrow to Saumarez, 24 May 1810; Croker to Saumarez, 24 May and 26 September 1810.
9. SRO, HA/93/6/1/1609, Fenwick to Saumarez, 29 October 1810.
10. SRO, HA/93/6/1/1643, Croker to Saumarez, 27 November 1810.
11. SRO, HA/93/6/1/1270/1, Fenwick to Admiralty, 7 March 1810.
12. Shrubland, Saumarez to Lady Saumarez, 14–19 and 25 May 1810.
13. Tiselius, 'Landshövdingen Axel Von Rosen': 'De borde icke tillåta något engelsk

flagg förande fartyg, som icke för liden betydlig sjöskada nödgades söka räddning, ingå i en egentlig hamn eller passera eller lägga till under kanonerna av den fästning, som kommenderar inloppet därtill.'

14. SRO, HA/93/6/1/1178, Pickmore to Saumarez, 2 November 1809.
15. Tiselius, 'Landshövdingen Axel Von Rosen'.
16. Shrubland, Saumarez to Lady Saumarez, 14 June 1810.
17. NMM, YOR/16A, Saumarez to Yorke, 20 June 1810; Yorke to Saumarez, 28 June 1810.
18. SRO, HA/93/6/1/1367, Barrow to Saumarez, 6 June 1810.
19. SRO, HA/93/6/1/1391 and 1390, Foster to Saumarez, 16 June 1810 and Krusenstjerna to Saumarez, 14 June 1810.
20. Professor Feldbaek has kindly pointed out that this was the name by which he was known in Sweden whereas in Norway he was called Kristian August.
21. SRO, HA/93/6/1/1257 and 1259, Fenwick to Saumarez, 19 February and 21 February 1810.
22. Von Rosen, Ep.E.10:9, 24 June 1810.
23. Shrubland, Saumarez to Lady Saumarez, 1 July 1810.
24. Shrubland, Saumarez to Lady Saumarez, 26 July 1810.
25. Ross II, pp. 209–10; NMM, YOR/16A, Saumarez to Yorke, 21 August 1810.
26. NA, Kew, FO 73/57, Foster to Bathurst, 31 October 1809.
27. Palmer, *Bernadotte*, p. 172.
28. Kermina, *Bernadotte et Desirée Clary*, p. 134.
29. Suremain, *Mémoires*, p. 228.
30. Kermina, *Bernadotte et Desirée Clary*, p. 93.
31. Von Rosen, Ep.E.10:10, 17 August and 25 August 1810.
32. Ross II, p. 204.
33. SRO, HA/93/6/1/1504, Fenwick to Saumarez, 27 August 1810.
34. SRO, HA/93/6/1/1577/1, Barrow to Saumarez, 18 October 1810.
35. Von Rosen, Ep.E.10:9, 20 August 1810.
36. Von Rosen, Ep.E.10:10, fol. 98B, 25 August 1810.
37. NA, Kew, ADM 1/10, secret letter, Saumarez to Yorke, 21 August 1810.
38. NMM, YOR/16A, private letter, Saumarez to Yorke, 21 August and 27 August 1810; Krusenstjerna to Saumarez, 29 August 1810.
39. SRO, HA/93/6/1/1531, Newman to Governor of Gothenburg, 16 September 1810.
40. NMM, YOR/16A, Krusenstjerna to Saumarez, 29 August 1810; SRO, HA/93/6/1/1538, Krusenstjerna to Saumarez, 20 September 1810.
41. Von Rosen, Ep.E.10:10, 17 September 1810.
42. Ibid., 19 September 1810.
43. SRO, HA/93/6/1/1544 and 1555, Krusenstjerna to Saumarez, 23 and 28 September 1810; NMM, YOR/16A, Saumarez to Yorke, 21 September 1810.
44. Von Rosen, Ep.E.10:10, 26 September 1810.
45. SRO, HA/93/6/1/1571 and 1607, Krusenstjerna to Saumarez, 10 and 28 October 1810.
46. NMM, YOR/16A, Yorke to Saumarez, 19 October 1810.
47. Ibid., Saumarez to Yorke, 21 September 1810.
48. Ross II, p. 221.
49. Ibid., pp. 214–15.

50. Bernadotteska Familie Arkivet, Karl XIV Johan, fol. 52, Journal, 17 October 1810.
51. Von Rosen, Ep.E.10:10, 8 September 1810.
52. Ross II, p. 217.
53. NMM, YOR/16A, Krusentjerna to Saumarez, 29 August 1810.
54. Palmer, *Bernadotte*, pp. 177–9.
55. Kermina, *Bernadotte et Desirée Clary*, pp. 155/6.
56. *Napoléon* XXI, no.16890, Napoleon to Bernadotte, 10 September 1810.
57. Ibid., no.16906, Napoleon to Comte Mollien, Ministère du Trésor Public, 15 September 1810.
58. NMM, YOR/16A, Saumarez to Yorke, 23 October and 20 November 1810.
59. Von Rosen, Ep.E.10:9, fol. 112, 15 October 1810.
60. Coquelle, 'La Mission d'Alquier', pp. 196–8.
61. *Napoléon* XXI, no.16768, Napoleon to Champagny, 7 August 1810.
62. Ibid., no.16930, Napoleon to Eugène, 19 September 1810.
63. Ibid., no.17062, Napoleon to Champagny, 19 October 1810.
64. Ibid., no. 17040, Napoleon to Champagny, 13 October 1810.
65. SRO, HA/93/6/1/1606, unnamed translation of decree into English, dated 27 October 1810.
66. *Napoléon* XXI, no.17173, Napoleon to Prince Lebrun, 28 November 1810.
67. Ibid., no.17071, Napoleon to Alexander I, 23 October, 1810.
68. Ibid., no.17099, Napoleon to Champagny, 4 November 1810.
69. Ibid., no.17197, M. de Champagny – Rapport à SM L'Empéreur et Roi.
70. *Bernadotte*, pp. 7–8.
71. Archives Nationales, Paris, Archives des Affaires Etrangères, Suède, Correspondance, 249, fol. 294: rapport de Ranchoup, quoted in Coquelle, *Napoléon*, p. 199.
72. *Bernadotte*, p. 79, Bernadotte to Napoleon, 11 November 1810.
73. Von Rosen, Ep.E.10.9, 23 November 1810.
74. Coquelle, 'La Mission d'Alquier', pp. 200–1.
75. Ibid., p. 206.
76. *Napoléon* XXI, no.16906, Napoleon to Comte Mollien, 15 September 1810.
77. *Bernadotte*, pp. 79 and 81–3, Bernadotte to Napoleon, 11 November and 19 November 1810.
78. Ibid., pp. 84–7, Bernadotte to Napoleon, 8 December 1810.
79. SRO, HA/93/6/1/1609, Fenwick to Saumarez, 29 October 1810.
80. SRO, HA/93/6/1/1660, account of Bernadotte's election.
81. *Napoléon* XXI, no.17229, Champagny to Alquier, 22 December 1810.
82. *Bernadotte*, pp. 88–93, Napoleon to Bernadotte, 8 March 1811; pp. 96–9, Alquier to Bernadotte, 26 December, 1810; pp. 100–6, Engeström's reply, undated.
83. *Napoléon* XXII, no.17580, Napoleon to Charles Jean, Prince Royal, 6 April 1811.
84. SRO, HA/93/6/1/1648, Declaration of War, 17 November 1810.
85. Ryan, *Saumarez Papers*, p. 83 n.1.
86. SRO, HA/93/6/1/1641, Johnson to Saumarez, 27 November 1810.
87. NMM, YOR/16A, Saumarez to Yorke, 20 November and 3 December 1810.
88. SRO, HA/93/6/1/1570 and 1610, Fenwick to Saumarez, 9 and 29 October 1810.
89. NMM, YOR/16A, Saumarez to Yorke, 26 November 1810.
90. SRO, HA/93/6/1/2500, pp. 96–101, von Rosen to Saumarez, 15 June 1827.

91. *Napoléon* XXI, no.16916, Napoleon to Decrès, 17 September 1810; XXII, no.17824, Napoleon to Decrès, 19 June 1811; no.18160, Napoleon to Missiessy, 3 October 1811; XXIII, no.18264, Napoleon to Decrès, 16 November 1811.
92. *Napoléon* XXI, no.17034, Napoleon to Decrès, 12 October 1810.
93. Ibid., no.16991, Napoleon to Decrès, 4 October 1810.
94. SRO, HA/93/6/1/1625, Saumarez to Yorke, 5 November 1810.
95. Shrubland, Saumarez to Lady Saumarez, 30 July 1809.
96. SRO, HA/93/6/1/1641, Johnson to Saumarez, 27 November 1810.
97. NMM, YOR/17, Minute on hemp, August 1810; Board of Agriculture memorandum, 3 May 1811; Thompson to Yorke, 20 October 1810.
98. NA, Kew, ADM 2/1372, Lords Commissioners to Navy Board, 28 June 1811.
99. NA, Kew, ADM 2/1373, Lords Commissioners to Hood, 21 September 1811.

8 The Affair of the Carlshamn Cargoes, pp. 128–140
1. NA, Kew, ADM 1/11, Barrett to Saumarez, 10 November 1810.
2. NA, Kew, ADM 1/11, Saumarez to Croker, 26 November 1810.
3. SRO, HA/93/6/1/1645, Consul Smith to Honeyman, 2 December 1810.
4. NA, Kew, FO 73/68, W. Fawkener to William Hamilton, 11 January 1811.
5. NA, Kew, FO 73/68, John Atkins to Lord Bathurst, 3 and 7 January 1811.
6. Rear Admiral H. Robinson, *Sea Drift* (London, 1858), p. 43, quoted in Adams, *Admiral Collingwood*, p. 20.
7. Wright and Fayle, *History of Lloyds*, pp. 261–74; NA, Kew, ADM 1/3993, Rowcroft to Croker, 17 December 1810.
8. Von Rosen, Ep.E.10:9, 23 November 1810.
9. *Napoléon* XXII, no.17916, Napoleon to Maret, 15 July 1811.
10. NA, Kew, FO 73/68, Berg to Freeling, 14 January 1811.
11. Von Rosen, Ep.E.10:9, 8 December 1810; NA, Kew, FO 73/68, Berg to Freeling, 16 January 1811.
12. NA, Kew, FO 73/68, Berg to Freeling, 25 January 1811.
13. NA, Kew, FO 73/68, Berg to Freeling, 8 March 1811.
14. Von Rosen, Ep.E.10:11, 14 March 1811.
15. Goodwin, *Nelson's Victory*, p. 81.
16. Ross II, pp. 223–4.
17. NMM,YOR/16a, Yorke to Saumarez, 16 March 1811.
18. Ibid., Yorke to Saumarez, 19 October 1810.
19. NA, Kew, ADM 1/11, Saumarez to Croker, 18 October 1810.
20. NA, Kew, ADM 2/1371, Croker to Maurice, 1 March 1811.
21. James, *Naval History* V, pp. 342–5; Lindeberg, *Englandskrigene*, pp. 156–7; Koch and Skovmand, *Dansk Daad*, p. 251.
22. BL, Add. MSS 41385, Byam Martin to Saumarez, 7 June 1812.
23. Shrubland, Saumarez to Lady Saumarez, 1/2 May 1811.
24. Shrubland, Lady Saumarez to Saumarez, 30 May 1811.
25. Ross II, p. 229.
26. SRO, HA/93/6/1/1731, Fenwick to Saumarez, 19 May 1811.
27. NA, Kew, ADM 1/12, Smith to Saumarez, 15 May 1811.
28. Von Rosen, Ep.E.10:9, 23 May 1810.
29. NA, Kew, HD 3/6, Memorandum from Capt. John Ross RN, 3 September 1834.
30. Ibid., 26 September 1810.

31. SRO, HA/93/6/1/2060, Thornton to Saumarez, 6 June 1812.
32. SRO, HA/93/6/1/1664, Fenwick to Saumarez, 22 February 1811.
33. SRO, HA/93/6/1/1731, Fenwick to Saumarez, 19 May 1811.
34. SRO, HA/93/6/1/1725, Foy to Saumarez, 14 May 1811.
35. SRO, HA/93/6/1/1738, Foy to Saumarez, 28 May 1811.
36. NMM, YOR/16a, Yorke to Saumarez, 21 May 1811.
37. NA, Kew, FO 73/68, L. Tarras to O. Irving, 11 March 1811.
38. SRO, HA/93/6/1/1728, Admiralty to Saumarez, 16 May 1811.
39. SRO, HA/93/6/1/1740, Saumarez to Baron Tawast, 30 May 1811.
40. NA, Kew, FO 73/68, Saumarez to Croker, 24 May 1811.
41. NA, Kew, FO 73/68, Smith to Saumarez, 5 June 1811.
42. NA, Kew, ADM 1/12, Saumarez to Croker, 23 May 1811.
43. Ross II, p. 229.
44. Ibid., p. 237.
45. Shrubland, Saumarez to Lady Saumarez, 24 and 29 May 1811.
46. Shrubland, Lady Saumarez to Saumarez, 15 June 1811.
47. NMM, YOR/16a, Saumarez to Yorke, 28 May 1811.
48. Ibid., Saumarez to Yorke, 26 June 1811.
49. NA, Kew, ADM 1/12, Saumarez to Croker, 26 June 1811.
50. NMM, YOR/16a, Saumarez to Yorke, 9 April 1811.
51. SRO, HA/93/6/1/1703, Instructions from the Admiralty to Saumarez, 12 April 1811; NMM, YOR/16a, Yorke to Saumarez, 21 May 1811.
52. Shrubland, Saumarez to Lady Saumarez, 18 June 1811.
53. *Napoléon* XXII, no.17892, Napoleon to Marshal Davout, 5 July 1811.
54. SRO, HA/93/6/1/1833, Yorke to Saumarez, 16 August 1811.
55. Sherwig, *Guineas and Gunpowder*, p. 8.
56. SRO, HA/93/6/1/1834, Lords Commissioners to Saumarez, 17 August 1811.
57. SRO, HA/93/6/1/1797, Foy to Saumarez, 21 July 1811.
58. SRO, HA/93/6/1/1868, Johnson to Saumarez, August 1811.
59. SRO, HA/93/6/1/1866 and 1874, Foy to Saumarez, 30 August and 5 September 1811.
60. SRO, HA/93/6/1/1887, Foy to Saumarez, 9 September 1811.
61. SRO, HA/93/6/1/1907/1, Foy to Saumarez, 27 September 1811.
62. NA, Kew, ADM 1/1372, Croker to Saumarez, 10 August 1811.
63. NA, Kew, FO 73/68, Atkins to Thos. Wharton, 23 July 1811.
64. Ibid., Chetwynd to Culling Smith, 27 July 1811.

9 The Von Rosen Letters, pp. 141–154

1. NA, Kew, HD 3/6, letter in French from Sir James Saumarez, 23 January 1813.
2. Ross II, p. 245.
3. Von Rosen, Ep.E.10.9, fol. 105, 19 September 1810.
4. Ibid., 15 October 1810.
5. *Svenskt Biografiskt Lexikon* 30, p. 381, 'skämtsam, uppsluppen, och världsvan'.
6. Heckscher, *The Continental System*, p. 236.
7. Von Rosen, Ep.E.10:9, fol. 83, 22 May 1810.
8. Ibid., fol. 89, 29 June 1810.
9. Ibid., fol. 88, 24 and 29 June 1810.
10. Ibid., fol. 90, 7 July 1810.
11. Ibid., fol. 98A, 17 August 1810.

12. Ibid., fol. 96, 4 August 1810.
13. *Napoléon* XXI, no.16787, Napoleon to Montalivet (Minister of the Interior), 11 August 1810.
14. Von Rosen, Ep.E.10:9, fol. 99, 20 August 1810.
15. Ibid., fol. 107, 26 September 1810.
16. Ibid., fol. 118, 23 November 1810.
17. SRO, HA/93/6/1/1609, Fenwick to Saumarez, 29 October 1810.
18. Von Rosen, Ep.E.10:9, fol. 104, 17 September 1810.
19. NA, Kew, FO 73/68, Berg to Freeling, 21 December 1810, 14, 16 and 25 January 1811, 8, 15 and 25 March, *inter alia*.
20. Von Rosen, Ep.E.10:11, fol. 102, 1 June 1811.
21. NA, Kew, FO 73/69, Berg to Freeling, 14 October 1811.
22. Von Rosen, Ep.E.10:12, fol. 181, 17 June 1812.
23. Scott, *Bernadotte and the Fall of Napoleon*, p. 8.
24. Coquelle, 'La Mission d'Alquier', p. 233.
25. NMM, YOR/16A, Saumarez to Yorke, 20 November 1810.
26. Shrubland, SA/3/1/3, 1809–11, signature indecipherable, 20 July 1810.
27. Von Rosen, Ep.E.10:9, fol. 118, 23 November 1810.
28. Ibid., fol. 122, 8 December 1810.
29. Von Rosen, Ep.E.10:11, fol. 58, 9 January 1811.
30. Ibid., fol. 72, 6 April 1811.
31. Ibid., fol. 91, 11 May 1811.
32. NMM, YOR/16A, Saumarez to Yorke, 20 November 1810.
33. Bernadotteska Familie Arkivet, Karl XIV Johan, fol. 51 letterbooks, Bernadotte to Essen, 28 May 1811.
34. Von Rosen, Ep.E.10:11, fol. 94, 22 May 1811.
35. Von Rosen, Ep.E.10:11, fol. 95, 23 May 1811.
36. Ibid., fol. 98, 29 May 1811.
37. Ibid., fol. 100, 31 May 1811.
38. Ibid., fol. 102, 1 June 1811.
39. SRO, HA/93/6/1/1733, Yorke to Saumarez, 21 May 1811.
40. SRO, HA/93/6/1/1740, Saumarez to Tawast, 30 May 1811.
41. Von Rosen, Ep.E.10:11, fol. 102, 1 June 1811.
42. Von Rosen, Ep.E.10:11, fol. 109, 8 June 1811.
43. Ibid., fol. 110, 27 June 1811.
44. Ibid., fol. 123, 7 August 1811.
45. Ibid., fol. 24, 10 August 1811.
46. Ibid., fol. 115, 5 July 1811.
47. Coquelle, 'La Mission d'Alquier', p. 209–11.
48. Ibid., pp. 225–6, Alquier to Engeström, 20 July 1811.
49. Shrubland, Saumarez to Lady Saumarez, 15 May 1811; SRO, HA 93/6/1/1984, Count Ernst Robert von Rosen to Saumarez, 30 December 1811.
50. Von Rosen, Ep.E.10:11, fol. 120, 26 July 1811.
51. Ibid., fol. 123, 7 August 1811.
52. Archives Nationales, Paris, Archives des Affaires Etrangères, Suède, Correspondances, 296, fol. 55, quoted in Coquelle, 'La Mission d'Alquier', pp. 225–6.
53. Von Rosen, Ep.E.10:11, fol. 130, 30 August 1811.

10 Diplomatic Intrigues: Napoleon's Fateful Decision, pp. 155–176

1. Coquelle, 'La Mission d'Alquier', p. 213.
2. Bazin, *Bernadotte*, pp. 131–2.
3. Vandal, *Napoléon et Alexandre 1er*, pp. 10–12.
4. NA, Kew, FO 22/60, Barrow to Bagot, 8 September 1809; Von Rosen, Ep.E.10:12, fol. 211, 16 December 1812.
5. *Napoléon* XXI, no.16804, Order, 18 August 1810; XXII, no.17892, Napoleon to Davout, 5 July 1811.
6. Ibid., XXI, no.17099, Napoleon to Champagny, 4 November 1810.
7. Ibid. XXI, no.17200, 10 December 1810; XXIII, no.18454, Observations – Dictée en conseil des Ponts et Chaussées, 27 January 1812.
8. Marzagalli, *Les Boulevards de la Fraude*, p. 108.
9. Ibid., p. 105.
10. Esdaile, *Wars of Napoleon*, pp. 104–6.
11. Thompson, *Letters of Napoleon*, p. 275 n.
12. Niven, *Napoleon and Alexander I*, p. 61.
13. Knight, *Pursuit of Victory*, pp. 393–4.
14. NA, Kew, ADM 2/1370, Croker to Saumarez, 11 May 1810; Von Rosen Ep.E.10:9, 22 May 1810.
15. NA. Kew, FO 22/62, Fenwick to Culling Smith, 4 February 1811.
16. SRO, HA/93/6/1/1362, Victualling Office to Saumarez, 5 June 1810.
17. Shrubland, Saumarez to Lady Saumarez, 13 July 1809; 7 June 1810, 15 July 1811.
18. Shrubland, Saumarez to Lady Saumarez, 24 May, 11 and 18 June 1811; Lady Saumarez to Saumarez, 8 June 1811.
19. Hansson, *Engelske flottan*, pp. 118–23.
20. A study by Kristina Sandberg, 'England, Sverige och Hanöbukten 1810–1812' (1978), in Karlshamn Kommun Biblioteket, gives interesting details of the British occupation of Hanö during these three years, and I am most grateful to Harriet Rydberg, Librarian, for letting me have a copy.
21. Coquelle, 'La Mission d'Alquier', pp. 229–31.
22. SRO, HA/93/6/1/1957, Foy to Saumarez, 16 November 1811.
23. Letters from Krusenstjerna to Engeström in Riksarkivet, dated 22 September and 29 October 1810, quoted in Sandberg, 'England', p. 23 but without further details.
24. Suremain, *Mémoires*, pp. 256–7.
25. Coquelle, 'La Mission d'Alquier', p. 235.
26. Von Rosen, Ep.E.10:11, fols 147, 150 and 151, dated 12, 15 and 17 October 1811.
27. Quoted in Palmer, *Bernadotte*, p. 50.
28. Ibid, p. 88.
29. Kermina, *Bernadotte et Desirée Clary*, p. 115.
30. Ibid., p. 116.
31. Ibid., pp. 145–50.
32. *Byam Martin Letters* II, pp. 176–7, Byam Martin to H. Martin, 26 May 1812.
33. Kermina, *Bernadotte et Desirée Clary* pp. 155–6.
34. Bazin, *Bernadotte*, p. 273.
35. Shrubland, Saumarez to Lady Saumarez, 18 June 1811.
36. Shrubland, Saumarez to Lady Saumarez, 15 September 1811.

37. SRO, HA/93/6/1/2499/3, Admiralty to Saumarez, 14 September 1811.
38. SRO, HA/93/6/1/1885, Gneisenau to Saumarez, 8 September 1811; HA/93/6/1/2499/7, Saumarez to Gneisenau, 28 September 1811.
39. *Napoléon* XXIII, no.18325, Napoleon to Lacuée, 13 December 1811.
40. SRO, HA/93/6/1/1907/1. Foy to Saumarez, 27 September 1811.
41. *Napoléon* XXII, no.17549, Napoleon to Champagny, 1 April 1911.
42. Ibid., no.17571, Napoleon to Champagny, 4 April 1811.
43. NA, Kew, ADM 2/1373, Barrow to Saumarez, 26 September 1811; ADM 1/12, Saumarez to Croker, 6 November 1811; Shrubland, Saumarez to Lady Saumarez, 7 October 1811.
44. Aspinall, *Correspondence of George, Prince of Wales*, fol. 3142. Wellesley to Prince Regent, 15 August 1811.
45. Shrubland, Saumarez to Lady Saumarez, 18 October 1811.
46. Ross II, p. 251.
47. Shrubland, Saumarez to Lady Saumarez, 25 October 1811.
48. Von Rosen, Ep.E.10:12, fols 155 and 157, 5 and 22 November 1811.
49. SRO, HA/93/6/1/1917, Yorke to Saumarez, 5 October 1811.
50. NA, Kew, ADM 2/1372, Barrow to Saumarez, 9 September 1811.
51. Ibid., 2/1373, Croker to Saumarez, 11 December 1811.
52. *Napoléon* XXIII, no.18378, Napoleon to Bassano, 27 December 1811.
53. SRO, HA/93/6/1/1954, Foy to Saumarez, 12 November 1811.
54. SRO, HA/93/6/1/1964, Fenwick to Saumarez, 21 November 1811.
55. SRO, HA/93/6/1/1996, Fenwick to Saumarez, 16 January 1812.
56. Coquelle, 'La Mission d'Alquier', pp. 215–16.
57. SRO, HA/93/6/1/1976, Bickerton to Saumarez, 4 December 1811.
58. Ryan, *Saumarez Papers*, p. 227, Buller to Cooke, 25 May 1812.
59. SRO, HA/93/6/1/1708, Fenwick to Saumarez, 18 April 1811.
60. SRO, HA/93/6/1/1804, Watts to Reynolds, 29 July 1811.
61. SRO, HA/93/6/1/1871, Ernst Von Rosen to Saumarez, 2 September 1811.
62. SRO, HA/93/6/1/1873. Fenwick to Saumarez, 5 September 1811.
63. SRO, HA/93/6/1/2499/29–31, Croker to Saumarez, 5 October 1811.
64. SRO, HA/93/6/1/1916, Yorke to Saumarez, 5 October 1811.
65. All these letters are in the Shrubland archive, now at SRO, SA/3/1/2/1, unnumbered but kept in folders in order of date.
66. Shrubland, Saumarez to Lady Saumarez, 24 June 1810 and 1 June 1812.
67. SRO HA/93/6/1/2499/17–19, Yorke to Saumarez, 5 October and Saumarez to Yorke, 13 October 1811.
68. Shrubland, Saumarez to Lady Saumarez, 15 July 1811.
69. Ryan, *Saumarez Papers*, pp. 197 and 210–11.
70. Hughes, *Private Correspondence of Admiral Lord Collingwood*, fol. 96, Collingwood to Mrs. Stead, 5 March 1806.
71. Ibid., fol. 153, Collingwood to his sister, 25 June 1808.
72. SRO, HA/93/6/1/1946/1, Reynolds to Dashwood, 7 November 1811.
73. SRO, HA/93/6/1/1726, Croker to Saumarez, 15 May 1811.
74. *Napoléon* XXI, no.16971, Napoleon to Savary, 1 October 1810.
75. Ryan, *Saumarez Papers*, pp. 205–6, Saumarez to Croker, 2 December 1811; pp. 208–9, Narrative of the loss of the *St George* and *Defence*; Shrubland, Saumarez to Lady Saumarez, 1 December 1811.
76. Shrubland, Saumarez to Lady Saumarez, 11 November 1811.

77. SRO, HA/93/6/1/1959 and 1971, Dashwood to Saumarez, 17 and 29 November 1811.
78. SRO, HA/6/1/1995, Dashwood to Saumarez, 10 January 1812.
79. ADM 1/14, Hope to Saumarez, 29 December 1811.
80. SRO, HA/93/6/1/1996, Fenwick to Saumarez, 16 January 1812.
81. Ross II, p. 256.
82. SRO, HA/93/6/1/1999, 'Loss of HMS *Defence* by a survivor'.
83. SRO, HA/93/6/1/1996, Fenwick to Saumarez, 16 January 1812.
84. Ryan, *Saumarez Papers*, pp. 210–11.
85. Ross II, pp. 268–9.
86. SRO, HA/93/6/1/1969, Foy to Saumarez, 26 November 1811.
87. Von Rosen, Ep.E.10:12, fol. 156, 9 November 1811.
88. SRO, HA/93/6/1/1952 and 1953, Thornton to Saumarez, 11 and 12 November 1811; HA/93/6/1/2007, Croker to Saumarez, 21 March 1812.
89. *Napoléon* XXII, no.18239, Napoleon to Jerome, 3 November 1811.
90. WYAS, WYL250/8/43, Thornton to Canning, 15 April 1808.

11 The Final Year, pp. 177–197

1. Muir, *Britain and the Defeat of Napoleon*, p. 222.
2. Von Rosen, Ep. 10:12, fol. 163, undated.
3. SRO, HA/93/6/1/2031, Fenwick to Saumarez, 11 May 1812.
4. Harris, *Talleyrand*, pp. 192–6.
5. Esdaile, *Napoleon's Wars*, pp. 437–9.
6. Muir, *Britain and the Defeat of Napoleon*, pp. 182–5.
7. Wellesley, *The Wellesley Papers* II, pp. 44–55.
8. Thompson, *Letters of Napoleon*, pp. 236–7.
9. *Napoléon* XXIII, nos 18447 and 18461, Napoleon to Davout, 19 and 28 January 1812.
10. Ibid., no.18458, Napoleon to Jerome, 27 January 1812.
11. Coquelle, 'La Mission d'Alquier', pp. 237–9; Bazin, *Bernadotte*, pp. 131–43.
12. Bazin, *Bernadotte*, pp. 140–1.
13. Ibid., pp. 249–50.
14. Von Rosen, Ep.E.10:11, fols 136–7, 14 September 1811.
15. Von Rosen, Ep.E.10:12., fol. 162, 14 December 1811.
16. Shrubland, Saumarez to Lady Saumarez, 18 October 1811.
17. Shrubland, Saumarez to Lady Saumarez, 28 August 1812.
18. Shrubland, Saumarez to Lady Saumarez, 21 September 1812.
19. SRO, HA/93/6/1/2412, Thornton to Saumarez, 18 December 1812.
20. Mackesy, *War in the Mediterranean*, p. 383.
21. Nicolas, *Dispatches and Letters* V, p. 204.
22. Hughes, *Private Correspondence of Admiral Lord Collingwood*, no.175, 25 April 1809.
23. Maurice, *Diaries of Sir John Moore*, p. 198.
24. SRO, HA/93/6/1/1630, Fenwick to Saumarez, 7 November 1810.
25. SRO, HA/93/6/1/2396, Bornemann to Saumarez, 3 November 1812.
26. Quoted in Adams, *Admiral Collingwood*, p. 272.
27. Ibid., p. 226.
28. Shrubland, Saumarez to Lady Saumarez, 9 April 1808.
29. Shrubland, Saumarez to Lady Saumarez, 14 May 1808.

30. Von Rosen, Ep.E.10:9 and 10:11, fols 90 and 102, 7 July 1810 and 1 June 1811.
31. Fremantle, *Wynne Diaries* II, p. 183.
32. Von Rosen, Ep.E.10:11, fol. 110, 27 June 1811.
33. Von Rosen, Ep.E.10:12, fol. 171, 27 March 1812; SRO, HA/93/6/1/2025, Saumarez to Thornton, 4 May 1812.
34. Shrubland, Lady Saumarez to Saumarez, 11 July 1812.
35. Tracy, *Naval Chronicle* V, p. 72.
36. SRO, HA/93/6/1/2025 and 2027, Saumarez to Thornton, 4 May; Thornton to Saumarez, 6 May 1812.
37. SRO, HA/93/6/1/2027, Thornton to Saumarez, 6 May 1812.
38. Ryan, *Saumarez Papers*, p. 221, n.1.
39. SRO, HA/93/6/1/2499/17–18, Yorke to Saumarez, 5 October 1811.
40. Von Rosen, Ep.E.10:9, fol. 96, 4 August 1810.
41. Von Rosen, Ep.E.10:12, fol. 171, 27 March 1812.
42. SRO, HA/93/6/1/2024, Fenwick to Saumarez, 3 May 1812.
43. Von Rosen, Ep.E.10:12, fol. 177, 11 May 1812.
44. Ibid.
45. SRO HA/93/6/1/2034, Von Rosen to Saumarez, 15 May 1812.
46. Shrubland, Saumarez to Lady Saumarez, 22 July, 30 July and 28 August 1812.
47. Shrubland, Saumarez to Lady Saumarez, 23 September 1811.
48. Ross II, pp. 265–6.
49. Ross I, pp. 27–8; Knight, *Pursuit of Victory*, p. 191 n.
50. SRO, HA/93/6/1/2012, 2013 and 2015 Melville to Saumarez and Saumarez to Melville, 12 April 1812 and Melville to Saumarez, 18 April 1812.
51. Owen, 'Lord Collingwood', p. 154.
52. NA, Kew, ADM 1/14, Heywood to Saumarez, 22 April 1812.
53. Unknown author, 'Fregatten Najadens Ødelæggelse', available online at <http://www.idi.ntnu.no/~anders/books/Fra_Krigens_Tid/Najaden.html>; James, *Naval History* VI, pp. 53–4; Ross II, pp. 275–8.
54. Ross II, pp. 278–80.
55. Ibid., p. 284.
56. SRO, HA/93/6/1/2049, Fenwick to Saumarez, 31 May 1812.
57. SRO, HA/93/6/1/2032, Smith to Saumarez, 12 May 1812.
58. NA, Kew, ADM 1/14, Saumarez to Croker, 6 May 1812.
59. SRO, HA/93/6/1/2026 and 2044, Thornton to Saumarez, 6 and 29 May 1812; *Byam Martin Letters* II, pp. 186–7.
60. Engeström Letters, Ep.E.10:12, Dashwood to Smith, 24 March 1812; NA, Kew, ADM 1/14, Dashwood to Saumarez, 24 March 1812.
61. SRO, HA/93/6/1/2043, Morris to Saumarez, 27 May 1812.
62. Ryan, *Saumarez Papers*, pp. 227–8, Morris to Martin, 11 June 1812.
63. Riksarkivet, Stockholm, Gietta-Pukesta Ark., III, 17 May 1812.
64. *Byam Martin Letters* II, 176–9.
65. Riksarkivet, Stockholm, Giertta-Pukesta Ark III, 27 May 1811.
66. *Napoléon* XXIII, no. 18664, Napoleon to Bassano, 25 April 1812.
67. Ibid., no.18669, Napoleon to Alexander I, 25 April 1812.
68. Ibid., no.18652, Bassano to Castlereagh, 17 April 2006.
69. Ibid., no.18652, Bassano to Castlereagh, 17 April 1812; Muir, *Britain and the Defeat of Napoleon*, p. 198.

70. *Napoléon* XXIII, no.18841, 1er Bulletin de la Grande Armée, 20 June 1812.
71. Ibid., nos 18683 and 18702, Napoleon to Bassano and to the Prince de Neuchatel, both 20 May 1812.
72. Metternich, *Memoirs* I, p. 153, quoted in Esdaile, *Napoleon's Wars*, p. 461.
73. *Napoléon* XXIII, no.18720, Napoleon to the Prince de Neuchatel, 23 May 1812.
74. *Bernadotte*, pp. 88–9, Napoleon to Bernadotte, 8 March 1811.
75. SRO, HA/93/6/1/2040. Saumarez to Thornton, 23 May 1812.
76. SRO, HA/93/6/1/2053 and 2057, Thornton to Saumarez, 31 May and Morris to Saumarez, 4 June 1812.
77. Quoted in Briggs, *England in the Age of Improvement*, p. 142.
78. Muir, *Britain and the Defeat of Napoleon*, pp. 194–6.
79. SRO, HA/93/6/1/2093, Fenwick to Saumarez, 25 June 1812.
80. Von Rosen, Ep.E.10:12, fol. 179, 3 June 1812.
81. SRO, HA/93/6/1/2060, Thornton to Saumarez, 6 June 1812.
82. SRO, HA/93/6/1/2057, Morris to Saumarez, 4 June 1812.
83. SRO, HA/93/6/1/2077, Thornton to Saumarez, 15 June 1812.
84. SRO, HA/93/6/1/2074 and NA, Kew, ADM 1/14, Thornton to Saumarez, 14 June 1812.
85. SRO, HA/93/6/1/2075, Thornton to Saumarez, 14 June 1812.
86. SRO, HA/93/6/1/2075/1, Gyllenskold to Thornton, 14 June 1812.
87. Von Rosen, Ep.E.10:12, fol. 181, 17 June 1812.
88. Ibid., fol. 184, 15 July 1812.
89. Shrubland, Lady Saumarez to Saumarez, 13 June 1812.
90. SRO, HA/93/6/1/2057 and 2060, Morris to Saumarez, 4 June and Thornton to Saumarez, 6 June 1812; NA, Kew, ADM 1/14, Ross to Morris, 17 June 1812.
91. Ross II, pp. 281–2, Thornton to Saumarez, 17 July 1812
92. Von Rosen, Ep.E.10:12, fol. 184, 15 July 1812.
93. Ibid., fol. 185, 2 August 1812.
94. Shrubland, Saumarez to Lady Saumarez, 9 August 1812.
95. Bernadotteska Familie Arkivet, Karl XIV Johan Letterbooks, fol. 51, Bernadotte to von Platen, 28 March 1811.
96. Shrubland, Saumarez to Lady Saumarez, 6 September 1812.
97. Von Rosen, Ep.E.10:12, fol. 201, 19 September 1812.
98. Shrubland, Saumarez to Lady Saumarez, 16 September 1812.
99. Ryan, *Saumarez Papers*, p. 263, Saumarez to Wilkinson, 24 October 1812.
100. *Byam Martin Letters* II, pp. 189–315.
101. Ryan, *Saumarez Papers*, pp. 262–4, Melville to Saumarez, 22 October 1812; Hope to Saumarez, 30 October 1812; Saumarez to Hope, 31 October 1812; Ross II, pp. 288–92.

12 Conclusions, pp. 198–220

1. Muir, *Britain and the Defeat of Napoleon*, p. 21.
2. WYAS, WYL250/8/42, Canning to Thornton, 10 June 1808.
3. Ryan, *Saumarez Papers*, pp. 44–5, Thornton to Saumarez, 4 September 1808; WYAS, WYL250/8/43, Thornton to Canning, 4 September 1808; SRO, HA 93/6/1/449, Thornton to Saumarez, 22 December 1808.
4. WYAS, WYL250/8/23, Canning to his wife, 20 September 1809.
5. Ryan, *Saumarez Papers*, p. 56, *Aboukir*, *Majestic* and *Minotaur*.
6. SRO, HA/93/6/1/1728, Admiralty to Saumarez, 16 May 1811.

7. NA, Kew, HD 3/6, letter from Sir James Saumarez, 23 January 1813.
8. BL, Add. MSS 75805, quoted in Knight, *Pursuit of Victory*, p. 241.
9. Shrubland, Saumarez to Lady Saumarez, 31 May 1808 and 11 June 1810.
10. Shrubland, Saumarez to Lady Saumarez, 15 July 1709.
11. NA, Kew, ADM 1/9, Saumarez to Captains and Commanders, 31 July 1809.
12. NA, Kew, ADM 2/1371, Circular to all Commanders-in-Chief and Port Admirals, 8 October 1810.
13. Shrubland, Lady Saumarez to Saumarez, 5 October 1808.
14. SRO, HA/93/6/1/1129, von Platen to Saumarez, 22 September 1809.
15. *Byam Martin Letters* II, p. 176.
16. NA, Kew, HD 3/6, Memorandum for His Majesty from Capt. John Ross RN, 3 September 1834 (I am grateful to Professor Rodger for drawing this to my attention); Von Rosen, Ep.E.10:9, 16 July 1810.
17. Ross II, p. 229.
18. Von Rosen, Ep.E.10:12, fol. 208, 4 November 1812.
19. NA, Kew, HD 3/6, memorandum for His Majesty from Capt. John Ross RN – 3 September 1834
20. Shrubland, SA/3/2/2/8, log of HMS *Russell*; Ross I, p. 77.
21. Ross I, p. 82.
22. Clarke and McArthur, *Life of Admiral Lord Nelson*, quoted in Ross I, p. 194.
23. Ross I, p. 150.
24. Shrubland, Saumarez to Lady Saumarez, 18 June 1800.
25. Shrubland, Bertie to Saumarez, 24 June 1808.
26. Stirling, *Pages and Portraits* II, p. 307.
27. Shrubland, Lady Saumarez to Saumarez, 20 September 1811; Saumarez to Lady Saumarez, 23 and 29 September 1811; SRO HA/93/6/1/1770, Yorke to Saumarez, 27 June 1811.
28. BL, Spencer Papers, Add. MSS 75847, St Vincent to Spencer, 27 December 1800.
29. Muir, *Britain and the Defeat of Napoleon*, pp. 260 and 309–10; Horne, *How Far From Austerlitz?*, p. 351n.
30. BL, Liverpool Papers, Add. MSS 38258, Saumarez to Lord Liverpool, 18 June 1814.
31. Hampshire Record Office, Phillimore Papers, 115M88/N30, Saumarez to Lord Liverpool, 26 January 1818.
32. Von Rosen, Ep.E.10:11, fol. 102, 1 June 1811 and fol. 110, 27 June 1811.
33. Shrubland, Saumarez to Lady Saumarez, 18 June 1800.
34. NA, Kew, FO 174/11, Saumarez to Consul at Tangier, 7 July 1801.
35. Shrubland, Saumarez to Lady Saumarez, 8 July 1808.
36. Shrubland, Saumarez to Lady Saumarez, 14 May 1808.
37. Shrubland, SA/3/1/2/4, Saumarez to Richard Saumarez (younger), 27 August 1810.
38. Captain Sir Jahleel Brenton, quoted in Ross II, p. 329.
39. Hampshire Record Office, Phillimore Papers, 115M88/N30, Saumarez to Lord Spencer, 20 June 1800.
40. Shrubland, Lady Saumarez to Saumarez, 17 March 1798.
41. Shrubland, Lady Saumarez to Saumarez, 30 May 1811.
42. Ross II, p. 303.
43. Shrubland, Saumarez to Lady Saumarez, 10 September 1808.

44. Shrubland, Saumarez to Lady Saumarez, 15 May and 11 June 1810.
45. Shrubland, Saumarez to Dobree, 15 February 1800.
46. Shrubland, Saumarez to Lady Saumarez, 27 July 1808.
47. Shrubland, Saumarez to Lady Saumarez, 15 May 1810.
48. Shrubland, Saumarez to Lady Saumarez, 15 April 1808.
49. SRO, HA/93/6/1/2062, Saumarez to Smith, 7 June 1812.
50. Shrubland, Saumarez to Lady Saumarez, 4 August 1812.
51. NA, Kew, ADM 1/10, Saumarez to Admiralty, 27 July 1810.
51. BL, Byam Martin Correspondence, Add. MSS 41366, Saumarez to Byam Martin, 17 June 1812.
53. Ross I, p. 204, Saumarez journal to his family.
54. Shrubland, Mrs. Richard Saumarez to Lady Saumarez, February 1797.
55. Shrubland. Saumarez to Lady Saumarez, 9 April 1808.
56. Ross II, p. 307.
57. Shrubland, Lady Saumarez to Saumarez, 8 June 1811.
58. Ross II, p. 328, quoting Sir Jahleel Brenton.
59. Shrubland, 'Notes on Love and Marriage' in an undated Commonplace Book.
60. Shrubland, Saumarez to Martha, 21 June 1790; to Lady Saumarez, 9 August 1812.
61. Shrubland, Saumarez to Lady Saumarez, 27 August 1808.
62. Shrubland, Saumarez to Lady Saumarez, 10 July 1810 and 11 June 1811.
63. Shrubland, Saumarez to Lady Saumarez, 7 August 1812.
64. Shrubland, Lady Saumarez to Saumarez, 21 January 1795.
65. Shrubland, Lady Saumarez to Saumarez, 17 March 1797 and 17 January 1798.
66. Shrubland, Lady Saumarez to Saumarez, 22 May 1811.
67. Shrubland, Lady Saumarez to Saumarez, 1 November 1811.
68. Shrubland, Saumarez to Lady Saumarez, 18 October; Lady Saumarez to Saumarez 25 October 1811.
69. Shrubland, Saumarez to Lady Saumarez, 18 December 1811.
70. *Byam Martin Letters* II, p. 164.
71. Shrubland, Lady Saumarez to Saumarez, 22 June and 20 July 1812.
72. Shrubland, Lady Saumarez to Saumarez, 30 May 1811.
73. Shrubland, Lady Saumarez to Saumarez, 8 June and 20 July 1811.
74. Shrubland, Saumarez to Lady Saumarez, 6 August 1812.
75. Shrubland, Lady Saumarez to Saumarez, 20 July 1809.
76. Shayer, *James Saumarez*, p. 28.
77. Shrubland, Saumarez to Lady Saumarez, 15 July 1811.
78. Shrubland, Lady Saumarez to Saumarez, 25 October 1811.
79. Heaps, Leo, *Log of the* Centurion, p. 86.
80. Esdaile, *Napoleon's Wars*, p. 458.
81. A. Beugnot, ed., *Mémoires du Comte Beugnot, Ancien Ministre, 1783–1815* (Paris, 1868) I, pp. 309–10, quoted in Esdaile, *Napoleon's Wars*, p. 444.
82. SRO, HA/93/6/1/2500, Count Rosen to Saumarez, 15 June 1827.

Epilogue, p. 221

1. Ross II, pp. 313–14.
2. Ibid., p. 304.
3. I am grateful to Professor Andrew Lambert for this information.
4. Ross II, pp. 320–5.

5. Priaulx Library, Guernsey, Dobree–Mann MSS, Family Letters II, 1824–41.

Bibliographical Note, pp. 227–232

1. Ryan, 'Defence of British Trade' and 'Trade with the Enemy in Scandinavian and Baltic Ports'.
2. Shrubland, T.14279, Box 17, Lord de Saumarez to his mother, undated; J.G. Lockhart to Lord de Saumarez, 6 March 1839 (probable year); SA/3/1/8/2/45, Count von Platen to Lady Saumarez, 9 January 1840.
3. James, *Naval History* V, p. 215.
4. Greenwood, 'James, Lord de Saumarez', pp. 247 and 269.
5. Shayer, *James Saumarez*, p. 132.
6. Bienkowski, *Admirals in the Age of Nelson*, pp. 214–37.
7. Marcus, *Age of Nelson*, p. 410.
8. Muir, *Britain and the Defeat of Napoleon*, pp. 179–80.
9. Hall, *British Strategy*, p. 165.
10. Kennedy, *The Rise and Fall of British Naval Mastery*, pp. 150, 169 and 171.
11. Warner, *The Sea and the Sword*, p. 107.
12. Lewis, *A Social History of the Navy*, p. 68.
13. Kennedy, *Nelson's Band of Brothers*, p. 81.
14. Fitchett, *Nelson and his Captains*, pp. 200–1 and 203–7.
15. Rodger, *Command of the Ocean*, p. 560.
16. Padfield, *Maritime Power and the Struggle for Freedom*, p. 299.
17. *Napoléon*, XV, XXI, XXII and XXIII.
18. Heckscher, *The Continental System*, p. 236.
19. Coquelle, *Napoléon et l'Angleterre*.
20. Coquelle, 'La Mission d'Alquier'.
21. *Bernadotte*.
22. *Byam Martin Letters* II, pp. 130–3; I, pp. 29–30; II, ix.

Bibliography

Primary sources

United Kingdom

Suffolk Record Office, Ipswich
HA/6/3/1–2500: Official correspondence of Admiral Sir James Saumarez
SA/3/1/1–7: Private papers of the Saumarez Family, formerly at Shrubland Hall, Suffolk

National Archives, Public Record Office, Kew
ADM 1/6–15: Baltic Reports, 1807–12
ADM 1/3993: Correspondence with Lloyds
ADM 2/1102–3: Convoys 1808–10
ADM 2/1365–75: Secret Letters 1808–12
ADM 7/793: Convoy Lists
ADM 50/Admirals' Journals: /50, Hood; /51, 56, and 59, Saumarez; /58, Keats; /59 and 94, Bertie; /90, Hope; /98, M. Dixon; /100, Reynolds
ADM 51/Captains' Logs: /1813, *Mars*; /1857, *Devastation*; /1887, *Aetna*; /1905, *Orion*
ADM 52/3874 and 3878: Masters' Log, *Victory*
ADM 80/145 and 146: Keats Order Book and Letters 1809.
FO 22/51, 53–4, 57–8, 60–3: Denmark
FO 65/88: Russia
FO 73/49–50, 55–9, 66, 68–70, and 75: Sweden
FO 174/11: Tangier
FO 188/2: Swedish Embassies 1808, Naval Affairs
FO 189/11: Sweden, Merry
FO 353/56: Jackson Memoirs
FO 933/35: Thornton and Moore.
HD 3/6: Ross Memorandum 1834.
PRO 30/29/8/4: Canning to Leveson-Gower; 30/29/12/2: Leveson-Gower to Canning.
WO 1/189: Moore Dispatches
WO 6/14: Gambier
WO 6/42: Castlereagh/Moore.

British Library, London
Add. MSS 38258: Lord Liverpool Papers
Add. MSS 41365–6, and 41385: Byam Martin Correspondence

Add. MSS 42773: Canning Correspondence with George Rose
Add. MSS 51803: Foley Correspondence
Add. MSS.75847: Spencer Papers (Althorp)
Loan MS 57/3: Bathurst Papers

British Library Newspapers, Colindale, London
Microfilm copies of *The Times*, 1808

British Postal Museum, London
POST 43/120: Packet Boat Action
POST 6/1–37: Payments to Packet Officers and Crews
POST 30/1–4798: Registered Files
POST 39/2–5: Packet Reports

Devon Record Office, Exeter
152M/CA812/OA/200–2: Addington Papers

Guildhall Library, London
Baltic Exchange Papers.

Hampshire Record Office, Winchester
115M88/N30: Phillimore Papers

Harrowby Manuscripts Trust, Sandon Hall, Stafford
Harrowby (Ryder) MSS, vols 11, 94, 95, 97–9.

Long Melford Hall, Sudbury, Suffolk
Private correspondence of the Hyde Parker family.

Mulgrave Castle, Lythe, North Yorkshire
Mulgrave Archives, Box VII:
Bundle 19: 30, 34–7
Bundle 20: 30, 48, 84, 127–8, 131, 136, 160, 166, 180, 211, 368, 387–8, 412–13, 477, 507, 549, 568, 585, 648–9, 663, 696, 714, 725, 745, 759
Bundle 21: 344, 353.

National Maritime Museum, Greenwich
FOL/17: Foley Papers
MKH/113: Keats Letters to Samuel Hood
LBK/40: Mulgrave Letterbook
YOR/16A and 17: Yorke Correspondence

Somerset Archive and Record Service, Taunton
DD/CPL 31: Saumarez Letters to Sir Richard Keats

West Sussex Record Office, Chichester
L190: Bickerton Papers (Lyons Archive)

West Yorkshire Archive Service, Leeds (courtesy of Harewood House Trust)
Harewood Archive of George Canning Papers:
WYL250/8/23: Correspondence with his wife
WYL250/8/31: Correspondence with Chatham and Mulgrave
WYL250/8/32: Castlereagh and Portland
WYL250/8/33: Portland
WYL250/8/34: Bathurst
WYL250/8/41a: Cabinet Minutes
WYL250/8/42: Prussia and Sweden
WYL250/8/43: Sweden
WYL250/8/ 43a: Cabinet Minutes
WYL250/8/44: Denmark and Baltic
WYL250/8/50: Austria and Lord Pembroke
WYL250/8/57: Russia and Leveson Gower
WYL250/8/59b: D'Antraigues.

Guernsey

Priaulx Library, Candie
Saumarez Family File and various contemporary newspapers

Island Archives Service, St Peter Port
AQ 207/13–17 and 23–9, and AQ 252/02–02: Lt. Governor's Collection
AQ 283/42 and 79/062: De Havilland Collection,
AQ 365/02–10, and 13–14; AQ 365/03/01: Mansell Papers
AQ 79/105: Coombe S. Collection
Stevens-Guille Collection, 28/15–16, 36, 47, 57, 66 and 68

Scandinavia

Bernadotteska Arkivet, Kungliga Slottet, Stockholm
Karl XIV Johans Arkivet, vols 51–4 (Letterbooks 1810–11)

Kungliga Biblioteket, Stockholm
Lars von Engeström Collection, Ep.E.10:7, 9, 11, and 12

Riksarkivet, Stockholm
RA/720290.001: Esplunda arkivet
RA/720335:Giertta-Pukesta arkivet, vol. 3
RA/720791.009: Gustaf af Wetterstedt arkivet
C.J. Améer, *Aminnelse-tal öfver Grefve Johan Puke* (Karlskrona, 1818).

Rigsarkivet, Copenhagen
302/40, 302/1919 and 1920: Department for Udenlandske Anliggender,

Tøjhusmuseet, Copenhagen
Bon/04/15–17:
Carl Munnich: Kort 5 af.6 nr.9 and 10

United States
Huntington Library, San Marino, CA
Grenville Collection, STG Box 169(43)

Edited collections of letters and memoirs

Aspinall, A., ed., *The Later Correspondence of George III*, 5 vols (Cambridge, 1962–70).
—— *The Correspondence of George, Prince of Wales, 1770–1812*, 8 vols (London, 1963–71).
Aspinall, A. and Smith, E.A., *English Historical Documents, 1783–1832* (London, 1959).
Bail, M., ed., *La Correspondance de Bernadotte avec Napoléon, 1810–14* (Paris, 1819).
Bech, M.C., *En Kjøbenhavnsk Grosserers Ungdomserindringer 1787–1816* (Copenhagen, 1905–27, reprinted 1968).
Bonner-Smith, David, ed., *Letters of Admiral of the Fleet the Earl of St Vincent whilst First Lord of the Admiralty, 1801–1804*, 2 vols, Navy Records Society 55 and 61 (London, 1922–7).
Boteler, J. Harvey, *Recollections of my Sea Life from 1808 to 1830*, ed. David Bonner-Smith, Navy Records Society 82 (London, 1942).
Brenton, Sir Charles, *Memoirs of Sir Jahleel Brenton* (London, 1855).
Bromley, J.S., *The Manning of the Royal Navy: Selected Public Pamphlets, 1693–1873*, Navy Records Society 119 (London, 1974).
Chambers, C., 'The Bombardment of Copenhagen, 1807. Journal of Surgeon Charles Chambers of HM Fireship *Prometheus*' in *Naval Miscellany III*, ed. W.G. Perrin, Navy Records Society 63 (London, 1927), pp. 365–466.
Craig, Hardin, Jnr., ed., 'Letters of Lord St Vincent to Thomas Grenville, 1806–07', in *Naval Miscellany IV*, ed. C. Lloyd, Navy Records Society 92 (London, 1952), pp. 469–93.
Duffy, Michael, ed., *Naval Miscellany VI*, Navy Records Society 146 (Aldershot, 2003).
Fortescue, J.B., *Report on the Documents of J.B. Fortescue Esq. Preserved at Dropmore*, 10 vols (London, 1892–1927).
Fremantle, Anne, ed., *The Wynne Diaries*, 3 vols (Oxford, 1935–40).
Granville, Countess Castalia, ed., *The Private Correspondence of Lord Granville Leveson-Gower*, 2 vols (London, 1916).

Hamilton, Sir Richard Vesey, ed., *Letters and Papers of Admiral of the Fleet Sir Thos. Byam Martin*, 3 vols, Navy Records Society 12, 19 and 24 (1898–1903).

Hannay, David, ed., *Letters Written by Sir Samuel Hood, 1781–83*, Navy Records Society 3 (London, 1895).

Harcourt, L.V., ed., *Diaries and Correspondence of Rt. Hon. George Rose* (London, 1860).

Heaps, Leo, ed., *Log of the* Centurion (London, 1973).

Hughes, Edward, ed., *The Private Correspondence of Admiral Lord Collingwood*, Navy Records Society 98 (London, 1957).

Jackson, T. Sturges, ed., *Logs of the Great Sea Fights, 1794–1805*, vol. II, Navy Records Society 18 (London, 1900).

Koch, Hal og Hansen A.F., ed., *Dansk Daad* (Copenhagen, 1942–3).

Laughton, Sir John Knox, ed., *Letters and Papers of Charles, Lord Barham, Squadron, 1758–1813*, 3 vols, Navy Records Society 32, 38 and 39 (London, 1906–10).

Leyland, J., ed., *Papers Relating to the Blockade of Brest 1803–5*, 2 vols, Navy Records Society 14 and 21 (London, 1898).

Lloyd, Christopher, ed., *The Keith Papers*, vols II and III, Navy Records Society 90 and 96 (London, 1950–5).

—— *Naval Miscellany IV*, Navy Records Society 92 (London, 1952).

Malmesbury, Earl of, ed., *Diaries and Correspondence of James Harris, first Earl of Malmesbury*, 4 vols (London, 1844)

Maurice, Sir J.F., ed., *The Diary of Sir John Moore*, 2 vols (London, 1904).

Metternich, Prince Klemens Wenzel von, *Memoirs of Prince Metternich, 1773–1815*, 5 vols (London, 1880).

Morriss, Roger, *The Channel Fleet and the Blockade of Brest, 1793–1801*, Navy Records Society 141 (Aldershot, 2001).

Naish, G.B.P., ed., *Nelson's Letters to his Wife and Other Documents, 1785–1831*, Navy Records Society 100 (London, 1958).

Napoleon, *La Correspondance de Napoléon Ier 1769–1821*, ed. Jean-Baptiste Vaillant, 32 vols (Paris, 1858–69), vols XV, XXI, XXII and XXIII.

Newnham Collingwood, G.L., ed., *A Selection from the Public and Private Correspondence of Vice-Admiral Lord Collingwood* (London, 4th edn 1829).

Nicolas, Sir N.H., ed., *The Dispatches and Letters of Vice Admiral Lord Viscount Nelson*, 7 vols (London, 1844, reprinted 1997).

Owen, Captain C.H.H., 'Letters from Vice-Admiral Lord Collingwood, 1794–1809', in *Naval Miscellany VI*, ed. M. Duffy, Navy Records Society 146 (London, 2003), pp. 149–220.

Perrin, W. ed., *Naval Miscellany III*, Navy Records Society 63 (London, 1927).

Ralfe, James, *The Naval Biography of Great Britain* (London, 1828).

Robertson, Rev. James, *Narrative of a Special Mission to the Danish Islands* (London, 1863).

Rodger, N.A.M., ed., *Naval Miscellany V*, Navy Records Society 125 (London, 1984).

Ross, Sir John, *Memoirs and Correspondence of Admiral Lord Saumarez*, 2 vols (London, 1838).

Ryan, A.N., ed., *The Saumarez Papers: Selections from the Baltic Correspondence, 1808–12*, Navy Records Society 110 (London, 1968).

—— 'Documents Relating to the Copenhagen Operation, 1807', in *Naval Miscellany V*, ed. N.A.M. Rodger, Navy Records Society 125 (London, 1984), pp. 297–329.

Spavens, William, *Memoirs of a Seafaring Life: The Narrative of William Spavens*, ed. N.A.M. Rodger (London, 2000).

Stephen, James, *War in Disguise: or the Frauds of the Neutral Flags*, ed. Sir Francis Piggott (London, 1917).

Stirling, A.M.W., ed., *Pages and Portraits from the Past, Being the Private Papers of Sir William Hotham*, 2 vols (London, 1919).

Suremain, J.-B. de, *Mémoires du Lieutenant Général de Suremain (1794–1815)* (Paris, 1902).

Thompson, J.M., ed., *Letters of Napoleon* (Oxford, 1934).

Tracy, Nicholas, ed., *The Naval Chronicle*, 5 vols (London, 1998–9).

Warner, Oliver, ed., *The Life and Letters of Vice-Admiral Lord Collingwood* (London, 1968).

Wellesley, Marquess of, *The Wellesley Papers*, 2 vols (London, 1914).

White, Colin, ed., *Nelson: The New Letters* (Woodbridge, 2005).

White, Capt. Thomas, *Naval Researches* (London, 1836).

Secondary sources

Adams, Max, *Admiral Collingwood* (London, 2005).

Albion, R.G., *Forests and Seapower: The Timber Problem of the Royal Navy, 1652–1862* (Cambridge, MA, 1926).

Alm, Michael, 'Royalty, Legitimacy and Imagery', *Scandinavian Journal of History* 28 (2003), 19–36.

Andersen, Helge, *Orlogskibet Prinds Christian Frederik* (Holstebro, 1989).

Andersen, Henning Søby, 'Denmark between the Wars with Britain, 1801–07', *Scandinavian Journal of History* 14 (1989), 231–8.

Anderson, R.C., *Naval Wars in the Baltic, 1522–1850* (London, 1969).

Bagot, Jocelyne, *George Canning and his Friends* (London, 1909).

Baker, Norman, *Government and Contractors: The British Treasury and War Supplies, 1775–83* (London, 1971).

Bamford, P.W., *Forests and French Seapower, 1660–1789* (Toronto, 1956).

Barnes, Hilary, 'Canning and the Danes, 1807', *History Today* 14 (1965), 530–8.

Bartlett, C.J., *Castlereagh* (London, 1966).

Barton, D.P., *Bernadotte and Napoleon* (London, 1921).

Barty-King, Hugh, *The Baltic Exchange* (London, 1977).

Baugh, D., *British Naval Administration in the Age of Walpole, 1715–50* (Princeton, NJ, 1965).

Baynham, Henry, *From the Lower Deck: The Old Navy, 1780–1840* (London, 1969).

Bazin, C., *Bernadotte: Un Cadet de Gascogne sur le Trône de Suède* (Paris, 2000).

Benady, T., 'The Settee Cut – Mediterranean Passes', *Mariner's Mirror* 87 (2001), 281–96.

Bennett, Geoffrey, *Nelson the Commander* (London, 1972).

Bienkowski, Lee, *Admirals in the Age of Nelson* (Annapolis, 2003).

Black, J. and Woodfine, P., eds, *The British Navy and Use of Naval Power in the 18th Century* (Leicester, 1988).

Briggs, Asa, *England in the Age of Improvement* (London, 1999).

Bryant, Sir Arthur, *Years of Victory, 1802–1812* (London, 1944).

Buckland, C.B.S., *Friedrich von Gentz* (London, 1933).

Butterfield, Herbert, *The Peace Tactics of Napoleon, 1806–1808* (Cambridge, 1929).

Carr, R., 'Gustavus IV and the British Government, 1804–09', *English Historical Review* 60 (1945), 36–66.

Clarke, John, *British Diplomacy and Foreign Policy 1782–1865* (London, 1989).

Clarke, J.S. and McArthur, J., *The Life of Admiral Lord Nelson*, 2 vols (London, 1809).

Cobbett, William, *The Parliamentary History of England*, 36 vols (London, 1806–20).

Coquelle, P., *Napoléon et l'Angleterre, 1803–13* (Paris, 1904).

——'La Mission d'Alquier à Stockholm', *Revue d'Histoire Diplomatique* 23 (1909), 196–239.

Cormack, William S., *Revolution and Political Conflict in the French Navy, 1789–94* (Cambridge, 1995).

Creswell, John, *British Admirals of the Eighteenth Century: Tactics in Battle* (London, 1972).

Crimmin, Pat, 'Sir Thomas Troubridge', in *British Admirals of the Napoleonic Wars*, ed. P. Le Fevre and R. Harding (London, 2005), pp. 295–322.

Cronin, Vincent, *Napoleon* (Harmondsworth, 1971).

Crouzet, François, *L'Economie Britannique et le Blocus Continental* (Paris, 2nd edn 1987).

Crowhurst, Patrick, *Defence of British Trade, 1689–1815* (Folkestone, 1977).

Czisnik, Marianne, 'Nelson and the Nile: The Creation of Admiral Nelson's Public Image', *Mariner's Mirror* 88 (2002), 41–60.

Daly, Robert W., 'Operations of the Russian Navy during the Reign of Napoleon I, 1801–15', *Mariner's Mirror* 34 (1948), 169–83.

Davies, David, *Fighting Ships: Ships of the Line, 1793–1815* (London, 1996).

Davis, R., *The Industrial Revolution and British Overseas Trade* (Leicester, 1979).

Dixon, Peter, *Canning: Politician and Statesman* (London, 1976).

Dodge, E.S., *The Polar Rosses* (London, 1973).

Duckworth, Colin, *The D'Antraigues Phenomenon* (Newcastle, 1986).

Duffy, Michael, ed., *Parameters of British Naval Power, 1650–1850* (Exeter, 1992).

—— 'Sir Samuel Hood, 1762–1814', in *British Admirals of the Napoleonic Wars*, ed. P. Le Fevre and R. Harding (London, 2005), pp. 323–46.

Emsley, C., *British Society and the French Wars, 1793–1815* (London, 1979).

Esdaile, C.J., *The Wars of Napoleon* (Harlow, 1995).

—— *Napoleon's Wars: An International History, 1803–15* (London, 2007).

Fagrell, Gunnar, 'Amiralen Sir James Saumarez', *Unda Maris, 1973–4* (Kungsbacka, 1975), 145–88.

Feldbaek, Ole, *Denmark and the Armed Neutrality 1800–1801: Small Power Policy in a World War* (Copenhagen, 1980).

—— 'Denmark and the Baltic, 1720–1864' in *In Quest of Trade and Security: The Baltic in Power Politics, 1500-1990*, ed. G. Rystad, K.-R. Böhme and W.M. Carlgren (Stockholm, 1994), pp. 257–95.

—— *Dansk Søfarts Historie:* III, *1720–1864:Storhandelens Tid* (Copenhagen, 1997).

—— 'Denmark in the Napoleonic Wars: A Foreign Policy Survey', *Scandinavian Journal of History* 26 (2001), 89–101.

—— *The Battle of Copenhagen 1801* (Barnsley, 2002).

Fitchett, W.H., *Nelson and his Captains* (London, 1902).

Fleming, Fergus, *Barrow's Boys* (London, 1998).

Foreman, Amanda, *Georgiana, Duchess of Devonshire* (London, 1999).

Forester, C.S., *The Commodore* (London, 1945).

Fregosi, Paul, *Dreams of Empire: Napoleon and the First World War, 1792–1815* (London, 1989).

Galpin, W.F., *The Grain Supply of England during the Napoleonic Period* (New York, 1925).

Gash, Norman, *Lord Liverpool: The Life and Political Career of Robert Banks Jenkinson, 1770–1828* (London, 1984).

Glete, Jan, *Navies and Nations: Warships, Navies and State Building 1500–1860*, 2 vols (Stockholm, 1993).

Glover, Richard, *Britain at Bay, 1803–14* (London, 1973).

Goodwin, Peter, *Nelson's Victory* (London, 2004).

Greenwood, David, 'A Study of the Life and Career of James, Admiral Lord de Saumarez', unpublished manuscript (2001).

—— 'James, Lord de Saumarez' in *British Admirals of the Napoleonic Wars*, ed. P. Le Fevre and R. Harding (London, 2005), pp. 245–69.

Griffiths, A.J., *Observations on some Points of Seamanship* (Portsmouth, 1828).

Gulin, Sven, 'Kriget där inte ett enda skott avlossades', *Goteborgs-Posten*, 6 September 1975.

Hall, Christopher, *British Strategy in the Napoleonic Wars, 1803–1815* (Manchester, 1992).

—— *Wellington's Navy* (London, 2004).

Hansson, Hans, *Engelske flottan har siktats vid Vinga* (Stockholm, 1984).

Harding, Richard, *The Evolution of the Sailing Navy, 1509–1815* (Basingstoke, 1995).

—— *Seapower and Naval Warfare, 1650–1830* (London, 1999).

Harris, Daniel G., *F.H. Chapman: The First Naval Architect and his Works* (London, 1989).

Harris, Robin, *Talleyrand: Betrayer and Saviour of France* (London, 2007).

Harvey, A.D., *Collision of Empires: Britain in Three World Wars, 1793–1945* (London, 1992).

Harvie, David I., *Limeys* (Stroud, 2002).

Heckscher, E.F., *The Continental System* (Stockholm, 1922).

Henderson, James, *The Frigates* (London, 1970).

—— *Sloops and Brigs* (London, 1972).

Hepper, David J., *British Warship Losses in the Age of Sail, 1650–1859* (Rotherfield, 1994).

Herbert, J.B., *Life and Services of Admiral Sir Thomas Foley* (Cardiff, 1884).

Hibbert, Christopher, *Nelson: A Personal History* (London, 1994).

Hill, Richard, *The Prizes of War: The Naval Prize System in the Napoleonic Wars, 1793–1815* (Stroud, 1998).

Hinde, Wendy, *George Canning* (London, 1973).

—— *Castlereagh* (London, 1981).

Hobson, R. and Kristiansen, T., *Navies in Northern Waters* (London, 2004).

Hood, Dorothy, *The Admirals Hood* (London, 1942).

Hopkirk, Peter, *The Great Game: On Secret Service in High Asia* (London, 1990).

Horne, Alistair, *How Far From Austerlitz? Napoleon 1805–1815* (London, 1997).

Howarth, David, *Trafalgar: The Nelson Touch* (London, 1971).

James, W.M., *The Naval History of Great Britain during the French Revolutionary and Napoleonic Wars*, 6 vols (2nd edition 1837; reprinted London, 2002).

Jensen, O.L., *Introduction to the History of the Royal Danish Navy* (Copenhagen, 1994).

Jorgensen, Christer, *The Anglo-Swedish Alliance against Napoleonic France* (Basingstoke, 2004).

Kennedy, Ludovic, *Nelson's Band of Brothers* (London, 1975).

Kennedy, Paul, *The Rise and Fall of British Naval Mastery* (London, 1991).

Kermina, Françoise, *Bernadotte et Desirée Clary* (Paris, 1991).

Kirby, David, *The Baltic World 1722–1993* (London, 1995).

Kirby, D. and Hinkkanen, M.-L., *The Baltic and the North Seas* (London, 2000).

Knight, Roger, *The Pursuit of Victory: The Life and Achievement of Horatio Nelson* (London, 2005).

Krajeski, Paul, *In the Shadow of Nelson: Sir Charles Cotton* (Westport, CT, 2000).

Lambert, Andrew, *The Last Sailing Battlefleet: Maintaining Naval Mastery 1815–1850* (London, 1991).

—— 'Sir William Cornwallis', in *Precursors of Nelson: British Admirals of the Eighteenth Century*, ed. P. Le Fevre and R. Harding (London, 2000), pp. 352–75.

—— 'William, Lord Hotham, 1736–1813', in *British Admirals of the Napoleonic Wars*, ed. P. Le Fevre and R. Harding (London, 2005), pp. 23–44.

Lavery, Brian, *Nelson and the Nile* (London, 1998).

—— 'Lord Keith', in *Precursors of Nelson: British Admirals of the Eighteenth Century*, ed. P. Le Fevre and R. Harding (London, 2000), pp. 377–400.

Le Fevre, Peter, 'Sir John Borlase Warren', in *British Admirals of the Napoleonic Wars*, ed. P. Le Fevre and R. Harding (London, 2005), pp. 218–44.

Le Fevre, Peter and Harding Richard, eds, *Precursors of Nelson: British Admirals of the Eighteenth Century* (London, 2000).

—— *British Admirals of the Napoleonic Wars: The Contemporaries of Nelson* (London, 2005).

Lefebvre, G., *Napoléon* (Paris, 1969).

Lewis, M., *Social History of the Navy, 1793–1815* (London, 1960).

Lindeberg, Lars, *Englandskrigene, 1801–14* (Copenhagen, 1974).

Lloyd, Christopher, *British Seaman, 1200–1860* (London, 1968).

—— *The Nile Campaign* (Newton Abbot, 1973).

Lloyd, C. and Craig, H. Jnr, eds, 'Congreve's Rockets', in *Naval Miscellany IV*, Navy Records Society 92 (1952), pp. 423–68.

Lyon, David, *The Sailing Navy List: All the Ships of the Royal Navy, Built, Purchased and Captured, 1688–1860* (London, 1993).

Macdonald, Janet, *Feeding Nelson's Navy* (London, 2004).

Macintyre, Donald, *Admiral Rodney* (London, 1962).

Mackesy, Piers, *The War in the Mediterranean, 1803–1810* (London, 1957).

Maffeo, S.E., *Most Secret and Confidential: Intelligence in the Age of Nelson* (London, 2000).

Mahan, A.T., 'Admiral Saumarez', *Atlantic Monthly* 71 (1893), 605–19.

—— *The Influence of Sea Power upon the French Revolution and Empire, 1793–1812*, vol. II (London, 1893).

—— *Types of Naval Officers Drawn from the History of the British Navy* (London, 1902).

Marcus, G.J., *A Naval History of England*, II: *The Age of Nelson* (London, 1971).

Marzagalli, Silvia, *Les Boulevards de la Fraude, 1806–1813* (Lille, 1999).

Morley, David, *Out of Nelson's Shadow* (Guernsey, 2005).

Mörner, Magnus, 'Marskalk Bernadotte i Danmark', *Militarhistorisk Tidskrift 2002* (Stockholm, 2002), 13–60. An abbreviated abstract in Swedish from his work in Spanish: *El Mariscal Bernadotte y el Marqués de la Romana: la Epopeya Singular de la División del Norte en Dinamarca en 1808* (Madrid, 2006).

Morriss, Roger, *Royal Dockyards during the Revolutionary and Napoleonic Wars* (Leicester, 1983).

Muir, C.J.B. and Esdaile, C.J., 'Strategic Planning in a Time of Small Government: The Wars against Revolutionary and Napoleonic France, 1793–1815', in *Wellington Studies I*, ed. C.M. Woolgar (Manchester, 1990), pp. 1–90.

Muir, Rory, *Britain and the Defeat of Napoleon, 1807–1815* (London, 1996).

Muller, Leos, *Consuls, Corsairs and Commerce* (Uppsala, 2004).

Munch-Petersen, Thomas, 'A Prelude to the British Bombardment of Copenhagen: Viscount Howick and Denmark, 1806-1807', *Scandia* 65/1 (1999), 37–70.

—— 'Lord Cathcart, Sir Arthur Wellesley and the British Capture of Copenhagen in 1807', *Wellington Studies II*, ed. C.M. Woolgar (Southampton, 1999), pp. 104–22.

—— 'The Secret Intelligence from Tilsit', *Historisk Tidsskrift 102/1* (Copenhagen, 2002), 55–96.

—— *Defying Napoleon: How Britain Bombarded Copenhagen and Seized the Danish Fleet* (Stroud, 2007)

Niven, Alexander, *Napoleon and Alexander I: A Study in Franco-Russian Relations, 1807–1812* (Washington, DC, 1978).

Nordling, C., 'Capturing the "Gibraltar of the North": How Swedish Sveaborg Was Taken by the Russians in 1808', *Journal of Slavic Military Studies* 17 (2004).

—— *How Vice Admiral Cronstedt Surrendered Sveaborg* (Abingdon, 2004).

Oakley, Stewart, 'Trade, Peace and the Balance of Power', in *In Quest of Trade and Security: The Baltic in Power Politics, 1500-1990*, ed. G. Rystad, K.-R. Böhme and W.M. Carlgren (Stockholm, 1994), pp. 221–56.

Oman, Carola, *Nelson* (London, 1947).

—— *Sir John Moore* (London, 1953).

Østre Landsdelkommando, *Bornholms Militaere Domiciler* (Ringsted, 1985).

Owen, C., 'Lord Collingwood', in *British Admirals of the Napoleonic Wars*, ed. P. Le Fevre and R. Harding (London, 2005), pp. 139–63.

Padfield, Peter, *Broke and the Shannon* (London, 1968).

—— *Maritime Supremacy – 1588–1782* (London, 1999).

—— *Maritime Power and the Struggle for Freedom, 1788–1851* (London, 2003).

Palmer, Alan, *Bernadotte – Napoleon's Marshal, Sweden's King* (London, 1990).

Parkinson, C.N., *The Trade Winds: A Study of British Overseas Trade during the French Wars, 1793–1815* (London, 1948).

——, *War in the Eastern Seas, 1793–1815* (London, 1954).

Pope, Dudley, *The Great Gamble – Nelson at Copenhagen* (London, 1972).

Popham, Hugh, *A Damned Cunning Fellow* (Tywardreath, 1991).

Raven, G. and Rodger, N.A.M., eds, *The Anglo-Dutch Relationship in War and Peace, 1688–1988* (Edinburgh, 1990).

Roberts, Michael, *The Age of Liberty – Sweden 1719–72* (Cambridge, 1986).

Rodger, N.A.M., *The Admiralty* (Lavenham, 1979).

—— *Wooden World: An Anatomy of the Georgian Navy* (London, 1986).

—— *The Insatiable Earl: A Life of John Montagu, Fourth Earl of Sandwich, 1718–1792* (London, 1993).

—— *The Safeguard of the Sea: A Naval History of Britain, 1 660–1649*, vol. I (London, 1997).

—— 'George, Lord Anson', in *Precursors of Nelson: British Admirals of the Eighteenth Century*, ed. P. Le Fevre and R. Harding (London, 2000), pp. 177–99.

—— 'Honour and Duty at Sea, 1660–1815', *Historical Research* 75 (2002).

—— *The Command of the Ocean: A Naval History of Britain, 1649–1815*, vol. II (London, 2004).

—— 'The Idea of Naval Strategy in Britain in the 18th and 19th Centuries', in *The Development of British Naval Thinking: Essays in Memory of Bryan Ranft* ed. Geoffrey Till (London, 2006).

Rolo, P.J.V., *George Canning: Three Studies* (London, 1966).

Rose, J. Holland, 'A British Agent at Tilsit', *Transactions of the Royal Historical Society* 20 (1906), 61–77.

Rutter, Owen, *Red Ensign: A History of Convoy* (London, 1943).

Ryan, A.N., 'The Causes of the British Attack upon Copenhagen, 1807', *English Historical Review* 68 (1953), 37–55.

—— 'The Navy at Copenhagen in 1807', *Mariner's Mirror* 39 (1953), 201–10.

—— 'The Defence of British Trade in the Baltic, 1807–1813', *English Historical Review* 74 (1959), 443–6.

—— 'Trade with the Enemy in Scandinavian and Baltic Ports during the Napoleonic Wars', *Transactions of the Royal Historical Society* 12 (1962), 123–40.

—— 'An Ambassador Afloat: Vice-Admiral Sir James Saumarez and the Swedish Court, 1808–1812', in *The British Navy and Use of Naval Power in the 18th Century*, ed. J. Black and P. Woodfine (Leicester, 1988), pp. 238–58.

Rystad, G., Böhme, R.-R., and Carlgren, W.M., eds, *In Quest of Trade and Security: The Baltic in Power Politics, 1500-1990* (Stockholm, 1994).

Sainsbury, A.B., ' Sir John Duckworth, 1748–1817', in *British Admirals of the Napoleonic Wars*, ed. P. Le Fevre and R. Harding (London, 2005), pp. 165–96.

Samuel, Ian, *An Astonishing Fellow – Sir Robert Wilson* (Bourne End, 1985).

Sandberg, Kristina, 'England, Sverige och Hanöbukten, 1810–1812' (unpublished dissertation, Karlshamn, 1978).

Schroeder, Paul, *The Transformation of European Politics, 1763–1848* (Oxford, 1994).

Scott, F.D., *Bernadotte and the Fall of Napoleon* (Cambridge, MA, 1935).

Shayer, David, *James Saumarez: The Life and Achievements of Admiral Lord de Saumarez of Guernsey* (Guernsey, 2006).

Sherwig, J., *Guineas and Gunpowder: British Foreign Aid in the Wars with France, 1793– 1815* (Cambridge, MA, 1969).

Sparrow, Elizabeth, *Secret Service: British Agents in France, 1792–1815* (Woodbridge, 1999).

Stokeley, Jim, *Fort Moultrie, Constant Defender* (Washington, DC, 1985).

Syrett, D., *The Royal Navy in American Waters, 1775–83* (Aldershot, 1989).

Thompson, J.M., *Napoleon Bonaparte: His Rise and Fall* (Oxford, 1952).

Tiselius, Carl A., 'Landshövdingen Axel von Rosen: Ett Hundraårsminne', *Göteborgs Handels-och-Sjöfarts Tidning*, 20 October 1934.

Tolstoy, Leo, *War and Peace*, first published 1868/9, translated A. Briggs (London, 2005).

Tracy, Nicholas, *Navies, Deterrence and American Independence: Britain and Seapower in the 1760s and 1770s* (Vancouver, 1988).

—— *Attack on Maritime Trade* (London, 1991).

Trulsson, Sven, *British and Swedish Policies in the Baltic after Tilsit* (Lund, 1976).

Uden, G. and Cooper, R., eds, *Dictionary of British Ships and Seamen* (Harmondsworth, 1980).

Vandal, A., *Napoléon et Alexandre 1er: L'Alliance Russe sous le Premier Empire*, 3 vols (Paris, 1891–6).

Wandel, C.F., *Søkrigen i de dansk-norske Farvande, 1807–14* (Copenhagen, 1915).

Warner, Oliver, *The Sea and the Sword: The Baltic, 1630–1945* (New York, 1965).

—— *Command at Sea* (London, 1976).

Werdenfels, Ake, 'Engelska Flottan och Hanö 1810–12', *Blekingeboken 2006* (Karlskrona, 2007), pp. 47–96.

White, C., 'Sir Richard Goodwin Keats'; in *British Admirals of the Napoleonic Wars*, ed. P. LeFevre and R. Harding (London, 2005), pp. 347–68.

Wilkinson, C. 'Peter Rainier', in *British Admirals of the Napoleonic Wars*, ed. P. Le Fevre and R. Harding (London, 2005), pp. 91–112.

Willis, Sam, 'Capability, Control and Tactics in 18th Century', unpublished thesis, University of Exeter, 2004 – to be published in 2008 as *Fighting at Sea in the 18th Century* (Woodbridge).

Wilson, A.M., *The Happy Warrior: A Life of Admiral Sir James Saumarez* (St. Leonards, 2006).

Woolgar, C.M., *Wellington Studies II* (Southampton, 1999).

Wright, C., and Fayle, C.E., *History of Lloyds from the Founding of Lloyds Coffee House to the Present* Day (London, 1928).

Zamoyski, A., *Rites of Peace: the Fall of Napoleon and the Congress of Vienna* (London, 2007).

Index

LaVergne, TN USA
18 December 2010

209280LV00002B/64/P